The
RetailGreen
Agenda

Sustainable Practices for
Retailers and Shopping Centers

Rudolph E. Milian

International Council of Shopping Centers

Copyright © 2008 by the International Council of Shopping Centers. All rights reserved. No part of this publication may be reproduced, stored in a retrieval system or transmitted in any form or by any means, electronic, mechanical, photocopying, recording or otherwise, without the prior written permission of the publisher.

No Warranties and Limitation of Liability

The information in this publication is meant for informational purposes only and is subject to change without notice. All information in this publication is provided "as is," without guarantee of completeness, accuracy, timeliness or of the results obtained from the use of this information, and without warranty of any kind, expressed or implied, including but not limited to warranties of performance, leasability, salability, merchantability and fitness for any particular purpose and noninfringement. All statements about persons, companies, governments, places and other entities described in this publication are the subjective opinions of the author based on his understanding from personal observations, research and interviews. Others may disagree with these statements. The content of this book is provided with the understanding that the author, the reviewers, the International Council of Shopping Centers (ICSC) as primary publisher, or any other publisher whom the author may grant rights to reproduce all or part of this work are not engaged to render advice on legal, investment, accounting, architecture, environmental, economic or other professional issues and services. ICSC and the author assume no liability or responsibility for any errors or omissions or for any decision made or action taken based on information contained in this publication or for any consequential, special or similar damages, even if advised of the possibility of such damages. Your use of this work and your relying on its accuracy are at your own risk. Under no circumstances and under no legal theory shall ICSC, the author, the suppliers, or any other party involved in creating, producing, or delivering this publication's contents be liable to you or any other person for any indirect, direct, special, incidental, or consequential damages arising from your review or the review of this work by others. Additionally, ICSC and the author are not responsible for the content of Web sites and information resources that were referenced in this publication. The links provided to the Web sites do not constitute an endorsement by ICSC, the author or the reviewers of the sponsors of the Web sites or the information contained therein. The author used reasonable effort to ensure that the information contained in this work was obtained from reliable and up-to-date sources. Due to the changing nature of statistics, laws, rules, regulations, and practices delays, omissions or inaccuracies in information may be contained in this publication. However, neither ICSC nor the author makes any warranties or representations as to its accuracy or completeness. Unless expressly stated, the observations, opinions, findings, interpretations and conclusions expressed in this publication are those of the author and do not necessarily represent the views of ICSC or the reviewers of this work.

Companies, professional groups, clubs and other organizations may qualify for special terms when ordering quantities of more than 20 of this title.

Published by
International Council of Shopping Centers
Publications Department
1221 Avenue of the Americas
New York, NY 10020-1099
www.icsc.org
International Standard Book Numbers 1-58268-084-1
                      978-1-58268-084-2
ICSC Catalog Number: 298

Cover: *Earth image taken on August 25, 1992, by NOAA GOES-7 weather satellite depicts Hurricane Andrew as it makes landfall on the Louisiana coast after devastating South Florida. Photo by F. Hasler, M. Jentoft-Nilsen, H. Pierce, K. Palaniappan and M. Manyin is courtesy of the U.S. National Aeronautics and Space Administration (NASA). Photo illustration by Joseph Rutt shows the image of Earth floating in serene, starry-night space, illustrating a planet full of life sustained by a vulnerable, thin atmosphere in danger of thickening by deforestation and emissions of greenhouse gases.*

Book design by Level C

For the next generation of retail and shopping center professionals. May you enjoy the environment and natural resources in the same abundance as the generation before you, and may you allow the generation after you the same opportunity.

Contents

About the International Council of Shopping Centers

The International Council of Shopping Centers (ICSC) is the trade association of the shopping center industry. Serving the shopping center industry since 1957, ICSC is a not-for-profit organization with more than 75,000 members in 100 countries worldwide. ICSC members include shopping center

- owners
- developers
- managers
- marketing specialists
- leasing agents

- retailers
- researchers
- attorneys
- academics
- public officials

- architects
- contractors
- consultants
- investors
- lenders and brokers

ICSC holds more than 250 meetings a year and provides a wide array of services and products for shopping center professionals, including publications and research data.

For more information about ICSC, please contact:
International Council of Shopping Centers
1221 Avenue of the Americas
New York, NY 10020-1099
Telephone +1 646 728 3800
info@icsc.org (for general ICSC information)
publications@icsc.org (for information about ICSC publications)
Fax: +1 732 694 1755
www.icsc.org

About This Publication

This publication was printed with soy-based inks on Finch Fine Paper, which contains 30% post consumer recycled content and is Forest Stewardship Council Certified (FSC). The FSC is an international organization that brings people together to find solutions that promote responsible stewardship of the world's forests. By utilizing Finch Fine Paper, we estimate:

➡ 491 trees preserved
➡ 1,418 pounds (638 kilograms) of waterborne waste not created
➡ 208,733 gallons (793,185 liters) of wastewater flow saved
➡ 23,096 pounds (10,393 kilograms) of solid waste not generated
➡ 45,475 pounds (20,463 kilos) net greenhouse gases prevented
➡ 348,072,960 BTUs of energy not consumed

The printing company selected for this publication is AGS Custom Graphics, a Consolidated Graphics Company (NYSE:CGX). CGX is a strategic partner with American Forests (americanforests.org), an organization that works to protect, restore and enhance the natural capital of trees and forests. CGX has secured Forest Stewardship Council (FSC) certifications for all of its 70 facilities throughout North America.

AGS Custom Graphics
8107 Bavaria Road
Macedonia, OH 44056
USA
+1 800 362 6134
www.agscustomgraphics.com

FSC
Mixed Sources
Product group from well-managed
forests, controlled sources and
recycled wood or fiber

Cert no. SW-COC-1530
www.fsc.org
© 1996 Forest Stewardship Council

Acknowledgments

WITH APPRECIATION AND gratitude to Patricia Montagni and Geeta Sobha for their work in seeing this project through to publication; to Jeffrey M. Bedell, LEED AP, CEM, CPP, Benjamin A. Bross, LEED AP, Michelle Corti, Mario Castro Frías, CSM, CMD, CDP, Robert L. Furlan, P.Eng., David V. Green, AIA, LEED AP, Lisa Loweth, Elsa Rodrigues Monteiro, Richard P. O'Leary, CDP, Joseph Pettipas, LEED AP, IDC, ARIDO, IIDA, Arcadio Gil Pujol, CSM, CMD, CDP, and John Rutte, PE, LEED AP, for the thorough review of the manuscript and their many suggestions and guidance; to Joseph Rutt and Ellen Rosenblatt for their collaboration on the book design; to Esther Boyce for her general assistance; and to all who contributed by making themselves available for interviews and supplied photographs, information, material and encouragement; and to Mark Milian and Martha Milian for their assistance in reviewing multiple manuscript drafts and suggesting changes.

ICSC and the author of this book express appreciation to the following professionals for reviewing this work and making suggestions or comments.

Jeffrey M. Bedell, LEED AP, CEM, CPP
Vice President, Operations
The Macerich Company
Santa Monica, California, USA

Benjamin A. Bross, LEED AP
Design Director
Constructora Planigrupo, S.A.
D. F. Mexico

Michelle Corti
EES Coordinator
Master's Class of 2008
Donald Bren School of Environmental
Science and Management
University of California, Santa Barbara
Santa Barbara, California, USA

Mario Castro Frías, CSM, CMD, CDP
Vice President, New Project
Development
Allard Industries Ltd.
Santo Domingo, Dominican Republic

Robert L. Furlan, P.Eng.
Director, National Green Services
and Standards
The Cadillac Fairview
Corporation Limited
Toronto, Ontario, Canada

David V. Green, AIA, LEED AP
Principal
Altoon + Porter Architects LLP
Los Angeles, California, USA

Lisa Loweth
Vice President, Sustainability
General Growth Properties, Inc.
Chicago, Illinois, USA

Elsa Rodrigues Monteiro
Head of Institutional Relations,
Environment & Communications
Sonae Sierra
Lisboa, Portugal

Richard P. O'Leary, CDP
Vice President, Director of
Construction Services
JCPenney Company, Inc.
Dallas, Texas, USA

Joseph Pettipas, LEED AP, IDC, ARIDO, IIDA
Vice President and Practice Leader
Retail-Hospitality
Hellmuth, Obata & Kassabaum, Inc.
(HOK Canada)
Toronto, Ontario, Canada

Arcadio Gil Pujol, CSM, CMD, CDP
Managing Director
LaSBA, S.A.
Consultoría Inmobiliaria Comercial
Madrid, Spain

John Rutte, PE, LEED AP
Vice President, Development
Cousins Properties Incorporated
Atlanta, Georgia, USA

Sustainability Through Innovation

SUSTAINABILITY RESONATES TODAY with policy makers, many retailers and a new breed of environmentally aware customers who are putting their *green* stamps of approval—or worse yet—of disapproval, when they think someone is standing idly by while the environment deteriorates.

Pressures from these three sources are compelling enough reasons to drive a green agenda in the shopping center industry. Yet we have found other forces influencing the budding popularity of the green movement.

Concerns relating to traditional sources of energy—mainly the burning of dwindling supplies of fossil fuels, such as crude oil, coal and natural gas—are central to the societal shift toward sustainability.

It should come as no surprise after years of warnings by the world's scientists that we face the risk of irreversibly damaging the climate systems by continuing to release into the atmosphere massive amounts of carbon dioxide, the most prevalent form of greenhouse gases.

There remains little doubt that these heat-trapping pollutants contribute to climate change, and with that comes scientific predictions, such as more frequent and fiercer storms occurring in some areas and periods of drought occurring in others.

Unfortunately, there is more: Melting polar ice caps are already contributing to rising sea levels, which climatologists say threaten coastal cities with erosion, and create the potential for increased flooding from swollen rivers.

Today's persistent high cost of energy and diminishing freshwater supply forewarn us that conservation is going to be a new way of life, underscoring the business justification for retail buildings to operate in a more sustainable fashion.

However, the green movement is not all about dwindling resources, energy and climatic changes. There are other environmental issues that are just as important. Air pollution (smog), water pollution, land use and habitat alteration are all issues

that arise when real estate development is proposed for entitlement today. These issues tend to play a role in the sustainability movement at the local community level, much more in some than in others.

The retail real estate industry is addressing many of these concerns through densification of existing real estate, a movement to develop (or redevelop) sustainable mixed-use real estate that encourages a walkable, live-work-shop-play lifestyle with convenient access to public transportation.

Mixed-use development is no longer difficult to finance. There is capital available for this type of so-called *responsible property investment,* which earns high returns for the risk that a skillful developer considerably reduces.

Like other businesses, retail property companies should have flexible strategies that consider contingency measures to deal with legislation frequently introduced at all levels of governments to curb greenhouse gases and help preserve the environment.

Peer-to-peer learning is essential. Shopping center professionals should be aware of the great progress the industry is making to be able to respond to the groundswell of support by their stakeholders—civic groups, government, employees, retail tenants, customers and shareholders—touting today's popular green movement, also know as "sustainable development."

Sustainability is a conviction that suggests that today's generation of industries, governments and the people of Earth share in the responsibility to consume and preserve natural resources in a manner that will sustain the same quality of life for future generations to provide for themselves—much as we do today.

Many retailers and shopping center companies are leading the way with great innovations in many areas of sustainability. They are implementing green tactics quite economically and are achieving measurable cost savings with a payback of as little as two years. Some retailers simply set out to employ such green building practices as daylight harvesting to help reduce operating costs, only to learn that daylighting could also improve retail sales by as much as 40 percent.

While this book highlights many examples of those best practices, it is by no means an attempt to provide an exhaustive list of recommendations or promulgate minimum acceptable standards of practice. Because of space limitations, this sampling does not attempt to endorse or cover all retailers and shopping center companies that have effective green programs.

This publication functions as a source of news and as an educational tool to inform the reader about key issues regarding this much talked about subject that is frequently misunderstood and sometimes inaccurately portrayed.

Reasonable effort was employed to ensure that the information contained in this work came from reliable, up-to-date sources. A distinguished team of experts from around the world reviewed, commented and contributed to this compendium.

In addition, every effort was made to acknowledge correctly and contact the source and/or copyright holder of each photo and image used to illustrate this com-

plex subject. ICSC thanks those sources for their kind permissions and apologizes for any unintentional errors or omissions, which we would endeavor to correct in future editions.

As a not-for-profit trade association for the retail real estate industry, the International Council of Shopping Centers (ICSC) offers considerable discounts to individuals, companies, governmental agencies and academic institutions that wish to purchase this book in large quantities for educational use.

ICSC invites your inquiries and feedback by e-mail, to publications@icsc.org, on this and other ICSC educational textbooks and publications.

The
RetailGreen
Agenda

Sustainable Practices for
Retailers and Shopping Centers

·

Chapter 1

The Green Movement

As THE 20TH century concluded, the green, or ecological, movement was relatively unknown, with some people looking down at its proponents as if they were fanatics or downright kooky. Today, the modern environmental movement is widely recognized and readily accepted. Caring for the environment is considered mainstream, especially in building design and operations. But that was not the case when the modern eco-movement started in the late 1960s.

SANTA BARBARA OIL SPILL

On the afternoon of January 29, 1969, oil workers for the Union Oil Company drilling from a platform located six miles off the coast of Summerland near Santa Barbara, California, were faced with a nightmare when an offshore well blowout occurred.

The pressure buildup caused breaks on the ocean floors. Oil and gas from deep beneath Earth began to gush into the Pacific Ocean. Oil workers desperately tried to cap the rupture for 11 straight days as 200,000 gallons (757,000 liters) of crude oil covered the once-pristine Pacific Ocean waters, spreading 800 square miles (2,070 square kilometers).

People viewed in horror—on television, in person and in hundreds of photographs published in newspapers across the world—as animal life began dying in the contaminated waters. The lungs of dolphins with oil-clogged blowholes collapsed. Oil filled the gills of fish and splattered across the feathers of birds diving into the polluted water in search of food.

For weeks, every morning brought nightmares from the evening before. Tides washed to shore the floating corpses of birds, fish, dolphins and seals—and much of the devastation was televised.

This environmental disaster aroused public anger and awoke the world to how man can inadvertently affect the environment while simply going about his routine business to reap Earth's natural resources.

APOLLO 10

Perhaps the most widely attributed catalyst for the modern environmental movement occurred in May 1969 when astronauts from the *Apollo 10* reconnaissance mission (preceding the *Apollo 11* lunar landing) brought back dozens of photographs of an earthrise.

Everyone who looked at the images was in awe. This was home—Earth from a distance of 36,000 nautical miles. One photo in particular stood out. It featured Earth—with its colorful blue, green, brown and white hues—floating serenely in starry, black space. It was unlike any other stellar body ever before observed by telescope—so peaceful, alive and fragile.

We began to ask ourselves the fundamental question: Who is claiming stewardship over this planet?

"It was not until we saw the picture of the earth from the moon that we realized how small and how helpless this planet is—something that we must hold in our arms and care for," said Margaret Mead, an American researcher and cultural anthropologist of that era.

PHOTO COURTESY OF NASA AND JPL

Some 40 years later, a new generation wants answers and expects swift action. "While the planet may seem helpless, human beings are not," said Michelle Corti, a Class of 2008 graduate student working on her master's degree at the Donald Bren School of Environmental Science and Management of the University of California, in Santa Barbara.

"We are the ones that will be affected by climate change, and we are the ones with the power to reduce its negative effects—now," asserted Corti, demonstrating that today's generation will not tolerate inaction when the health of the environment is at stake.

EARTH DAY

A few months after man first landed on the moon, the United Nations Educational, Scientific and Cultural Organization (UNESCO) held its Conference on the Environment in San Francisco, California, entitled Man and His Environment.

One of the presenters on the final day of the conference, November 25, 1969, was young Cynthia Wayburn. Representing the idea of John McConnell, a small town newspaper publisher and an activist for the environment, Wayburn proposed a holiday to celebrate Earth.

During its flight in 1992, the *Galileo* spacecraft returned images of Earth and the Moon. NASA and JPL combined separate images to generate this view. The image shows the lifeless moon contrasted by Earth, full of life in vibrant colors, with a partial view of Earth centered on the Pacific Ocean. This photo-illustration contains same scale and relative color/albedo images of Earth and the moon. False colors occur via use of the 1-micron filter as red, 727-nm filter as green and violet filter as blue. The Jet Propulsion Laboratory manages the *Galileo* project for NASA's Office of Space Science.

"It was not until we saw the picture of the earth from the moon that we realized how small and how helpless this planet is—something that we must hold in our arms and care for."
—Margaret Mead, 1969

McConnell already had a name for it—Earth Day—when he proposed his idea to a few members of the San Francisco Board of Supervisors and other community leaders a month earlier.

McConnell even designed a two-sided, dyed flag using the noteworthy photo of Earth taken from space during the *Apollo 10* mission, floating on a navy blue field. The flag was made from recyclable, weather-resistant polyester.

McConnell imagined a day of celebration in which people around the world would concentrate on the need for preserving the ecological balance on which all forms of living things depend for their existence. Thus a movement for environmental protection was unleashed throughout the globe with unstoppable force. By the end of 1969, the U.S. Congress passed The National Environmental Policy Act (NEPA) of 1969 (42 U.S.C. 4321-4370a) and established the Environmental Protection Agency (EPA) in 1970 to enforce it.

NEPA, which became law on January 1, 1970, continues to be the foundation of environmental policy in the United States. Congress has amended NEPA throughout the years to keep it relevant.

Congressional records from 1969 show that Congress recognized the profound impact of human activity on the environment, particularly from population growth, high-density urbanization, industrial expansion, resource exploitation, and new and expanding technological advances. Congress had understood the critical importance of restoring environmental quality and outlined a policy for the federal government to work with state and local governments as well as with public and private organizations.

Congressional minutes dating back to 1969 referred to the concept of environmental sustainability more than a decade before a U.N. committee later known as the Brundtland Commission coined the term *sustainable development* in 1987.

In drafting the language for NEPA, Congress wisely fashioned a national environmental policy for Americans "to create and maintain conditions under which man and nature can co-exist in productive harmony to fulfill the social, economic and other requirements of present and future generations of Americans." A *greening* agenda had risen in 1969 from the halls of Capitol Hill in Washington, DC, and from the UNESCO floor in San Francisco, California, to the world stage, and it has remained there ever since.

San Francisco Mayor Joseph Alioto issued the first Earth Day proclamation on March 21, 1970, and Gaylord Nelson, a U.S. senator from Wisconsin, insisted that Earth Day be held on April 22, 1970. About 20 million people participated, reinforcing the hope that this movement would prevail.

United Nations secretary-general U Thant (from Myanmar in Southeast Asia) later agreed with McConnell that this annual event should be celebrated on the day of the vernal equinox in March. He signed a proclamation on February 26, 1971, to that effect. His successor, Austrian-born Secretary-General Kurt Waldheim, also observed Earth Day on the vernal equinox in 1972.

The significance of the equinoctial Earth Day is to commemorate the actual be-ginning of spring in the Northern Hemisphere and the beginning of autumn in the Southern Hemisphere. The Earth Day ceremony continued to be held on the first day of spring in the Northern Hemisphere each year, while more than 500 million people in 175 countries hold a much larger global observance every year on April 22.

Following the first Earth Day celebration in 1970, Congress amended the Clean Air Act and set national air quality, auto emission and antipollution standards. That same year, Congress also created the Occupational Safety and Health Administration (OSHA) as part of the Occupational Safety and Health Act. OSHA would help to ensure worker safety and health in the United States. President Richard M. Nixon signed it into law on December 29, 1970.

In the years that followed, more milestones were set to preserve the environ-ment. In 1971, Congress restricted the use of lead-based paint in buildings. (Lead is a highly toxic metal that can be ingested, especially by children, in the form of chipped-off paint. If absorbed by humans, it can cause a range of health effects from behavioral problems and learning disabilities to death.)

Further headway came in 1972. After 33 years of regular use of the effective pesticide called dichlorodiphenyltrichloroethane (DDT), EPA banned it as a cancer-causing agent and began to place restrictions on many other forms of pesticides. DDT, an organochlorine contact insecticide, exterminated insects by acting as a nerve poison, but environmental experts later found that it posed a substantial en-vironmental hazard.

Later in 1972, the United States and Canada approved the Great Lakes Water Quality Agreement, agreeing to clean up the Great Lakes, the source of 95 percent of the freshwater supply in North America, used by 25 million people for drinking water.

Prior to this time, industrial waste flowed regularly from rivers, dumping oil, sludge, sewage and chemicals into the precious Great Lakes.

One such waterway was the Cuyahoga River, which runs through Cleveland, Ohio, and empties into Lake Erie. The river was so polluted that the sludge floating over the waters caught on fire on June 25, 1969, and people joked that anyone who fell into the river would decay rather than drown.

At the time, it may have seemed funny to some people, but the situation was a grim and urgent reminder that the environment needed to be preserved, and that included the water as much as the land and air. Congress subsequently passed the Clean Water Act in 1972 to curb pollution that was being diverted to rivers, lakes and streams.

By 1973, EPA began phasing out leaded gasoline due to the damage it caused to the environment. At that time, gasoline and other products made from crude oil were cheap and were taken for granted. However, that would soon change.

ENERGY CRISIS

The Organization of Petroleum Exporting Countries (OPEC) formed in 1960, but its impact did not become evident until autumn 1973. OPEC (plus Egypt and Syria) cut back on oil production abruptly and placed an embargo on shipments of crude oil to Western nations. Crude prices dramatically climbed very quickly.

OPEC's actions demonstrated the relationship among politics, geography, demography and economics, and thus it became evident that the foreign policy of nations in the Middle East could easily affect economic conditions in Latin America, Europe and other parts of the world.

The oil crisis that the industrialized world experienced between 1973 and 1975 propelled the building industry into the green building movement as operators looked for ways to cut energy consumption in response to threats of fines and systematically induced brownouts. Many schools and offices in the United States closed down to save on heating oil, and in many places, the law mandated that retailers and shopping centers close early to save fuel.

By March 1974, Arab oil ministers, with the exception of Libya's, announced the end of the oil embargo against the United States. The oil crisis soon ended, but the effects of high prices of crude oil and gasoline and the concerns relating to energy dependence remained long afterward.

U.S. President Jimmy Carter created the Department of Energy (DOE) in 1977, making it responsible for nuclear safety, energy conservation, energy-related research, radioactive waste disposal and domestic energy production.

LEGIONNAIRES' DISEASE

The latter part of the 1970s brought new issues for building operators to address, beyond energy conservation and preserving the environment. The green building movement began focusing on making the indoor environment healthier for building occupants.

This part of the movement gained traction in July 1976 as Legionellosis—better known as Legionnaires' disease—made newspaper headlines all over the world.

The malaise acquired its name when an outbreak of pneumonia-like symptoms afflicted 221 persons, most of whom had attended the 58th convention of the American Legion Department of Pennsylvania at the Bellevue-Stratford Hotel in Philadelphia, Pennsylvania, commemorating the bicentennial celebration of America's independence from Great Britain.

A contagious virus was ruled out almost immediately when initial tests of family members who were living with those afflicted, but had not attended the convention, showed no probability for those suffering the flu-like condition to transmit the ailment directly to others.

Everyone was baffled as to how a group of World War II veterans could have contracted the mysterious illness about the same time, since the only thing they had in

common was that they all were Legionnaires and they all had spent time together in the same hotel. More than 4,000 Legionnaires, along with their families and friends, had participated in the convention.

U.S. Centers for Disease Control and Prevention (CDC) epidemiologists, Environmental Information Systems (EIS) officers and Pennsylvania health officials took on the case. They interviewed thousands of people with any connection to the epidemic, including more than 4,400 Legionnaires and their families, searching for clues. They also collected samples from the air, water, soil and materials from the hotel and its surroundings.

They learned that of the 221 people who became sick, 182 persons were either involved with the American Legion convention or had been inside the Bellevue-Stratford Hotel in July 1976. However, 39 sick people had not been inside the hotel or were not connected at all with the convention, except that they had walked past the hotel or had been within a block of the hotel during the same period. In fact, many of the convention delegates who became ill watched a parade from the sidewalk in front of the hotel, suggesting an airborne transmission of an agent in the environment.

In January 1977, investigators finally disclosed that the CDC's Dr. Joseph McDade and his team had discovered a bacterium responsible for the outbreak. Almost two years later, the bacterium was given the scientific name Legionella pneumophila—Legionella (in honor of the victims who were Legionnaires); *pneumophila* (for the pneumonia-like symptoms of those afflicted in Philadelphia).

Although the exact source was never definitively concluded, the Legionnaires' disease bacillus was likely breeding in the cooling tower of the hotel's air-conditioning system and was spread by the air handling system air intake in aerosolized water droplets. This single incident of building contamination, which caused 34 deaths from what initially appeared to be a mysterious epidemic, prompted worldwide indoor environmental regulations and hygiene provisions of climate control systems to prevent similar health risks.

The Legionella bacteria continue to pose a threat in buildings even today. It affects mostly smokers, the elderly and people with weak immune systems. Less than 5 percent of people exposed to the bacteria actually acquire the disease, which is consistent with the experience of Legionnaires attending the convention at the Bellevue-Stratford Hotel.

Legionella transmission occurs when humans inhale a mist of droplets containing the bacteria. The most common source in buildings is a cooling tower used in conjunction with a central plant air-conditioning system that the bacteria have colonized.

The bacteria can also spread to humans from the misty spray of cooling towers, evaporative condensers, hot and cold potable water taps, showers, whirlpool baths, heated spas, humidifiers, architectural decorative fountains, and grocery store produce misters. In addition, contaminated wet soil, freshwater ponds, creeks and natural hot springs can be sources of Legionella bacteria. Warm water ranging in

temperatures from 77 to 108°F (25 to 42°C) helps the bacteria multiply, and cases increase in warm weather. Legionella bacteria can survive in temperatures from 68 to 122°F (20 to 50°C).

The American Society of Heating, Refrigeration and Air Conditioning (ASHRAE) Guideline 12: Minimizing the Risk of Legionellosis Associated with Building Water Systems provides design and control measures for sources where Legionella can breed. Growth of Legionella may occur in infrequently used portions of the plumbing system, in stagnant water and in portions of the system with tepid temperatures, such as shower nozzles, tap faucets, hot water tanks and reservoirs, according to the ASHRAE guideline.

There has never been a report of Legionella bacteria spreading from person to person.

SICK BUILDING SYNDROME

Buildings became the focus of attention in the 1970s when different health threats were publicized. One such threat involved asbestos-containing materials (ACM), which were widely used in buildings in the 1960s for insulation.

Throughout the 1970s, news reports had widely circulated warnings of asbestos-related dangers to the health of workers and other building occupants. Therefore, it was no surprise to anyone in the building industry when in the latter part of the decade the U.S. Consumer Product Safety Commission banned the use of asbestos in building construction.

This red flag alerted architects, contractors, developers and property managers that buildings are not always a safe haven for occupants. They can make people sick, and operators share in the responsibility to promote health and safety.

By 1984, when a committee of the World Health Organization (WHO) warned of the dangers of the sick building syndrome (SBS), the building industry understood the negative effects buildings can have on the health of their occupants and on the environment.

The building industry responded with a swift action plan and expanded the plan over the years, making way for the so-called green building concept.

WHAT IS A GREEN BUILDING?

One of the key organizations in the United States that began making headway in green buildings as early as the 1970s was the Natural Resources Defense Council (NRDC), a New York City-based, not-for-profit environmental advocacy organization founded in 1970.

One young man in particular, Robert K. "Rob" Watson, a scientist for NRDC, focused on the impact buildings have on the environment and energy consumption. Today Watson is considered one of the pioneers of the modern green building movement in the United States, along with Rick Fedrizzi.

Rob Watson chaired the first LEED (Leadership in Energy and Environmental Design) Green Building Rating System committee for the United States Green Building Council (USGBC). Fedrizzi is the founding chairman of the USGBC and serves as its president and chief executive officer.

In the early 1990s, Watson and Fedrizzi touted the benefits of green buildings, a metaphor for nature's green-colored plant life. *Green buildings* refers to the design, construction and operations of buildings that are environmentally responsible and profitable, and are healthy places to live, visit, shop and work.

Others call it sustainability, sustainable design, sustainable development and green architecture. It all refers to similar concepts: the practice of increasing the efficiency of the resources that buildings consume—such as energy, water and materials—while at the same time reducing the impacts that buildings have on human health and the environment throughout the building's life cycle, from initial development through construction and ongoing operations.

From the early workings of the USGBC, green buildings represented an opportunity to transform the building industry. Fedrizzi and Watson professed that buildings are a human habitat and integral to our quality of life. The USGBC promulgated an alternative to the status quo of the time and has since grown its influence over all types of U.S. buildings, capitalizing on a hot trend that is not about to cool off.

Volunteers of the USGBC tried to convince the building industry that it had a choice between buildings that are healthier, have a smaller environmental footprint and use less energy—thus costing less to operate—versus energy-guzzling sick buildings, but the organization was at first met mostly with deaf ears.

As new concerns for the environment rose with such far-reaching issues as climate change and the depletion of natural resources, the building industry began to embrace the movement. Architects and building operators found ways to address these concerns with new building designs and systems of operation.

As the green building movement gained momentum in the first years of the 2000s, its impact mostly related to public buildings. These buildings included child-care facilities, schools, universities, libraries, firehouses, museums and government offices but not initially commercial real estate.

Commercial buildings, primarily office buildings, soon followed in the green movement. Residential properties were next. Operators of retail properties were not far behind in creating a plan to implement a green agenda, hence RetailGreen, the title of this work.

AN INCONVENIENT TRUTH

Today the mass media is increasingly giving more prominence to the subject of sustainability and the dangers to the environment. In 2006, former U.S. vice president Albert Arnold "Al" Gore Jr. starred in a documentary film entitled *An Inconvenient Truth*. The film focused on global warming and the need for humans to reduce the amount of greenhouse gases (GHGs) being emitted into the atmosphere.

Recognizing the work that went into the film and its achievement, the Academy of Motion Picture Arts and Sciences gave it two Oscars during the 2006 Academy Awards ceremony in Hollywood. A year later, the Norwegian Nobel Committee awarded the Nobel Peace Prize for 2007 in equal parts to Gore and to the Intergovernmental Panel on Climate Change (IPCC) for their efforts to build up and disseminate greater knowledge about climate change.

Through his crusade to help prevent further pollution to the atmosphere and for his strong commitment to keep these issues highly visible through frequent lectures, books, and his documentary film, Gore has done more for public awareness than any other person has, according to the Norwegian Nobel Committee.

In 2007, 19 million people watched the Live Earth concerts that took place over a 24-hour period throughout seven continents. The highly publicized event brought performers together to raise the public's awareness and help solve what has become a modern-day crisis—climate change.

On July 7, more than 1.2 million people attended the concerts, which took place in many cities from Sydney, Australia, to New York City. Gore partnered with Emmy Award–winning producer Kevin Wall, producer-singer-rapper-songwriter Pharrell Williams and Cameron Diaz to launch Save Our Selves (SOS): The Campaign for a Climate in Crisis.

The Alliance for Climate Protection, the Climate Group and other international organizations coordinated the highly visible event to drive individuals, corporations and governments to address climate change. Gore is a key figure in the bipartisan Alliance for Climate Protection, a private lobbying group he helped to set up and still chairs.

Then, in October 2007, Leonardo DiCaprio released *The 11th Hour,* an intentionally somber documentary that was yet another global-warming warning. DiCaprio produced the motion picture and acted as the narrator, warning the audience that we have not only reached the 11th hour, but that it is actually 11:59, the time to take action. "Global warming is not only the number one environmental challenge we face today but one of the most important issues facing all of humanity," DiCaprio stated in advance promotional material.

Protecting the environment and preserving the atmosphere have become priorities all over the world, and the news media are doing their share to shape public opinion.

Each segment of the economy is considering various ways to do its part to reduce its impact on climate change. Retailers and retail real estate professionals are no exception.

Opposite page: The Nobel Peace Prize laureates, Al Gore (left) and Rajendra Pachauri, appear on the podium with their diplomas and gold medals during the Nobel ceremony in Oslo in December 2007. Former U.S. vice president Al Gore and the U.N.'s top climate panel, the IPCC, received the 2007 Nobel Peace Prize at a ceremony in Oslo for their work to help combat climate change.

PHOTO: SIGURDSON, BJORN/AFP/GETTY IMAGES

© ® THE NOBEL FOUNDATION

RETAIL FOCUS ON A GREEN AGENDA

In the late 1990s and early 2000s, shopping center executives began to make headway in the green arena, particularly in Europe. However, the green building movement in the shopping center industry finally mushroomed when the membership of the International Council of Shopping Centers (ICSC) elected John L. Bucksbaum, SCSM, as the 47th worldwide chairman of the global industry trade group during the annual ICSC spring convention (now known as RECon) held in Las Vegas, Nevada, on May 22, 2006.

John L. Bucksbaum, SCSM (left), ICSC chairman from 2006 to 2007 and chief executive officer of General Growth Properties Inc., introduced former U.S. president William Jefferson "Bill" Clinton at ICSC's convention in Las Vegas in May 2006. In different lectures during the same convention, both leaders advised the attendees about the importance of green building practices.

PHOTO: LAWRENCE M. ROMORINI—ONE OF A KIND ART STUDIO

The day before he took office, Bucksbaum, chief executive officer of General Growth Properties Inc., introduced William Jefferson "Bill" Clinton, the keynote speaker at the same convention, to address conventioneers on sustainable development practices.

The former president of the United States lectured several thousand retail and shopping center executives on how to be good stewards of the environment while undertaking their responsibilities with regard to their retail properties.

Bucksbaum, an executive who puts his words into action, embarked on a one-year campaign to get the word out about the environment and to share valuable examples of how the industry is tackling sustainability. During his 2006–2007 term as ICSC chairman, Bucksbaum became a spokesman for the shopping center industry, positioning green development as one of the most important trends in retail real estate.

Bucksbaum took his convincing message to industry gatherings including the Canadian Convention in Toronto, Ontario, on September 19, 2006; the ICSC Fall Conference in Chicago, Illinois, on September 22, 2006; and the ICSC European Conference in Warsaw, Poland, on April 25, 2007.

He called for sound green building practices at every talk he gave—not just to ICSC members but to students at the Wharton Zell-Lurie Real Estate Center, executives at the Real Estate Roundtable and participants from other real estate groups.

Bucksbaum delivered an impassioned speech at the multidisciplinary Conference on Mixed-Use Development in which he called upon the audience to embrace sustainability, mixed use, densification and other forms of projects that are more in tune with development principles being touted by governments, urban planners and environmentalists.

"There are sound, financial, ethical and goodwill reasons for our industry to get out in front with respect to sustainability and energy efficiency initiatives," Bucksbaum told the audience of 1,500 members from six real estate organizations gathered at the Westin Diplomat in Hollywood, Florida, on November 16, 2006.

"Our abundant dependency on imported fossil fuels—namely gasoline and barrels of oil to provide energy to run our buildings—tends to drain the purchasing power of consumers, deplete Earth's natural resources and risk polluting the environment," Bucksbaum explained. "If we want to ensure our children and grandchildren have the same opportunities to enjoy life as we know it today, we must change in this regard."

By the time Bucksbaum's term as chairman ended, ICSC had set up a large display at the 2007 ICSC convention in Las Vegas, labeled ICSC Green Pavilion. The display depicted hundreds of sustainable practices undertaken by shopping centers and retailers worldwide. In addition to the display, the organization ran "green sessions" to educate ICSC members on how they can do their part to reduce environmental impacts.

René Tremblay, president and chief executive officer of Ivanhoé Cambridge, headquartered in Montréal, Québec, succeeded Bucksbaum as chairman of ICSC for

the 2007–2008 term on May 22, 2007. As the French Canadian business leader assumed his role as head of the 72,000-member retail real estate organization during the 2007 convention, Tremblay reaffirmed ICSC's commitment to share sustainability practices in order to help educate ICSC's membership.

"Environmental sustainability has moved beyond a regulatory inconvenience to become a legitimate win-win by offering compelling financial, ethical and goodwill reasons to go green," Tremblay said, outlining his prescient sustainable development aspiration.

During the same convention, Jon Ratner, vice president and director of sustainability initiatives for Cleveland, Ohio-based Forest City Enterprises—another large operator of retail, office and residential properties in the United States—expressed his satisfaction with the progress the shopping center industry had made in a relatively short period

In an interview with *The Wall Street Journal,* Ratner pointed to the Green Pavilion and said, "This would have been unheard of five years ago." Ratner explained his projects showcased in the Green Pavilion and discussed his company's commitment to sustainability to a *Journal* reporter.

He noted that Forest City began its green building practices ahead of most other shopping center companies. "This is an industry that's historically not been environmentally conscious," said Ratner, explaining that the retail industry was at its infancy regarding environmental conservation.

"Conservation is all about being smart," said Gordon T. "Skip" Greeby Jr., CDP, PE, the co-chairman of ICSC's Certified Development, Design and Construction Professional (CDP) Admissions and Governing Committee and a member of the ICSC Board of Trustees.

The Lake Bluff, Illinois, executive who heads up The Greeby Companies worked with his committee to make sustainability an important component of the exam specifications for CDP certification, saying that sustainability is merely part of best practices in development, architecture and construction principles. "We should and must go in that direction," said Greeby, adding that the retail real estate development industry is adopting the challenge and seems to be adapting with great enthusiasm.

On December 5, 2007, then-ICSC chairman Tremblay addressed an audience of about 2,000 professionals responsible for designing and building stores and shopping centers. "Sustainability is one trend that the retail profession must embrace," said Tremblay, explaining that as time passes, new shopping center construction will include more sustainable practices. He called upon the audience to help expedite this change.

"Right now, sustainability is more emerging than established," Tremblay told the builders. And its growth seems to have occurred quite suddenly, taking many unprepared retailers and shopping center companies by surprise.

"While the sustainability movement may seem rather sudden to most of us in the shopping center and retail world, it really isn't," said Mary Lou Fiala, chief opera-

tions officer of Regency Centers, a leading national owner, operator, and developer of grocery-anchored, neighborhood and community retail centers, and successor to Tremblay as ICSC chairman from 2008 to 2009.

"I say this because, in general, our industry has simply lagged behind the progress of other sectors such as institutional and commercial, which have been practicing sustainability for a number of years," Fiala noted. "This movement is undoubtedly important; we can have a positive effect within our communities by becoming more sustainable throughout our business practices. At the same time, we can continue to operate in a practical and economically responsible way that continues to be attractive to our stakeholders. These approaches are not at odds with each other."

Rubberstamped by two successors, Bucksbaum's 2006 message helped mold opinion about sustainability across the entire retail real estate industry. Heeding the message from Bucksbaum, many executives from prominent shopping center companies, including some from his own company—the second largest owner and operator of retail properties in the United States—refined their previous green practices and began implementing new ones.

"We started surveying all the general contractors we work with to learn of the sustainable practices they are undertaking when working with various developers," said Timothy E. Gardels, CDP, first vice president of design and construction for General Growth Properties. "This way we can implement the most efficient sustainable best practices."

Operators of retail buildings have been showing increasing support for the green building movement. Many now strive to make their shopping centers and retail stores into "greener" sustainable buildings by following a few techniques that minimize the negative impact on the environment and help lower building operating costs.

These sustainability techniques are becoming common practice as the environmental movement continues to flourish. The Green Building Initiative's Green Globe system, the U.S. Green Building Council's LEED program, the Building Research Establishment's Environmental Assessment Method (BREEAM) and other green building rating standards around the world are in the forefront of this movement.

Most of the criteria for these green building standards compare the same basic categories. Some categories are combined in some rating systems, others are more segmented. In some systems, corporate social responsibility issues are measured as well.

The green building environmental factors to be addressed in new construction and ongoing building operations—those that specifically affect building occupants and the ecosystem in general—primarily fall into the following key areas:

- Building new or renovated construction in sustainable (often remediated, previously contaminated brownfield) urban sites with access to mass transportation, reducing habitat alteration, minimizing light pollution and heat island effect, and managing stormwater runoff to avoid water pollution

- Optimizing water efficiency, conservation and reuse
- Using renewable energy and minimizing emissions of climate-changing gases and other air pollutants into the atmosphere
- Recycling; using rapidly renewable, recycled or locally available materials; and conserving natural resources
- Promoting indoor environmental quality, proper ventilation, thermal control, natural lighting and healthy conditions for building occupants

Green building standards vary from organization to organization and from country to country, but the guiding principles are similar across the board in what is now part of a worldwide movement. According to the DOE, the 81 million buildings in the United States use more energy than any other industry, including agriculture, manufacturing and transportation.

A significant opportunity exists for buildings to become greener, but green building practices comprise much more than energy efficiency and mitigating the factors attributed to climate change. In addition to improving energy efficiency, sustainability practices generally involve an integrated design, development, construction and ongoing operations approach that considers the sometimes unintended environmental, social and economic consequences buildings can pose.

Retailers and shopping center professionals are catching on quickly about value-added green efficiencies and are applying these standards with great success. Green building strategies are here to stay—forever. We simply know more today than we ever did before about how to operate buildings efficiently, and the technology exists to enable us to do so.

As technology continues to improve and such things as renewable forms of energy become widely available, the retail building industry is poised to advance on the road to sustainability. The question is: How long will it take retail buildings to reach the highest levels of sustainability?

Chapter 2

The Premise for Going Green

AS THE FIRST decade of the 21st century reached the halfway mark, sustainable building design and operation was one of the least understood and obfuscating issues, rarely discussed among retailers and shopping center professionals. That is no longer the case.

Today, the subject of sustainability is better understood as it relates to well-publicized environmental concerns. Think of sustainability in terms of Earth's abundant but limited resources. Consider the planet's ability to provide all living creatures with what they need and what they have relied upon for their existence for millions of years. Is it sustainable?

WORLD POPULATION EXPLOSION

As Earth continues to age and humans continue to multiply, our natural resources will undoubtedly dwindle beyond a point at which the planet is able to replenish these needed resources at a rate that can meet the needs of humans and other life forms.

Two primary factors are at play that have not existed in Earth's 4.5-billion-year history: the exponential growth of the human population and humankind's tendency to draw from Earth's resources much faster than can be replenished.

As the 2000s decade was concluding, Earth's population stood at about 6.7 billion. At the present rate of growth of between 65 and 70 million people a year, the population will increase to roughly 9.2 billion by 2050, and estimates put the population by 2100 as high as 12 billion. Some population experts believe that the world's population will stabilize in the 10 to 12 billion range, and actually decline thereafter.

Policy makers have to ask themselves the most fundamental question: At what point will Earth's resources fail to sustain the human population? Some scientists put Earth's human-carrying capacity at between 10 and 20 billion human beings.

But maybe that is too many. Perhaps Earth's capacity for sustaining a quality life for humans has already been surpassed.

About half of the world's population lives in conditions of poverty by Western living standards, and perhaps not surprisingly, it is the other half—the well-to-do-consuming population—that is using up substantial energy by burning fossil fuel.

LIMITED ENERGY SUPPLIES, SOARING COSTS

Experts project that by 2050, Earth's increased population will require 50 percent more energy from all types of energy sources compared to today's energy demands. The fuels our society relies upon today for our energy needs, carbon-based fossil fuels, such as coal, petroleum and natural gas, are not renewable forms of energy because once the supply available runs out, it will take years—perhaps millions—before new supplies are created by the ecosystem.

Yet there are still plenty of carbon-based fuels on reserve to supply our energy needs for several decades.

Coal—used primarily to generate electricity—is Earth's most abundant fossil fuel. Worldwide reserves are projected to last as long as 250 years. The United States alone has an abundant coal supply beneath its land to meet its own needs for 200 years.

Global natural gas reserves-to-production ratio is estimated to last between 65 and 75 years depending on who is doing the estimating. Natural gas reserves are more widely dispersed than coal and oil. Nearly two-fifths of the world's natural gas reserves are in Russia and countries that were once a part of the former Soviet Union, and one-third are in the Middle East.

On the other hand, three-fifths of proved world crude oil reserves are buried in the Middle East. The world crude oil supply is more abundant than natural gas but more limited than coal. There is perhaps one century's worth of crude oil reserves, although projections frequently increase as sources of oil are found to contain more oil than previously thought.

The U.S. Energy Information Administration estimates the world's total proved reserves at roughly 1.2 trillion barrels of oil and 6.3 quadrillion cubic feet (178.4 billion cubic meters) of gas as of 2007. An additional 1.7 trillion barrels of oil are locked in Venezuela's Orinoco tar sands near the Orinoco River that starts at the Venezuela-Brazil border and ends in the Atlantic Ocean at the Gulf of Paria.

With the selling price of a barrel of oil at more than US$100, oil from the Orinoco tar sands is now more economical to extract at a cost of US$16 per barrel than in previous times when crude oil sold for US$60 a barrel. Extracting oil from oil wells costs on average between US$4 and US$9 per barrel.

However, the process of extracting oil from tar sands is not simple or environmentally sound. A great deal of water is necessary for refining oil from tar sand, and the resulting toxic water has to be placed in holding tanks—all of which adds to the cost of crude oil.

The complete cost of oil production including capital and operating cost is under US$30 per barrel. The presumption is that the balance between the cost and the selling price compensates the seller for the underlying value of the resource.

The high cost of crude oil is definitely a factor encouraging conservation and sustainability. In early 2008, the current price of crude oil was hovering around US$100 per barrel. This represented a dramatic increase over the previous five years, and it continued to rise in a gyrated fashion.

Crude oil prices fluctuated in commodity trading throughout most of the 2000s decade. In mid-2005 (as well as in January 2007) crude was trading at US$50 a barrel. In autumn 2006, a barrel of oil sold for US$60. A year later, in autumn 2007, a barrel of oil commanded US$90 in the open market. That was 13 times the price of natural gas per million British thermal units (BTUs), which is considerably higher than the historical average traded price between 6 and 10 times.

Light, sweet crude oil trading for April delivery passed the key psychological level of US$100 on the New York Mercantile Exchange during the last week of February 2008. As the U.S. dollar fell to record levels at the end of February and U.S. oil supplies dwindled in March, the price of crude oil settled at the end of trading on March 5, 2008, at US$104.52. This record price was 69 percent higher than the trading price of crude oil a year earlier, and surpassed what experts believe was until then the all-time high record set almost three decades earlier.

In inflation-adjusted terms, the cost of crude oil peaked at US$103.76 a barrel in April 1980, when inflation was rampant and when geopolitical turbulence in the Middle East—Iran in particular—created an uncertainty about the adequacy of oil supplies from the world's most important oil-exporting region.

Many geopolitical events were occurring in spring 1980. One was the historical Iranian Revolution that toppled the ruling shah of Iran. Others included a failed U.S. attempt to rescue American hostages held in Iran, threats by Iran to choke off supplies from the Persian Gulf to the West, oil fields set ablaze and a suspension of Iranian oil exports to Japan. A few months later, war broke out between Iran and Iraq. Such geopolitical occurrences can reduce oil consumption in the West when supplies tighten or prices increase.

Today, U.S. consumers use about 9.7 million barrels of gasoline each day in the summer compared to a seasonal low of 8.8 million barrels in February. The OPEC organization supplies almost 40 percent of the world's demand of 86 million barrels of crude oil per day. The high cost of crude oil is responsible for the increase in gasoline prices in U.S. filling stations.

One reason for this is that OPEC prices crude oil in U.S. dollars. When the value of the U.S. dollar goes down, foreign suppliers to the United States receive less from selling their crude and then have to exchange the dollars they receive into their own currency.

To compensate for this currency fluctuation, OPEC countries tighten the spigots on crude supplies to drive up the price of crude oil. This can help them achieve their target price when converting dollars to their own currency. The cost of crude oil

makes up almost 60 percent of the price of gasoline. Oil producers can reduce the supply line arbitrarily to prop up prices and to make crude a more valuable resource.

In 2006, two significant cuts in crude supplies by OPEC—one in autumn and one in December—helped it achieve higher crude prices in the months that followed. All of this occurred in the wake of a falling U.S. dollar.

However, the fallen dollar alone does not totally account for the hike in crude prices. In a three-month period from mid-August to mid-November 2007, the value of the U.S. dollar fell by 8 percent compared to other benchmark currencies yet oil prices rose by a whopping 40 percent—five times higher.

Also, other factors such as lower supplies due to poor inventory management, news of shrinking crude supplies in developed nations, advancing commodity futures from trading speculation, concerns about turmoil in the Middle East and bottlenecks at refineries also influence crude oil prices as well as gasoline prices.

Crude oil prices are poised to increase in the near term and perhaps in the mid term unless the value of the U.S. dollar goes higher or consumption drops because of an economic recession or a mild winter in the Northern Hemisphere.

Winter in the Northern Hemisphere (the half of the globe north of the equator) occurs in December, January and February. That period is important to world energy consumption because the Northern Hemisphere contains most of the planet's land and about 90 percent of the human population.

The International Energy Agency (IEA), created during the oil crisis of 1973–74, acts as energy policy advisor to 27 developed member nations in their effort to ensure reliable, affordable and clean energy for their citizens, and coordinate measures in times of oil supply emergencies.

The IEA, acting as an energy watchdog based in Paris, France, carefully monitors the supplies of crude oil stockpiled in the United States and elsewhere because as the stockpiles tighten, the price of crude rises.

Typically, the number of days of cover offered by oil stockpiles in the Organization for Economic Cooperation and Development nations ranges between 50 and 60. Any slip in the number of days—even by one day—is considered problematic, particularly if it occurs at a time of year when inventories commonly build, mostly preceding peak use.

As economies around the world expand, so does oil consumption. According to the IEA, the economy of the People's Republic of China's grew in 2007 by 6.1 percent over the previous year. India was not far behind, and the economy in the Middle East grew by 4.5 percent.

Despite the increase in the economic expansion of developing countries, high prices of crude oil curtailed demand. Oil consumption in the United States fell by 1.3 percent in 2006 while demand grew by only 0.6 percent worldwide, according to BP. World demand is projected to be flat in 2007 compared to 2006.

Consuming nonrenewable energy from carbon fuels is one concern. A more publicized concern is the damage humans are doing to Earth's ecological system by polluting the environment in the process of consumption.

CLIMATE CHANGE IS UNEQUIVOCAL

"The time for doubt has passed," U.N. secretary-general Ban Ki-moon (from the Republic of Korea) told a gathering of 80 national leaders that made up the U.N. General Assembly in New York City on September 24, 2007.

California's environmentalist governor, Arnold Schwarzenegger, took the podium to make his point to this international forum of national presidents, prime ministers and envoys. Known worldwide for his motion-picture celebrity status, the governor of the most populous U.S. state, representing some 37 million Americans, called for "action, action, action." Former prime minister of Japan Yoshiro Mori agreed. So did German chancellor Angela Merkel and French Republic president Nicolas Sarkozy.

Secretary-General Ban and Governor Schwarzenegger were referring to the worst pollutant of all—carbon-based emissions of greenhouse gases (GHGs)—largely blamed for causing climate change and the apocalyptic consequences climatologists and environmental experts around the world are predicting.

GREENHOUSE GASES: BELIEVERS AND SKEPTICS

The enormous increase in the formation of greenhouse gases that has occurred in the past two centuries is causing climate change, and there is an almost certain 90 percent chance that humans are mostly to blame, according to a report by the Intergovernmental Panel on Climate Change (IPCC).

The IPCC comprises 2,500 reputable researchers representing governments, institutions of higher learning, sustainability proponents and businesses from more than 140 nations. The World Meteorological Organization (WMO) and the United Nations Environment Programme (UNEP) established the IPCC in 1988 to monitor climate change.

In every report it has issued since its inception, the IPCC has been warning anyone willing to listen of the dangers associated with fossil fuel pollutants.

Two decades after the IPCC first organized as an authoritative order, Rajendra K. Pachauri, the laureate U.N. chief climate scientist, pointed to mounting evidence of climate change and squarely pinned the blame on human activity.

"We, the human race, have substantially altered the earth's atmosphere," Pachauri told the U.N. General Assembly in September 2007. "In 2005, the concentration of carbon dioxide exceeded the natural range that has existed over 650,000 years," claimed Pachauri, who also serves as chairman of the IPCC.

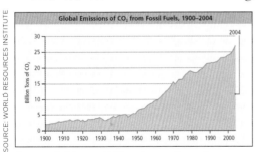

SOURCE: WORLD RESOURCES INSTITUTE

Global Emissions of CO₂ from Fossil Fuels, 1900–2004

Souces & Notes: WRI estimates based on IEA, 2004; EIA, 2004; Marland et al., 2005; and BP, 2005. Emissions include fossil fuel combustion, cement manufacture and gas flaring.

Despite the overwhelming evidence, naysayers have continued to dispute the connection between GHG emissions from human activity and the warming trends recorded in the 1990s and 2000s.

U.S. senator James Inhofe, a Republican from Oklahoma and a ranking member on the Senate Environment and Public Works Committee, gave a blazing 50-minute speech on September 25, 2006, on the Senate floor, challenging the news media to take a more skeptical approach when reporting the causes of climate change.

Two months later, Senator Inhofe, as chairman of the Environment and Public Works Committee, released a Senate Committee booklet to the public, but primarily aimed at the U.S. news media, titled "A Skeptic's Guide to Debunking Global Warming Alarmism, Hot and Cold Media Spin Cycle: A Challenge to Journalists Who Cover Global Warming."

Senator Inhofe's "Skeptic's Guide" included hard-hitting critiques of the *New York Times, Time Magazine, Newsweek,* the Associated Press, Reuters, the *Los Angeles Times,* the *Chicago Tribune* and the *Washington Post* for their supposed one-sided reporting of climate change, and he suggested media sources with opposing points of view.

For example, the report stated, "The April 3, 2006, global warming special report of *Time Magazine* was a prime example of the media's shortcoming . . . *Time Magazine* did not make the slightest attempt to balance its reporting with any views with scientists skeptical of this alleged climate apocalypse."

Then, in December 2007, Senator Inhofe released another report, entitled "U.S. Senate Report: Over 400 Prominent Scientists Disputed Man-Made Global Warming Claims in 2007—Senate Report Debunks Consensus."

Senator Inhofe timed the release of his second report to refute a U.N. conclusion by climatologists working with world leaders earlier that month in Bali, Indonesia, to hash out a draft for a successor to the Kyoto Protocol.

Senate Inhofe's report contained writings and references from other previously published information by contrarian so-called scientists—some claiming to be former members of the IPCC—challenging both Secretary-General Ban's assertion that the debate on the cause of climate change is over and the Bali consensus that Earth is in imminent danger.

Inhofe's report debunking man-made global-warming claims quoted one source stating that global warming—and global cooling—are part of natural climate changes that Earth has experienced for billions of years and that climate change is caused primarily by cyclical variations in solar output.

Despite claims by Inhofe and the references in his 2007 report that a link between GHG emissions associated with energy consumption and climate change is inconclusive, worldwide carbon dioxide emissions have indeed surged to about 33 billion tons (29.9 billion metric tons) from a minimal level two centuries ago, and global temperatures have risen in the 1980s, 1990s and 2000s.

The National Oceanic and Atmospheric Administration (NOAA) Earth System Research Laboratory (ESRL) Atmospheric Baseline Observatory, located in Barrow, Alaska, on the most northerly inhabited point of land in the United States, has been continuously measuring meteorological parameters since 1977.

In November 2007, the average temperature at the observatory was 14.3°F (7.9°C) warmer than the monthly norm. In the first 10 days of December 2007, the average temperature was 22.2°F (12.3°C) warmer than the long-term average for December.

According to NOAA, these unusually warm temperatures are likely due to heat from the warmer Arctic Ocean, offshore from Barrow, that had not yet frozen for the winter. The Barrow Observatory chief, Dan Endres, who has been at the observatory since 1984, notes that in the 1980s, the ocean would generally freeze by the middle of October. In the 2000s, however, freeze-up has been occurring progressively later.

This warming trend coincides with the increases in global emissions of atmosphere pollutants, which grew as much as 70 percent from 1970 to 2004 due to man-made activity such as burning natural gas and coal to produce electricity.

Scientists from NOAA's ESRL have a powerful data and modeling system called CarbonTracker that tracks carbon monitoring from 28,000 global atmospheric observations.

The study, based on an estimate of net atmospheric carbon dioxide (CO_2) exchange across North America every week from 2000 to 2005, shows that humans release two billion tons (1.81 billion metric tons) of CO_2 into the atmosphere each year by burning fossil fuels and manufacturing cement. Forests, grasslands, crops, soil and the ocean generally absorb between one-third and one-fourth of those emissions.

However, carbon dioxide figures are sometimes conflicting and often confusing. The U.S. Energy Information Administration (EIA) noted in a May 2007 report that the United States emitted 5,877 million (5.9 billion) metric tons of energy-related carbon dioxide ($MMTCO_2$) in 2006 compared to about 5,955 (6.0 billion) million metric tons of $MMTCO_2$ in 2005.

The EIA is a statistical agency of the U.S. Department of Energy whereas NOAA is an agency of the U.S. Department of Commerce, studying the role of the oceans, coasts and atmosphere in the global ecosystem for policy makers and businesses to make the best social and economic decisions.

The IPCC, whose role is to provide decision makers with an objective source of information about climate change, forewarned that even if atmosphere pollutants were stabilized, Earth would keep warming from the CO_2 already in the atmosphere.

Even if all factories were to shut down today and cars were taken off the roads, the average sea level would gradually continue to rise over the next 1,000 years. "We have already committed the world to sea level rise," chief U.N. climate scientist Pachauri said.

Sea level could reach perhaps as high as 4.6 feet (1.4 meters) above where it stood in 1850, the year before the preindustrial period began, according to IPCC's Pachauri.

Carbon dioxide and other greenhouse gases are not to be blamed exclusively on the human race, though. These gases blend naturally with the atmosphere, commensurate with the natural range that Pachauri said has existed over 650,000 years and make Earth livable and comfortably warm to sustain life. But that is not the case for our neighboring planets.

VENUS IS HOT!

Scientists have learned what happens when there is an imbalance of greenhouse gases by analyzing the atmospheres of nearby planets. Venus, in particular, provides a cryptic case study because of the abundance of greenhouse gases in its atmosphere and the warming effect these gases have created.

From the 1960s to the early 1990s, unmanned former Soviet Union and American explorers have been studying Venus by intensively probing its surface and atmosphere. After the last American probe in 1994, the European Space Agency (ESA) picked up where the Americans left off. The agency's first mission to Venus, called *Venus Express,* is now the only spacecraft in orbit around the planet, having successfully been inserted in April 2006.

This highly sophisticated probe, exploring one of the most mysterious planetary bodies in the solar system, has been revealing planetary details of enormous scientific value. The following is what we collectively know from scientific papers written over many years.

Venus, Earth and Mars formed about the same time (approximately 4.5 billion years ago), and all three are about the same distance from the Sun. Many scientists estimate that several million years ago the three planets likely had similar moderate surface temperatures to support life.

The radius of Venus is 95 percent of Earth's radius and has about 82 percent of Earth's density. Proximity from the Sun is very close for both planets. Venus is 0.72 Astronomical Units (AUs) from the Sun in comparison to Earth, which is a relative 1.0 AUs.

This image of Venus is a mosaic of several images photographed by the NASA *Mariner 10* spacecraft in 1974 showing the thick cloud coverage of greenhouse gases that keep surface temperatures melting hot.

Because of these traits, scientists have referred to Venus and Earth for many decades as the "twin planets." But this is where their similarities end.

The hyperactive greenhouse effect that permeates the atmosphere of Venus likely resulted from extensive water vapor. Many scientists hypothesize that Venus had oceans similar to the ones we have on Earth. Those oceans boiled and evaporated over millions of years, releasing water vapor and carbon dioxide into the atmosphere, where a dense greenhouse gas blanket formed.

On Earth, liquid water creates chemical reactions that trap volatile carbon and sulfur compounds, sequestering them in rocks. When all the water on Venus dis-

PHOTO: NATIONAL AERONAUTICS AND SPACE ADMINISTRATION (NASA)

sipated, these volatile gases remained in Venus's atmosphere, which added to the immense greenhouse effect.

As water vapor reached the upper atmosphere of Venus, a strong flux of ultraviolet radiation from the Sun broke up the water vapor's molecular components into separate molecules of oxygen and hydrogen. They then separated as ions, two hydrogen ions for every one oxygen ion, and mostly escaped into space, leaving largely thick carbon dioxide to make up most of the remaining atmosphere. Note that the hydrogen and oxygen escaping into space is in the same ratio as a water molecule, H_2O: two hydrogen ions for every oxygen ion.

This process, which continues to this day, also liberates some of the oxygen atoms, which migrate from the high atmosphere to a lower layer, called the exosphere.

Similar to a comet, subsolar and antisolar atmospheric circulation picks up ions from Venus's oxygen exosphere and hurtles them in the antisolar direction (the night side of the planet). The oxygen atoms, though few in volume, migrating from the day side to the night side of the lower portion of the atmosphere in Venus give the planet a fluorescent airglow at night, which is how *Venus Express* detected the atmospheric contents.

It is a long process, as one full day on Venus lasts 243 Earth days. Because of the very slow rotation of Venus on its axis and its thick atmosphere, the atmospheric circulation patterns follow what is called a Hadley circulation.

As the Sun radiates its warmth over one side of Venus for months, the hottest area near the equator creates havoc with the weather. Hot air rises and flows at high altitude toward the poles. It then sinks at the poles and flows back toward the equator, low near the surface, in the redundant Hadley circulation pattern.

The Sun on Venus rises in the west because Venus rotates in the opposite direction of Earth's rotation. The atmosphere in Venus rotates in the same direction as the planet, and the winds reach speeds of 220 miles (354 km) per hour traveling in the Hadley pattern.

Despite the fluorescent airglow from the oxygen in Venus, not much remains in the atmosphere today. "The oxygen in the atmosphere of Venus is a very rare element," said Pierre Drossart, coprincipal investigator on *Venus Express'* Visible and Infrared Thermal Imaging Spectrometer (VIRTIS) instrument.

The greenhouse gas on Venus allows the Sun's radiation to pass through and heat up the surface of Venus, but it prevents the radiation from escaping. The surface of Venus has continued to get hotter because of this. The hotter the surface gets, the more radiant heat it traps. It is now a vicious cycle.

This natural process tends to function much the same way as a nursery greenhouse on Earth in the winter. A greenhouse allows the Sun's radiation to filter through the glass to heat up the nursery, but mostly closed windows prevent the heat from escaping the greenhouse.

Similarly, on Venus, the thick atmosphere, made up mostly of greenhouse gases, maintains the planet's unbearably hot, unlivable atmospheric temperature. The very

thick atmosphere of Venus is made up of 96 percent carbon dioxide (CO_2), 3.5 percent nitrogen (N_2) and 0.5 other gases.

Without having a natural reservoir for its atmospheric carbon dioxide, such as provided by Earth's terrestrial limestone and oceans, the surface air pressure on Venus is about 92 times greater than it is on Earth's surface and about as intense as diving half a mile below sea level on Earth. Worst of all, the surface temperature on Venus, roughly 900°F (482°C), is hot enough to melt lead.

Venus is the most extreme example we know of the warming effect that occurs when the Sun's radiation interacts with a hellish, thick atmosphere composed of mostly greenhouse gases.

The present movement to reduce greenhouse gas emissions on Earth is rooted in containing the amount already in our atmosphere to prevent them from ever reaching uncontrollable levels.

Despite an enormous increase in GHGs released into Earth's atmosphere over the past 150 years, the total quantity now hovering above us is practically insignificant compared to that of Earth's neighboring planets, which is why climate change is a glacially slow—though progressive—process.

The atmospheres of both Venus and Mars, the latter being Earth's other neighbor, are composed of 95 to 96 percent carbon dioxide while Earth's atmosphere only has 0.04 percent carbon dioxide. Earth's oceans contain about 60 times more carbon dioxide than its atmosphere.

Mars is different from Earth and Venus in several ways. Mars has a land mass about one-tenth the size of Earth. Scientists believe that in its early life, Mars cooled much faster than Earth and Venus, as smaller objects usually do. Scientists concluded that Mars once had oceans and lakes, but its low-density gravity was unable to hold the atmosphere as Venus and Earth do.

The weak gravity and thin atmosphere of Mars prevented greenhouse gases from forming as they did on Earth and Venus. The chemical reaction that existed in Mars consumed most of the carbon dioxide from the atmosphere and the oceans to form carbonate rocks, which solidified much of the CO_2.

As the interior of Mars cooled in its planetary infancy, most of the atmosphere became trapped within the rocks. Today most of the carbon dioxide in Mars is frozen on or beneath the ground. The water in Mars is sealed in permafrost, and the landscape in some parts is dotted with snowcaps.

This prevents the greenhouse effect on Mars despite the abundance of CO_2, compared with the moderate amount on Earth and the rampant amount on Venus. By volume, the carbon dioxide greenhouse gases on Mars—although excessive by percentage of atmospheric substance—are indeed infinitesimal compared to Earth because of the very thin atmosphere that exists in Mars; hence no greenhouse effect.

By contrast, the carbon dioxide greenhouse gases in the atmosphere of Venus are thousands of times more plentiful by volume and percentage of atmospheric elements than all greenhouse gases that make up the atmosphere of Earth. The net

effect is that Mars is colder than ice and therefore unlivable. Average surface temperatures on Mars are -81°F (-63°C) but vary throughout the planet.

According to NASA, the temperature on Mars may reach a comfortable high of 70°F (21°C) at noon around the equator in the summer (albeit without a breathable atmosphere) and a low of about -225°F (-143°C) at the poles.

With its warm and cold seasons caused by the Earth-Sun geometry, the rotation of Earth on its axis, Earth has precisely the correct amount of greenhouse gases to support life. This phenomenon results in the hemispherical variance in climate.

Like Earth, Mars rotates on its axis as it circles the Sun, but with Mars's thin atmosphere, the temperature variances between day and night and between winter and summer are astronomical.

As previously noted, greenhouse gases are indeed good for Earth—but only in limited quantities. Earth's gravity holds the thin layers of gases that make up our atmosphere. This atmosphere is a mixture of approximately 78 percent nitrogen (N_2), 20.95 percent oxygen (O_2) and 1.05 percent other gases such as argon (Ar), ozone (O_3) and water vapor (H_2O). Only 0.038 percent of the other gases in the atmosphere are made up of carbon dioxide—the most common form of greenhouse gas found on Earth.

We breathe air from the atmosphere. But the atmosphere has another function equally as important. It protects life on Earth because the atmosphere, with the right amount of CO_2, absorbs some ultraviolet radiation from the Sun.

The atmosphere also allows radiant heat to escape to outer space to create a cooling process. As sunlight radiates heat to Earth, a balanced amount of infrared radiation must travel from the surface of Earth back to outer space.

On warm, humid days, the moisture in the air traps the heat, but on a clear, dry evening, the air will cool because the lack of humidity and clouds let infrared radiation escape quickly into space. The coldest winter days on Earth are always the driest and the clearest because there are no clouds in the sky to absorb the radiant heat released from Earth's surface.

Without the atmosphere to which we are accustomed, temperature extremes between day and night would burn or freeze living things on the planet. The atmosphere acts like a thermal blanket keeping us comfortable—relatively speaking.

Plants—namely the cyanobacteria we call blue-green algae—produce almost all the oxygen in Earth's atmosphere. Whereas nitrogen is four times more abundant than oxygen in Earth's atmosphere, oxygen is about 10,000 times more plentiful than nitrogen on Earth's surface, when considering the entire planet's oxygen contained within all living and some nonliving things.

Even though such gases as nitrogen and oxygen make up most of Earth's atmosphere, neither element is a greenhouse gas because nitrogen and oxygen do not absorb the Sun's radiation in the way that greenhouse gases do.

Among the known climate-changing greenhouse gases in Earth's atmosphere are water vapor (H_2O), carbon dioxide (CO_2), methane (CH_4), nitrous oxide (N_2O), chlorofluorocarbons (CFCs), hydrofluorocarbons (HFCs), sulfur hexafluoride (SF_6), and ozone (O_3).

The atmospheric buildup of greenhouse gases that climatologists attribute to humans and causes climate change is a result of two major activities: fossil fuel burning and deforestation.

The most damaging of all causes of climate change is the release of carbon dioxide from burning fossil fuels. Scientists estimate that carbon dioxide gases have increased by 25 percent in our atmosphere over the past 150 years.

Humans are the only creatures on Earth that burn fossil fuel to produce energy for manufacturing, for comfort and for cooking. That process produces carbon dioxide gases and simultaneously releases them into the atmosphere.

The second leading source of greenhouse gases is deforestation because forests absorb carbon dioxide through photosynthesis. Humans are primarily blamed for deforestation, although forest fires (naturally induced by lightning) and droughts cause some level of deforestation.

Other human activities also result in carbon dioxide emissions but to a much lesser extent. These activities include manufacturing cement, improper land use, changing the makeup of wetlands, covered vented landfills, and certain methods of farming and raising livestock.

Earth's atmosphere is essential to sustaining life, but it is extremely thin compared to the massive body of land and water that covers our planet. The atmosphere is akin to a thin coat of paint on the surface of a huge bus. Without the paint, the bus would rust and corrode.

Scientists worry that Earth's atmosphere is thickening with heat-trapping greenhouse gases that can persist in the air for centuries, and they have brought the matter to governments all over the world to take remedial action. And so, worldwide pressure is mounting for reducing the amounts of greenhouse gases entering the atmosphere from all sources.

KYOTO PROTOCOL

The Kyoto Protocol to the United Nations Framework Convention on Climate Change (UNFCCC) entered into force on February 16, 2005. The treaty requires the 36 industrialized nations and the European Union (EU), which ratified the Kyoto agreement, to reduce GHG emissions over a five-year period.

These governments have to ensure a reduction of pollutants emitted into the atmosphere from 2008 to 2012 (the latter date being the target year) to levels below those specified for each of them in the treaty, ranging from 5 to 8 percent lower than that nation emitted in 1990 (the base year).

Most of the world's countries eventually agreed to the Kyoto Protocol, but some nations chose not to ratify it. About 175 nations have ratified the treaty since the first signature was penned on the document in March 1998. These countries accounted for about 62 percent of carbon dioxide emissions in 1990.

A total of 190 nations participated in the U.N. meetings, which included the United States. Part of the 190 also includes 40 classified as industrialized (or de-

veloped) nations but excludes six developing nations classified merely as observers. However, not all 190 countries have agreed to abide by the goals set for reducing their own GHG emissions in the pact.

China and the United States are the world's largest emitters of GHG. However, the United States is not a party to the Kyoto agreement, and China—although a signatory to it—is exempt from mandatory GHG reductions. According to a Netherlands Environmental Assessment Agency study conducted in 2007, China produced 6.8 billion tons (6.2 billion metric tons) of carbon dioxide, and the United States produced 6.4 billion tons (5.8 billion metric tons).

Therefore, by volume China is now the world's largest emitter of GHGs, although the United States far surpasses China on a per capita basis. Studies have shown that about one-fourth of the pollutants that China emits into the atmosphere results from its manufacturing and transporting exports out of the country.

China, India, Brazil and many other developing (as opposed to developed) nations are expected and authorized by the Kyoto pact to increase harmful GHG emissions as these countries heighten industrial production at a feverish pace in the next few decades. These countries have no obligation other than to monitor and report emission levels.

The Protocol places a heavier burden on developed nations under the principle of "common but differentiated responsibilities," and the document cites the U.N.'s rationalization.

The United Nations concludes that developed countries can pay more easily for the cost involved in cutting emissions. Secondly, the United Nations intimated in public disclosures that developed countries have historically contributed more to

This image is a composite of hundreds of photos made by the orbiting Defense Meteorological Satellites Program (DMSP) satellites to show Earth without cloud cover. We can see the environmental footprint of many regions simply from the carbon dioxide emissions generated by lights clearly visible in this image.

CREDIT: C. MAYHEW & R. SIMMON (NASA/GSFC), NOAA/ NGDC, DMSP

at Night
information available at:
/antwrp.gsfc.nasa.gov/apod/ap001127.html

Astronomy Picture of the Day
2000 November 27
http://antwrp.gsfc.nasa.gov/apod/astropix.html

the problem by emitting larger amounts of climate-changing gases per capita than developing countries over the past 150 years, and so it is now time to "call in the chips."

The United Nations estimates that China has increased GHG emissions by 47 percent in the period between 1990 and 2004, and India has increased its emissions by 55 percent during the same period. At the present rate of economic growth, China is opening two coal-fired power plants every week.

Presently, about 90 percent of the world's atmosphere-warming emissions are produced by only 17 countries. The irony is that this group consists of both developed and developing countries.

According to the U.S. Department of Energy, four of the top ten largest emitters of greenhouse gases from the consumption of petroleum as of 2005 (China, India, Brazil and Saudi Arabia) were developing nations not required to reduce GHG emissions by the Kyoto Protocol. The other six (United States, Japan, Russia, Germany, Canada and France) are developed nations.

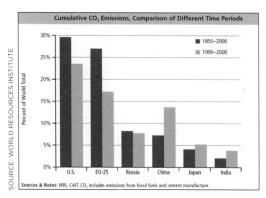

When you look beyond the top 10 largest emitters of greenhouse gases from oil consumption, the picture does not improve. Mexico, ranked eleven, is not required to reduce GHG emissions because it is considered a developing nation.

Negotiators for the Kyoto accord made concessions to the Russian Federation, and the pact now only requires Russia to maintain emissions at a neutral level in the target period.

The main activity responsible for releasing most of the heat-trapping carbon dioxide gas into the atmosphere is predominantly from the combustion of fossil fuels used in power generation, transportation, industrial processes and buildings devoted to residential and commercial purposes.

Certain industrial processes such as cement manufacturing, hydrogen production and the combustion of biomass also emit CO_2 in large quantities. When analyzing all sources of CO_2 emissions from fossil fuel combustion around the world, about 60 percent is caused by stationary emission sources such as power plants.

Four regional clusters account for the majority of stationary CO_2 emissions: North America (particularly the East and Midwest), Europe (the northwest region), East Asia (the eastern coast of China) and South Asia (the Indian subcontinent).

A system such as the Kyoto treaty that does not require reduction from these four clusters cannot effectively reduce GHG emissions to the extent necessary to curb climate change, not even with the practice of allowing the trading of carbon credits.

Carbon credits are created when developed countries achieve certain greenhouse gas emission reductions through special programs that the nations implement. These credits can be sold to other industrial countries that fail to meet their goals.

The Kyoto treaty also provides for an international carbon-traded market to allow developed countries, mainly Canada, Japan and members of the European Union, to earn credits by paying for carbon-reducing projects in developing countries.

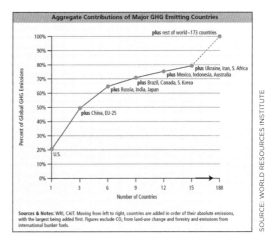

SOURCE: WORLD RESOURCES INSTITUTE

These credit earnings could range from planting trees in Brazil to subsidizing electric company enhancements in China, India and Mexico. For example, Tractebel Electricity and Gas International built a cogeneration plant in the Municipality of García in the state of Nuevo León in Mexico that would burn natural gas, but with a modern, low-NO$_x$ burner and minimum GHG emissions. The cogeneration plant has a capacity to generate 245 MW of electricity and 180 tons (163 metric tons) of steam on average per hour. Because this plant replaces less efficient coal-burning, high-emission electricity plants, proponents hope that carbon allowances from other sources can help subsidize projects such as this one.

The World Bank reports that allowances traded in carbon markets around the world hovered around US$30 billion in 2006, much of it stemming from the EU secondary market. The United States, which has been of two minds regarding the Kyoto treaty from the very beginning, does not presently support this type of obligation.

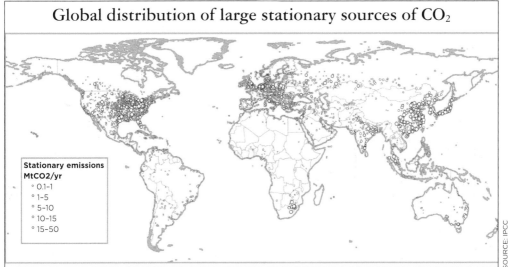

SOURCE: IPCC

Four regional clusters account for the majority of CO$_2$ emissions into the atmosphere, expressed above in circles depicting million tons of carbon dioxide (MtCO$_2$): North America (particularly the East and Midwest), Europe (the northwest region), East Asia (the eastern coast of China) and South Asia (the Indian subcontinent).

On July 25, 1997, the Senate passed a unanimous resolution (by a vote of 95 to 0) preventing the United States from becoming a signatory to the United Nations Framework Convention on Climate Change of 1992 or allowing federal officials from engaging in further negotiations in Kyoto. By passing this resolution, the Senate rejected the Kyoto Protocol while the treaty was still in the review phase.

According to U.S. *legem terrae,* whose principle lies in a constitutional balance of three branches of government, the legislative branch must ratify an accord of the Kyoto type that is made by the executive branch of government to become legally binding.

In the Byrd-Hagel Resolution (S. Res. 98), the Senate cited the exemption for developing countries as being inconsistent with the need for global action on climate change and the potential for the U.S. economy to suffer under an unevenhanded Kyoto mandate.

Then, on November 12, 1998, acting U.N. ambassador Peter Burleigh signed the Kyoto Protocol on behalf of the United States, at the direction of President Clinton and Vice President Gore, with the caveat that the Clinton administration would not take the document for ratification to the Senate until developing nations agreed to mandatory GHG reductions.

Later, in March 2001, after George W. Bush became president, he explained in a letter to various senators why he rejected the Clinton administration's support of the Kyoto treaty. "I oppose the Kyoto Protocol because it exempts eighty percent of the world, including major population centers such as China and India from compliance, and would cause serious harm to the U.S. economy," wrote President Bush. "The Senate's vote, ninety-five to zero, shows that there is a clear consensus that the Kyoto Protocol is an unfair and ineffective means of addressing global climate change concerns," the president's statement concluded.

The United States has continued to insist on a level playing field and has called upon all nations to participate in the reduction of climate-changing emissions.

Political pressures continue to mount, with "fairness" put forth as the overriding complaint. Developing nations contend that the Western nations' economic growth in the 20th century surged by burning fossil fuel, and now it is their turn to thrive without the emission restrictions that have become an assumed obligation in the 21st century.

The U.S. government is looking for alternative ways to reduce GHG emissions by the large-emitting countries by doing an end run around to the Kyoto Protocol's principle of "common but differentiated responsibilities."

The George W. Bush administration, through EPA and Congress, has considered a series of administrative regulations and legislation intended to level the playing field of the world's largest emitters of carbon dioxide. The measures are geared to reducing U.S. atmosphere-warming emissions by 2020 as well as forcing other developing countries that export raw material to the United States to reduce their own emissions.

One proposal in Congress would cap GHG emissions of U.S. companies by 2012 and impose reserve allowances on imports of raw materials that require a

great deal of energy to make. This might include cement, glass, paper, aluminum, iron and steel.

Reserve allowances are assigned a market value by a governmental entity, giving the party assigned an incentive to emit fewer GHGs in order to conserve these allowances. This aspect of the measure would serve to compel some developing countries exporting to the United States to reduce emissions.

According to proponents, these types of restrictions would allow economic competitiveness for purchasing materials such as cement, iron and steel if they were produced worldwide under carbon restraints as in the United States. The developing countries exporting to the United States would have to pay a premium. This functions in essence as a trade tariff on countries such as China and India.

The Netherlands Environmental Assessment Agency, under the auspices of the Hague as the seat of the Dutch government, released a report in 2007 noting that China produced 44 percent of the world's cement by relying mostly on burning coal—a greenhouse gas emitter—for two-thirds of its energy consumption.

Other estimates place China manufacturing as low as 37 percent of the world's cement, followed by India with 6 percent and the United States with 5 percent. Whether China produces 37 or 44 percent of the world's cement is immaterial. The fact remains that China produces a staggering amount of cement and releases a proportionate share of GHGs. This is particularly troubling since most cement-producing facilities in China are outdated and inefficient, causing cement production to contribute from 6 to 8 percent of all CO_2 emissions in China.

Cement production adds CO_2 emissions from various processes, including the calcination process (a chemical reaction from heating limestone), generation of power needed to make the cement, and the combustion of fuels to heat the material in the kiln. Combustion accounts for roughly 40 percent and calcination for the balance of 60 percent of the total CO_2 emissions from cement manufacturing facilities. The manufacturing of cement produces just under one pound (0.45 kilograms) of CO_2 for every pound of cement created.

According to the World Business Council for Sustainable Development, global cement production increased approximately 20 percent during the 1990s and continues to increase as the world becomes more industrialized. Cement manufacturing accounts for approximately 5 percent of CO_2 emissions worldwide.

For comparison, the Portland Cement Association says that the average U.S. household is responsible for emitting 28,400 pounds (12.9 metric tons) of CO_2 in a year. Two U.S. family vehicles emit 26,500 pounds (12 metric tons) of CO_2 in a year and a Boeing 747 commercial passenger jetliner emits 880,000 pounds (403 metric tons) of CO_2 while flying one-way between London and New York.

However, climate-changing emissions are not to be blamed exclusively on cement production, living in a comfortable suburban house, driving your car, flying commercially or using energy produced from burning carbon fuel.

A substantial amount of carbon dioxide regularly absorbed by the roughly 12 million square miles (31 million sq km) of currently arable land with trees and other

vegetation on Earth is now escaping into the atmosphere because of unchecked deforestation.

This is due to the rampant harvesting of forests and through certain land use changes that are resulting in a loss of arable land occurring at a rate of 38,610 square miles (100,000 sq km) per year. With today's burgeoning population, arable land is priceless because less than one-fourth of Earth's 57 million square miles (148 million sq km) of land is arable.

According to the World Wildlife Fund (WWF), an organization working for the preservation of species, Earth's forest cover has shrunk about one-third since the last ice age to approximately 15 million square miles (39 million sq km). Slightly less than half (47 percent) of the forests around the world are tropical, 9 percent are subtropical, 11 percent are temperate and 33 percent are boreal.

The WWF notes that 60 percent of the world's forests are located within Brazil, Canada, the People's Republic of China, Indonesia, the Russian Federation, the United States and the Democratic Republic of Congo.

According to Greenpeace, an environmental activist organization with 2.5 million members worldwide, only sixteen ecoregions contain 50 percent of the world's most important intact forest landscapes. Among the key forests in Eurasia, cites Greenpeace, are the Scandinavian and Russian taiga, the West Siberian taiga and the East Siberian taiga. In Central Africa, the most important are the Central and Northeastern Congolian lowland forests.

In North America, the interior Alaska/Yukon lowland taiga, the southern Hudson Bay taiga, the midwestern Canadian shield forests, the eastern Canadian forests, and the northern and eastern Canadian shield taiga are the most significant intact forest landscapes.

In South America, the Guyanan moist forests and Guyanan highlands moist forests, the Uatuma-Trombetas rainforests, the Madeira-Tapajos rainforests and the southwest Amazon rainforests are key forests.

However, there are many smaller but vital imperiled ecosystems such as southern Chile's Valdivian coastal range, which contains important forests necessary to absorb Earth's now abundant carbon dioxide in the air.

When combining the damages of deforestation with the heat-trapping effects of fossil fuel combustion, countries such as Brazil, China, Indonesia and Malaysia move up to the world's top emitters of GHG, according to published reports.

Conservation International attributes about 20 percent of global CO_2 emissions escaping into the atmosphere to tropical deforestation, which is more than all the world's cars, trucks, trains and airplanes combined.

Critics of the Kyoto pact call for a tighter agreement in Bali to curtail deforestation, and they are quick to point out that no blame can be pinned on North America for GHGs resulting from loss of forestland. The Kyoto Protocol expires in 2012, but the United Nations began talks in 2007 to create the next multination initiative to replace the Kyoto agreement in 2013.

A major U.N. conference, hosted by the government of Indonesia, took place at the Bali International Convention Centre in December 2007, bringing together representatives from more than 180 countries with observers from intergovernmental and nongovernmental organizations, and the media. They plan to take part in setting new GHG reduction targets. Although most countries agree that the largest emitters should mitigate GHG emissions, not all concur with the methods or the targets because of conflicting interests.

Island nations worried about rising sea levels that could wipe out large amounts of their land are exerting the most pressure, while developing countries fear that reducing their emissions will slow their now robust economic growth. Oil-producing countries have expressed concern that a reduction of GHG emissions will cut their oil revenues and thus slow their economic growth.

Japan, an island nation that is also industrialized, ratified the Kyoto Protocol in 2002. Japan's Foreign Ministry's director-general estimates that the United States and China together now account for 40 to 45 percent of the world's GHG emissions, and as such is exerting pressure on those two countries to take action.

After almost 10 years since its introduction, Australia's prime minister, Kevin Rudd, signed the Kyoto Protocol in December 2007 as the first official act of a newly elected Australian government. Australia committed to meeting its Kyoto Protocol target and voluntarily set a new target to reduce GHG emissions by 60 percent on 2000 levels by 2050.

Australia also agreed to participate constructively in the negotiations, working toward a post-2012 agreement with the caveat that it would do so providing the new agreement be equitable and effective. In outlining its position, Australia issued a warning to the United Nations stating that any binding commitments toward Kyoto's successor need to encompass both developed and developing countries to be truly successful in tackling climate change.

GHG emissions are measured both as total output and on a per capita basis. The United Nations has considered Australia one of the largest contributors of carbon emissions per capita, although it ranks it among the lowest when measuring emissions per square mile, because of Australia's vast land mass coupled with its low population density.

The United Nations estimates that the European Union produces about 22 percent of global atmosphere-warming emissions. The global association of governments facilitating cooperation in international law, security, economic development and social equity has worked closely with the European Union, a staunch supporter of the Kyoto Protocol.

The European Union is also an advocate of a worldwide low-carbon economy, whereby a freeze would be imposed on the tonnage of CO_2 emissions from burning carbon-based fuels such as coal, natural gas, gasoline and oil. Under this concept, a reduction of carbon-based fuels compared to the level frozen by law would occur at some point in the 21st century.

Each of the EU's initial 15 members signed off on the goal of curbing their carbon emissions by 8 percent by 2012 compared to 1990 levels.

Germany is the most aggressive EU nation, proposing to cut GHG emissions in half by 2050 compared to 1990 levels. Some climatologists advocate that a 50 percent reduction over this period is necessary to avert the worst consequences of climate change.

As the European Union has grown its member states to 27, the European Commission (EC), the EU's governing body, has been pressuring all its member nations to achieve a new accelerated goal of reducing GHG emissions by as much as 20 percent compared to 1990 levels. Central European nations are the most conflicted because their continued economic growth requires increased energy consumption.

CLIMATE DISRUPTION

The worldwide pressure to prevent climate change—now broadly accepted as a serious threat—is rooted in the fear of the threatened consequences. That is, any activity that causes climate disruption would eventually result in the catastrophic effects being predicted, and therefore must be stopped.

The UNEP Intergovernmental Panel on Climate Change (IPCC) is one of the most reliable sources on monitoring climate change even though some scientists still dispute its claims. The IPCC regularly conducts studies and publishes its findings for the United Nations and national governments to act upon them. Because of this work, the 2007 Nobel Peace Prize was awarded to the IPCC to equally share with Al Gore, who has positioned himself as a champion for the cause.

"Eleven of the warmest years since instrumental records have been kept (1850) occurred during the last twelve years and therefore climate change is accelerating," warned IPCC chief Pachauri.

Many scientists concluded that one piece of evidence that Earth's climate has already begun a path of change is shown in weather-related records, which have been repeatedly broken during the 2000s. Land surface temperatures throughout the world in January and April 2007 were about 3°F (1.6°C) warmer than the average for the same months since record keeping began in 1880, according to the World Meteorological Organization.

According to climatologists at NASA's Goddard Institute for Space Studies, Earth's surface temperature has increased by 1.44°F (0.8°C) over the past 100 years.

SOURCE: NATIONAL CLIMATIC DATA CENTER (NCDC)—U.S. DEPARTMENT OF COMMERCE, THE NATIONAL OCEANIC AND ATMOSPHERIC ADMINISTRATION (NOAA)

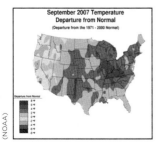

September 2007 Temperature Departure from Normal
(Departure from the 1971 - 2000 Normal)

To track climate variability and change, the U.S. National Climatic Data Center (NCDC) tracks temperatures across the continental United States and compares them to averages for 1971 through 2000. In this example, the areas depicted in red and dark red show September 2007 temperatures between 4 and 8°F (2.2 and 4.4°C) warmer than average. The areas in pink are 2°F (1.1°C) warmer while the areas in light blue are 2°F cooler.

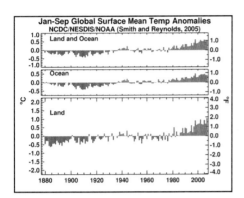

Jan-Sep Global Surface Mean Temp Anomalies
NCDC/NESDIS/NOAA (Smith and Reynolds, 2005)

Land and ocean temperatures all over the world have increased substantially since 1980. NCDC calculated long-term mean temperatures on Earth by processing data from thousands of worldwide observation sites on land and sea for the entire period of record of the data beginning approximately in 1880.

SOURCE: NATIONAL CLIMATIC DATA CENTER (NCDC)— U.S. DEPARTMENT OF COMMERCE, THE NATIONAL OCEANIC AND ATMOSPHERIC ADMINISTRATION (NOAA), NATIONAL ENVIRONMENTAL SATELLITE, DATA, AND INFORMATION SERVICE (NESDIS)

The IPCC concurs. In a report released on November 17, 2007, the IPCC claims that temperatures have risen 1.3°F (0.7°C) in the last 100 years and that 11 years of the 12-year period between 1996 and 2007 are among the warmest since 1850.

John R. Christy, director of the Earth System Science Center at the University of Alabama in Huntsville and a member of the IPCC, said temperatures are increasing over time but not drastically.

The Great Ocean Conveyor Belt is crucial to maintaining climate stability by circulating warm water across the globe. It affects both seawater and coastal land temperatures.

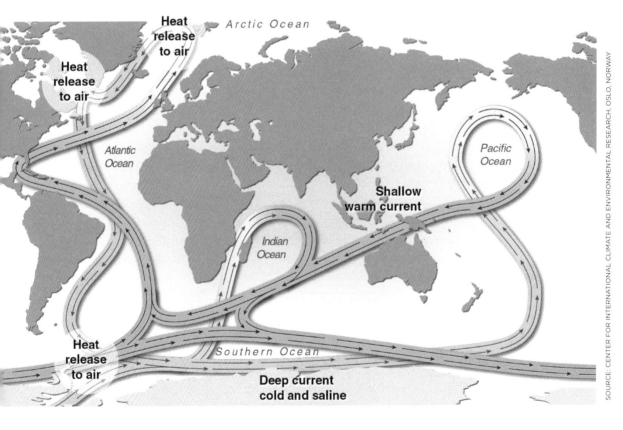

SOURCE: CENTER FOR INTERNATIONAL CLIMATE AND ENVIRONMENTAL RESEARCH, OSLO, NORWAY

Christy pointed to satellite data from the U.S. National Oceanic and Atmospheric Administration to support what he referred to as a modest warming trend of 2.5°F (1.4°C) for the past century or about 0.25°F (0.14°C) per decade.

However, mild temperature hikes in the tropics can result in severe temperature differences in the polar caps, primarily due to ocean currents distributing Earth's warmth across the globe.

One example is the Gulf Stream, a warm ocean current that flows northeast-wardly from the U.S. Southeastern coasts and the Gulf of Mexico toward Western Europe. Some scientists predict that an intrusion of ice-cold fresh water from melt-ing Arctic ice caps can divert this current southward and significantly chill Western Europe, which now remains relatively warm because of the Gulf Stream despite its very northerly latitudes.

Another phenomenon that aids in heat transfer from sea to land to air and works in conjunction with the Gulf Stream is known as the Great Ocean Conveyor Belt. This Conveyor Belt of ocean currents is crucial to maintaining a balance in our climate. It transfers warm water from the Pacific Ocean to the Atlantic Ocean in a relatively shallow current. It then returns deep-current cold water from the Atlantic back to the Pacific.

The IPCC warns that climate change could alter the currents as we know them. A warming of the polar caps is likely to increase precipitation runoff and melt fresh-water ice, which if substantial enough could then flow from the Arctic Ocean into the Atlantic Ocean.

A significant amount of fresh water pouring into the salt water of the Gulf Stream may prevent the diluted water from sinking deep enough in the ocean to allow the belt to effectively conduct the heat throughout the continents. The weakening of the Conveyor Belt could lead to even greater climate change in Europe and other continents.

It is critical to maintain the integrity of the Conveyor Belt in the wake of new evidence of melting polar caps, which can also contribute to rising sea levels.

THE BIG THAW

The year 2005 was a wake-up call for climatologists. It was one of the worst on record for ice sheet melt in Greenland. In 2006, a NASA-funded research study found, through satellite photos of the northern ice cap, that more days of snow melting were evident at high altitudes in Greenland than the average measured over the previous 18 years.

Conditions worsened in 2007. Greenland's ice sheet melted almost 19 billion tons (17.2 billion metric tons) more in summer 2007 than the previous high mark, making the volume of Arctic sea ice at half the size of summer 2003. Greenland's ice sheet melt that summer was 552 billion tons (500 billion metric tons) of ice or 12 percent worse than 2005, according to University of Colorado research and NASA satellite data.

Greenland is a climate change bellwether because ice covers most of the land surface. If the Greenland ice sheet melts, the IPCC will not begin to speculate by how many more feet the seas will rise, but the panel expects that a rise would inundate coastal cities and overflow many inland rivers. Some scientists predicted that if this ice melted completely, the world sea level could rise more than 22 feet (6.7 m).

The U.S. National Oceanic and Atmospheric Administration (NOAA) published a benchmark State of the Arctic report in 2006, and then gave a follow-up report in 2007 to update its findings. According to the report, winter and spring 2007 temperatures were considerably above historical averages, and a shrubifying effect was evident on the arctic tundra.

As shrubbery begins to grow in areas formerly covered with ice, the shrub cover absorbs more radiation from the Sun and accelerates the warming effect in the polar regions. The Geophysical Institute of the University of Alaska in Fairbanks reported that the permafrost in Alaska and Siberia is warming, although not quite thawing.

Sea ice cover in 2007 was 39 percent smaller than average and 23 percent less than 2005, according to Jacqueline Richter-Menge of the Hanover, New Hampshire-based Cold Regions Research and Engineering Laboratory.

Experts tracking climate variances point to satellite photos of the northern section of a large floating ice mass on the eastern side of the Antarctic Peninsula—known as Larsen B—as evidence that climate change is well underway. The ice shelf is slowly disintegrating into the Weddell Sea, as noted in photos that show huge structural differences in 2002 when the ice mass began collapsing.

This collapsing Larsen B shelf, the size of Rhode Island, was no minimal event. It consisted of 1,255 square miles (3,250 sq km) of ice approximately 700 feet (213 m) thick and weighing 720 billion tons (653 billion metric tons).

This ice shelf likely formed between 10,000 and 12,000 years ago toward the end of the last major global glaciation known as the Wisconsin Ice Age, when ice covered much of Earth. At one point during the Wisconsin Ice Age, ice covered 97 percent of what is present-day Canada.

Glacial retreating is also evidenced on the opposite pole. The Columbia Glacier, one of the best-known tidewater glaciers of Alaska, is melting into the Prince William Sound. The glacier is about 400 square miles (1,000 sq km) and 1,800 feet (549 m) thick but has thinned to about 1,300 feet (396 m) in some parts since 1980.

According to a study by the University of Colorado at Boulder Institute of Arctic and Alpine Research, it has shrunk in length by 9 miles (14 km) since 1980 (now 32 miles [52 km] long) despite the enormous amount of annual snowfall that accu-

2002 MODIS IMAGE COURTESY OF NASA'S TERRA SATELLITE

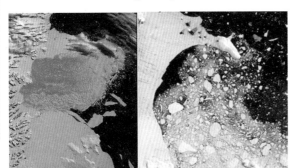

Moderate Resolution Imaging Spectroradiometer (MODIS) photographs taken from NASA's *Terra* satellite of the northern section of the Larsen B ice shelf on Antarctic Peninsula collapsed and separated from the continent, leaving thousands of smaller icebergs floating in the Weddell Sea.

mulates on the glacier, covering the Chugach Mountains where the glacier descends. Experts say the Columbia Glacier retreat is North America's single largest contributor to rising sea level.

Muir Glacier, the tidewater glacier in Glacier Bay National Park and Preserve in Alaska, is also retreating. John Muir, the naturalist, wrote stories about the glacier in the *San Francisco Bulletin* during his first two visits in 1878 and 1880. Muir died in 1915, but if he were alive today, he likely would not recognize the substantially thawed glacier named for him.

Climatologists contend that glacial retreat is a clear sign that the climate is changing. Glaciers have been receding since 1980, and ice shelves have been disintegrating substantially since 1995. Some scientists estimate that the thickness of the polar ice caps may have already diminished by as much as 40 percent in the past 40 years.

According to the IPCC, sea levels have gone up by an average 0.07 inches (1.7 centimeters) per year since 1961. EPA estimates that sea level has already risen six to eight inches over the past century, but the real danger to sea level lies in the polar caps, particularly the Southern Hemisphere, which houses the bulk of the world's ice.

Antarctica, more commonly known as the South Pole, contains about 90 percent of the world's ice and 70 percent of the fresh water, albeit in a frozen state, found in glaciers and polar ice caps. Any significant melting of the Antarctic ice would send global sea levels soaring a dozen feet or so, and fresh water dumped into the sea from melting ice could alter global ocean currents, causing massive climate disruption. "Manhattan, Venice, Maracaibo and Buenos Aires are all at risk," said Benjamin A. Bross, LEED AP, design director of Constructora Planigrupo, S.A., a leading Mexican shopping center developer.

CONFUSED ANIMALS

Climate change is disrupting the life patterns of many wild animals living near the poles. The goose population in northern lands has increased, and with it, overgraz-

Muir Glacier in Alaska. Photo on left taken August 13, 1941, by glaciologist William O. Field; photo on right taken from the same vantage point on August 31, 2004, by geologist Bruce F. Molnia of the United States Geological Survey (USGS). According to Molnia, Muir Glacier has retreated more than 7 miles (11 km) and thinned by 875 yards (800 m) between 1941 and 2004.

PHOTOS COURTESY OF NSIDC/WDC FOR GLACIOLOGY, BOULDER, COMPILER, 2002, UPDATED 2006, GLACIER PHOTOGRAPH COLLECTION. BOULDER, CO: NATIONAL SNOW AND ICE DATA CENTER/ WORLD DATA CENTER FOR GLACIOLOGY.

On the left is a photograph of Qori Kalis Glacier taken in July 1978, and on the right, a photograph taken from the same vantage in July 2004. Lonnie G. Thompson took both photographs.

The Qori Kalis Glacier is the largest ice outlet from the Quelccaya Ice Cap in Peru's southeast corner. The ice cap has diminished by 20 percent since 1963 and melted at an accelerated rate between 1998 and 2001.

PHOTOS: LONNIE G. THOMPSON, BYRD POLAR RESEARCH CENTER, THE OHIO STATE UNIVERSITY/COURTESY NSIDC.

ing is evident in some areas. Because of altering climate conditions, the population of caribou around Alaska and Canada is declining, partly due to their inability to migrate to new feeding grounds.

In late summer, early autumn 2007, Pacific walruses arrived ashore earlier on the Russian side of the Bering Strait, which separates Alaska from Russia, and stayed longer than usual. Some herds grew to 40,000 at Point Shmidt, resulting in disaster as crowding and stampeding killed thousands.

PHOTO CREDIT: CAPTAIN BUDD CHRISTMAN, NOAA CORPS

Polar bears are also vulnerable. In Churchill, Manitoba, located on the Canadian sub-Arctic western tip of Hudson Bay, polar bears are waiting several weeks longer into November to migrate to solid ice—their hunting grounds—because of increasingly warmer weather every year.

Hudson Bay is melting about three weeks earlier and is freezing later than it did in the mid-1980s. The ice mass was thinner and smaller during the 2000s than it was during the two previous decades. Because the icy surface is less stable, the polar bears wait until the ice is thick enough to venture out.

The walrus is at home at Bering Sea Island, but melting ice caps can crowd its habitat. Climate disruption forces polar bears to return to land in July from Hudson Bay.

This climate disruption gives the white behemoths less time to venture into the Arctic ice, where they prey primarily on ringed seals. According to Polar Bears International, a nonprofit group dedicated to worldwide conservation of polar bears, the Western Hudson Bay polar bear population declined from 1,140 to 950 between 1997 and 2007. Scientists are predicting a decline of three-quarters of the polar bear population by 2050.

While about 74 percent of the world's polar bears live in North America's Arctic region, all penguins live in the Southern Hemisphere in Antarctica, along the west-

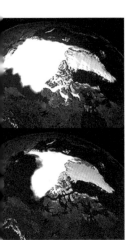

Left photos show sea ice extent on September 21, 1979, and September 14, 2007 (lower photo).

Emperor penguins enjoy their scenery in the Antarctic ice in the Southern Hemisphere, where the ice is slowly disintegrating into the Weddell Sea.

SOURCE: IMAGES COURTESY NASA/GODDARD SPACE FLIGHT CENTER SCIENTIFIC VISUALIZATION STUDIO

PHOTO: BERNARD BRETON © 2008 ISTOCK INTERNATIONAL INC.

ern and southern coasts of South America and the tips of southern Australia, New Zealand and South Africa, where the thawing phenomenon mirrors the Northern Arctic.

The IPCC says that more pollution could bring abrupt and irreversible changes in this century, such as polar sea ice diminishing by another 40 percent and a corresponding rise in sea levels between 4 and 6 inches (10 and 15 cm) because warming in the polar regions happens relatively quickly.

When the sun's rays strike the white arctic ice, the rays reflect about 80 percent of the sun's heat upward. But as the ice melts and dark water appears below, 90 percent of the sun's rays and heat are instead absorbed into the ocean water, which warms sufficiently enough to melt the ice that surrounds it.

Climatologists all over the world now predict almost unanimously that unless humans significantly curtail the vast release of heat-trapping pollutants into the atmosphere in the next few decades, climate adjustments of unprecedented magnitude will cause costly disruption of human and natural systems throughout the world.

In this apocalyptic scenario, which proponents maintain can still be averted, many weather-related fatalities would occur. One such prediction in which deaths might result is extensive evaporation of soil moisture content and drought. Drought would degrade cropland and spoil the quality of water sources.

PROPENSITY FOR WILDFIRES

Extreme heat draws the moisture out of the soil and causes vegetation to wilt and die—and with that comes the danger of wildfires. Forces of nature or human negligence cause forest fires. When lightning from frequent storms hits the dry vegetation on the ground, temperatures can reach 572°F (300°C), the flash point necessary for woody material to catch on fire, in an instant. Many other fires start because of careless human activity, but in either case, wind and dry vegetation drive fires to spread uncontrollably.

Was climate change responsible for Southern California's runaway brushfires of October 2007? Some say yes; others dispute it. However, it is indisputable that climate change makes droughts more persistent, which exacerbates the potential for fires.

Some scientists link higher summer temperatures to large wildfires in the U.S. western states, according to a research report by the Institute for the Study of Planet Earth of the University of Arizona.

Climate change causes earlier snowmelt in mountain forests. An increase in drought and the lengthier dry periods between rainfalls boost the risk of wildfires.

The University of Arizona study also shows that invasive grasses thrive in warmer temperatures. As they dry up, they can quickly succumb to flying sparks and burn—igniting nearby combustible material into flames and spreading over many miles.

Senate Majority Leader Harry Reid of Nevada blamed the droughts and global warming for causing the October 2007 California fires that horribly scorched many homes in San Diego, Orange and Los Angeles Counties.

IPCC member John R. Christy refuted those claims, saying it is a stretch to link those droughts to climate change. "If you look at a one thousand-year climate record for the U.S. Southwestern states, you will see not five-year cycles of droughts—such as the one that caused conditions for the California 2003 and 2007 fires to spread—but fifty-year-long droughts," said Christy. "The twelfth and thirteenth centuries were dry."

However, incidences of major wildfires in the western United States between 1986 and 2004 quadrupled over the period between 1970 and 1986. The forest acreage burned was even worse: six times greater from 1986 to 2004 compared to the 1970-to-1986 period.

Officials blamed arsonists for setting some of the 2007 wildfires and the Santa Ana winds for spreading them. However, dry conditions caused by warming temperatures and infrequent rain can result in the *perfect firestorm*, as was the case with the wildfires that ravaged Southern California in October 2007.

A total of 23 brushfires—15 huge ones—ravaged uncontrollably when the powerful Santa Ana westward winds whipped dry air from the desert and spread flames over nearly three-quarters of a million acres in Southern California. The firestorms reduced 1,760 homes and 338 commercial buildings to ashes, and although the death toll was small at just seven, the damages were estimated at around US$2.6 billion. The 2007 disaster caused almost 1 million people to flee their homes.

Two researchers, one from the University of Arizona's Laboratory of Tree-Ring Research and another from the University of California-San Diego's Scripps Institution of Oceanography, co-published a scientific paper in 2006 that concluded that the changing climate had a greater influence on wildfire activity and intensity than forest management.

Fires are not only destructive to surfaces and structures on the ground; they also pollute the atmosphere. Extremely hazardous air quality remained for weeks in the aftermath of the October 2007 wildfires, which spewed massive amounts of smoke into the atmosphere. Smoke contains microscopic particles of burned wood and other organic matter mixed with gases.

Mother polar bear and cub (*Ursus maritimus*) in 2006. Bears need to survive the summers when they are on solid land and without access to their food source—seals.

CREDIT: NOAA CLIMATE PROGRAM OFFICE, NABOS 2006 EXPEDITION/MIKE DUNN, NC STATE MUSEUM OF NATURAL SCIENCES

PHOTO: T. J. MILIAN - OCTOBER 27, 2007   SOURCE: NOAA

Santa Ana winds spread wildfires over 100 miles (160 km) almost to the California coast in October 2007 (top photo).

Extremely hazardous air quality remained for weeks in the wake of the Southern California October 2007 wildfires that spewed massive amounts of smoke into the atmosphere. The lower photo depicts a smoky, hazy skyline of Glendale, California. The setting sun barely shows through the thick atmosphere that has been polluted by the smoke that lingered days after the blazes were mostly contained. The California Environmental Protection Agency warned that the elderly, children and people suffering from heart and respiratory conditions were particularly vulnerable to high pollution levels.

The biggest health threat after massive fires have been contained comes from these fine toxic particles, which irritate the eyes and clog the respiratory system. Symptoms include burning eyes, runny nose and respiratory illnesses, such as bronchitis.

"The air [in some parts] has been going from unhealthy to hazardous, which means everyone's advice is to stay indoors," Patricia Rey, a spokeswoman for the California Environmental Protection Agency Air Resources Board told reporters at a news conference three days after the 2007 fires were contained.

Pollution levels in the atmosphere shot up three times higher than normal, while ash and soot polluted the ground. Retailers and shopping center operators in Southern California had to react to the heavy pollution levels by limiting outside activity and optimizing their heating, ventilating and air-conditioning (HVAC) units, which included replacing air filters clogged with ash and soot buildup.

During the same news conference, Rey also warned about the long-term effects of pollution and the greenhouse gases emitted by the fires.

Almost 30 percent of all the CO_2 released into the atmosphere every year comes from burning forests. With the help of sunlight, plants and trees absorb carbon dioxide from the atmosphere through photosynthesis. Plants and trees also release about half of the CO_2 they assimilate through photosynthesis back to the atmosphere by plant respiration. When plants and trees burn, they release the carbon dioxide back into the atmosphere.

This process is known as the carbon cycle, which over time circulates the carbon atoms on Earth. The same carbon atoms in your body have been in many other molecules since the beginning of time. This is because the carbon stored in plants and other living organisms remains within them only while they are alive.

Plants, animals and humans typically return the carbon to the soil when they die, through decomposition. Subsequently, new plants or small microorganisms absorb the carbon atoms from the soil.

The vast amount of carbon dioxide from the animals, plants, wood and other organic matter that burned in the California fires of 2007 could have taken several

courses, including being absorbed into the atmosphere, adding to the greenhouse effect or being absorbed by oceans and land plants.

Scientists believe that between one-fourth and one-third of all the carbon dioxide regularly emitted into the atmosphere is naturally absorbed where it can cause no harm, and the remainder mixes with other natural gases in the atmosphere to add to the greenhouse effect.

Typically, the oceans absorb one-quarter of the CO_2, and land plants absorb an additional one-quarter through photosynthesis. When animals and humans eat those plants, the carbon becomes part of their bodies. Animals and humans use the carbon to build up their own tissue. These animals and humans exhale carbon dioxide when they breathe. In turn, other plants absorb that carbon with the help of the sun as part of photosynthesis, which helps the plants convert the carbon atoms from the carbon dioxide to produce sugars.

The carbon cycle actually recycles carbon atoms in living things, but the process is slow. Large wildfires release much more carbon than can be absorbed by other living things for several months—even years. Particularly when thousands of large trees are lost in forest fires, the balance between new plants absorbing carbon dioxide to dying plants releasing CO_2 is disturbed drastically.

The California Air Resources Board estimated that the 2007 Southern California fires released into the atmosphere the equivalent greenhouse gas emissions of 440,000 cars over the course of a year, according to spokesperson Rey.

Christine Wiedinmyer, a member of the Biosphere-Atmosphere Interactions group at the National Center for Atmospheric Research (NCAR) in Boulder, Colorado, used satellite observations of the October 2007 wildfires and a new computer model she developed to estimate carbon dioxide emissions based on the mass of vegetation burned.

Wiedinmyer estimated that the 2007 fires emitted 8.7 million tons (7.9 million metric tons) of carbon dioxide in just the one-week period of October 19–26. This is equivalent to 25 percent of the monthly emissions from all fossil fuel burning throughout California. Wiedinmyer's model has a wide margin of error of about 50 percent, putting the actual GHG emissions between four and 4.4 and 13.2 million tons (12 million metric tons).

And so, what began as a concern for personal safety and property when the Santa Ana winds started spreading fires in Southern California in 2007 eventually became an environmental issue regarding emissions and brought about questions of whether climate change will cause wildfires more frequently.

In a November 2007 report, the IPCC noted that climate change is already occurring and predicted the change will bring more heat waves and raise the risk of wildfires in the future.

Warmer, windier weather and longer, drier summers could mean higher firefighting costs and greater loss of lives and property, according to researchers at the Lawrence Berkeley National Laboratory in Northern California and the U.S. Forest Service.

CATASTROPHIC WEATHER EVENTS

But the dangers of climate change do not end there. Evaporation of soil moisture and ocean surface waters draws the moisture into the air and causes other types of weather-related disasters. Massive moisture in the air results in increased floods in some regions and droughts in others. Climate change causes more precipitation but relocates where it falls, which is the reason for the droughts.

The prognosis for the future includes the likelihood that there will be more flood-causing downpours in some areas and longer droughts in others, accompanied by more intense heat waves.

Among various dire predictions by the IPCC are more common extreme weather conditions. Rising sea levels could be accompanied by torrential coastal storms that tend to erode beaches, inundate coastal areas, and damage buildings.

Tropical storms will be more frequent and more intense. Heavy rains will affect some areas and spread diseases. As glaciers severely retreat, they can cause landslides, flash floods, and increased water flowing into rivers.

Climate change is contributing to river flows by melting the glaciers of the Himalayas. Swollen rivers result in floods, and with added storms, the situation worsens quickly.

In 2007, one of the worst torrential monsoons in South Asia made the rivers flowing from the Himalayan peaks in Nepal through the northern Bihar and Uttar Pradesh states of India extremely swollen. As the rivers crested, they flooded thousands of villages.

Without proper historical weather records, Bihar's Disaster Management Office called the storms unprecedented, saying people 80 years of age had never witnessed such heavy rainfall. In total, 38 million people in India were driven from their homes or had family members killed from these weather events.

About 38 million people in India were driven from their homes by a destructive monsoon in 2007.

Nearby densely populated areas in Nepal, Pakistan and Bangladesh also suffered from the aftermath of this South Asia storm. Millions were also left homeless in Bangladesh and Nepal.

In 2007, several U.S. cities experienced their hottest recorded August temperatures—ever—including Charleston, South Carolina; Cincinnati, Ohio; Louisville, Kentucky; Memphis, Tennessee; and Phoenix, Arizona. In Louisville, average daily temperatures—taking into account the high and low each day of the month—averaged 85.1°F (29.5°C) in August compared to the normal average temperature of 77.1°F (25°C) degrees, 8°F (4.4°C) above the August historical norm.

Whereas hot temperatures over land draw moisture into the clouds, much worse conditions can occur when these hot temperatures warm up ocean waters. Hurricanes are among

SOURCE: U.S. NATIONAL OCEANIC AND ATMO-SPHERIC ADMINISTRATION (NOAA)

the most destructive of all weather events. They occur in the North Atlantic when cool air travels south and passes over deep and warm ocean waters of at least 78°F (26.5°C) in the summer.

As water vapor rises and condenses within the body of the storm, latent heat is released, making the storm stronger and more intense. When the water temperature cools off some months later in late autumn, hurricanes subside and totally disappear until the next summer, when the cycle starts all over again.

As these tropical storms travel northwest over the warm current above the Gulf of Mexico, they can gain enormous strength—as was the case with Hurricanes Katrina and Rita in 2005—and become destructive Category 5 hurricanes.

Hurricane Katrina slammed the Gulf Coast on August 29, 2005, as a powerful Category 5 hurricane, and the colossal Hurricane Rita followed less than one month later, making landfall between the Louisiana and Texas coasts on September

The warm Gulf Coast was a critical ingredient in intensifying Hurricane Katrina's wind velocity and strength, converting it into a Category 5 hurricane. Hurricane Katrina caused severe destruction across the entire Mississippi Gulf Coast, especially in Alabama, Louisiana and Mississippi

Two-thirds of the land in Africa is arid or semiarid. In the Nature Reserve of Popenguine, Senegal (depicted), the lack of rain and the sun's intense heat crack the earth's surface. Most of Senegal's territory is in the Sahel zone, regularly susceptible to ongoing cycles of drought and floods. Climate change disrupts weather patterns causing persistent droughts in some areas and floods in others.

SOURCE: U.N. PHOTO BY EVAN SCHNEIDER

24. Rita became the fourth most intense Atlantic storm in history, according to the U.S. National Hurricane Center.

Meteorologists measure storm intensity in the western hemisphere by the Saffir-Simpson Hurricane Scale. This classification scale divides hurricanes into five categories, distinguished by the intensities of their sustained winds.

To be classified as a hurricane, a tropical cyclone must have maximum sustained winds exceeding 74 miles (119 km) per hour, which makes it a Category 1 hurricane. Below that would be a tropical storm or tropical depression. The highest classification in the scale, Category 5, is reserved for storms with winds greater than 155 miles (249 km) per hour.

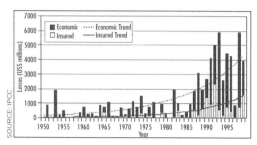

Inflation-adjusted losses from extreme weather events around the world have risen substantially since the late 1980s. The shopping center industry has evidenced rising costs for insurance premiums, which have translated into higher common area costs relating to tenant insurance reimbursable charges. In many cases, the landlord has had to absorb some or all of these increases.

The warming effect of the oceans make it likely that these types of storms will appear more frequently in Central and North America, and maybe as far south as South America.

In 2004, Brazil experienced a hurricane for the first time ever. The Category 1 storm, dubbed Catarina by meteorologists, made landfall about 520 miles (840 km) southwest of Rio de Janeiro, packing sustained winds of 74 miles (119 km) per hour. The U.S. National Weather Center in Miami pronounced it the first hurricane on record in the South Atlantic Ocean.

The worldwide insurance industry—accounting for US$3.4 trillion in annual premium revenue—is facing a dilemma from trying to manage risk involving extreme weather events.

Hurricanes Katrina and Rita, in combination with other weather-related losses, made 2005 the costliest year ever for property insurers. Global natural disasters caused US$230 billion in damage. According to reinsurer Swiss Re, only about one-third was insured at US$83 billion. Katrina alone cost the insurance industry about US$45 billion.

While the news media colloquially refers to climate change as global warming, the former is a more accurate term than the latter because some areas tend to become warmer, others cooler, some wetter and others drier, according to Michelle Corti, a researcher studying the impact of climate change at the University of California Donald Bren School of Environmental Science and Management.

To illustrate this point, Corti cites several climate changes that Europe experienced in 2007. Massive flooding struck England and Wales, recording the wettest May-to-July period compared to the same three-month period every year since records were first kept in 1766.

People do not have to live on the coast or by rivers to suffer from floods. Some homes and businesses in England that were miles away from cresting rivers experienced the flood backup through the sewers.

Germany had the least amount of rainfall in April 2007 and the most amount of rainfall in May 2007 since their countrywide records began in 1901.

Also in 2007, Romania suffered its worst drought in 60 years. The Netherlands experienced unusual drought conditions, recording 0.04 inches (0.10 cm) of precipitation in April compared to a normal average of 1.7 inches (4.3 cm). Greece experienced its worst heat wave in 110 years, causing many forest fires.

These climate change examples are not only phenomena of 2007. They have been occurring throughout the 21st century. One of the most widespread droughts hit a third of the European Union's land area in 2003, which affected 100 million people and resulted in US$12.5 billion in damages.

By consensus, scientists and environmental experts representing the IPCC now anticipate that these frequent and irregular weather patterns and storms will intensify as global temperatures keep rising.

Another prediction about the consequences of climate change is that we could expect greater concentrations of smog to accompany the more frequent and extreme heat waves.

POTENTIAL FOR CONFLICTS

Some world leaders have begun to recast climate change as more than an environmental issue. It is becoming a matter of national security.

Margaret Beckett, a former British foreign minister, brought the matter of the crisis in the Darfur region of western Sudan to the U.N. National Security Council in April 2007 and blamed the conflict on climate change.

SOURCE: U.N. PHOTO BY ESKINDER DEBEBE

More than 12,000 refugees struggle for survival in the Zam Zam Camp for Internally Displaced Persons in the Darfur region of Sudan.

A combination of drought, desertification, tribal cultural differences and over-population caused a massive migration around the Darfur region and across the border into Chad where thousands assembled in refugee camps.

The reduction in rainfall in northern Darfur was unprecedented, turning millions of acres of semidesert grazing land into lifeless desert.

The Baggara (Arabized cattle) nomads and other pastoralist societies fled south with their livestock, seeking scarce resources such as fertile land and water, to foreign land mostly occupied by non-Arab farmers. The farmers clashed with nomadic and seminomadic herders who settled with their cattle, horses, sheep and other domestic animals on the lands of Chad farmers. The herders lived in tents to protect themselves from intermittent periods of intense heat and cold.

The result of the conflict in Darfur, a region smaller than France, is that more than 200,000 have died and 2.5 million Darfuris have been displaced from their homes, as the region's ethnic African rebels have been fighting the Arab-dominated Sudanese government and its militia allies between 2003 and 2008.

In January 2008, the U.N. Security Council sent 6,500 peacekeeping soldiers into the region. Additionally, the international community has been spending more than US$1 billion a year to alleviate suffering in Darfur.

U.N. secretary-general Ban Ki-moon said in 2007 that the slaughter in Darfur was caused "at least in part from climate change."

"It is a question of war and peace," said Jan Egeland, the former U.N. undersecretary for humanitarian affairs. Egeland, who is now a director of the Norwegian Institute of International Affairs, pointedly explained that the situation in the Sahel belt of Africa is evidence that climate change has the potential to cause conflict among nations.

Former U.N. secretary-general Kofi Annan warned, "Climate change is not just an environmental issue, as too many people still believe. It is an all-encompassing threat."

DISRUPTION OF LIVING SPECIES

The impact of climate change has even further possible implications. The ecosystem of the planet would be knocked off kilter through rising temperatures, and this could disrupt many forms of life. Animals would be forced to migrate, disrupting even the regions that had not suffered from the effects of climate change.

About 20 to 30 percent of all plant and animal species face the risk of extinction if temperatures increase by 2.7°F (1.5°C), as claimed in a 2007 IPCC report. But if temperatures rise by 6.3°F (3.5°C), between 40 and 70 percent of species could disappear, the IPCC warned.

The loss of just one species alone can have a ripple effect on an entire ecosystem. This would affect not only human activities but also animals, plants and insects that have adapted to climate condition throughout the centuries. Some species would be forced to migrate out of their habitats while others would begin to overpopulate uncontrollably.

Entomologists fear that climate change could prompt Central American locust (*Schistocera piceifrons*) swarms to migrate into North America in sudden search of food.

Normally, locusts are solitary insects, but lack of rain and shrinking of food supply resulting from climate change in Central America could cause them to swarm, seeking rainfall and more available food supply as is abundant in the North American Great Plains.

These insects can cause devastation and famine not seen in the Great Plains and western United States since 1877, when the last massive swarm of the Rocky Mountain locust (*Melanoplus spretus*) devoured every vegetable, weed and blade of grass in sight.

PHOTO: THORSTEN RUST © 2008 ISTOCK INTERNATIONAL INC.

Above is the Great Barrier Reef located in the Coral Sea, off the coast of Queensland in northeast Australia. Mass coral bleaching due to rising ocean temperatures in the summers prevents the coral from reproducing fast enough and threatens destruction of the world's biggest single structure made by living organisms. More than 1,500 species of fish live in and depend on the coral reef for protection from predators, for food from smaller sea species and plants and for spawning.

The acidification (lowering in pH) of the ocean has been attributed to climate change. The oceans absorb carbon dioxide produced by living organisms and turn it into carbonic acid. In low levels, the ecosystem supports this activity quite normally.

Climate observers estimate that 70 million tons (64 million metric tons) of CO_2 are released into the atmosphere every day. Another 25 million tons (23 million metric tons) of CO_2 are absorbed into the oceans every day, making the ocean more acidic. Scientists contend that the ocean's average pH has already decreased to about 8.2 and will continue to lower to unprecedented levels. Increased acidity of seawater may slow the reproduction of fish and affect plankton such as krill, which is what nonpredatory fish eat to sustain their existence.

Krill, a Norwegian term meaning "small fry," refers to many species of planktonic crustacean known as euphausiids, which look like tiny shrimp. It is the most abundant food resource in the Southern Ocean, and it is also prevalent in northern ocean waters.

The dilemma involving saltwater fish is that predatory fish eat plankton-eating fish, which in turn eat plankton. If climate change significantly reduces plankton, most fish in the ocean will suffer.

Many species of jellyfish actually thrive in acidic seawater and their population is soaring. Some gargantuan Nomura jellyfish—the size of a white shark—have been observed in the 21st century in the warm waters of the Atlantic Ocean

Warmer ocean temperatures have been blamed for making ocean waters more acidic, a condition that helps jellyfish thrive. In this photograph, a diver attaches a sensor to a gigantic Echizen jellyfish off the coast of Komatsu in Ishikawa prefecture in northern Japan. The sensor sends information about water depth and temperature via satellite to scientists.

PHOTO CREDIT: YOMIURI SHIMBUN/AFP/GETTY IMAGES

and Eastern Sea, reminiscent of a circa 1980s Japanese film airing on the Sci Fi cable television channel.

The massive sea creatures, which can grow 6.5 feet (1.9 m) wide and weigh up to 450 pounds (204 kg), have proliferated by a hundredfold in some areas off Japan, causing a crisis in the local fishing industry.

Below the ocean waves, coral reef bleaching has been increasing all over the world since the 1980s. Reefs form naturally from colonies of tiny coral polyps. When the coral dies, other polyps growing over the dead coral limestone skeletons replace them, making them rise higher to create a safe habitat for marine life. The bleaching process stresses the symbiotic algae, which can cause the coral host to die and ultimately destroy entire reef tracts.

Various causes for the destruction of coral reefs are linked to climate change. These include higher ocean temperature, solar irradiance from increased ultraviolet radiation attributed to the depletion of the ozone, the dilution of fresh water into saltwater—a condition that occurs from melting ice and excessive precipitation—and more frequent hurricanes that in less than an hour can wipe out a reef that was created over thousands of years.

Some reefs are a few feet long, but the largest known reef, facing the coast of Australia, covers 1,400 miles (2,250 km).

A study conducted by the University of North Carolina in 2007 found that coral reefs from the Indo-Pacific—an area that contains three-quarters of the world's coral reefs—had declined by 20 percent in the past two decades, mostly from diseases, coastal development and higher ocean temperatures above the ideal condition for coral reefs to thrive.

New technology is emerging to create man-made reefs, including a concrete structure for small fish to spawn and live, but treating the symptoms is not the solution.

Coral reefs must be preserved because they act as shelter for marine plants and sea creatures. These, in turn, fuel the livelihood of fishermen and help tourism in seacoast communities. But economic loss is not the only danger of coral reef reduction.

Dying coral reefs have had a highly detrimental impact on the inhabitants of the Carteret Islands. These islands, located northeast of Bougainville in New Guinea, are disappearing below the sea because of sinking volcanic activity and a series of other activities linked to climate change.

About 2,500 people live on the atoll, which makes up the islands, and these islands are quickly sinking under the sea. The cause is rising sea level from melting ice caps and a loss in coral reefs that serve as a natural barrier to coastal destructive storm surges that erode the land.

Most of the Carteret Islands are so small that natives can walk from one coast to the opposite in five or ten minutes, yet soon they will be forced to evacuate their homeland forever.

Ironically, the carbon footprint of the islanders is practically zero because the only electricity on the islands is powered by a single generator. Showing old movies twice a week is one of the few pastimes that the islanders enjoy that requires using carbon-based fuel.

Africa, which has one of the smallest carbon footprints, is also suffering from climate-changing effects. The IPCC projects that by 2020, 75 million to 250 million people in Africa will suffer water shortages, partly from the amount of pollutants already in the atmosphere.

In its 2007 report, the IPCC warned that climate change would cause widespread food shortages and other destabilizing effects such as flooding in parts of Asia, fiercer storms and prolonged droughts. Residents of Asia's large cities will be at a greater risk of river and coastal flooding.

The change in climate could benefit northern regions of North America and Europe with increased agricultural productivity, but southern Africa, southern Asia and South America may bear the brunt, according to some climate experts.

The IPCC also warned that GHG emissions must be reduced in the next 15 years to avert the worst consequences of climate change. It is no surprise that residents from many of these underdeveloped countries have their eyes squarely pointed toward the largest emitters of GHGs.

Offsetters Climate Neutral Society (OCNS), a Canadian not-for-profit organization that sells carbon offset credits, says each person in the United States emits 19.7 tons (17.9 metric tons) of CO_2 per year. The average American car (getting 23.9 miles [38.5 km] per gallon) produces 0.93 pounds (0.42 kg) of carbon dioxide for every mile driven.

Using just one gallon of gasoline in an automobile produces 19.6 pounds (8.9 kg) of CO_2 on combustion, according to the U.S. Energy Information Administration (EIA). The OCNS claims about 20 pounds of carbon dioxide produced per gallon of gasoline, or roughly three times the weight of a gallon of gasoline.

Gasoline consists mostly of hydrocarbons encircled by atoms of hydrogen. The carbon from the gasoline mixes with oxygen from the air, adding the weight of the oxygen to the weight of the carbon from the gasoline to create a much denser carbon dioxide gas emission.

CARBON FUELS POWER BUILDINGS

Global Green USA—the U.S. affiliate of Green Cross International that was founded by former president of the Soviet Union Mikhail S. Gorbachev—claims that there are significant reasons to look beyond manufacturing and the transportation industry to achieve carbon reduction.

Excessive consumption is largely blamed for the depletion of natural resources worldwide and the acceleration of climate change—but some green building advocates believe that enormous consumption occurs in buildings of all types, from residences to offices, shopping centers and industrial buildings.

Retail buildings have diverse loads, long operating hours and high occupancy in the evenings. Planning for energy-efficient retail buildings should begin in the design stage and continue throughout the life of the building by analyzing new technology involving lighting, refrigeration and space conditioning.

Shopping center professionals and retailers tend to flinch when confronted with figures from the U.S. Department of Energy (DOE) and the U.S. Department of Transportation (DOT), both of which agree that buildings account for about 39 percent of all energy use in the United States—more than industrial and transportation—while vehicles used for transportation comprise only 27 percent.

However, that is where the agreement relating to estimates of energy consumption by U.S. buildings ends. Global Green USA notes that the construction, operations and maintenance of buildings are responsible for roughly 40 percent of the total energy use in the United States. The energy use number varies only 1 percent from the figures quoted by the DOE and DOT.

Global Green also says that U.S. buildings—commercial, public and residential—are a main contributor to climate change because they produce 30 percent of the world's carbon dioxide emissions, a figure we have been unable to tie to any other source. Furthermore, U.S. buildings account for 30 percent of the consumption of wood products and raw materials in the country.

Bill Wehrum, acting assistant administrator for the EPA Office of Air and Radiation, said that buildings contribute about 20 percent of the U.S. national greenhouse gas emissions.

In testimony before the U.S. Senate subcommittee of the Senate Energy and Natural Resources Committee, The American Institute of Architects (AIA) president, RK Stewart, FAIA, testified that buildings consume 71 percent of the U.S. electricity production. "Buildings in the United States account for 9.8 percent of the carbon dioxide production emissions worldwide," Stewart told the subcommittee. U.S. percentage of world emissions as quoted by the AIA is one-third the amount stated by Global Green.

The United States Green Building Council (USGBC) has a completely different set of building consumption statistics posted on its Web site. The site claims that buildings in the United States account for:

- 65 percent of electricity consumption

- 36 percent of energy use

- 30 percent of greenhouse gas emissions

- 30 percent of raw materials use

- 30 percent of waste output (136 million tons [123 million metric tons] annually)

- 12 percent of potable water consumption

Yet another set of numbers comes from the World Resources Institute (WRI), which posts extensive research data from various sources on its Web site, http://www.wri.org/.

Using IPCC reporting categories, the WRI attributes 15.3 percent of emissions of GHGs from the United States to U.S. residential buildings and 12 percent to U.S. commercial buildings, which include office, hotel and shopping centers.

The WRI estimates that the buildings sector all over the world, which encompasses residential, commercial and institutional buildings, accounts for 15.3 percent of global GHG emissions, including 9.9 percent for commercial buildings and 5.4 percent for residential. According to WRI, these emissions mostly come from energy consumption from three broad categories: public electricity use, direct fuel combustion, and district heating.

Public electricity use includes lighting, appliance use, refrigeration, air conditioning, and to some extent space heating and cooking. These activities account for 65 percent of commercial building emissions and 43 percent of residential building emissions. According to WRI, the building sector worldwide consumes more electricity, 42 percent, than any other sector.

The variance of building energy use and emissions being reported is all over the board, which is confusing to green building executives who are seeking the facts. "I have seen a broad range of building numbers reported . . . ranging from twenty percent to seventy-one percent," said Lisa Loweth, vice president of sustainability for General Growth Properties Inc., referring to energy consumption and GHG emissions data reported in a multitude of sources.

In order to understand the true impact and optimize the environmental demands that buildings have on energy consumption, we would need to explore the concept of embodied energy of buildings, building materials and construction components throughout the building's life cycle. "Embodied energy" means the total energy that can be attributed to bringing a building to its existing state. It includes the energy consumed in raw materials, processing them and manufacturing composite items as well as transporting materials to the site and the energy consumed in the operation of the building, all the way up to its disassembly and deconstruction.

Sources and notes: WRI, IEA, 2004. Absolute emissions in this sector, estimated here for 2000, are 6,418 MtCO$_2$.

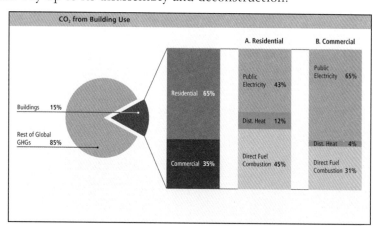

A realistic estimate of the embodied energy of a building can be very complex, and there are diminishing returns with respect to the accuracy of the calculation. However, it is important to understand the concept to consider all the energy a building actually consumes.

From the wide range of statistics quoted by various sources and not having truly reliable embodied energy estimates, we can only infer that buildings consume quite a bit of energy. That makes them responsible for an extensive amount of GHG emissions but exactly how much, we do not know.

Irrespective of the numbers, reducing fossil fuel energy is an essential strategy for green building operators because it makes good business sense.

Green building practices offer more direct benefits to shopping centers and retailers than promoting good environmental disciplines. One such benefit comes with the reduction of costs to operate shopping centers and retail stores simply by reducing the consumption of utilities, such as water, natural gas and electricity.

The Alliance to Save Energy released a 77-page study in July 2005 entitled "Building on Success: Policies to Reduce Energy Waste in Buildings." The report suggests buildings can reduce their energy use by 14 percent by 2020 by implementing new short-term but effective energy-saving strategies.

The escalating cost of utilities hurts retailers, shopping center companies and consumers in many ways. High utility costs affect the ability of consumers to acquire goods and pay for services because it takes a chunk out of their budgets and minimizes the disposable spending needed to improve quality of life. This budget reduction has a detrimental effect on the economy as it means less revenue for businesses due to a drop in consumer spending and higher costs from energy spikes—a combination that results in lower profits.

WATER CONSERVATION

Another goal of sustainability in the building industry is maintaining replenishable water resources. The U.S. Geological Service estimated in 1999 that buildings in the United States use 12.2 percent of all potable water (15 trillion gallons [57 trillion liters] per year).

Withdrawal of freshwater from the ecosystem should not exceed its natural replacement rate to ensure availability for future generations and naturally occurring market-based migration to desired localities. Only 3 percent of the world's water is freshwater, and more than two-thirds of it is frozen in the form of glaciers. Water is therefore a finite resource that cannot be wasted or disregarded.

As economies expand, populations grow and they consume more water. The dangers of water shortages are becoming more eminent. According to a report by the U.S. Government Accountability Office (GAO), 36 U.S. states will suffer from some type of water shortage in the 2010s. The IPCC predicts that North Americans will experience longer and hotter heat waves and greater competition for water. Policy makers are taking legislative and regulatory steps to protect the water resources

within their jurisdictions, and building operators are being asked to help conserve this valuable resource. Many city codes require new installation of toilets with low-flow flushing and now include many other water conservation restrictions.

Presently, the world has sufficient supply of freshwater resources, but it is not available uniformly. Many areas suffer from shortages. The U.S. Southwest, North Africa and the Middle East have perennial water shortages, but new areas of China, India and other countries are experiencing shortages as well.

About 300 million people in China (roughly the population of the United States) do not have access to clean drinking water. Many of China's rivers and freshwater bodies are polluted to such an extreme that the government grades fresh water quality from Grade I (least polluted) to Grade V (most polluted). In significant cities such as Beijing and Tianjin in Northern China, water scarcity is threatening China's economic vitality.

One thing is for sure: population growth results in increased consumption of fresh water, which is a limited resource.

Water consumption is not limited to the personal use of water, but is also essential to the infrastructure that supports the increasing world population. Industrial development and factories, irrigation of ornamental landscaping and agriculture to feed the masses, and other large water users consume water just to sustain the needs of the increased population.

Early projections indicate that developing countries will outpace the use of water for industrial purposes in the 2010s, far greater than the developed countries. Moreover, the water supply faces risks from many threats beyond the growing demands being placed by a growing population. Water supplies are vulnerable to chemical, biological and radiological terrorist attacks. Climate change also makes water conservation more critical. As temperatures rise, the demand for cooling and irrigation increases.

The production of corn-based ethanol fuel alone requires a vast amount of water, and virtually every locale where farmers grow corn is experiencing water shortages. To produce one gallon (3.8 liters) of ethanol fuel, ethanol farmers require three to four times that amount in water. A farm producing 30 million gallons (114 million liters) of ethanol will consume between 90 and 120 million gallons (340 and 450 million liters) of water, which is about what many small towns require for all their water uses.

As the United States prepares to cut 20 percent of gasoline use in the 2010s, ethanol production will double, requiring six to eight times the amount of water used now to produce the required ethanol.

Possibly, more low-quality water, even wastewater will be used to produce corn and other inedible plant material for growing ethanol and other biofuels. This would help conserve potable water.

Continued waste of valuable water resources, contamination of source water from pollution and the changes in precipitation from climate-changing trends may all

contribute to water scarcity in some regions. If not already evident to many, the need to conserve this precious resource will become more evident to this and future generations.

HEALTHY INDOOR ENVIRONMENT

The primary goal of sustainable building operators is to minimize the impact of buildings on the environment, while ensuring the health and well-being of the occupants. Ensuring indoor environmental quality (IEQ) is critical when considering all aspects of the interior of a retail building, whether that relates to the inside of a store or the interior common area of a shopping center.

IEQ refers to the quality of the air and overall environment inside the building, based on concentrations of pollutants and conditions that can affect the occupants' health, comfort and their performance within the building. IEQ can affect employee productivity and the customer's receptiveness within the indoor environment. Factors include building contaminants, indoor temperature, relative humidity, light and sound, among others.

Indoor air quality (IAQ)—not to be confused with IEQ, which stands for the more extensive factors of indoor quality—is important to minimize the risks that affect the health and comfort of building occupants.

Despite the efforts of well-intentioned building management to provide a safe, climate-controlled and comfortable interior environment, buildings, from residences to retail properties, are contaminated with a variety of biological pollutants, hazardous substances and toxic gases that threaten the health of customers, employees, patrons, residents and visitors.

Some studies attribute asthma-related illness and other ailments to dampness and mold in interior settings. These are considered microbial contaminants, but indoor environmental quality is much more than that.

Among the leading sources of contaminants in building interiors are:

- Inorganic contaminants (carbon monoxide, radon, asbestos, lead, and gypsum used on drywall)

- Organic gases called volatile organic compounds (VOCs) and semivolatile organic compounds (SVOCs) (aldahydes, paints, lacquers, paint strippers, cleaning supplies, chemicals used in office supplies and equipment such as copiers and printers, correction fluids, craft materials including glues and adhesives, permanent markers, and photographic solutions)

- Pesticides (fungicides, insecticides and biocides)

- Biological allergens (dust, pollen, pet and rodent dander, bacteria, viruses, dust mites, insects and cockroach excrements, and mold infestation)

- Contaminants from combustion (wood burning and flue gas from vented sources; gas stoves, gas heating appliances and unvented gas fireplaces; tobacco smoke, candles and incense burning; equipment powered by propane and flue gas reentry into interior space)

With this long list of contaminants threatening IAQ, it is not surprising to learn that testing of indoor air in offices, retail stores and shopping centers has shown that indoor air is sometimes more polluted than outdoor air. The poor air quality in some buildings can pose health risks to employees and patrons frequenting these facilities.

Proper ventilation to dilute contaminants, filtration of air, and elimination of contaminants at the source are the most effective methods to achieve high IAQ in retail stores and enclosed shopping malls.

SUSTAINABILITY IS HERE TO STAY

Clean air and the environment have become sources of concern for many in outdoor settings as well as indoors. Sustainability will continue to gain prominence at school, at work, in the news media and even in the entertainment arena.

Responding to public outcry and pressures from former Washington, DC Mayor Anthony Allen "Tony" Williams (now chief executive officer of Arlington, Virginia-based Primum Public Realty Trust), the Washington Metropolitan Area Transit Authority (Metro) began purchasing compressed natural gas buses in 2001. These buses are popular with the public because they help avoid nitrogen oxides, a major cause of smog, from accumulating over the region surrounding the U.S. capital. By replacing diesel buses with compressed natural gas buses, Metro cut diesel emissions of particulate matter, which contains more than 40 toxic chemicals.

PHOTO: R. E. MILIAN

THIS BUS IS RUNNING ON CLEAN NATURAL GA[S]

metrobus

Cross like your life depends on it.
Use crosswalks. Obey signals.
Look left, right, left.
STREET SMART
streetsmart.mwcog.org
Police are enforcing safety laws!

The positive reception to Nobel laureate Gore's *An Inconvenient Truth* is indicative that people care more today about the environment and are more keenly aware of how rampant consumption and waste can endanger the world order.

This type of exposure tends to heighten public awareness that translates into public support for sustainability. Retailers and shopping center owners recognize the groundswell of public support for the green movement. They see an opportunity for cost savings and other health benefits associated with green buildings.

This realization is causing developers and operators of retail buildings to come to terms with this "now convenient truth" and join the sustainability movement that government officials, developers, design professionals, retailers and shopping center managers are touting from Atlanta to Auckland.

Sustainability is the term commonly used to express the changes needed to ensure that future generations on Earth can enjoy the same quality of life that we enjoy today. The Brundtland Commission, known more formally as the World Commission on Environment and Development (WCED), convened by the United Nations in 1983, coined this often-used term.

Chairman Gro Harlem Brundtland led the Brundtland Commission, which defined *sustainable development* as development that "meets the needs of the present without compromising the ability of future generations to meet their own needs."

Retailers and retail property owners recognize the importance that buildings play on sustainability. They are shifting strategies and implementing new tactics. All of this focuses on one goal: to ensure a safe built environment for building occupants and to reduce the impact to the greater environment outside these buildings. Continued progress toward this goal by all industries—not just by retailers and shopping center companies—will ultimately ensure the ability of future generations to provide for themselves.

PHOTO ILLUSTRATION: R. E. MILIAN (PHOENIX, ARIZONA. APRIL 2008)

whole
living

body+so

The key to weight loss

**25 Green
Ideas for
Under $25!**
Perfect eco-chic
solutions for every
room in your home

Chapter 3

Legislation Mandating Change

SUSTAINABILITY, FORMERLY CONSIDERED expensive and unfeasible, is sweeping legislative halls across the world with officials at all levels of government leading the way. However, legislating energy efficiencies and other building mandates is not a new phenomenon. The California Energy Efficiency Standards for Residential and Nonresidential Buildings were established in 1978 as a response to a legislative mandate to reduce California's energy consumption. Officials have been updating these standards periodically to allow consideration and possible incorporation of new energy-efficiency technologies and methods.

According to the California Energy Commission, California's building efficiency standards (along with those for energy-efficient appliances) have saved more than US$56 billion in electricity and natural gas costs since 1978. The Commission estimates these standards will save an additional US$23 billion by 2013.

In the 2000s, three different versions governed buildings in California. The first one went into effect in 2001, the second in 2005 and now a new version, the Building Energy Efficiency Standards contained in the California Code of Regulations, Title 24, Part 6 (also known as the California Energy Code) for 2008, will go into effect in 2009 to cover the remainder of the decade.

Projects that apply for a building permit in 2008 must comply with the 2005 standards, whereas the projects that apply in 2009 must comply with 2008 standards. California is only one of many states and municipalities getting tougher on legislation to curb GHG emissions.

As political leaders commit to reducing GHG emissions, e.g., the Kyoto Protocol, their lawmakers have to set a legislative agenda to achieve these reductions. This is not always easy, as lawmakers are faced with the challenge of legislating meaningful mandates to reduce carbon emissions while at the same time protecting the vitality of their economies.

These mandates can take the form of punitive taxes, dictating vehicle fuel-economy standards, requiring use of renewable energy, imposing transportation

and infrastructure limitations, and setting standards for appliances, equipment and lighting. Some or all restrictions can be imposed at the local, state (or province) and federal level. They can even be mandated regionally as is the case with the European Commission, which directs each EU member nation to comply.

Whether these energy policies come in the form of a decree or inducement, they all trickle down from global pressures, such as the Kyoto Protocol, to country-specific local mandates and incentives. Even the United States, which is not obligated to reduce GHG emissions by the Kyoto Protocol, has its own requirements to control carbon use at the foundation of local government.

Since the new century began, many U.S. municipalities have passed ordinances requiring municipal buildings larger than 10,000 square feet (930 sq m) to be constructed as sustainable buildings. These municipal governments include Arlington, Virginia; Austin and Dallas, Texas; Los Angeles, San Francisco and San Jose, California; Portland, Oregon; and Seattle, Washington. Most of these cities require public buildings to achieve minimum Leadership in Energy and Environmental Design (LEED) certification. In December 2007, San Francisco went as far as changing its building code to require all residential and commercial—even privately owned— buildings to be LEED certified.

In 2008, a new tougher law went into effect in Greensburg, Kansas, a rural city of 1,450 residents devastated by a massive tornado in 2007. The law now mandates all new city-owned buildings greater than 4,000 square feet (370 sq m) to be certified LEED Platinum—the greenest level—and they are required to reduce energy use by 42 percent over the previously existing building code requirements.

Shortly after the resolution went into effect, representatives of 10 commercial and public buildings in Greensburg pledged to rebuild to at least some level of the green building standard. Greensburg is focusing its recovery on rebuilding as a model green community that will truly live up to its name.

With the support of the U.S. Conference of Mayors, more than 720 mayors from all states have signed the U.S. Mayors Climate Protection Agreement. The intermunicipal pact calls for each of the signatory cities to implement carbon dioxide restrictions at the local level.

The mayors—representing 75 million Americans, one-quarter of the U.S. population—have committed their cities to meet or exceed the Kyoto Protocol targets within their own communities.

They are planning to lower GHG emissions armed with anti-sprawl land use policies, and by planting trees and vegetation, promoting the use of bicycles and carpooling, encouraging use of mass transit, revising building codes regarding energy efficiency and passing many regulations they believe will help them achieve their goals.

Many city and county mayors are taking an extra step by also urging their state and federal legislative bodies to enact policies and programs that will help them meet their planned CO_2 reduction of between 5 and 8 percent by 2012 compared with 1990 emission levels.

Fifteen states have already banded together to enact new automobile standards that will reduce GHG emissions, although EPA has not set a process to enforce it.

Policy makers all over the world have targeted the building industry with sustainability-focused legislation directed at both privately owned and public buildings. Some regulations are tougher than others are. Twenty-two states and more than 50 municipal governments have passed legislation mandating LEED-certified public buildings when using public funds to build them.

Commercial buildings not supported financially by public funds to go green are making headway on their own initiative and within their economic constraints. They must quantify the benefits of green building design and operation.

Some cities and states are incorporating green building requirements into building codes. Just east of New York City, the town of Babylon, located on Long Island, New York, became the first municipality in the United States in 2006 to adopt a comprehensive green building code for commercial buildings tied directly to LEED certification.

Babylon's green building initiative covers all new commercial, retail, industrial and multiresidential buildings over 4,000 square feet (370 sq m), according to Town of Babylon supervisor Steve Bellone, who holds a position similar to an elected city mayor.

The first large-scale retail project in this municipality faced with mandatory minimum LEED compliance was a new hybrid outlet center called the Arches at Deer Park. The center (planning a late-2008 opening) is a partnership of Tanger Outlet Centers, the Blumenfeld Development Group and Apollo Real Estate Advisors.

The 800,000-square-foot (74,300 sq m) retail center (685,000 square feet [63,600 sq m] on phase one) is being positioned as a "smart-style outlet center" because it combines big-box stores, outlet stores, restaurants and a Regal multiplex theater.

Adam's Architecture designed the Arches. The construction carefully focused on green building construction practices, as the building was erected on a sustainable reuse site. Among the project's green building initiatives was a railway system used to deliver and haul construction materials and debris by train. This reduced truck traffic and the carbon fuels the trucks would have burned.

"Since our buildings consume forty percent of the energy we use, the easiest, quickest and cheapest way for us to significantly reduce our reliance on fossil fuels, protect our environment and save on energy costs is to build green," Bellone remarked as he introduced the newly created extension of the Long Island Rail Road into the Arches shopping center site. The Arches builder expects to meet at least the minimum LEED requirements when the project is completed.

Many cities across the United States have green initiatives for municipal buildings, but Babylon was the first to require LEED certification for privately owned buildings. According to Babylon officials, the new code could reduce greenhouse gas emissions from the city by 1.37 million tons (1.24 million metric tons), which

has the same effect as removing 300,000 passenger cars from the Long Island Expressway (LIE) per year.

Throughout the entitlement process and before the new code became effective, the Town of Babylon encouraged the developer of The Arches at Deer Park to apply for LEED certification. Deer Park is a residential hamlet located on the northwest corner of the Town of Babylon. Under the new green building code, the Town of Babylon will not issue a building permit unless the permit application includes a completed LEED checklist or other comparable reporting mechanism that shows that the proposed building will achieve sufficient LEED points to attain the minimum LEED-certified status.

Many developers oppose codes and ordinances that require LEED certification because of the costs imposed in applying for certification and the potential for delay if the USGBC were to run into a backlog for processing applications.

Ordinances with language that calls for LEED certification also leave it up to the sole discretion of the USGBC to change building code standards without customary review by city officials, as the USGBC has the wherewithal to change the LEED specifications independently anytime it chooses.

According to the USGBC, as of mid-2007, various LEED green building initiatives including legislation, executive orders, resolutions, ordinances, policies, and incentives were incorporated into 55 cities, 11 counties, 8 townships, 22 states, 33 schools and 11 federal agencies across the United States and Canada.

Most of these measures are not as strictly tied to achieving LEED certification as the ordinance enacted by the Town of Babylon. However, the list is long and the details greatly vary. Some are geared to only publicly owned buildings, while others extend to commercial buildings as well.

A synopsis of where these policies existed in the United States and Canada as of 2007 follows:

Resolution

Asheville, NC
Athens, GA
Austin, TX
Babylon, NY
Berkeley, CA
Bowie, MD
Chicago, IL
Clayton, MO
Dallas, TX
Eugene, OR
Fort Collins, CO
Houston, TX
Kansas City, MO

Minneapolis, MN
Morgantown, WV
Portland, OR
Saanich, British Columbia
Sacramento, CA
San Antonio, TX
Sarasota County, FL
Scottsdale, AZ
Suffolk County, NY
Tucson, AZ
Tybee Island, GA
Vancouver, BC

Ordinances

Alameda County, CA
Atlanta, GA
Calabasas, CA
Chapel Hill, NC
Chatham County, GA
Cincinnati, OH
Cook County, IL
Cranford, NJ
Frisco, TX
Gainesville, FL
Honolulu, HI
Livermore, CA
Los Angeles, CA
Los Angeles County, CA
New York, NY
Normal, IL
Oakland, CA
Pasadena, CA
Pleasanton, CA
Salt Lake City, UT
San Francisco, CA
San Mateo County, CA
San Jose, CA
Santa Cruz, CA
Santa Monica, CA
Saint Louis, MO

Executive Orders

Albuquerque, NM
Arizona
California
Colorado
King County, WA
Maine
Maryland
Massachusetts
Michigan
New Jersey
New Mexico
New York
Rhode Island
Salt Lake City, UT

Virginia
Wisconsin

Green Building Policies including LEED

Boston, MA
Calgary, Alberta
Grand Rapids, MI
Long Beach, CA
Madison, WI
Phoenix, AZ
Plano, TX
Princeton, NJ
San Diego, CA
Seattle, WA
Washington, DC (Dept. Parks and
   Recreation)

Private Sector Initiatives

Acton, MA
Arlington, VA
Baltimore County, MD
Calabasas, CA
Chatham County, GA
Cincinnati, OH
Cranford, NJ
Gainesville, FL
Issaquah, WA
Long Beach, CA
Maryland
Nevada
New Mexico
New York
Normal, IL
Oregon
Pasadena, CA
Pleasanton, CA
Portland, OR
San Antonio, TX
San Diego, CA
San Francisco, CA
Santa Monica, CA

Sarasota County, FL
Seattle, WA

Legislation

Arkansas
Baltimore County, MD
Colorado
Hawaii
Maryland
Montgomery County, MD
Nevada
New Mexico
Pennsylvania
Washington State

Federal Initiatives

National Aeronautics and Space
  Administration
U.S. Department of Agriculture
U.S. Department of Defense
U.S. Air Force
U.S. Army
U.S. Navy
U.S. Department of Energy
U.S. Department of Health and
  Human Services
U.S. Department of Interior
U.S. Department of State
U.S. Environmental Protection Agency
U.S. General Services Administration

MANDATING GREEN BUILDING STANDARDS

The pressure to reduce carbon dioxide emissions in the United States no longer depends on future legislation, codes and ordinances. Some jurisdictions control green building practices by licensing the contractors that install the equipment to ensure they are knowledgeable enough.

Other government officials feel the need to rate equipment to assure sustainable practices. They do this by certifying the efficiency of the equipment, such as an HVAC unit or luminaire fixture, so that a buyer knows exactly how it will perform.

Even the utility companies are being required by some jurisdictions to disclose to energy purchasers information about the type of energy they are buying. This information can range from facts on emissions of GHGs to fuel mix. Awareness is the objective when regulators require general disclosure to buyers of energy.

Environmental groups expect EPA to tighten operating standards more than ever due to a lawsuit settled by the U.S. Supreme Court in the case of *Massachusetts v. EPA*, brought by 12 U.S. states, three cities and numerous environmental groups to force EPA to take action to curb GHG emissions.

In this April 2007 case, the Supreme Court rebuked EPA for refusing to comply with its clear statutory responsibility to regulate greenhouse gas emissions, by ruling in a vote of five to four that EPA violated the Clean Air Act by improperly declining to regulate new vehicle emissions standards to curb the greenhouse gases that contribute to climate change.

"Under the clear terms of the Clean Air Act, EPA can avoid taking further action only if it determines that greenhouse gases do not contribute to climate change or if it provides some reasonable explanation," wrote Supreme Court Justice John Paul Stevens for the majority.

EPA argued that because it has not regulated CO_2 emissions in the past, the agency cannot regulate CO_2 emissions going forward without new legislation that would require it to do so.

In granting a permit to a coal-burning power plant four months after the landmark Supreme Court's decision, EPA refuted the Supreme Court's assertion, stating that CO_2 is not "subject to regulation" by the agency under the Clean Air Act because CO_2 is not yet regulated by "a statutory or regulatory provision that requires actual control of emissions."

From country to country, rules, regulations, and public policy covering the required use of renewable energy alone can influence renewable energy standards, require net metering and generation disclosure, control contractor licensing and equipment certification, and provide for specific design standards.

Building energy code regulations can specify energy standards for public buildings and require these buildings to purchase or generate their own green power. Some regulations go as far as to allow local government to buy renewable energy by aggregating the purchasing power of several communities to spread discounts from quantity buying to all purchasers.

This has resulted in increased federal regulation to curb fossil fuel consumption in the United States throughout the 2000s. In 2005, Congress mandated oil refiners to blend about 7.5 billion gallons (28.4 billion liters) of cleaner-burning, corn-based ethanol or other renewable fuels by 2012 into gasoline pumped in the approximately 200,000 U.S. filling stations serving Americans nationwide.

By 2007, the United States produced 6.8 billion gallons (25.6 billion liters) of ethanol (almost meeting the 2012 target). A mixture of 85 percent ethanol (E85)

Shopping centers can reduce GHG emissions by using sedan- and SUV-flexible fuel vehicles (FFVs) as security vehicles, and light trucks for maintenance purposes. FFVs use E85 fuel (85 percent ethanol and 15 percent gasoline). These vehicles are equipped with modified components designed specifically to be compatible with ethanol's chemical properties as described in this illustration. To learn more about FFVs, visit: http://www.eere.energy.gov/afdc/progs/vehicles_search.php.

Flexible Fuel Vehicle Features

Engine calibration updates: Fueling and spark advance calibrations directed by vehicle computer and software to optimize combustion, enable cold start, and meet emissions requirements

Insulated wiring: Made from special materials to handle ethanol's increased conductivity and corrosiveness

Fuel pump assembly: In-tank components made from ethanol-compatible materials; larger capacity fuel pump to deliver more fuel to compensate for ethanol's lower energy density

Updated piston rings, cylinder heads, valve seats, and valves: Special materials used to minimize wear from ethanol's alcohol properties, which wash lubrication from parts

Fuel filler neck: Anti-siphon and spark arrestor features included to handle ethanol's increased conductivity

Fuel sensor: Automatically senses the composition of fuel to adjust for ethanol blends

Updated fuel injectors: Made from ethanol-compatible materials; designed to deliver greater fuel volume required by ethanol's lower energy density

Fuel rail and fuel lines: Made from ethanol-compatible materials; designed to handle increased fuel volume requirements to compensate for ethanol's lower energy density

Fuel tank: Composed of special materials to minimize evaporative emissions from ethanol

SOURCE: NATIONAL RENEWABLE ENERGY LABORATORY (NREL), A U.S. DEPARTMENT OF ENERGY NATIONAL LABORATORY OPERATED BY MIDWEST RESEARCH INSTITUTE AND BATTELLE

to gasoline can be used as fuel for vehicles. Gasoline stations could have sold all the ethanol produced had they installed an adequate amount of E85 pumps projected in the mid-2000s.

By early 2007, less than 2,000 stations in about 45 states sold E85, according to the National Renewable Energy Laboratory (NREL), a U.S. Department of Energy National Laboratory operated by Midwest Research Institute and Battelle. As more gasoline stations add E85 pumps, more consumers are likely to purchase vehicles capable of using E85 fuel.

Today, all U.S. vehicle manufacturers sell flexible fuel vehicles (FFVs). These are vehicles—sedans, pickups, SUVs and minivans—capable of operating on strictly gasoline, E85 fuel (85 percent ethanol, 15 percent gasoline), or a mixture of both. There are more than five million flexible fuel vehicles on U.S. roads today, but many FFV owners do not know their vehicle is one. Furthermore, most automobiles that normally use unleaded gasoline for fuel can also use E10 fuel, a blend of 10 percent ethanol and 90 percent gasoline.

California governor Arnold Schwarzenegger mandated gasoline reformulation so that all California refineries will have to blend 10 percent ethanol into the gas offered for sale in the state by 2012, and some analysts are projecting that the target will be reached sooner if enough ethanol plants can be built to produce the required corn-based ethanol.

In 2012, when all gasoline sold in California is mixed with a minimum of 10 percent ethanol, which the California Air Resources Board estimates will consist of 1.5 billion gallons (5.7 billion liters) of ethanol, the burgeoning ethanol market will shift into high gear because California is the world's fifth largest economy and the largest consumer of transport fuels in the United States.

Biofuel analysts project the production capacity between 2008 and 2009 to reach 12 billion gallons (45 billion liters) in the United States, which may increase with legislative action mandating that more ethanol be mixed with gasoline, as is the case with California's goal and the energy law the U.S. Congress passed in 2007. By comparison, between 2004 and 2006, worldwide ethanol production grew to 13.5 billion gallons (51.1 billion liters), a 25 percent increase.

Biodiesel doubled in the same period worldwide to 6.1 million metric tons (6.7 million tons), but ethanol and biodiesel combined still account for only 1 percent of the world's supply of transportation fuel.

The U.S. House of Representatives and the U.S. Senate are regularly introducing bills to curb the country's reliance on foreign oil. Congress intends for these measures to encourage the use of renewable energy.

On December 19, 2007, President George W. Bush signed into law the Energy Independence & Security Act of 2007 (H.R. 6.), a measure that raises fuel economy standards for cars and light trucks for the first time in 32 years and mandates the use of renewable biofuels by energy producers.

The act also establishes new efficiency requirements for household appliances and government buildings and requires the production of 36 billion gallons (136 billion liters) of renewable fuels by 2022, an almost fivefold increase from 2007 ethanol

production levels. This and other U.S. federal legislation under consideration and the EPA administrative regulations may change many things we take for granted.

Federal officials are feeling the pressures from all sides. They are listening to state and local leaders and are responding by creating their own laws to address the environment and the consumption of carbon-based energy.

For example, incandescent lightbulbs will be phased out by 2017 pursuant to the Energy Independence and Security Act, and appliances such as television sets and stereo systems that use power when they are supposedly turned off but are actually placed on standby may become a thing of the past with other potential legislation.

Title IV of the Energy Independence and Security Act also contains some "Energy Savings in Buildings and Industry" provisions that will influence government and commercial buildings. In summary, those are:

1. Requires improved federal and commercial building energy efficiency with green building standards for new federal buildings

2. Includes a "zero net energy" initiative to develop technologies, practices and policies to reach the goal of having all commercial buildings use no "net carbon energy" by 2050

3. Provides new incentives to promote industrial energy efficiency through converting waste heat into electricity

The third provision illustrates how mandates to reduce carbon fuel consumption can also be administered in the form of a "carrot," such as providing lucrative incentives to help reduce carbon emissions.

The building sector is poised for this type of inducement whether it comes from federal or local government. Some municipal officials are encouraging sustainable building design and construction not with ordinances but with financial incentives under existing zoning, tax credits and rebates. (See Chapter 4.)

Many municipalities are also expediting the review of building permits for green buildings. The type of energy consumed by buildings, whether it is carbon-based or renewable, is not necessarily within the building's control. Buildings typically rely on electricity purchased from utility companies for their energy source, and the utility company decides what fuel to burn to generate the power it retails.

Utility companies that produce secondary energy, such as electricity, are responsible for a significant amount of GHG emissions before they distribute power to buildings and other users.

Fossil fuels supply 85 percent of the energy in the United States. According to the U.S. Energy Information Administration (EIA), more than three-quarters of the U.S. CO_2 emissions from electricity generation comes from burning coal (roughly two billion metric tons [2.2 billion tons]).

Coal-burning electricity plants in the United States account for half of the country's electricity and one-third of all U.S. CO_2 emissions from all sources, according to the Department of Energy.

Therefore, the elimination of GHGs is not only the responsibility of the user—such as retailers and shopping centers—but it is also the responsibility of generators of electricity that all users purchase from and consume.

These electricity-producing power companies have various alternatives to reduce emissions. One obvious option is to use more renewable forms of energy fuels such as hydro, wind and solar to produce electricity. (See Chapter 16.)

Another option is to use better technology to prevent unnecessary emissions, such as more efficient smokestacks. In the United States, the federal Clean Air Act (CAA) and state air quality laws regulate emissions from coal-fired power plants. For example, in 2002, the North Carolina General Assembly adopted the Clean Smokestacks Act.

A lesser-known method for power plants to reduce emissions of heat-trapping gases is to sequester the carbon dioxide these plants produce deep underground, rather than release it into the atmosphere.

CARBON DIOXIDE SEQUESTRATION

The U.S. Department of Energy (DOE) Office of Fossil Energy has two major programs to reduce carbon emissions. One program involves the capturing and sequestering of greenhouse gases. The other one deals with making fossil energy systems more efficient.

The first approach involves testing new technology on capture and sequestration systems that store, convert or recycle greenhouse gases to prevent them from reaching the atmosphere. The DOE National Energy Technology Laboratory (NETL) is helping to develop these technologies to capture, purify and store carbon dioxide gas, which can significantly reduce greenhouse gas emissions without reducing conventional energy consumption or slowing economic growth.

The NETL will spend about US\$197 million between 2008 and 2018 on underground carbon sequestration. The laboratory is still studying ways of conducting permanent CO_2 storage programs and ensuring safety from these storage systems and expects to have an extensive carbon sequestration program consisting of safe, cost-effective, commercial-scale CO_2 capture, storage, and mitigation technologies in place by 2012.

The EPA plans to have a set of regulations for carbon sequestration in place by mid-2008, which will encourage utility companies to begin using technology for carbon sequestration. Once EPA issues proper guidelines, new and existing power plants and fuel-processing facilities can be retrofitted with proper CO_2 capture technology.

The Department of Energy estimates that the vast lands of North America have the capacity to store 3.5 trillion tons (3.2 trillion metric tons) of carbon dioxide underneath Earth's surface, which is enough to sequester all of the CO_2 emissions that power companies would produce in Canada and the United States for centuries.

Experts believe that power plants have the ability to capture and store approximately 90 percent of their carbon dioxide emissions. This technology already exists, and power plants are using it to capture the carbon dioxide produced from burning coal and other fossil fuels and safely store it thousands of feet below Earth's surface for centuries. But few power plants do this, according to a study conducted by the Massachusetts Institute of Technology (MIT) under its Carbon Capture and Sequestration Technologies Program, which MIT started in 1989.

Captured carbon dioxide is already commonly used for enhanced oil recovery in Canada. The Dakota Gasification Company (DGC) has an agreement with PanCanadian Petroleum Limited to sell and ship carbon dioxide to an EnCana oil field located in Weyburn, a small city in the southeastern part of Saskatchewan, Canada.

The Dakota Gasification Company Great Plains Synfuels Plant in central North Dakota captures its CO_2 and ships it as a heavy liquid along a 200-mile (320 km) pipeline from the United States to Weyburn. DGC is a subsidiary of the Basin Electric Power Cooperative.

Coal-fired power plants all over the world normally use enormous smokestacks to vent CO_2 into the atmosphere, so the Weyburn sequestration project is of tremendous environmental benefit as it mitigates climate change.

PanCanadian Petroleum injects the carbon dioxide it buys from DGC into the ground to force oil pockets from deep underground closer to the surface, where it can easily pump the crude out while storing the CO_2 beneath Earth's surface.

In addition to carbon dioxide, the Synfuels Plant produces natural gas, fertilizers, solvents, phenol and other chemicals. DGC is considering other markets to sell them the CO_2 gas. The Synfuels Plant has a production capacity in excess of 200 million standard cubic feet of CO_2 per day.

Secretary of Energy Samuel Wright Bodman said that by 2005, the DOE-funded "Weyburn Project" had successfully sequestered five million tons (4.5 million metric tons) of carbon dioxide and had doubled the Weyburn oil field's oil recovery rate by pumping CO_2 to help extract oil.

If this technology were used on a worldwide scale, one-third to one-half of carbon dioxide emissions would be eliminated in the next 100 years, and billions of barrels of deeply trapped oil could be recovered, according to the DOE.

"Just by applying this technique to the oil fields of Western Canada, we would see billions of additional barrels of oil and a reduction in CO_2 emissions equivalent to pulling more than 200 million cars off the road for a year," said Bodman.

Instead of emitting CO_2, power plants would need to separate the heat-trapping gas from the flue gas using available technology. This is currently both costly and energy intensive, but as new technology emerges, the NETL anticipates a potential for cost reductions between 30 and 45 percent of mid-2000s levels.

Geologic sequestration of carbon dioxide involves capturing the gas from power plants and other stationary GHG sources, then injecting it into geologic formations for storage deep underground in a similar fashion to the Weyburn Project. The

SOURCE: INTERNATIONAL ENERGY AGENCY AND NATURAL RESOURCES CANADA

Various governmental agencies are collaborating on the Weyburn project involving the use of carbon sequestration technology. Among them are Natural Resources Canada (NRCan), the United States Department of Energy, the Saskatchewan Industry and Resources (SIR), the Alberta Energy Research Institute (AERI), the European Community and the International Energy Agency Greenhouse Gas Research and Development Programme (IEA GHG).

final—and most important—step is ensuring the CO_2 will remain permanently trapped below the surface.

Geologic formations such as oil and gas reservoirs, unmineable coal seams and underground saline formations are possible areas to store CO_2, according to the NETL. Mark Stewart, a geologist from the University of South Florida, agrees. According to a *USA Today* report, Stewart explained that the underground zones where oil and gas have been trapped for millions of years have the capacity to hold the greenhouse gases that are presently being emitted into the atmosphere.

Key areas of the NETL's research and development technology are the capture, storage, monitoring, mitigation and verification of CO_2, all essential components of the carbon sequestration process.

Carbon dioxide is one of the most frequently overlooked toxic gases, an asphyxiant, a potent respiratory stimulant, and both a stimulant and depressant of the central nervous system. According to the Canadian Centre for Occupational Health and Safety, exposure of healthy individuals for prolonged periods to air made up of more than 10 percent of carbon dioxide gas can result in unconsciousness in about one minute. That is because at higher concentrations, carbon dioxide will displace the oxygen in the air.

Because of this and the potentially harmful effects to the environment if the sequestered CO_2 were to escape accidentally into the atmosphere, the DOE and EPA must be certain the sequestration methods are reliable before issuing routine permits to sequester.

Another approach by the DOE Office of Fossil Energy to reduce carbon emissions deals with developing technologies that boost the fuel-to-energy efficiencies of natural gas- and coal-fired power plants and emit less GHGs.

Observers believe that new legislation to prevent utility companies from emitting GHGs or a carbon tax coupled with a cap and trade system will propel energy producers to invest in new technology to reduce emissions and equipment to sequester carbon dioxide.

As systems that are more efficient surface, more regulations will likely pass to prompt immediate upgrades. Time will tell, but lobbyists predict that power plants will bear the brunt of significant legislation to curb GHGs by the end of the first decade of the 21st century.

More than 30 states have passed laws to address climate change, and several states have legislation requiring statewide reduction of carbon dioxide emissions from all sources.

California, Minnesota and New Jersey are among these states, and many more are expected to follow suit. California, Hawaii and New Jersey have enacted the most aggressive laws to curb the leading cause of climate change.

CARBON CAP AND TRADE

State government is the most likely government entity to first institute a carbon cap-and-trade system in the United States by targeting electricity-producing companies, which are among the highest emitters of GHGs.

State governments can allocate carbon credits to users or sell them at a nominal cost—say between US$2 and US$3 per ton of GHG emissions—then use the revenue to give subsidies for wind, solar and other clean energy installations.

Under a state law signed by Governor Jon S. Corzine in July 2007, New Jersey must reduce GHG emissions by 20 percent by 2020 (relative to New Jersey's projection of business-as-usual energy use) and make further cuts to achieve an 80 percent reduction by 2050.

A carbon cap-and-trade system is likely to become law in New Jersey, in New York and perhaps in as many as another eight states, to force electricity producers to mitigate GHG emissions.

In the U.S. Northeast, 10 states voluntarily signed a regional pact to reduce global greenhouse gases emitted from smokestacks of power plants by 2019. Power companies operating in the states covered by the pact are required to abide by these limits. Those that fail to meet this goal can make it up by purchasing carbon credits from other power companies that exceed the reduction permits, thereby helping them recoup some of the capital invested in smokestack technology upgrades to help them reduce greenhouse gases.

Just like fuel surcharges, these utility companies will likely pass on the cap-and-trade charges—along with higher cost of gas, oil or coal burned to generate power—to their customers, whether that is a business, a store, a shopping center or a residential customer.

Utility costs already account for the single largest operating expense category in regional and superregional shopping centers, second only to labor costs.

Governor Corzine made an announcement during a meeting of the International Carbon Action Partnership (ICAP) in Lisbon, Portugal, on October 29, 2007, regarding the trading of carbon credits. ICAP is working to bring together regions and governments that are committed to mandatory cap-and-trade programs to reduce greenhouse gas emissions.

"We are enthusiastically seeking to create a carbon trading system called the Regional Greenhouse Gas Initiative (RGGI), which along with my colleague from New York, [former] Governor Spitzer, and eight other governors, we are working to establish," said Governor Corzine, in an official statement on October 29, 2007.

The New Jersey governor was referring to what will likely be the first mandatory

market-based program (S.2976) to reduce carbon emissions in the United States. Observers anticipate that the RGGI cap-and-trade program will cap New Jersey regional power plant CO_2 emissions at approximately 2007 levels from 2009 through 2014 and further reduce emissions by 10 percent by 2019.

Former New York governor Eliot Spitzer added, "New York is implementing a greenhouse gas emissions trading program that will achieve a sixteen percent reduction in power plant emissions by 2019."

In addition to New Jersey and New York, other states attempting similar caps of electricity generators relying on the Northeast power grid are Maryland, Delaware, Connecticut, Rhode Island, Massachusetts, New Hampshire, Vermont and Maine, with proponents for the RGGI alliance hoping that Pennsylvania will join them.

A carbon allowance trading system does not have limited application to energy companies. It can be legislated to any emitter of GHGs by placing a limit on the total amount of CO_2 that they would be allowed to emit. This system can affect an entire country, a whole state, an incorporated city, an industry or even an individual business.

Beyond what is already known about cap and trades involving RGGI-aligned U.S. states, a similar system may become law in the United States some time in the 2010s, according to business leaders and policy makers that have been monitoring proposed legislation involving carbon cap and trade.

The Climate Security Act of 2007 (S. 2191), sponsored by Senators Joseph I. Lieberman and John W. Warner, was the most sobering cap-and-trade bill introduced in Congress in 2007. The measure, which made it out of subcommittee, could be up for a Senate vote in 2008.

If the measure was eventually passed in some form, the legislation would cap carbon emissions by polluting industries at 15 percent below 2005 levels by 2020 and set up a system to let them trade carbon emissions credits.

Senator Jeff Bingaman from New Mexico, the chairman of the U.S. Senate Energy and Natural Resources Committee, and Pennsylvania senator Arlen Specter sponsored a competing piece of legislation in 2007. The bill, the Low Carbon Economy Act, targets a reduction of carbon emissions to 2006 levels by 2020 and to 1990 levels by 2030, via a cap-and-trade program that EPA would administer.

In 2006, the Energy Information Administration (EIA), a statistical agency of the U.S. Department of Energy, estimated the sources of GHG emissions from energy production and industry. Natural gas accounts for 1,282 million tons (1,163.1 million metric tons) of CO_2 emissions. Petroleum accounts for only 2,845 million tons (2,581.2 million metric tons). Coal accounts for 2,352 million tons (2,134.1 million metric tons). Renewables account for 13.1 million tons (11.9 million metric tons) and all other sources produce a mere 48.6 million tons (44.1 million metric tons) of CO_2 emissions.

President George W. Bush has not signaled support of carbon caps, and observers predict that 2008, a presidential election year, is not the likely time for Congress to adopt these bills into law.

However, Eileen Claussen, president of the Pew Center on Global Climate Change in Arlington, Virginia, thinks there is a chance Congress will pass cap-and-trade legislation in 2008. "If not, I think it's inevitable by 2009 or 2010," said the president of this independent, nonprofit, nonpartisan group dedicated to providing information on climate change.

A system involving carbon cap and trade is designed to let the free market dictate the way to mitigate climate change. The cap-and-trade concept intrinsically recognizes that government can *cap* the amount of pollutants it permits a company to emit per year predicated on a lesser amount of pollutants than it emitted in previous years. This limit would gradually decrease in future years, in essence capping emissions at even lower levels.

Once the system is in place, if a restricted emitter manages to reduce its polluting emissions by a greater amount than it was legally required to, it has a right to *trade* or sell the permits (to pollute) in the open market to other restricted emitters that exceed their allowable polluting emissions.

To illustrate how a cap-and-trade program would work if stores were to become a target for this type of legislation, let us suppose that Store A is allocated a permit for 33 tons (30 metric tons) of carbon dioxide emissions a year, and the store implements a carbon reduction program that reduces emissions to 27 tons (24.5 metric tons).

That store will be able to sell six tons of carbon emission credits to another store, one that has used up its credits. If Store B were to have the same requirements but emitted 39 tons (35.4 metric tons) of CO_2 instead—or six more tons than was allocated under the cap and trade system—Store B could in essence purchase credit permits for the six tons from Store A.

In this hypothetical example, Store A is taking advantage of the incentive to cut emissions because it can sell excess permits. Store B, on the other hand, is penalized for not investing capital or equipment and systems to help it reduce emissions to achieve the level of carbon dioxide that it is permitted to release into the atmosphere.

The carbon cap-and-trade system gives two options to carbon emitters. In order to comply, they have to evaluate the pros and cons of purchasing credits as opposed to investing in systems to reduce their carbon footprint. "At the end of the day, the market will bear out whether simply paying the bill will be cheaper than producing or investing in sustainable approaches," said Benjamin A. Bross, LEED AP, design director of Constructora Planigrupo S. A., in Mexico City.

Greenhouse gas emissions trading is now common in Europe and has been since January 1, 2005. The European Union Emission Trading Scheme requires large emitters of carbon dioxide within the European Union to limit their amount of CO_2 emissions to no more that it allows for that year. If these emitters do not use up their allowances, they may sell them to other emitters. If instead an emitter reaches its cap and needs to emit more, it has to buy emission allowances from other large emitters that did not reach their caps.

A U.S. research professor at Northwestern University in Illinois launched the Chicago Climate Exchange (CCX) in 2003. It is now the only legally binding

greenhouse gas emissions trading system in North America, although unlike the European Union, U.S. law does not presently require emissions trading.

CCX members such as Ford Motor Company, DuPont, IBM and Motorola typically commit to reducing GHG emissions by 6 percent by 2010. If they fail to meet those targets, they can buy credits from members who reduce beyond their allowances or they can buy offsets from sources that neutralize greenhouse gases.

The U.S. EPA has successfully operated a cap-and-trade system to limit human-generated emissions of sulfur dioxide (SO_2) that cause acid rain and nitrogen oxide (NOx), a precursor of ozone formation. EPA sets a cap on total SO_2 emissions by issuing allowances that are equal to the cap, then auctions off 2.8 percent of the total allowances each year for about US$515 a ton.

Notwithstanding restrictions such as a cap-and-trade system, some retailers are purchasing energy credits voluntarily. Whole Foods Market, the world's largest retailer of natural and organic foods, operating stores under its corporate namesake and Wild Oats Farms, began purchasing wind energy credits on a voluntary basis in 2005. It also sells cards to its customers for those who want to contribute toward renewable energy credits. Boulder, Colorado-based Renewable Choice Energy administers the program.

Ultimately, cap-and-trade systems function similar to a tax, levying costs and penalties that businesses pass on to consumers in the way of higher retail prices.

THE EUROPEAN COMMISSION

In Europe, policy is getting stricter, and the European Commission (EC) has been setting sustainability policies to enforce energy efficiencies, reduction of GHG emissions and water conservation that member states are expected to enforce. The Commission of the European Communities (the formal name for the European Commission) is the executive branch of the European Union. The EC imposed caps on GHG emissions in 2005 on member states, and European legislation observers expect further tightening in the future.

The Luxembourg European Council called on the European Union to implement Article 6 of the consolidated EC Treaty, which states that all community activities and policies must integrate the intent of environmental protection. Toward that goal, the European Union formulated a long-term strategy to adopt policies that support economically, socially and environmentally sustainable development.

The European Union now has in place an energy policy regarding all energy sources from fossil fuels (oil, gas and coal) to nuclear energy and renewables (solar, wind, biomass, geothermal, hydroelectric and tidal). European policy makers hope to create a low-energy economy that would result in using primarily more competitive, secure and sustainable energy resources.

This policy will involve taxes, subsidies and CO_2 emissions trading to encourage the use of technologies for energy efficiency and renewable or low-carbon energy. Among the EU's objectives involving its present and new policy setting are:

1. Reducing energy consumption by 20 percent by 2020 consistent with the EU Action Plan for Energy Efficiency (2007–2012)

2. Developing minimum efficiency requirements for appliances

3. Improving efficiency of production, transportation and distribution of electricity, heating and air conditioning

4. Developing new energy technologies including renewable forms of energy

5. Improving the energy performance of buildings

Each member of the European Union is required to submit its own action plan outlining energy efficiency measures to cut fossil fuel energy consumption and GHG emissions.

Each country's action plan—covering a myriad of measures from motor vehicle gasoline efficiency to building equipment standards—is intended to help the European Union cut total energy consumption by 20 percent by 2020 to meet the goals outlined in the EU's multinational action plan.

One suggestion for drastically reducing GHG emissions is an Energy Performance Certificate that, if adopted, buildings would need to have in place upon initial construction, substantial renovation or when offered for sale. Some proponents of the Energy Performance Certificate have gone as far as suggesting that if buildings are offered for lease—such as is regularly done with apartment, office and retail buildings in Western Europe—this certification of energy performance should be required by law as a condition for leasing.

ICSC's European Sustainability Working Group is a task force that concentrates on defining the best way to measure the environmental performance of retail buildings, taking into consideration varying requirements by EU member nations.

The group is considering using the British Research Establishment's Environmental Assessment Method (BREEAM) for measuring the efficiency of retail buildings across Europe.

In 2007, the European Union met with the Group of Eight (G8), the influential group of powerful industrialized nations, to discuss action involving energy and GHG emissions. The G8 comprises Canada, France, Germany, Italy, Japan, Russia, the United Kingdom and the United States, and represents about 65 percent of the world economy. The leaders of the G8 decided to set up a Sustainable Buildings Network. This network is considering ways to assess and recommend the implementation of energy-efficiency systems in all types of buildings and will suggest ways to employ renewable forms of energy in the building sector.

Water conservation is also high on the EU sustainability agenda, having conducted studies that estimated that between 20 and 40 percent of potable water goes to waste regularly. The European Union is considering various policy options including "user pays" water pricing with compulsory metering. It is strongly encouraging installation of water-saving devices on taps, showerheads and toilets in residential, public, industrial and commercial buildings.

RECYCLING LEGISLATION

Recycling laws can take many shapes and forms. Some laws mandate that certain forms of waste be separated and sent for recycling to keep recyclable waste out of landfills. Various jurisdictions can set targets for consumers and businesses to recycle a certain percentage of recyclable waste. Current legislation in California requires 50 percent of waste to be recycled statewide.

Once local governments in charge of waste management begin to track volumes of waste—as many do today—they can increase recycling rates simply by charging households and businesses more if they produce more garbage. Some jurisdictions have resorted to reducing the frequency of trash collections while increasing the collection of recyclable waste.

Recycling laws are arguably one of the most efficient methods to encourage recycling for both consumers and businesses. Lawmakers are aware of this reality, which can result in tighter recycling regulations in the future.

Since the inception of New York State bottle deposit laws in the 1980s, five million tons (4.5 million metric tons) of recyclable waste, including 90 billion bottles, has been recycled in the state.

Another 10 states—including California—have *deposit laws* that require consumers to pay US$0.05 or more up front as deposit for purchasing beer and sodas such as Coke and Pepsi that will be reimbursed by the store when they bring back the containers.

California's bottle and can recycling law diverts nearly 100,000 tons (91,000 metric tons) of plastic alone from landfills every year and much more recycled waste when adding the aluminum and glass that is recycled.

These types of laws usually pertain to plastic, aluminum cans or glass bottles for beer and soda. Some state legislators are advocating broadening the deposit laws to cover not just beer and soda containers but also bottles for noncarbonated beverages such as bottled mineral water.

The not-for-profit Container Recycling Institute estimates that the beverage container recycling rate is 70 percent in states where recycling is mandatory or where deposit laws exist. By comparison, only 34 percent of containers are recycled in states where recycling is not required by law.

Consumers are beginning to question the impact that bottled water has on the environment. Some eco-conscious consumers point to the millions of disposable containers that do not get recycled and to the GHG emissions from fuel used to transport bottled mineral water via truck, railway, sea vessel or other means from the manufacturing point to the ultimate consumer.

Recycling saves energy and preserves raw materials. It also reduces pollution. One such pollutant is GHG emissions, and recycling curbs these emissions in several ways.

Recycling keeps materials out of the landfill, reducing the amount of waste that is buried or burned there. These landfills generate landfill gas, which is 50 percent methane, a greenhouse gas—some of which escapes into the atmosphere.

Recycling also conserves natural resources and reduces the need to mine and refine resources such as aluminum cans and to transport these resources great distances using fossil fuel. It also reduces emissions of pollutants that can cause smog and acid rain and contaminate freshwater resources.

Recycling one ton (0.9 metric tons) of aluminum cans results in four tons (3.6 metric tons) of GHG reductions, according to Californians Against Waste, a nonprofit environmental organization that advocates waste reduction and recycling policies and programs.

Recycling aluminum requires 95 percent less energy than making it from scratch. Other recycled material is not as energy saving. Recycling plastics requires 70 percent less energy. Steel requires 60 percent less energy, paper 40 percent less energy and glass 30 percent less energy than producing those materials from scratch.

Additionally, there is money to be made in recycling some products rather than sending them to a landfill, even before taking into consideration the costs of landfill hauling and dumping. Waste paper now commands about US$90 a ton throughout the United States for purchasing as basic material for recycling.

Recycling legislation continues to ramp up all over the world. Europe, Japan and a few U.S. states have passed *take back* laws that require electronics manufacturers to recycle their products.

The Green Dot (Der Grüne Punkt) is the official logo of a European network of industry-funded systems enforced by the European Commission for recycling the packaging materials of consumer goods. By joining the Green Dot program, a manufacturer agrees to contribute to the cost of recovering and recycling the packaging and containers.

Most companies that manufacture packaged products in European countries are obligated under Packaging and Packaging Waste Directive 94/62/EC to either join the Green Dot program or collect recyclable packaging themselves. Most do either, but if they did not, they would face a stiff fine for noncompliance. More than 130,000 companies generating some 460 billion packages now use the Green Dot. Europe's Packaging and Packaging Waste Directive also requires member states to recycle 60 percent of their glass and paper, half of their metals and almost a quarter of plastic packaging by the end of 2008.

In 2007, the European Parliament voted to increase recycling rates by 2020 to 50 percent of municipal waste and 70 percent of industrial waste.

The U.S. EPA estimates that recycling a ton of a mixed recyclables avoids emissions equivalent to 2.8 tons (2.5 metric tons) of CO_2. According to the nonprofit advocacy group, the National Recycling Coalition, the amount of energy saved by recycling aluminum and steel cans, plastic PET (polyethylene terephthalate) and glass containers, and newsprint and corrugated packaging, in 2006, was equal to the amount of electricity consumed by 17.8 million Americans in one year.

ICSC volunteers from around the United States gathered at the nation's capitol on March 5, 2008, to lobby legislators on Capitol Hill on matters of importance to the retail real estate industry including extending the Energy Efficient Commercial Building Tax Deduction beyond its expiration of December 31, 2008. The measure offers incentives for retailers and owners of commercial buildings for improvements in interior lighting, HVAC, hot water systems and other energy-saving systems.

Chapter 4

Financial Incentives

WHILE IN SOME jurisdictions around the globe certain green building standards are forced upon building owners by law, there are many sources of incentives for rewarding such efforts.

In the United States, there are local, state and federal financial incentives for switching to renewable energy. These include grants, loans, rebates, tax incentives, public benefit funds, industry recruitment and bond programs.

FINANCIAL INCENTIVES TO GO GREEN

The leading U.S. federal incentive, Energy Efficient Commercial Building Tax Deduction (26 U.S. Code § 179D) for energy efficiencies in retail stores, shopping centers and other commercial buildings, expires on December 31, 2008. The original tax incentives would have expired in 2007, but the incentives were extended through 2008 by Section 204 of the Tax Relief and Health Care Act of 2006 (H.R. 6111).

This series of tax deductions and credits are for energy-efficient building expenditures made by the building's owner. Partial deductions are also available for improvements in interior lighting, heating, ventilation and air conditioning, and hot water systems.

The building industry continues to lobby Congress to extend the Energy Efficient Commercial Buildings Tax Deduction—a part of the Energy Policy Act of 2005 (EPACT)—at least until 2013 and to increase the size of the deduction from US$1.80 per square foot (US$19.37 per square meter) to at least US$2.25 per square foot (US$24.22 per square meter).

Business leaders are hoping that Congress will extend the incentives perhaps through various bills in 2008.

CORPORATE TAX INCENTIVES NOT FOR REITS

Several corporate tax incentives in the United States provide credits or deductions from 10 to 35 percent of the taxable income to recapture part of the equipment and installation costs involved in using renewable energy such as solar, wind, hydro and biomass. However, shopping centers operated by real estate investment trusts (REITs) often cannot take advantage of these types of incentives, depending on many factors relative to the financial treatment of a particular REIT company.

A shopping center REIT is a company that owns, and in most cases operates, the income-producing retail real estate. To qualify as a U.S. REIT, a company must distribute at least 90 percent of its taxable income to its shareholders annually, and as such, U.S. law permits it to deduct dividends paid to its shareholders from its corporate taxable income.

Most REITs remit 100 percent of their taxable income to their shareholders and therefore owe no corporate tax. Most states honor this federal treatment by not requiring REITs to pay state income tax. Accordingly, most REITs cannot take advantage of many income tax credits or deductions available for energy savings such as the Energy Efficient Commercial Buildings Tax Deduction, although they can take advantage of other forms of incentives.

Among the incentives available to retail stores and to (non-REIT) shopping centers through EPACT are:

- An income tax credit of between US$250 and $3,400 depending on the fuel economy and the weight of the vehicle is available for buying or leasing a new hybrid gas-electric car or truck.

- A 30 percent tax credit is available for the purchase price for installing qualified solar energy equipment.

- For solar, wind and geothermal equipment property, the Modified Accelerated Cost Recovery System (MACRS) property class is five years for the businesses to recover investments through depreciation deductions. The Energy Policy Act of 2005 also classified solar hybrid lighting technologies as five-year property. Refer to 26 USC § 168 references 26 USC § 48(a)(3)(A) with respect to classifying property as "five-year property" and EPAct 2005, which added these technologies to the definition of energy property in § 48 as part of the business energy tax credit expansion.

- A tax deduction is available for energy-efficient commercial buildings that reduce annual energy consumption by 50 percent compared to the American Society of Heating, Refrigerating, and Air Conditioning Engineers (ASHRAE) 2001 standard. The deduction would equal the cost of energy-efficient property installed during construction, with a maximum deduction of US$1.80 per square foot (US$19.37 per square meter) of the building. Additionally, a partial deduction of US$.60 per square foot (US$6.46 per square meter) would be provided for building subsystems.

According to the DOE, this information is of a general nature and must be verified for applicability to each circumstance. The Internal Revenue Service would make the final determination on the tax credit and deduction amounts.

OTHER INCENTIVES FOR GREEN BUILDINGS

Energy efficiency standards are also incorporated in rules, regulations and policies by many jurisdictions to provide specific incentives regarding the use of certain equipment and appliances that consume energy in amounts that are lower than what is required by regulations.

The Database of State Incentives for Renewables & Efficiency (DSIRE) operates an excellent Web site offering a very valuable, consistently updated list of financial incentives available in the United States for green initiatives.

DSIRE is affiliated with the North Carolina State University through its College of Engineering. The college operates the North Carolina Solar Center and works with the Interstate Renewable Energy Council (IREC) to make a list available to companies and consumers regarding incentives and legislation covering all 50 states.

The U.S. Department of Energy funds IREC. Its main goals are to accelerate the use of renewable energy through state and local governments, and the private sector. The Web site address is http://www.dsireusa.org and lists a host of incentives available in 10 broad categories for each U.S. state and for federal incentives.

These incentives are available to individuals, corporations, public entities or a combination of them. Four of the categories relate to tax reduction incentives, such as sales tax, corporate tax, personal tax and property tax.

Six categories cover grant programs, industry recruitment incentives (for renewable energy companies only), leasing or lease/purchase programs for efficient equipment, loans, production incentives and rebate programs.

For upgrades relating to energy, the main areas to consider are energy-efficient equipment and generating or purchasing renewable energy. A number of incentives cover both.

INCENTIVE CATEGORIES

Some grant programs offer funds between US$500 to US$1 million to shopping center and retail companies for energy efficiencies and renewable energy. The leasing or lease/purchase incentives relate to energy users that lease certain technology to achieve efficiencies, such as to lease photovoltaics with the intent to purchase several years later.

1. Low-interest and even no-interest loan programs are available in many states for retailers and shopping center companies to purchase energy-efficient or renewable energy equipment.

2. Production incentives offer cash incentives to project owners that generate renewable energy. This is based on the amount of energy produced rather than amounts invested. Some states offer this incentive for producing ethanol. The Federal Renewable Production Incentive works in the same fashion.

3. Several retail companies are installing solar power with the intent of giving back any extra solar power they are unable to consume to the electricity companies to put back on the grid for other users. Thus they may be able to qualify for renewable energy production incentives.

4. Property tax incentives usually ignore the additional value of equipment that produces renewable energy in assessing the building's value. In other words, the property owner does not pay higher property taxes because of a potential increase in property value gained from installing expensive sustainability equipment. Property tax incentives collected by local sources, such as cities and counties, often need multiple government approvals. Various states—including Connecticut, Iowa, Maryland, New Hampshire, Vermont and Virginia—allow local governmental authorities to offer these types of incentives for renewable energy equipment and reimburse local government.

5. Rebate programs are offered to retailers and shopping centers by the government or utility companies to purchase and install renewable energy equipment.

6. Sales tax incentives exempt the cost of renewable energy from state sales tax, although in some jurisdictions, sales taxes are excluded from capital improvements, and as such negate the effect of the incentive on expensive equipment.

UNDERSTANDING AND MAXIMIZING INCENTIVES

It is important to plan ahead when it comes to budgeting and applying for available incentives. In some cases, only the ultimate user or owner is eligible to receive these incentives. In other cases, rebates and incentives are for intermediate parties such as contractors when using renewable energy during the construction phase of a project.

If you are looking to take advantage of these incentives, watch out. You may leave too much money on the table if you make mistakes. This is why it is important to use knowledgeable engineering consultants to review the incentives available, which change from jurisdiction to jurisdiction, and can help complete the application and provide satisfactory documentation as required.

Sometimes more than one source will supply incentives, but these sources cannot be combined. Some incentive programs will pay upon installation of green building systems while others pay only on the efficiencies achieved, such as reduction of kilowatts consumed.

Property owners cannot simply rely on their suppliers to obtain the incentives, as many are not well versed on what is available. It is advisable to seek expert counsel on ways to take advantage of what is available.

In the United States, many states are in the forefront by offering incentives that can be combined with federal programs for optimum benefit. Among the most aggressive states that provide incentive programs for energy-efficient installations are California, Florida, Hawaii, New Jersey, New York and Texas.

When it comes to offering incentives to businesses, utility companies and private individuals for installing solar photovoltaic cells to harness energy from the sun, California clearly dominates the U.S. market with 57 percent share of all U.S. solar power systems in operation as of the end of 2007, according to a report prepared by Navigant Consulting Inc. for the DOE. This includes residential, commercial and government systems.

The second runner-up is—believe it or not—the northeastern state of New Jersey with an 8 percent share. Colorado has four, Nevada has three and Arizona has 2 percent of the share with the other 45 states combined accounting for 26 percent of the solar power systems.

California set a budget in 2006 of US$42 million for self-generation of electricity using solar power but had to expand the incentives to US$342 million based on demand. California has earmarked US$3 billion in incentives over the course of 10 years (starting in 2007) for self-generation of solar power.

For a retail store or shopping center to take advantage of this incentive, the solar power must be generated within the premises. Purchasing solar energy from a third party transmitted through the electric power grid is insufficient to comply with these requirements.

California's goal is to install 3,000 megawatts in the state by 2017. By comparison, the combined 50 states had only 700 megawatts of installed generation of electricity by solar panels connected to the electricity grid as of 2007.

There is a clear correlation between the incentives California and New Jersey are offering for solar power installation and their budding share of the solar power market. It is easy to understand why major retailers such as Kohl's, Target, Wal-Mart, JCPenney and Macy's are getting in on the action for California's golden sun rush to install solar systems in the state while most of their stores in other states resort to conventional fossil fuel energy. (See Chapter 9.)

Even in states such as California and New Jersey with generous incentives to install solar panels, the payback is roughly three to seven years, according to consultants' calculations, which vary extensively. The payback period is much longer in states without the lucrative incentives and those locales where the sun does not shine enough on the photovoltaic cells to generate sufficient power.

Incentives by some utility companies, added to state and other incentives, have brought the cost of solar energy to roughly US$.10 to US$.12 per kilowatt-hour, which suggests a payback of five to seven years, according to Solarbuzz, an international solar energy research and consulting company.

INCENTIVES FOR LEED COMPLIANCE

Some U.S. cities, counties and states provide incentives of different kinds for green-building standards connected with Leadership in Energy and Environmental Design (LEED) certification. These incentives range from tax abatements and grants to fast-tracking the entitlement process for LEED-targeted developments.

A synopsis of jurisdictions offering these incentives as of 2007 follows:

Incentives for LEED

Tax-related incentives

Baltimore County, MD
Chatham County, GA
Cincinnati, OH
Maryland
Nevada
New Mexico
New York
Oregon
Portland, OR
Pasadena, CA

Issaquah, WA
Los Angeles, CA
San Francisco, CA
Santa Monica, CA
Sarasota County, FL

Grant program

Cincinnati, OH
Pennsylvania (public school districts)
Santa Monica, CA

Density bonus

Acton, MA
Arlington County, VA
Bar Harbor, ME
Nashville, TN
Portsmouth, NH

Other

Babylon, NY *(certification fee rebate)*
Cranford, NJ *(incentives vary by request)*
San Antonio, TX *(waiver/reduction of development fees based on scorecard)*
Pasadena, CA *(rebates)*
San Diego, CA *(expedited discretionary processes)*
Seattle, WA *(economic incentives)*
Washington, DC *(incentives in development)*

Expedited permit review incentive

Chicago, IL
Gainesville, FL

Source: USGBC

LANDLORD-TENANT INCENTIVES

Some shopping center owners are beginning to provide incentives to their tenants to implement green tactics in their buildings, something that is becoming a win-

win for all parties involved. Forest City launched a program at its LEED-certified project in Denver called The Shops at Northfield Stapleton Tenant Sustainability Program—a first-of-its-kind program—to encourage tenants to embrace green building and sustainable design.

Forest City intended for these practices to help reduce the amount of energy and natural resources required to operate and maintain the center and the stores while helping to create a healthier environment for employees and customers.

One component of the program is a handbook that shows retailers how they can build green and motivates them to do so via benefits. Forest City offered these incentives on top of the lowered operating costs Northfield Stapleton retailers now enjoy because of this sustainable building effort. Tenants seemed responsive to this initiative from the outset.

In selling the idea to prospective tenants, Forest City leasing personnel explained that sustainable construction means that everyone—retailers, their employees and customers—would enjoy a healthier, more enjoyable place to shop and live. For merchant employees it means reduced absenteeism, better retention and better morale if they took advantage of this program—and many did.

The following merchants participated in Northfield Stapleton's Tenant Incentive Program:

American Eagle Outfitters	Hot Topic
Ann Taylor Loft	Journeys
Aveda	Justice
Bar	La Sandia Mexican Kitchen and Tequila
Bar Louie	Lane Bryant
Bath & Body Works	Lenscrafters
Brendan Diamonds	Ling and Louie's Asian Bar and Grill
Brookstone	New York & Company
The Buckle	PacSun
Charlotte Russe	Perfumania
The Children's Place	Select Comfort
Christopher & Banks	Sunglass Hut
Cingular Wireless	T-Mobile
Claire's	Verizon Wireless
Cold Stone Creamery	Victoria's Secret
Eddie Bauer	Yankee Candle
Finish Line	Zumiez
Helzberg Diamonds	

Specific tenant incentives included up to US$2 per square foot (US$21.53 per sq m) incentives toward their tenant allowance, free exposure in media advertising and recognition of their efforts throughout the center.

Additionally, the center placed signs on store windows to indicate the retailer's commitment to sustainability, which is important to environmentally aware customers.

Forest City also worked with Xcel Energy, the local utility company that services The Shops at Northfield Stapleton, on the Xcel Design Assistance Program (XDAP) to help facilitate incentives for the merchants. Through XDAP, Xcel Energy made cash incentives available to the retailers that followed Xcel's green building requirements.

Xcel's new construction equipment rebates encouraged retailers to install major energy-saving equipment in their stores under the Energy Design Assistance (EDA) program, and it included minor incentives under its ConservationWise rebates for lighting efficiency, motor efficiency and cooling efficiency.

EDA by ConservationWise from Xcel helps retailers and businesses design a new facility, addition or renovation with efficiency to lower energy bills, while some equipment they purchase in the process qualifies for rebates from Xcel. Other utility companies offer similar incentives to their residential and business accounts.

Xcel provided a comprehensive approach to energy savings for the retailers at The Shops at Northfield Stapleton at no charge, and included personalized computer energy modeling for each of the stores that took advantage of the program. These retailers can now use this valuable modeling to project their energy use. The software program also suggests energy-saving strategies for the retailers and projects energy-cost savings for implementing the strategies.

Chapter 5

Responsible Property Investing

BELIEVE IT OR not, there is a great deal of capital available for real estate deals that have an element of social responsibility and address environmental concerns. This capital is available in debt and equity form all over the world because in such so-called *responsible projects* there is usually a higher degree of risk and potentially greater returns.

SOURCING CAPITAL

Many capital sources already have allocations for real estate as part of their overall investment strategy in core funds that get average returns. For what some refer to as *responsible properties*, there are separate allocations from many value-added funds for investments that give opportunistic returns.

"We are finding investors—be it in public plans, corporate investors, insurance companies or major banks—with an appetite for what I would call 'responsible investments' that get risk adjusted returns north of twenty percent," said Kirk A. Sykes, president of Urban Strategy America Fund, a New Boston Real Estate Fund. Sykes explained that he does not call them "social funds"—although that is a common term—because that sounds like investors who just want to do good with their money.

Many investors are willing to take a higher risk on certain real estate to get a higher financial return. Many of these types of real estate investments revolve around responsible development. For example, Sykes said that a development in an urban area that sits undeveloped because other developers have ignored it is attractive to responsible investment funds when the right developer comes forth with a skill set to make the project work. "The project could be an environmentally

PHOTO ILLUSTRATION COURTESY OF EBL&S DEVELOPMENT

Station Park Green was envisioned as an example of environmental sensitivity, and while still on the drawing boards and going through the entitlement process it is one of 60 projects worldwide to serve as case studies for the U.S. Green Building Council's new LEED for Neighborhood Development (ND) certification.

challenged brownfield that is being proposed for redevelopment," said Sykes. "It could also be a project that is challenged by crime issues or by lack of available tenants."

These redevelopment projects are usually in urban areas near public transportation and in sustainable sites that municipalities with jurisdiction over them want to see restored and revitalized in an environmentally sustainable manner for their constituencies to enjoy in the 21st century.

One such proposition for Sykes's investment capital sources is a proposed green development in San Mateo, California, being developed by Philadelphia, Pennsylvania-based EBL&S, named Station Park Green.

The project's main emphasis is on sustainability. It adjoins the Hayward Park Caltrain station and features two parks, trees, walking paths, 599 residential units, 60,000 square feet (5,575 sq m) of retail, 10,000 square feet (930 sq m) of office space and almost two acres of open space on a 12-acre site.

An underutilized Kmart department store, with enough parking to satisfy hundreds of procrastinating shoppers wishing to complete their last-minute gift shopping on the Saturday before Christmas, has dominated the site and is the reason to redevelop it.

ICSC past trustee Edward B. Lipkin and president of EBL&S Development made connections with Sykes and other capital sources through the Responsible Property Investing Center (RPIC). Although Lipkin already had capital sources for his project, he feels that many opportunities will come about for retail developers and capital sources that share an interest in responsible property investing.

In 2007, the Boston College Institute for Responsible Investment brought together representatives from real estate and investment circles in an attempt to form the RPIC as a not-for-profit organization. RPIC plans to create a conduit where fund sources can be identified to further the green building movement by expanding information and networking.

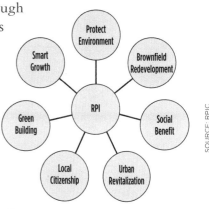

SOURCE: RPIC

Responsible Property Investing Center's mission seeks to find and create value through the economic, social and environmental profile of real estate investments.

RPIC is an organization of academics, lenders, fund managers, investors and real estate developers that focuses on responsible development financing, all of which emphasize environmental sustainability as one component of responsible development.

The RPIC fills a void in the real estate landscape by bringing together executives from these sectors to discuss best practices, conduct research and promote professional networking within the field of responsible property investing.

Responsible property investing is an investment principle that is becoming almost as popular today with major institutional investors as green development is with environmentalists.

UNEP FINANCIAL INITIATIVE

The United Nations even has a suborganization—not affiliated with RPIC—that studies this type of investing and encourages the acceleration of sustainable development across the world. This entity falls under the United Nations Environment Programme Finance Initiative (UNEP FI), which is a global partnership between the UNEP and private financial markets.

UNEP FI works closely with 170 financial institutions that are signatories to the UNEP FI statement and a range of partner organizations to develop and promote linkages between the environment, sustainability and financial performance.

According to UNEP FI, responsible property investing (RPI) means property investment or management strategies that go beyond compliance with minimum legal requirements, in order to address environmental, social and governance issues.

TIAA-CREF, one of the largest financial services companies in the United States, incorporated its Corporate Social Real Estate Portfolio into its Socially Responsible

Ten Elements of Responsible Property Investing

■ Energy Conservation: green power generation and purchasing, energy efficient design, conservation retrofitting,

■ Environmental Protection: water conservation, solid waste recycling, habitat protection

■ Voluntary Certifications: green building certification, certified sustainable wood finishes

■ Public Transport Oriented Developments: transit-oriented development, walkable communities, mixed-use development

■ Urban Revitalization and Adaptability: infill development, flexible interiors, brownfield redevelopment

■ Health and Safety: site security, avoidance of natural hazards, first aid readiness

■ Worker Well-Being: plazas, childcare on premises, indoor environmental quality, barrier-free design

■ Corporate Citizenship: regulatory compliance, sustainability disclosure and reporting, independent boards, adoption of voluntary codes of ethical conduct, stakeholder engagement

■ Social Equity and Community Development: fair labor practices, affordable/social housing, community hiring and training

■ Local Citizenship: quality design, minimum neighborhood impacts, considerate construction, community outreach, historic preservation, no undue influence on local governments

SOURCE: UNEP FI

Investment (SRI) division as a way to broaden its investment opportunities that address the needs and values of its investors, according to Kirk Sykes.

The portfolio has about US$500 million in commitments, comprising a variety of tax credit funds, hybrid debt/equity instruments and private placements in real estate. The portfolio strategy includes equity investments focused on a variety of affordable housing developments, transit-oriented urban infill and sustainable development projects.

For sustainable development projects, TIAA-CREF prefers high-performance buildings that meet LEED certification standards and brownfield redevelopment projects.

Like TIAA-CREF's Corporate Social Real Estate Portfolio, other major public plans, corporate investors, insurance companies and major banks have indeed demonstrated great interest in investing in sustainable real estate.

Listed below is a sampling of a few major capital sources, many of which have funds for responsible property investing or are at least considering this investment strategy:

Public plans:

- California Public Employees' Retirement System (CalPERS)

- California State Teachers' Retirement System (CalSTRS)

- Connecticut Retirement Plans and Trust Funds (CRPTF) (The CRPTF holds assets on behalf of the State Employees' Retirement Fund; Teachers' Retirement Fund; Municipal Employees' Retirement Fund; Probate Court Retirement Fund; Judges' Retirement Fund; State's Attorneys' Retirement Fund; Soldiers', Sailors' & Marines' Fund; Endowment for the Arts; Agricultural College Fund; Ida Eaton Cotton Fund; Andrew Clark Fund; School Fund; Hopemead Fund and Police & Fireman's Survivors' Benefit Fund)

- Los Angeles City Employees' Retirement System (LACERS)

- Massachusetts Pension Reserves Investment Management Board (MassPRIM)

- New York City Employees' Retirement System (NYCERS)

- TIAA-CREF New York Teachers Insurance and Annuity Association-College Retirement Equities Fund

Corporate investors:

- General Electric Capital
- Blue Cross

Insurance companies:

- John Hancock Funds
- AXA Equitable Life Insurance Company (AXA Funds Management Group)

Major banks:

- Bank of America Corporation
- Citigroup Inc.
- The Hong Kong and Shanghai Banking Corporation (HSBC Holdings plc)
- Merrill Lynch & Company Inc.

The largest 200 U.S. public sector pension funds are valued at roughly US$1.65 trillion. Many of the plan managers regard urban development as an economic opportunity with investment determined solely by potential rates of return. However, some capital sources in the 2000s suggest there is more: Are these major public pension funds using other measuring sticks for investing in urban development?

Lisa Hagerman is delving into U.S. public sector pension funds and urban revitalization to understand why public pension funds would engage in alternative investments.

Hagerman quit her job as vice president of Economic Innovation International, a Boston consulting firm that builds privately capitalized market-rate community equity funds, to find out.

Hagerman went back to school and is studying full-time for her doctoral degree in Economic Geography at the Oxford University Centre for the Environment (OUCE). She is examining the investment strategy process used by fund officials, money managers and consultants.

The aim of her research is to advance urban revitalization by increasing capital flows to emerging U.S. domestic markets. The Rockefeller Foundation is supporting Hagerman's research project, the U.S. Public Sector Pension Funds and Urban Revitalization.

Hagerman has already completed case studies on CalPERS: Real Estate, CalPERS: Private Equity, NYCERS and New York Common: Fixed Income, and the MassPRIM Economically Targeted Investment (ETI) program, geared to responsibly investing locally to promote job growth, business development and affordable housing.

The complete case studies can be found at http://urban.ouce.ox.ac.uk.

In the second phase of her research, Hagerman is conducting case studies at Cal-STRS, Texas Teachers and six urban revitalization investment vehicles.

According to David Wood, director of the Institute for Responsible Investment of the Center for Corporate Citizenship at Boston College in Chestnut Hill, Massachusetts, four features make responsible real estate attractive to investors. "We've

found that walkable, mixed-use, energy-efficient and transit-oriented properties are among the highest rated for value by responsible real estate investors," said Wood.

Wood explained that these types of investors are finding and creating value through the economic, social and environmental profile of these real estate investments, and this activity led to the formation of the RPI Center.

Many projects developed in the late 2000s and those on the drawing board for the 2010s are increasing their green building focus because their urban sites are already sustainable by nature and help them qualify for LEED and BREEAM points. The green focus also helps developers with entitlements and permitting.

Among the most popular asset classes for real estate investors focusing on responsible projects are sustainable urban mixed-use properties with a significant retail component, which are connected to mass transit.

"Mixed use is where investors will seek to focus on their share of social and environmentally friendly investments," said Wood, who also oversees the networking and educational activities for RPIC along with Gary Pivo, senior fellow from the Office of Economic Development and a professor of planning and professor of natural resources with the University of Arizona.

"Responsible property investing lies at the nexus of real estate investing, corporate social responsibility and socially responsible investing," wrote Pivo in a position paper. It includes strategies, such as urban reinvestment or energy conservation, that produce social and environmental benefits while also generating market rates of return, according to Pivo.

Participating investors, which hold more than US$100 billion combined in real estate, include Caisse des Depots, CalPERS, Calvert, Domini, Prudential, Morley, Hermes, Lend Lease, Cherokee, Melaver and Land Securities, according to Pivo.

Urban regeneration infill provides great opportunity for growth of all real estate asset classes as the U.S. property sector shifts toward a densification trend much like in Europe, where a vibrant retail component becomes crucial.

"Many people believe there are quality investment properties in low-to-moderate [household] income areas that because of information asymmetry [between the seller and the buyer] provide opportunities for real returns when adjusted for risk," said Wood.

The UNEP Financial Initiative Property Working Group (PWG) agrees conceptually with Wood. The PWG is made up of investors and real estate executives, and together they explore issues relating to responsible property investing under the auspices of the U.N. subsidiary.

This group published a report in 2008 in which the financial experts suggested that rental income could someday become greater in sustainable properties if tenants demonstrate a willingness to pay a premium to lease in green real estate.

"For example, if tenants exercise a preference for occupying more 'sustainable' properties, then the income growth from such investments should prove superior to that from less sustainable, less desirable, stock," co-wrote Paul McNamara

(PRUPIM) and Jean Pierre Sicard (Caisse des Depots), who serve as the co-chairmen of the UNEP FI Property Working Group.

The group took its findings a step further, and surmised that sustainability could also affect liquidity. "Similarly, if investors exercise the same preference, then less sustainable assets will prove less liquid, more risky and potentially less valuable than more sustainable assets," the joint statement said.

McNamara and Sicard also suggested, "If new social standards based around improved sustainability lead to existing landlords having to improve the performance of their properties, then less sustainable assets will probably require greater expenditure and deliver poorer returns."

Time will tell whether the hypotheses of the PWG prove to be correct in the long term. However, the rationale proposed by the co-chairmen of the PWG—because of their influence over financial institutions—tends to hint that buyers of nonsustainable properties could begin to discount property value for needed green upgrades similar to the way buyers now often discount deferred maintenance.

More than 160 institutions, including banks, insurers and fund managers, work with UNEP to understand the effects of environmental and social considerations on financial performance. Many of these financial institutions are establishing real estate funds that focus on responsible property investing and use methods of bottom-line assessment that go beyond traditional investment models.

Funds devoted to sustainable development are not new. Headquartered in Basel, Switzerland, Bank Sarasin & Cie AG launched its first eco-efficiency fund in 1994. Since then, the popularity of all types of funds that invest in projects deemed favorable to the environment has increased in the 2000s, as more fund products have been made widely available.

One of the funds that Sykes taps into for investing in sustainable developments in urban markets such as the Station Park Green is the USA Fund. That fund is a triple bottom line-oriented fund because it:

1. Promotes economic development through job and tax generation
2. Employs sustainable design strategies
3. Provides a reasonable rate of return for its investors

In 1998, SustainAbility, a firm that consults with Starbucks and Wal-Mart, coined the term "triple bottom line (TBL)," to define companies that factor social and environmental responsibility into their business plans as well as financial results.

Deborah La Franchi, a principal of Strategic Development Solutions (SDS), believes in this three-prong approach of investing in certain types of real estate. SDS invests in properties that foster economic opportunity in low-income communities and promotes positive environmental effect. SDS, working with an investment partner, is one of the pioneers creating double bottom line (DBL) and triple bottom line private equity investment funds.

Economic Innovation International Inc. and SDS have jointly developed (or are in the process of capitalizing) more than US$2 billion in funds within this US$10- to US$12-billion industry.

According to SDS, the double bottom line fund industry gained popularity in 2000 and was expected to exceed US$7 billion by 2008. The investment goals of SDS's double bottom line funds are:

1. Risk-adjusted market rates of return for institutional investors
2. Measurable job, wealth and community revitalization for community stakeholders in targeted low-income neighborhoods

The objectives of triple bottom line funds, according to SDS, are:

1. First bottom line: Provide market rate private equity returns to its investors
2. Second bottom line: Invest in real estate projects located in predominantly low-income communities in order to create jobs and economic opportunities
3. Third bottom line: Support environmentally friendly and sustainable green buildings

Triple bottom line banking has become so popular that in 2006 the International Finance Corporation (IFC), the private sector arm of the World Bank Group, and the *Financial Times* (FT) launched the FT Sustainable Banking Awards to recognize banks that have shown leadership and innovation in integrating social, environmental and corporate governance objectives into their operation.

According to Haydeé Celaya, director of Private Equity and Investment Funds for the IFC, her financial institution is committed to investing in and financing ventures all over the world that are financially, environmentally and socially sustainable.

She believes that a triple bottom line approach to investing can make money and thereby meet the demands of the commercial marketplace and still be environmentally and socially responsible. "In fact, we show that environmental and social responsibility will support and enhance the achievement of financial imperatives," said Celaya, in an IFC press release in May 2007.

Triple bottom line returns can be lucrative not only because these real estate investments help a community advance and contribute to preserving the environment but because of the financial returns involved.

Many of these investments handsomely reward the risks associated with responsible property investing, particularly for rehabs involving mixed use in densely populated urban areas. Value-added returns compensate for that risk.

"These value-added returns are not part of a tree hugger agenda," said Sykes. "It is a capitalistic agenda."

Chapter 6

Starting a Green Building Program

STARTING A GREEN building program is not all that difficult. Most companies are already implementing green tactics without realizing it. Companies with no green strategy are leaving money on the table, as being green often means doing simple things like conserving water, energy and other resources that have high costs associated with them—and wasted energy means wasting money.

The largest part of the savings on a long-term basis will come from entirely retrofitting a retail building to be more energy efficient. This might include installing effective daylight harvesting systems, adding solar panels on the roof to generate electricity, reclaiming heat from refrigeration equipment to heat water, replacing boilers and air conditioning systems for better efficiency and adding a monitoring system to control energy creation and electricity use within the building envelope and exterior areas. However, in starting a green program you do not have to change everything your company does all at once to make a difference.

TAKE SMALL STEPS

You and others in your company can take many small steps in the interim. Keep in mind that every little bit helps. "We should show people how to take baby steps rather than go from zero to LEED," said Stephen Gallant, CDP, vice president of facilities and development for JoS. A. Bank Clothiers Inc., a retailer of men's tailored suits, footwear, formal and casual apparel established in 1905.

Gallant took his real estate on the road of sustainability by taking simple actions such as installing recycled carpets, wood floors and ceiling tiles at Jos. A. Bank stores. "We only use compact fluorescent lamps [CFLs] and other energy-efficient lighting," said Gallant.

Simple energy-saving measures that anyone can do at home or at work, such as replacing incandescent lightbulbs with energy-efficient CFLs, will help every business operate more eco-friendly.

Yet look around and you will notice how many commercial establishments continue to use the outdated incandescent lightbulbs. CFLs are inexpensive and will save at least three-quarters of the energy consumed by incandescent bulbs. But that is only one of thousands of small steps you can take.

Since many of the largest shopping center companies grew through acquisition, the variety of different fixtures across a portfolio of properties can be staggering, reaching hundreds of types. This requires evaluating the special needs of individual properties to retrofit lighting in a way that makes sense and results in a more efficient approach.

A wide array of energy-saving lighting products is now available for use in large commercial settings, including halogen, high-output fluorescent and high-intensity discharge (HID) lights, such as metal halide, high-pressure sodium and mercury vapor. Some are better suited for interior settings, while others have exterior applications. Light-emitting diodes (LEDs) are typically for signs and special lighting display needs.

One of General Growth Properties' first moves when it started a green program was to focus on lighting, and the company did not waste time. It conducted studies, evaluated alternatives and launched a massive lighting replacement program across its portfolio of operating properties with a quick payback in mind. "During its first year, General Growth's portfolio-wide lighting replacement program contributed twenty-five percent of the year's energy savings," said Brian F. Griffin, vice president of national operations for General Growth Properties. This type of results can make believers of the most skeptical observers when starting a new green building program.

There are many ways to start a green program at a shopping center or retail company. Two important steps to ensure success from the outset are to obtain management buy-in and to understand the criteria. Different measures exist for qualifying a building as green, but the primary factors are usually using renewable energy, reducing fossil fuel consumption, conserving water, promoting a healthy condition for building occupants, properly sourcing materials, managing waste through careful reuse and recycling techniques, and preserving the environment.

There are a host of things a retail building can do to contribute to preserving rather than hurting the environment. There is typically one rule of thumb: less is better. Heat or cool the premises a little less. Run electrical equipment less and consolidate vehicle trips. Use less water. Buy more regionally produced material and supplies. Upgrade your equipment to the most energy efficient possible.

Fossil fuel used for building energy is the worst type of fuel when it comes to striving to go green. But so is sourcing building materials that have to be flown or trucked from long distances, burning fossil fuel during transportation to the property.

Other considerations are reusing material, using renewable resources, recycling and considering the health and well-being of building occupants in all elements of building design, construction and operation.

Retailers and shopping center professionals need to get up to speed in the green building arena. "We are studying every possibility and looking at the educational process because if we wait until sustainability is mandated by law, it will be too late to properly execute," said Mark Trommsdorff, CDP, director of construction and property management at Kimco Realty Corporation in New Hyde Park, New York.

Trommsdorff's colleague, Richard P. "Rich" O'Leary, agreed: "We have to expand on the value of education and changing human awareness and behavioral change." O'Leary is vice president, director of construction services for the JCPenney Company, a retailer leading the way in exploring sustainable building practices.

The well-intentioned cannot make progress without adequate knowledge and some guidance. How do you deploy human capital and financial capital to invest in green strategies? Start with educating your management personnel, and look internally for talent in your organization.

If the first step is educating about what really constitutes green, the second step to starting a program is to assign a point person to take on leading this challenge. He or she should be well suited to create achievable goals, set new standards, change procedures and get the organization well underway to sustainability. That point person should be committed to the cause and receive support from the highest-ranking member of management.

The point person should assemble a sustainability team of department heads to share in the responsibility of carrying out a green building program. As team leader, he or she should call meetings with department heads on a regular basis to determine what information is needed to make decisions on sustainability. The team leader should also undertake a fact-finding mission to examine the organization's current environmental management policies, procedures and practices, while paying special attention to the organization's purchasing and contracting policies, procedures and practices.

CONDUCT A GREEN AUDIT

Soon after the program gets started, the team leader should commission a sustainability (or green) audit. This will highlight what is already being done as well as what can be done to take the store, shopping center or company to a higher level of sustainability. This green audit can be done with the help of an architect and a green building consultant who are knowledgeable about green building design, construction and operations. LEED-accredited professionals, BREEAM assessors, Green Globes verifiers and other green building experts make effective green building consultants. These professionals are trained to highlight areas to assess and address.

An excellent form to use in comparing the performance of any building to green building standards is the Green Globes Design v.1—Post-Construction Assessment.

This self-assessment form is a simple-to-use online auditing tool especially made by the Green Building Initiative (GBI) for designers, property owners and managers to use. (See Chapter 8.) While a nonprofessional using this form to assess the level of sustainability of a store or shopping center may not constitute a reliable green audit, it helps to identify many things to consider.

GBI has a list of independent third-party verifiers trained to conduct Green Globes audits. For an up-to-date list of verifiers in Canada, contact info@greenglobes.com. In the United Kingdom, you may contact amy.garrod@fabermaunsell.com and in the United States, contact info@thegbi.org.

A proper green audit will help the sustainability team leader and the department heads of the organization sort out priorities and set realistic short- and long-term goals. If you are starting a new green program, your goals should be reasonable, achievable and measurable.

At first, do not try to reach for the highest level of sustainability as it pertains to an operating building. Look for the small things that make the most impact. Immediate goals should include programs that help the environment, promote the health of building occupants and reduce operating costs from wasteful consumption of potable water and energy generated from the burning of fossil fuels.

One example to look at is Citigroup's efforts. Citigroup first undertook the arduous task to quantify the energy consumption across its entire real estate portfolio and identify potential savings opportunities. Then, armed with that information, Stephen Lane, executive vice president of Citigroup, has implemented energy-savings measures across the financial organization's 92 million square feet (8.5 million sq m) of offices and retail banks. One of these measures involved having larger windows that add natural lighting. Increasing natural light helps to economize on artificial lighting during the day. Another energy-saving measure consisted of installing sensors.

Hundreds of green building tactics may surface during a green audit. Many of these can be implemented quickly and for relatively little money. Some are just commonsense initiatives such as installing motion sensors that turn off lights inside stores, corridors and stockrooms when these areas are not occupied, keeping appliances off when not being used and adding economizers to HVAC units.

Utility companies can also help make suggestions to reduce energy consumption. Many stores and shopping centers can cut 10 percent of the electricity bill simply by instituting a series of well-thought-out conservation techniques that do not require major capital investments.

These green audits go beyond reducing consumption of water, electricity and natural gas. Green audits will also examine indoor environmental quality to optimize the health of building occupants.

How green does your organization need to be? Determine what makes the most sense, and then chart the course. It is important to recognize that there are different shades of green. Recycling efforts, energy-efficient enhancements and water conservation practices can take a retail store or shopping center a long way toward sustainability.

The point person should identify what is being done already and perhaps what can be achieved with relatively little effort. As with all business practices, a cost-benefit analysis helps to set priorities in getting the most impact for the amount spent to green up a building. A company that makes quick advances toward green building tactics can inspire many people to help make the organization greener. As the point person becomes the company's flag-waver on the subject, these simple tactics make everyone believers in what can be achieved.

Managers at all levels must be made to realize that the company has entrusted this person with accountability and authority to carry out the sustainability mission. It is critical that the point person receive the full support and cooperation of all department heads, each of which will need to carry out their part of the mission.

Sustainable tactics cross many areas. Although the point person is championing the cause, it is everyone's job to implement the strategy. This point person can be an internal executive or an outside consultant.

Alberta Development looked outside for sustainability guidance when the developer decided to build The Streets at SouthGlenn in Centennial, near Denver, Colorado. YRG Services became the point of contact to take Alberta's team "greenbound."

"We hired YRG Services as our sustainability consultant, and we tasked them to work with our architect, our construction company, even our tenants," said Bryan McFarland, principal of development for Greenwood Village, Colorado-based Alberta Development Partners LLC.

YRG worked as an integrated part of the project team, aligning itself with design, construction and operations people to integrate sustainable practices into the project, targeting a summer 2008 completion.

"We've brought together leaders in architecture and design, including Callison Architects, Communication-Arts, SEM Architects, EDAW and Shook Kelly, to create a regional, mixed-use shopping destination with local culture and universal appeal," said ICSC trustee Don Provost, principal of Alberta Development Partners.

The Streets at SouthGlenn redevelopment transformed the formerly enclosed regional mall into an open-air lifestyle mixed-use project by integrating shaded walkways and public spaces with retail, office, residential and urban convenience in a suburban setting. Anchors include Sears, Macy's, Whole Foods Market, Barnes & Noble, a movie theater and other shops.

YRG performed several tasks for Alberta, including LEED training and education, design assistance and technical support, green building strategy evaluation assessment, cost-benefit analysis, LEED certification coordination and management, plan and specification review, technical support and building commissioning, coordinating available incentives and even marketing support.

"We are adopting sustainability as a corporate policy," McFarland summed up.

Each company does it differently, but the green structure should address the needs of the company and take into consideration what it will take to accomplish the objectives.

CROSS-FUNCTIONAL TEAMS

In 2006, General Growth Properties, the second largest retail real estate company in the United States, set out to convert its organization into a more sustainable and efficient development and management company by implementing high-performance building techniques to new properties, renovated properties and throughout the operating network. The company also wanted to promulgate green practices among the workplace environment to ensure that sustainability becomes ingrained throughout the organization.

To achieve its goal, General Growth established an active network of collaborative cross-functional planning teams across the organization. Lisa Loweth, vice president of sustainability for General Growth Properties, became the company's point person. She now oversees a core planning team made up of the leaders of each of the network teams to orchestrate an integrated overall plan. The General Growth model revolves around three key components:

1. Designing and developing places

The sustainable design and development group (headed by Kenneth G. "Ken" Maynard, vice president of planning and design) has responsibility over the development, architectural and construction aspect for new properties and properties undergoing substantial redevelopment.

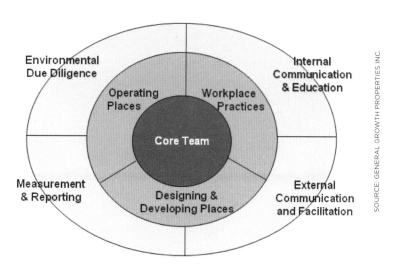

General Growth Properties established an active network of collaborative cross-functional planning teams to ensure that sustainability becomes an intrinsic part of how the company does business. These teams focus on different areas of the business, including sustainable design and development, sustainable operations, sustainable workplace practices, external sustainability communication and facilitation, internal sustainability communication and education, environmental research projects and measurement. Lisa Loweth, vice president of sustainability for General Growth Properties, oversees the core planning team to orchestrate an integrated overall plan.

2. Operating places

Julie Jones, SCMD, SCSM, senior vice president of national operations, oversees sustainable operations. She concentrates primarily on the operating properties to ensure that they run efficiently and sustainably.

3. Workplace practices

Communications, both internal and external, are essential to advance a green program for an organization of any size. At General Growth Properties, Mary Vermillion, CMD, group vice president of marketing, is responsible for sustainable workplace practices, external sustainability communication and facilitation. Kacie Walters, director of knowledge management, is responsible for internal sustainability communication and education.

One financial component crosses over to all areas. Measuring costs and quantifying benefits are critical to the successful implementation of sustainability measures from a business perspective. Madalyn Stein Kandelman, senior financial analyst, oversees all environmental research projects and measurement.

Timothy E. Gardels, CDP, first vice president of design and construction for General Growth Properties, said that in the design-built and operations areas of the company, there are subgroups for design, construction, operations and tenant coordination. Gardels works with the design and construction groups and reports to Loweth and Maynard on the goals and progress of his teams. Loweth in turn bears the responsibility to report to the highest levels of corporate management on the company's collective progress toward a total green makeover.

The most significant positive impact on the bottom line when a company starts a new program will come from energy savings. These types of initiatives frequently achieve a full payback on the capital invested in systems and equipment in as little as two to four years.

GUIDELINES FOR ENERGY MANAGEMENT

EPA has a program known as Energy Star Guidelines for Energy Management that outlines a road map for starting a program. EPA's seven-step strategy can assist any organization to improve its energy and financial performance and is available free on the EPA Web site: http://www.energystar.gov/index.cfm?c=guidelines.guidelines_index.

The highlights of the EPA recommended program consist of seven key steps with detailed recommendations for each of the steps:

STEP 1: Make Commitment
Form the Team
1.1 **Appoint an Energy Director**—Set goals, track progress and promote the energy management program.

1.2 **Establish an Energy Team**—Execute energy management activities across different parts of the organization and ensure integration of best practices.

Institute a Policy
1.3 **Institute an Energy Policy**—Provide the foundation for setting performance goals and integrating energy management into an organization's culture and operations.

ENERGY STAR Guidelines For Energy Management

- Make Commitment
- Assess Performance & Set Goals
- Create Action Plan
- Recognize Achievements
- Implement Action Plan
- Evaluate Progress

STEP 2: Assess Performance
Data Collection
2.1 **Gather and track data**—Collect energy use information and document data over time.

Baselining and Benchmarking
2.2 **Establish baselines**—Determine the starting point from which to measure progress.

2.3 **Benchmark**—Compare the energy performance of your facilities to one another, peers and competitors, and over time to prioritize which facilities to focus on for improvements.

Analysis and Evaluation
2.4 **Analyze**—Understand your energy use patterns and trends.

2.5 **Technical assessments and audits**—Evaluate the operating performance of facility systems and equipment to determine improvement potential.

STEP 3: Set Goals
Setting Goals
3.1 **Determine scope**—Identify organizational and time parameters for goals.

3.2 **Estimate potential for improvement**—Review baselines, benchmark to determine the potential and order of upgrades, and conduct technical assessments and audits.

3.3 **Establish goals**—Create and express clear, measurable goals, with target dates, for the entire organization, facilities and other units.

STEP 4: Create Action Plan
4.1 **Define technical steps and targets**

4.2 **Determine roles and resources**
Get buy-in from management and all organizational areas affected by

the action plan before finalizing it. Work with the Energy Team to communicate the action plan to all areas of the organization.

STEP 5: Implement Action Plan

    5.1 **Create a communication plan**—Develop targeted information for key audiences about your energy management program.

    5.2 **Raise awareness**—Build support in all levels of your organization for energy management initiatives and goals.

    5.3 **Build capacity**—Through training, access to information, and transfer of successful practices, procedures and technologies, you can expand the capacity of your staff.

    5.4 **Motivate**—Create incentives that encourage staff to improve energy performance to achieve goals.

    5.5 **Track and monitor**—Use the tracking system developed as part of the action plan to track and monitor progress regularly.

STEP 6: Evaluate Progress

    6.1 **Measure results**—Compare current performance to established goals.

    6.2 **Review action plan**—Understand what worked well and what did not in order to identify best practices.

STEP 7: Recognize Achievements

    7.1 **Provide internal recognition**—Give credit to individuals, teams and facilities within your organization.

    7.2 **Receive external recognition**—Apply for available awards and other forms of recognition from government agencies, the media and other third-party organizations that reward achievement.

The EPA program offers detailed suggestions and tips for planning an effective program. It even provides an example, using the retail chain Food Lion as a case study on how to start an effective program. EPA also adopted a model in cooperation with 18 U.S. government agencies entitled Guiding Principles for Federal Leadership in High Performance and Sustainable Buildings. The EPA guide suggests green building principles such as integrated design, energy performance, water conservation, indoor environmental quality and materials specifications.

Various factors should be considered when a retail property attempts to gauge its sustainability program. These include risk management, regulatory forces and compliance, shareholder activism and advocacy groups claiming a stake. Each of these factors weigh upon the level of sustainability that a retail property is expected to achieve.

Upon implementing a program, many benefits will become obvious. Some benefits can be measured because they have a financial impact, while others will be of

an operational nature. Yet other benefits will influence internal or external sources, such as stakeholders.

Financial benefits involve cost savings derived from reducing waste and using natural resources, such as water, electricity, natural gas, heating oil and other fuels, more efficiently. Also, insurance carriers may offer a reduction in premium if you are able to demonstrate proper risk management techniques that promote safety and environmental care.

Another benefit of having a well-documented green program is that it helps buildings comply with certain requirements that might otherwise be overlooked. This helps to avoid fines and penalties that may be imposed from not meeting environmental prerequisites prescribed by law.

A good program may result in improved overall performance and efficiency. Many retailers and shopping center professionals are often surprised by the reduction in waste after instituting a green building program. Internal communications and morale are frequently improved and sometimes lead to sound environmental solutions suggested by lower-ranking employees.

The formulating and implementing of a sound environmental policy often enhances the image of the retailer or shopping center as environmentally responsible. Once a policy is established, it should not be kept a secret from the outside world.

Many companies such as IKEA, The Home Depot and Limited Brands Inc. post their sustainability policies prominently on their Web sites for all stakeholders to read. Employee understanding of a company's environmental policy helps to promote the common goal, while better public perception can improve goodwill and patronage.

A green program can help foster community support by reducing the negative effects that some commercial buildings cause nearby residents such as increased traffic, noise, odors, dust and unwanted lighting—all common complaints by residents objecting to new retail development.

Sustainable practices also give a retailer and shopping center a certain level of credibility and integrity as well as a positive image with their stakeholders.

Chapter 7

Corporate Social Responsibility

SUSTAINABILITY IS A term often used by people who are referring to corporate responsibility and social responsibility. However, the proper term for that is corporate social responsibility (CSR). Environmental sustainability is more accurately portrayed as a subset of CSR, although the term has broader implications today.

ENVIRONMENTAL SUSTAINABILITY

Sustainability—referring to preserving the environment and resources for future generations—is often considered only one component of social responsibility. A company defined as socially responsible is expected to promote all principles of environmental sustainability and green building standards for obvious reasons. However, social responsibility goes beyond this.

Many companies that call themselves "socially responsible" delve into the supply line of the products they sell to ensure that work standards and wages are fair and competitive, without necessarily attempting to sustain the environment and resources for future generations.

When *sustainability* is used in the context of corporate social responsibility, it means: to improve or to sustain the quality of life for the citizens of the world. In this definition, the term has come to encompass economic, social and institutional qualities as well as environmental concerns. The term *sustainability* used in this broad sense is quite common in Europe, whereas many U.S. retailers that participate in community and social programs refer to this as CSR instead.

For example, Kohl's has raised more than US$85 million for children's initiatives in the United States. Kohl's calls this philanthropic CSR program "Kohl's Cares

PHOTO: R. E. MILIAN

CVS/Pharmacy, America's largest retail pharmacy, with more than 6,200 retail locations, helped with the relief effort during the October 2007 wildfires in Southern California. However, the efforts of CVS/Pharmacy in California cannot address the needs of its stakeholders in its Spring Valley, New York, store (pictured).

That CVS/Pharmacy store was among more than two dozen employers that were honored a year before the California wildfires at the National Disability Employment Awareness Month breakfast, an event held at the Palisades Center in West Nyack, New York. Rockland Employment Network, a consortium of nonprofit groups that helps match people with disabilities to jobs, sponsored the awards that CVS/Pharmacy earned through its CSR programs and fair-hiring practices.

for Kids." And CVS/Pharmacy showed its care for communities in Southern California when it donated more than US$300,000 in supplies to aid fire relief efforts during the 2007 wildfires that engulfed almost one million acres.

CVS demonstrated its CSR with a gift to needy victims of the fire. "We are deeply concerned about the impact these fires have had on our customers and employees and we are pleased to aid on-going relief efforts with these donations," said Ronald Day, CVS/Pharmacy's vice president for California, in a statement issued to the media in October 2007.

CVS shipped a truckload of health care and personal care items to San Diego's Qualcomm Stadium and other local shelters for distribution to evacuees. The retail chain gets its name from its first store that opened in Lowell, Massachusetts, in 1963, which operated under the name of Consumer Value Store.

The retail division of Woonsocket, Rhode Island-based CVS Caremark Corporation is America's largest retail pharmacy with more than 6,200 retail locations. With 6,200 locations all over the United States, CVS cannot solely rely on the CSR efforts in California to respond to the needs of its stakeholders living in New York State. As such, each store has to enact a CSR of its own.

BE RESPONSIVE TO STAKEHOLDERS

Every company and every organization has stakeholders—from a church or trade association to a shopping center developer or retailer. Social responsiveness and community involvement are important to shareholders, clients, investors, employees and customers, and collectively, these parties make up the stakeholders of a business. They are either individuals or organized groups that can be affected by a company's activities, products and services. Conversely, the actions of these stakeholders can affect the company's business positively or negatively. This is why it is good business for a company and its stakeholders to unite for mutual benefit.

Wal-Mart, the world's largest retailer, has one of the largest amounts of stakeholders representing the broadest base. Even governments—city, county and na-

tional—can be considered stakeholders of Wal-Mart. Entire companies that supply Wal-Mart's merchandise are stakeholders of Wal-Mart, and that includes their owners, employees and their own suppliers. Their destinies are intertwined with Wal-Mart's destiny. They all rely on Wal-Mart's success for their own success.

Individual shopping centers and retail stores have their own base of stakeholders. This is why a shopping center or store might sponsor a local football or soccer league activity, recognizing that this community exposure might boost sales.

In sponsoring such community activity, they are creating goodwill with their stakeholders who may be represented in the league by community leaders, customers, employees, city officials and the like.

Responding to social causes of interest to stakeholders is one of the best forms of public relations geared to promoting a sound CSR image.

STARBUCKS FAIR TRADE COFFEE

Starbucks has ongoing efforts to aid its suppliers, which is another example of CSR. Fair Trade Certified coffee is one initiative undertaken by Starbucks to be socially responsible with its coffee farmer suppliers all over the world. The Fair Trade system certifies cooperatives of family-owned farms, which only account for about 2 percent of the world's coffee supply.

Starbucks coordinates with several organizations to make credit available to coffee and cocoa growers. These organizations include the Calvert Foundation, Verde Ventures and EcoLogic Finance. They offer loans to coffee farmers. In turn, these growers are able to postpone selling their crops until the price is favorable.

Starbucks also collaborates with some of the farms to help improve the quality of life for farm workers and their families, with matching contributions going to social projects ranging from education programs in Nicaragua to expanding a hospital in Papua, New Guinea.

Some CSR initiatives are extensive while others are minimal. However, every company has its own version of CSR weaved into its policies and corporate culture. J.W. "Bill" Marriott, chairman and CEO of Marriott International brands of hotels and resorts, outlines his CSR version in five key areas under the acronym S.E.R.V.E.

"S" stands for *shelter and food*, which Marriott provides through organizations such as Habitat for Humanity International and the Federation of Red Cross

Fair Trade Certified coffee is one initiative taken by Starbucks to be socially responsible with its coffee farmer suppliers all over the world. Above is Starbucks in Shanghai, China.

and Red Crescent Societies. Marriott also donates leftover food from ballroom functions to soup kitchens in local communities. "E" stands for the *environment*, underscoring Marriott's commitment to environmental sustainability. "R" is for *readiness for hotel careers* and Marriott's support of education. "V" signifies *vitality of children* and support for youth programs, and "E" is for *embracing diversity and people with disabilities*.

The net contribution by Marriott Corporation in 2006 was US$6.6 million in cash donations and US$19.1 million in in-kind contributions. Additionally, the company keeps track of its employees' charitable and volunteer efforts and publicizes the aggregate statistics. Marriott employees raised US$6.8 million in their respective communities and contributed 210,000 hours of volunteer service.

Shopping centers in general and large centers in particular are considered socially responsible because of the contributions they make to the communities

Simon Property Group collects contributions at Menlo Park Mall in Edison, New Jersey, on behalf of the Simon Youth Foundation (SYF), which established a community scholarship to meet the financial needs of students in communities surrounding Simon regional shopping centers. At right, Macy's at Menlo Park Mall promotes the American Heart Association (AHA) Go Red for Women movement to help women live longer, stronger lives. By January 2008, the AHA had received more than US$8.5 million for its heart disease awareness and prevention campaign from the full scope of Macy's national sponsorship activities.

PHOTOS: R. E. MILIAN

surrounding them. This is evident by the scores of shopping centers recognized every year with the coveted ICSC MAXI Community Service Award, given by a jury of their peers. The awards featured several recycling and green building promotions in 2007.

Shopping centers also contribute to society. Along with their vast array of merchants, shopping centers account for a large employment base. The centers generate sales tax or value added tax (VAT) from the merchandise sold by retail stores and the services other merchants provide.

Shopping centers also contribute property tax revenues and employment tax. Despite such obligations conferred upon these large retail hubs, shopping centers willingly support local charities and community causes with events that help raise visibility for worthwhile community activities.

The companies that operate shopping centers are traditionally predisposed to connecting with the communities around them, even at the corporate level, because shopping center management inherently embraces community-mindedness universally. Few industries are as deeply ingrained in the fabric of community support as the shopping center industry.

General Growth Properties demonstrated one example of corporate social responsibility in a 2007 press release. The large U.S. REIT announced a program for its contract cleaning service vendors to require them to sign a commitment to meet minimum standards with respect to compensation and treatment of their employees doing housekeeping tasks at General Growth shopping centers.

The international retail developer is requiring its U.S. contractors to offer individual and family health insurance with affordable premiums in which the employer will cover 75 percent of the costs. Additionally, General Growth is requiring its U.S. contractors to undertake market-based compensation surveys and pay fair wages to the employees. Other large shopping center REITs have implemented similar programs.

Some investment companies are assessing how investments are structured to invest in green companies. As efforts are placed on preserving the environment and green buildings, companies positioned to take advantage of green technologies may prove to be winners in future years.

Many companies in the green categories that investors are considering are in the energy sector, but some real estate companies are also possible recipients of green investment funds. Corporate social responsibility is something that companies project to their stakeholders in the belief that stakeholders wish to deal with companies that share similar values as they do themselves and care about the community the company serves. It is all about public relations and maintaining a good relationship with stakeholders.

CULTURAL PRESERVATION

Cultural preservation is another concept that is sometimes associated with CSR or sustainability, particularly in Europe. For centuries, many architects have incorporated cultural preservation principles into all types of building design—including retail properties. Some architects do this at varying levels.

The concept of cultural preservation inherently tries to retain the identity and historic trademarks of the community where the project is located in order to preserve, rather than sustain, this culture for future generations.

One example of cultural preservation is often found in the United States in Arizona and New Mexico. Pueblo-style adobe architecture goes back 16 centuries to a time when Native Americans and Aztec tribes built their homes with sun-dried bricks using mud mortar and vigas, which are beams with their ends protruding outside of the building, lending strength and support to the structure. Villa Linda Mall in Santa Fe, New Mexico, includes some of these architectural features.

The warm tones of these buildings are symbolic of the reddish-colored soil that makes up the mountains surrounding this area. When an architect intends to preserve this look in a building—whether a residence, office building or shopping center—one of the primary motives is to preserve the culture.

Another aspect of cultural preservation in the United States might highlight the art deco architectural colors and design elements in South Miami Beach, Florida, in a new or renovated building.

Likewise, using traditional building designs reminiscent of 18th- and 19th-century Spain eight miles east in Coral Gables, Florida, is another example of cultural preservation.

Retail architect Benjamin Bross cautions that cultural preservation in a retail design is a highly philosophical issue. There is no right or wrong. "Regionalism has its place but so does an expression of Zeitgeist [German for "the spirit of the age"], said Bross. "Not to mention that the architect rarely dictates to the client; it's usually the other way around."

Wafi, one of the oldest shopping malls in Dubai, United Arab Emirates, has preserved the rich Arab culture through various architectural design elements of authentic 14th century souks, sculptures, mosaics and exquisite stained glass depicting the splendor of the Pharaohs.

PHOTOS: R. E. MILIAN

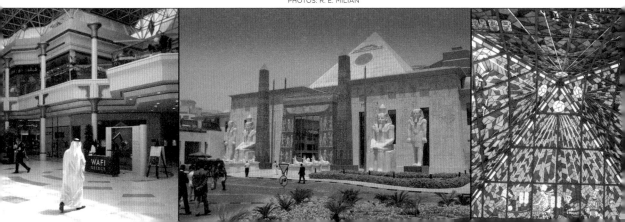

Chapter 8

Organizations Setting Green Thresholds

CERTIFYING GREEN BUILDINGS has become a large global business conducted by organizations, both for-profit and nonprofit. And there are independent consultants—some accredited by these organizations—available to work with building owners and operators to help design systems and prepare applications for green building certification.

These consultants can help interpret the building's level of sustainability and compliance with codes and green building legislation. In the United States, LEED is now a popular buzzword among real estate professionals. It has become one of the most reputable green building certifications in North America. A not-for-profit trade group in the United States certifies various types of buildings, at different levels of sustainability, with the prestigious LEED certification. A sister organization does the same in Canada.

Many green building programs are similar in scope, and there is no one-size-fits-all system. By having several acceptable options, companies can choose the certification source that meets their needs.

WHAT IS LEED?

The LEED Green Building Rating System stands for Leadership in Energy and Environmental Design, which is a point rating system devised by the U.S. Green Building Council (USGBC) to recognize the extent of environmental performance of a building, thereby encouraging environmentally sustainable design. The USGBC created LEED to be a voluntary, consensus-based national standard for developing high-performance, sustainable buildings.

USGBC members representing all segments of the building industry created LEED. The USGBC has some 12,500 members including corporations, govern-

mental agencies and nonprofit organizations. Volunteer members that continue to adjust the LEED rating system meet the objectives of owners of all types of high-performance buildings.

LEED offers project certification, professional accreditation and training and provides practical resources. The USGBC defined several objectives for LEED, which are to:

- Define a *green building* by establishing a common standard of measurement
- Promote integrated, whole-building design practices
- Recognize environmental leadership in the building industry
- Stimulate competition and innovation in the green arena
- Raise awareness of green building benefits
- Transform the building industry toward sustainability

The major areas promoting human and environmental health—sustainable site development, water conservation, energy and atmosphere, materials selection and use of resources, and indoor environmental quality—call for environmentally friendly actions and systems implemented during the design, construction and operations phases of many building types, including schools, industrial, residential, office and retail.

A property must receive at least 26 LEED-awarded points for minimum certification. The USGBC considers that the higher the point score, the greater the level of sustainability the property has achieved. Silver is the second level, ranking above the minimum certification threshold. Gold is the third level, and platinum is the highest level of green building standards set by the LEED system.

The origin of LEED and other green building rating systems are in the office sector. Because of this, and because it was originally designed for a single property owner, translating the concepts to produce meaningful environmental benefits in a multi-owner mixed-use or retail setting has been challenging.

Buildings can only apply for LEED certification under certain criteria. Commercial buildings are eligible for certification under:

- **LEED for New Construction**
  Intended for new construction and major renovations

- **LEED for Existing Buildings**
  Intended for existing buildings, focusing on operations, improvements and maintenance

- **LEED for Commercial Interiors**
  Intended for tenant improvement and interior space

- **LEED for Core and Shell Rating Systems**
  Intended for new core and shell construction

Three other rating systems have been undergoing pilot testing: These are the the LEED Portfolio program, the LEED for Neighborhood Development and the LEED for Retail, the USGBC's latest rating systems. They are scheduled for official roll-out in late 2008. All are promising for those parties wishing to certify their retail buildings.

- **The LEED Portfolio Program**
  This program enables retail companies and building owners to integrate LEED into their new and existing building projects using a cost-effective, streamlined certification process, mostly based on a consistent prototype design rollout.

The Portfolio program pilot (or volume program, as some call it) began in November 2006. The pilot includes 40 participating companies and institutions and covers 1,700 buildings comprising about 135 million square feet (125 million sq m) of building space.

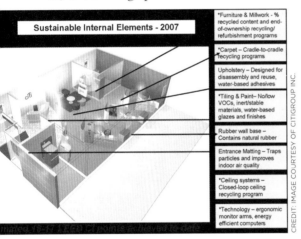

Citibank developed a sustainable internal elements design package in 2007 to roll out to all its new or renovated retail banking outlets. Citibank retail locations like the one featured in White Plains, New York, will follow a green model such as the portfolio features depicted below.

Pilot participants represent a cross-section of real estate sectors, including institutional investors, financial institutions, hoteliers, universities and retailers. The USGBC is working with pilot participants to develop submittal documentation for volume certification, quality control and education plans to help adopt LEED standards into design criteria, construction and operations practices.

One of the participants in the LEED Portfolio pilot program is Citibank, the preeminent financial services company with some 200 million customer accounts in more than 100 countries. Citibank developed a sustainable internal elements design package to roll out to all its retail banking outlets and coordinated the process with the USGBC. This design includes sustainable features that Citibank envisions can be implemented in the space fit-out and could give the institution from 16 to 17 credit points toward the commercial interior LEED certification, merely by following specified features such as

low-VOC tiles and paints, upholstery designed for reuse and its cradle-to-cradle carpet recycling program.

The banking retailer can achieve additional points in the portfolio design package with design elements it has already been using, such as energy-efficient signage, lighting and HVAC, as well as using building management systems and lighting controls.

Small-space retail users like Starbucks looking for an inexpensive way to have many stores certified economically stand the most to gain from a volume certification approach. However, big-box retailers such as Kohl's that build to a standard design can also benefit.

Kohl's developed a prototypical design and incorporated LEED standards throughout, according to Dan Booher, CDP, senior vice president of design, construction and store planning for Kohl's Corporation. Once Kohl's was happy with the design, Booher submitted the plans to the USGBC for consideration under the portfolio certification program while still being developed.

"We now have a LEED-accredited professional on staff," said Booher. He said that the internal LEED AP's role is to work with architects, construction contractors and other professionals to ensure the LEED-Kohl's program is built out according to the specifications of the new prototypical design for Kohl's store.

However, portfolio certification has limited applications, and other retail buildings may opt for two other LEED programs instead. The other two rating systems are:

- **LEED for Neighborhood Development**
  Intended to integrate the principles of smart growth, urbanism and green building into a standard for neighborhood design

- **LEED for Retail**
  Intended to recognize the unique nature of retail design and construction projects and addresses the specific needs of retail spaces

LEED for Retail—New Construction is a green building designation that the USGBC has been developing for adaptation to retail buildings with the help of retail executives during 2007 and 2008. LEED for Retail consists of two rating systems. One of them is similar to the LEED for New Construction (NC) (Version 2.2), and the other one pertains to the LEED for Commercial Interiors (CI) (Version 2.0).

"LEED NC and CI as they exist today do not acknowledge the retail environment," said Justin T. Doak, manager, LEED retail sector for the USGBC. Doak explained that the LEED for Retail committee and the USGBC are watching the participants of the retail pilot program to modify the point system awarded for new construction and commercial interiors involving retail to compensate for the high demands retail has over other real estate uses.

Retail spaces usually have high load demands for electricity to cool a building as

well as to power refrigeration and freezer equipment. Both LEED for Retail rating systems recognize the unique nature of retail design and construction and address the specific needs of retail spaces including lighting, project site, security, energy and water. In most cases, the system provides tailored credit language relaxed from office buildings and alternative compliance paths.

In the pilot LEED for Retail program, the USGBC sought specific representation from:

1. Quick Service Restaurants (QSRs)

2. Grocery Stores

3. Home Improvement Centers

4. Large Retail-Department Stores

5. Large Retail-Big Box

6. Clothing Retail

7. Banking/Financial Services

8. Salons

"There has never been a baseline for QSR," said Doak. These fast-food restaurants, considered retail buildings, have a high load for cooking, refrigeration and extensive water usage. QSRs consume considerable power and water. They cannot be compared with nonfood retail for the sake of measuring their level of sustainable design and operation.

The LEED for Retail system is still too new to speculate how it will evolve. However, observers' preliminary projections are that shopping center owners wishing to apply for LEED certifications will use the guidelines established in LEED for New Construction, and the retail tenants (not operating in big boxes or freestanding locations) will select Commercial Interiors as the rating system under which to apply.

Ben Packard, director of environmental affairs for Starbucks Coffee Company, chairs the LEED for Retail volunteer committee, and David A. Luick, manager for strategic development initiatives at Target Corporation, is the vice-chair.

Retailers on the committee include Chipotle, Kohl's, Office Depot, Whole Foods Market, Giant Food Inc. (a member of Royal Ahold that includes Stop & Shop and Giant Supermarkets), Falabella (the South American chain operating home improvement stores, department stores and supermarkets), Bank of America, Wachovia Bank, PNC Financial Services Group, Citibank, Office Depot, Tesco (Fresh & Easy), West Elm and Elephant Pharm.

Still under review at press time, LEED for Retail certification program—with a maximum of 70 possible points—was drafted as of October 2007 as follows:

LEED FOR RETAIL
New Construction and Major Renovations

The LEED-NC (short for new construction) Rating System is applicable to new commercial construction and major renovation projects.

(Not covered below is a completely different system called LEED for Retail Commercial Interiors intended for the interior space of shopping malls or retail stores.)

Criteria for sustainability   **Points**

Sustainable Sites – *16 possible points*
Prerequisite 1: Pollution prevention during construction activity is required
Credit 1 Site selection *(1 point)*
Credit 2 Development density and community connectivity *(1 point)*
Credit 3 Brownfield redevelopment *(1 point)*
Credit 4 Alternative transportation *(4 point maximum from A–H)*
    A. Public transportation access *(1 point)*
    B. Bicycle storage and commuting *(1 point)*
    C. Low-emitting and fuel-efficient vehicles *(1 point)*
    D. Parking capacity *(1 point)*
    E. Delivery service *(1 point)*
    F. Incentives *(1 point)*
    G. Car-share membership *(1 point)*
    H. Alternative transportation education *(1 point)*
Credit 5.1 Site development, protect/restore habitat *(1 point)*
Credit 5.2 Site development, maximize open space *(1 point)*
Credit 6.1 Stormwater design, quantity control *(1 point)*
Credit 6.2 Stormwater design, quality control *(1 point)*
Credit 7.1 Heat island effect, nonroof *(1 point)*
Credit 7.2 Heat island effect, nonroof *(1 point)*
Credit 7.3 Heat island effect, nonroof *(1 point)*
Credit 7.4 Heat island effect, roof *(1 point)*
Credit 8 Light pollution reduction *(1 point)*

                                                                          0–16

Water efficiency – *5 Possible Points*
Credit 1.1 Water-efficient landscaping, reduce by 50 percent *(1 point)*
Credit 1.2 Water-efficient landscaping, no potable use or no irrigation *(1 point)*
Credit 2 Innovative wastewater technologies *(1 point)*
Credit 3.1 Water use reduction, 20% reduction *(1 point)*
Credit 3.2 Water use reduction, 30% reduction *(1 point)*

                                                                          0–5

Energy and Atmosphere – *17 Possible Points*
Prerequisite 1: Fundamental commissioning of the building energy systems required
Prerequisite 2: Minimum energy performance required
Prerequisite 3: Fundamental refrigerant management required
Credit 1 Optimize energy performance *(1 to 10 points)*
Credit 2 On-site renewable energy *(1 to 3 points)*
Credit 3 Enhanced building commissioning *(1 point)*
Credit 4 Enhanced refrigerant management *(1 point)*

Credit 5 Measurement and verification *(1 point)*
Credit 6 Green power *(1 point)*

0–17

Materials and Resources – *13 Possible Points*
Prerequisite 1: Storage and collection of recyclables required
Credit 1.1 Building reuse, maintain 75% of existing walls, floors and roof *(1 point)*
Credit 1.2 Building reuse, maintain 95% of existing walls, floors and roof *(1 point)*
Credit 1.3 Building reuse, maintain 50% of interior nonstructural elements *(1 point)*
Credit 2.1 Construction waste management, divert 50% from disposal *(1 point)*
Credit 2.2 Construction waste management, divert 75% from disposal *(1 point)*
Credit 3.1 Materials reuse, 5% *(1 point)*
Credit 3.2 Materials reuse, 10% *(1 point)*
Credit 4.1 Recycled content, 10% (postconsumer + ½ preconsumer) *(1 point)*
Credit 4.2 Recycled content, 20% (postconsumer + ½ preconsumer) *(1 point)*
Credit 5.1 Regional materials, 10% extracted, processed and manufactured regionally *(1 point)*
Credit 5.2 Regional materials, 20% extracted, processed and manufactured regionally *(1 point)*
Credit 6 Rapidly renewable materials *(1 point)*
Credit 7 Certified wood *(1 point)*

0–13

Indoor Environmental Quality (IEQ) –*14 Possible Points*
Prerequisite 1: Minimum IAQ performance required
Prerequisite 2: Environmental tobacco smoke (ETS) control required
Credit 1 Outdoor air delivery monitoring *(1 point)*
Credit 2 Increased ventilation *(1 point)*
Credit 3.1 Construction IAQ management plan, during construction *(1 point)*
Credit 3.2 Construction IAQ management plan, before occupancy *(1 point)*
Credit 4 Low-emitting materials *(4-point maximum from A–F)*
      A. Adhesives and sealants *(1 point)*
      B. Paints and coatings *(1 point)*
      C. Flooring *(1 point)*
      D. Composite wood and agrifiber products *(1 point)*
      E. Furniture *(1 point)*
      F. Ceiling and wall systems *(1 point)*
Credit 5 Indoor chemical and pollutant source control *(1 point)*
Credit 6 Controllability of systems, lighting and thermal comfort *(1 point)*
Credit 7.1 Thermal comfort, design *(1 point)*
Credit 7.2 Thermal comfort, employee verification *(1 point)*
Credit 8.1 Daylight and views, daylight 75% of spaces *(1 point)*
Credit 8.2 Daylight and views, views for 90% of spaces *(1 point)*

0–14

Innovation and Design Process – *5 Possible Points*
Credit 1.1 Innovation in design *(1 point)*
Credit 1.2 Innovation in design *(1 point)*
Credit 1.3 Innovation in design *(1 point)*
Credit 1.4 Innovation in design *(1 point)*
Credit 2 Using a LEED-accredited professional *(1 point)*

0–5

Continued

Levels of sustainability based on points awarded
(Project totals 70 possible points)
Certified (minimum level) 26–32
Silver (second level)   33–38
Gold (third level)   39–51
Platinum (highest level)   52–70

Source: United States Green Building Council

As of January 2008, 9,516 commercial buildings worldwide were registered for LEED certification consideration while another 1,228 had already been awarded one of four levels of certification. Of those certified, 905 projects or slightly less than three-quarters represented new construction.

By the beginning of 2008, the USGBC had certified only two buildings under the new retail category, which the USGBC treated as a pilot under testing in 2007, although several retail buildings have been LEED certified under other categories such as new construction, commercial interiors, existing buildings, and core and shell. For more information, contact, leedinfo@usgbc.org.

The LEED system is spreading quickly across the globe, although it is not necessarily the green building certification for high-performance buildings of choice in every country.

IT'S A SMALL WORLD

By 2008, there were 10 green building councils affiliated with the World Green Building Council (WorldGBC), which operate around the world. Each offers a variation of the LEED rating system applicable to specific countries. Current members of the WorldGBC are GBCAustralia, CanadaGBC, EmiratesGBC, IndiaGBC, JapanSBC, MexicoGBC, New ZealandGBC, TaiwanGBC, United KingdomGBC and the USGBC.

The WorldGBC supports the efforts of its member councils to adopt and implement market-based rating tools besides LEED that meet local needs, such as BREEAM (in the United Kingdom), CASBEE (in Japan) and Green Star (in Australia).

For example, the United Kingdom Green Building Council (UKGBC) formally adopted the U.K. Building Research Establishment Environmental Assessment Method (BREEAM) as the environmental assessment method to measure U.K. buildings.

Why reinvent the wheel, the UKGBC figured. The U.K. BREEAM system has been around for more than two decades, serves to measure U.K. legislated standards and has served as a model for other sustainable building measurement systems.

AUSTRALIAN GREEN STAR RATING

The Green Building Council of Australia (GBCA) analyzed criteria from other green building systems to conceive the Green Star environmental measurement criteria by adapting it to the Australian building market and the environmental context of Australia's needs. Green Star places particular emphasis on commercial office buildings, but due to the rising popularity of Green Star within the six states of the Commonwealth of Australia in the 2000s, the GBCA developed rating systems for other real estate asset classes.

Green Star rating tools now cover different phases of the building life cycle and different building classes, e.g., office, retail, industrial, residential, etc. These rating tools use the best regulatory standards to encourage the real estate industry in Australia to improve the environmental performance of building development.

The retail version, the Green Star–Shopping Centre Design tool, was still in the pilot stage as of 2008.

The Green Star–Shopping Centre Design rating tool was designed for shopping center owners, developers and investors. Green Star–Shopping Centre Design will award certified ratings on the same comparable scale as other Green Star tools:

- 4-Star Green Star Certified Rating (score 45–59) signifies "Best Practice"

- 5-Star Green Star Certified Rating (score 60–74) signifies "Australian Excellence"

- 6-Star Green Star Certified Rating (score 75–100) signifies "World Leadership"

AUSTRALIA'S GREEN STAR
Green Star–Shopping Centre Design tool

Percent

Management
- Green Star Accredited Professional
- Commissioning – Clauses
- Commissioning – Building Tuning
- Commissioning – Commissioning Agent
- Building Users' Guide
- Environmental Management
- Waste Management – Construction
- Waste Management – Operations Plan
- Building Management Systems

10%

Indoor Environment Quality (IEQ)
- Ventilation Rates
- Air Change Effectiveness
- Carbon Dioxide Monitoring and Control
- Daylight
- Thermal Comfort

Continued

- Asbestos
- Internal Noise Levels
- Volatile Organic Compounds
- Formaldehyde Minimization
- Mold Prevention

12%

Energy
- Energy Improvement
- Electrical Submetering
- Tenancy Submetering
- Peak Energy Demand Reduction

24%

Transport
- Provision of Car Parking
- Small Parking Spaces
- Cyclist Facilities
- Proximity to Public Transport
- Trip Reduction – Mixed Use

8%

Water
- Occupant Amenity Potable

Water Efficiency
- Water Meters
- Landscape Irrigation Water Efficiency
- Cooling Tower Water Consumption
- Fire System Water Consumption

19%

Materials
- Recycling Waste Storage
- Reuse of Façade
- Reuse of Structure
- Shell and Core or Integrated Fitout
- Recycled Content of Concrete
- Recycled Content of Steel
- Polyvinyl Chloride (PVC) Minimization
- Sustainable Timber
- Recycled-Content Products & Materials
- Reused Products & Materials
- Disassembly & Adaptability

10%

Land Use and Ecology
- Ecological Value of Site
- Reuse of Land
- Reclaimed Contaminated Land
- Change of Ecological Value
- Topsoil and Fill Removal from Site

9%

Emissions
- Refrigerant Ozone Depletion Potential (ODP)
- Refrigerant Global Warming Potential (GWP)
- Refrigerant Leak Detection
- Refrigerant Recovery
- Watercourse Pollution
- Reduced Flow to Sewer
- Light Pollution
- Cooling Towers
- Insulant ODP

8%

TOTAL 100%

Source: GBCA

Green Star is simple to understand and provides a basis for easy comparisons among other rating systems such as LEED and BREEAM because the GBCA modeled the Green Star system on previously existing rating systems and tools in other parts of the world, including the British BREEAM system and the North American LEED system.

To compare the Australian system to LEED, take the Green Star Management category. Using an accredited professional would be applicable to Innovation and Design in LEED. Commissioning and building systems fall under LEED's Energy and Atmosphere category, and waste management systems pertain to the Materials and Resources LEED category.

The Green Star Transport and Land Use and Ecology categories cover sustainable practices found in LEED's Sustainable Site category. For example, anything in the Green Star Materials category is the same as the LEED Materials and Resources category. The Green Star IEQ is the same as the LEED IEQ category. Water is the same in the Green Star as it is in the LEED Water category. Anything under both Green Star Energy and Emissions categories is applicable to the LEED Energy and Atmosphere category.

SUSTAINABILITY IN JAPAN

The Japan Sustainable Building Consortium (JSBC) developed the Comprehensive Assessment System for Building Environmental Efficiency (CASBEE), a LEED-like system to measure the environmental performance of buildings. CASBEE, which attempts to take into consideration issues and problems peculiar to Japan and Asia, is applicable to a wide range of buildings.

CASBEE uses four assessment tools corresponding to the building's life cycle to conduct the appropriate evaluation. They are:

- CASBEE for Predesign
- CASBEE for New Construction

- CASBEE for Existing Building
- CASBEE for Renovation

The CASBEE-NC (new construction) tool has two parts. The assessor fills out each assessment form at each design stage: the main sheet and the score sheet.

The assessment results for each assessment items are given as scores on the scoring sheet for "Q" and "LR" sections.

The Q section covers Building Environment Quality and Performance. It is broken down into three categories:

1. Q-1 (Indoor Environment)
2. Q-2 (Quality of Service)
3. Q-3 (Outdoor Environment on Site)

The LR section covers Reduction of Building Environmental Loadings and is also subgrouped into three categories:

1. LR-1 (Energy)
2. LR-2 (Resources and Materials)
3. LR-3 (Off-site Environment)

CASBEE is scored on criteria for each assessment item, taking into consideration the level of technical and social standards at the time the assessment is conducted. The assessor uses a five-level scoring system. A score at the third level, otherwise the midpoint, defines an "average" green building.

The WorldGBC is attempting to organize an additional 18 green-building councils. They will cover Argentina, Brazil, Chile, China, Egypt, Germany, Greece, Guatemala, Hong Kong, Israel, Korea, Nigeria, Panama, Philippines, South Africa, Switzerland, Turkey and Vietnam.

GREEN GLOBES

Another body setting green building standards in the United States is Green Globes, established in 2004. It is not as prevalent as LEED. Green Globes-certified buildings are in the dozens compared to LEED-certified, which run into the hundreds.

Properties of all types that have applied for LEED certification number in the thousands, and the number continues to grow exponentially, consistent with the mushrooming green building movement.

The U.S. Green Globes system is similar to a Canadian Green Globes version that has the support of the Canadian government and the Building Owners and Manag-

ers Association of Canada (BOMA). Go Green Plus is a related trade name for the Canadian Green Globes environmental assessment system.

The U.S. version of Green Globes resembles a system used frequently in the United Kingdom known as BREEAM, in that it delves into a building's policies and practices, site issues, and consumption of energy and water resources. Green Globes also looks at the types of building materials used, solid waste management, emissions and effluents, and indoor environmental quality.

In Canada, two other popular certification bodies are the Canada Green Building Council's LEED program (affiliated with the USGBC) and Built Green Society of Canada. The Canada LEED program works similarly to the U.S. LEED program while the Built Green Canada is currently only used for residential buildings.

The Green Building Initiative (GBI) oversees Green Globes in the United States. GBI develops standards under the auspices of the American National Standards Institute (ANSI) and hopes to make Green Globes an official ANSI standard. For additional information on GBI, e-mail info@thegbi.org. For general information on ANSI, please visit http://www.ansi.org/.

Green Globes varies depending on whether the version relates to Canada, the United Kingdom or the United States, but in all cases, it generally offers an online auditing tool for building owners, architects and property managers to help them assess and rate existing buildings against green building best practices and standards.

The various online surveys address green building practices for various stages of project delivery, whether a renovation, a system upgrade or during the initial stage of designing a new building.

Although GBI did not specifically design the questionnaires for stores and shopping centers, many of the practices specified have relevance to retail properties. Currently, Green Globes questionnaires are available for Canada, the United States and the United Kingdom, with the U.K. system labeled GEM (Global Environmental Method) rather than Green Globes.

By registering a project online on the Green Globes Web site, the registrant can obtain a detailed report based on the confidential questionnaire he or she completes.

GREEN GLOBES DESIGN V.1
Postconstruction Assessment

A. PROJECT MANAGEMENT – POLICIES AND PRACTICES

Points
0–50

A.1 Integrated design
• Meet the environmental and functional priorities and goals of the project in an effective and cost-efficient manner

0–20

Continued

Points

A.2 Environmental purchasing
• Create demand for environmentally preferable products and equipment that have a less adverse environmental impact in terms of resource use, production of waste, energy use and water use

0–5

A.3 Building commissioning – documentation
• Help assure that building systems operate as intended.

0–20

A.4 Emergency response plan
• Minimize the risk of injury and the environmental impact of emergency incidents

0–5

B. SITE 0–115

B.1 Site development area
• Protect important existing land uses and reduce demands on municipal infrastructure and services
• Protect existing natural areas, reduce the impact on the site's biodiversity and minimize the soil compaction during construction

0–45

B.2 Reduce ecological impacts
• Avoid erosion on air and water quality and maintain the ecological integrity of the site
• Reduce impact on the microclimate and habitat
• Reduce impact on the nocturnal environment of fauna and flora

0–40

B.3 Enhancement of watershed features
• Reduce the amount of stormwater runoff entering storm sewers and increase ground infiltration of stormwater without negatively affecting the building or on-site vegetation

0–15

B.4 Site ecology improvement
• Increase natural biodiversity.

0–15

C. ENERGY   0–360

C.1 Energy consumption
(for buildings 20,000 square feet (1,860 sq meters) or less use C.3 instead)
• Reduce energy consumption for building operations by achieving a target that surpasses EPA Target Finder, taking into consideration intended use, occupancy, plug loads and other energy demands

0–110

C.2 Energy demand minimization   0–135
[Response to microclimate and topography (30 points)]
• Reduce loads by taking advantage of site and microclimate opportunities to reduce heat loss or gain through the envelope and use natural ventilation strategies

Points

[Daylighting (30 points)]
• Reduce loads on energy-using systems by using daylighting strategies, reducing electric lighting demand and using daylight photocontrols
[Building controls and energy metering (35 points)]
• Reduce loads on energy-using systems and encourage continuous energy efficiency and performance through monitoring energy consumption

C.3 "Right sized" energy-efficient systems
(for buildings 20,000 square feet or less)
• Reduce energy needed by using "right-sized" energy-efficient equipment

0–110

C.4 Renewable sources of energy
• Reduce the consumption of nonrenewable energy resources and the associated greenhouse gas emissions

0–45

C.5 Energy-efficient transportation
• Reduce fossil fuel consumption for commuting

0–70

D. WATER   0–100

D.1 Water
• Increase water efficiency and reduce the burden on municipal supply and treatment systems

0–40

D.2 Water-conserving features
Submetering
• Encourage water conservation through ongoing measurement of water consumption
Minimal use of water for cooling towers
• Reduce domestic water and sewer requirements
Minimal use of water for irrigation
• Eliminate or reduce the use of potable water required for landscape irrigation

0–40

D.3 Reduce off-site treatment of water
• Reduce the burden on municipal water supply and wastewater systems

0–20

E. RESOURCES, BUILDING MATERIALS AND SOLID WASTE   0–100

E.1 Materials with low environmental impact
• Select environmentally preferable products and materials with the lowest life cycle environmental burden and embodied energy
• Encourage the designer to consider relative environmental merits of products and materials

0–40

E.2 Minimized consumption and depletion of material resources
• Conserve resources and minimize the energy and environmental impact of extracting and processing nonrenewable materials

0–30

Continued

Points

E.3 Reuse of existing structures
• Conserve resources and minimize the energy and environmental impacts of extracting/ harvesting and processing resources

0–10

E.4 Building durability, adaptability and disassembly
• Extend the life of a building and its components, and conserve resources by minimizing the need to replace materials and assemblies

0–12

E.5 Reduction, reuse and recycling of waste
• Divert demolition waste from landfill and reduce landfill waste generated by occupants

0–10

F. EMISSIONS AND OTHER IMPACTS   0–75

F.1 Air emissions
• Reduce air emissions

0–15

F.2 Ozone depletion and global warming
• Avoid HFC and HCFC refrigerants that cause ozone depletion and global warming

0–30

F.3 Contamination of sewers or waterways
• Avoid contamination of waterways and reduce the burden on municipal wastewater treatment facilities

0–12

F.4 Land and water pollution
• Reduce the pollution of land and water and minimize risk to occupants' health and impacts on the local environment

0–9

F.5 Integrated pest management
• Eliminate infestations and reduce application of pesticides

0–4

F.6 Storage for hazardous materials
• Prevent pollution of water and indoor air

0–5

G. INDOOR ENVIRONMENT   0–200

G.1 Effective ventilation system
• Ensure occupant well-being and comfort by:
–Avoiding the entrainment of pollutants into the ventilation air path
–Providing sufficient ventilation
–Using effective zone air distribution (assurance that the outdoor air delivered to the space actually reaches the occupants)
–Monitoring air quality
–Reducing the indoor air quality problems resulting from construction/renovation

Points

–Providing mechanical ventilation in enclosed parking areas
–Providing effective filtration
–Building in easy access to the air-handling units (AHUs) for regular inspection and maintenance
0–60

G.2 Source control of indoor pollutants
• Measures to control moisture and prevent the growth of fungus, mold, and bacteria/microbial contamination
• Low VOC-emitting materials, e.g., adhesives, sealants, caulk, paints, carpets; environmentally certified by third party
0–45

G.3 Lighting design and integration of lighting systems
• Enhance occupant well-being by providing:
–Use of natural light (daylighting)
–Views to the exterior
–Suitable light levels for the types of tasks that are anticipated in the various building spaces
–Glare protection
–Control over lighting levels
0–45

G.4 Thermal comfort
• Provide a thermally comfortable environment, thereby helping to ensure the well-being and comfort of occupants
0–25

G.5 Acoustic Comfort
• Provide an acoustic environment that helps to ensure the well-being and comfort of occupants
0–25

Source: Green Building Initiative

BREEAM RETAIL

Throughout Europe—but most prevalent in the United Kingdom—the Building Research Establishment Limited's Environmental Assessment Method (BREEAM) is considered one of the leading measurements of green buildings and environmental compliance of existing laws relating to property, often superseding LEED.

The BREEAM program measures new construction as well as ongoing operation of various types of buildings relating to green building practices.

BREEAM now has a retail version—the BREEAM Retail evaluator—that BREEAM assessors can use on behalf of developers, retailers, real estate managing agents and owners of retail buildings to carry out an environmental assessment for most types of retail projects such as big-box stores and shopping centers.

BREEAM Retail assesses management, health and well-being, energy use, transport, water, materials, land use, ecology and pollution.

The BREEAM Retail Estimator assesses retail units and shopping centers at one of four stages in the building life cycle:

1. New build or major refurbishment
2. Postconstruction
3. Retail tenant fitout
4. Existing (occupied) operation and management

As with LEED, BREEAM Retail standards have no mandatory performance levels, but unlike LEED, BREEAM retail allows for rating criteria modification to measure statutory minimum requirements by jurisdiction. This enables building owners to adapt BREEAM retail standards to meet legal building environmental requirements, which vary from country to country in Europe.

A Microsoft Excel spreadsheet retail preassessment estimator is available for download from the BREEAM Web site, complete with macros that you can use to customize for different situations. Use this only for estimating the level of sustainability of a specific property prior to hiring a qualified BREEAM assessor, who will work closely with the Building Research Establishment to define the proper tools to make a reliable assessment. Visit: http://www.breeam.org/page.jsp?id=19.

BREEAM RETAIL
Management & Operation Stage Pre-Assessment Estimator BREEAM Retail 2006

MANAGEMENT SECTION CREDITS **Points**
0–16

M1 Commissioning
First credit:
Where evidence provided demonstrates that an appropriate project team member has been appointed to monitor commissioning on behalf of the client to ensure commissioning will be carried out in line with current Building Regulations and (where applicable), best practice
Second Credit:
Where evidence provided demonstrates that seasonal commissioning will be carried out during the first year of occupation, postconstruction (or post fitout)

0–2

M4 Considerate constructors
Where the project complies with either the Considerate Constructors scheme or an alternative independently assessed scheme and where a firm commitment is made to achieve certification under that scheme to the following standards:
First credit:
Where there is a commitment to comply with better than industry standard. Equivalent to the minimum score required to achieve Considerate Constructors Scheme certification or equivalent.
Second credit:
Where there is a commitment to go significantly beyond best practices regarding site management principles. Equivalent to *Considerate Constructors Scheme* certification with a minimum score of 32.

0–2

Points

M5 Construction site impacts
First credit
Where evidence provided demonstrates that there is a commitment by the contractor or a commitment by the client to require the fit-out contractor to: a) Monitor construction waste produced during, and as a result of fit-out works and b) Sort and recycle construction waste
Second credit
Where evidence provided demonstrates that there is a commitment by the contractor or a commitment by the client to require the fit-out contractor to adopt best practice policies in respect of air (dust) pollution arising from the site

0–2

M7 Environmental responsibility
One credit is awarded where evidence provided demonstrates that the assessment stakeholder has an appointed individual who has responsibility for monitoring and managing operational environmental impacts and responsibilities.

0–1

M11 Tenant engagement
One credit is awarded where evidence provided demonstrates ongoing formal engagement between the tenant and landlord, and vice versa, to raise awareness of environmental-related operational issues that affect both stakeholders.

0–1

M12 Building user guide
One credit is awarded where evidence provided demonstrates the provision of a simple guide that covers information relevant to the tenant/occupants and nontechnical building manager on the operation and environmental performance of the building.

0–1

M13 Building user education
One credit is awarded where evidence provided demonstrates that training is provided to the building occupants on the appropriate use of building controls and procedures to maintain efficient building operation and minimize operational environmental impacts.

M15 Public information dissemination
One credit is awarded where evidence provided demonstrates the publication and dissemination of the following:
1) details concerning the development's operational environmental impacts
2) the management team's monitoring and management strategies developed and employed to minimize and mitigate them
3) specific examples of good practice

0–1

M17 Customer information and interface
One credit is awarded where evidence provided demonstrates the existence of an environmental information center, open to all interested parties, with customer interface procedures to allow feedback to be channeled to those responsible for building management.

0–1

Continued

Points

M19 Environmental purchasing policy

One credit is awarded where evidence provided demonstrates that the assessment stakeholder has developed and implemented a formal environmental purchasing policy, which has been endorsed by senior director(s).

0–1

M22 Environmental management system

First credit:
Where evidence is provided to demonstrate that the assessment stakeholder has a BS8555 2003 compliant Environmental Management System
Second credit:
Where evidence provided demonstrates that the assessment stakeholder has a third party-certified EMS in place

0–2

HEALTH & WELL-BEING SECTION CREDITS   0–13
HW1 Daylighting

First credit: Where evidence provided demonstrates that ≥35% of the sales and common floor area is adequately daylit, (i.e., an average daylight factor ≥2%)
Second credit: Where ≥50% of the sales and common floor area is adequately daylit (i.e., an average daylight factor ≥2%)

0–2

HW4 High-frequency lighting

One credit is awarded where evidence provided demonstrates that high-frequency ballasts are installed on all fluorescent and compact fluorescent lamps.

0–1

HW5 Internal and external lighting levels

One credit is awarded where evidence provided demonstrates that all internal and external lighting, where relevant, is specified in accordance with the appropriate maintained illuminance levels (in lux) recommended by CIBSE.

0–1

HW9 Internal air pollution

One credit is awarded where air intakes serving occupied areas avoid major sources of external pollution and recirculation of exhaust air.

0–1

HW10 Indoor air quality

One credit is awarded where evidence provided demonstrates CO_2 levels are monitored in areas with unpredictable occupancy patterns and can be regulated accordingly.

0–1

HW11 Ventilation Rates

One credit is awarded where evidence provided demonstrates that each space within the development achieves recommended minimum fresh air rates (i.e., fresh air is provided at a rate in line with CIBSE Guide B2 "ventilation and air-conditioning" recommendations).

0–1

Points

HW12 Smoking policy

One credit is awarded where a smoking ban is in effect within and throughout the building.

0–1

HW14 Thermal comfort

One credit is awarded where thermal comfort levels are assessed at design stage; this is used to evaluate appropriate servicing options, and appropriate thermal comfort levels are achieved.

0–1

HW16 Microbial contamination

One credit is awarded where evidence provided demonstrates that the risk of waterborne and airborne Legionella contamination has been minimized by ensuring all water and HVAC (heating ventilation and air-conditioning) systems are designed to meet the requirements of HSE Approved Code of Practice (ACoP) and Guidance, L8, "Legionnaires disease; The control of Legionella bacteria in water systems," 2000.

0–1

HW18 Office space

Two credits are awarded where information provided demonstrates that office space within the development achieves best practice in terms of occupant comfort and control.
One credit for meeting best practice for three (or two credits for meeting four) of the following:
1) Provision of daylight
2) Potential for natural ventilation
3) Daylight glare control
4) Lighting zones
5) Thermal zoning

0–2

HW19 Safer parking

One credit is awarded where information provided demonstrates that the development's car park(s) (parking garage) has achieved the PARK MARK Safer Parking Award.

0–1

ENERGY SECTION CREDITS   0–43

E1 Reduction of CO_2 Emissions

Up to 10 credits are awarded where the building demonstrates a percentage improvement in CO_2 emissions above the notional building, as set out in the Building Regulations (Part L2A 2006). Credits awarded as follows:
- -20%=1 credit
- 0%=2 credits
- +20%=3 credits
- +35%=4 credits
- +45%=5 credits
- +50%=6 credits
- +60%=7 credits
- +70%=8 credits
- +85%=9 credits
- +100%=10 credits

0–10

Continued

Points

E2 Submetering of substantial energy uses
One credit is awarded where evidence is provided to demonstrate the provision of direct submetering of substantive energy uses within the building.

0–1

E3 Submetering of areas/tenancy
One credit is awarded where evidence provided demonstrates submetering of energy use by tenancy or areas or departments (for single-tenanted buildings) is installed within the building.

0–1

E4 External lighting
One credit is awarded where 80% of external luminaires have an efficacy of at least 100 luminaire-lumens/circuit-Watt and they are controlled through a time switch or daylight sensor to allow for daylight control.   0–1

E5 Building fabric performance & avoidance of air infiltration
Two credits are awarded where evidence is provided to demonstrate that goods loading/unloading and warehouse storage areas have been designed and detailed to ensure optimum building-fabric performance and to minimize unnecessary air infiltration.

0–2

E6 Maintenance schedules
Up to four credits are awarded where there are established periodic scheduled maintenance procedures in place covering the following:
1) calibration and operation of heating and cooling systems including boiler/burner systems
2) ventilation and humidification systems
3) lighting systems
4) domestic hot water systems
Note: To achieve any of the credits there must be adequate maintenance schedules covering the heating and cooling systems (where installed).

0–4

E10 Building services whole life performance
Four credits are awarded where evidence provided demonstrates that the project team has carried out quantitative analysis of the life cycle energy consumption for at least two viable design options for each of the following services, and they have specified the option that has the lower CO_2 emissions over a 60-year building life cycle.
–General lighting (fittings, control gear, lighting controls)
–Heating and hot water (boilers, distribution systems, controls)
–Mechanical ventilation (system & controls)
–Air conditioning (system & controls)

0–4

E11 Cold food storage
Up to four credits are awarded where evidence provided demonstrates best practice specification and operation of cold food storage cabinets.
• *One credit* where two of the following requirements are met
• *Two credits* where three of the following requirements are met
• *Third and fourth credit* where all the following requirements are met
1) Strip curtains specified on all fridge and freezer cabinets, or there are self-closing doors on cabinets
2) Night blinds on all fridge and freezer cabinets, or there are self-closing doors on cabinets

Points

3) Compressor controllers fitted to the refrigeration equipment
4) Low heat display lights used in cabinets, such as fiber optics, or no lighting
5) Waste heat recovery specified for at least 80% of refrigeration units and used to meet part of the space or water heating requirements

0–4

E12 Cold food storage—walk-in cold stores
Up to four credits are awarded where evidence provided demonstrates the energy-efficient specification and operation of walk-in cold food stores as follows:
Two credits; Where the walk-in cold store has a computerized monitoring system with either automated and/or programmable control to monitor operational variables
Third credit: Where the cold store's fans and pumps that circulate cold air are powered by variable speed drives
Fourth credit: Where strip curtains on the cold store entrance and a self-closing door or an air lock are specified

0–4

E13 Cold drink cooler
One credit is awarded where evidence provided demonstrates that all coolers use a bath of liquid refrigerant as the cooling agent instead of a water/ice bath.

0–1

E14 Catering areas
First credit:
Where evidence provided demonstrates that the kitchen/bakery layout is designed to minimize energy consumption
Second credit:
Where evidence provided demonstrates that the kitchen/bakery layout and catering equipment specified are designed to minimize energy consumption

0–2

E15 Laundry equipment
Up to two credits are awarded where evidence provided demonstrates that:
First credit: The equipment reuses water rather than discards it.
Second credit: Laundry facilities have "water-to-water" heat recovery.

0–2

E16 Dry-cleaning equipment
Up to two credits are awarded where evidence provided demonstrates that energy-efficient dry-cleaning equipment is specified as follows:
One credit where three of the measures outlined below are achieved
Two credits where five of the measures outlined below are achieved
1. Where steam traps are installed in the proximity of steam-heated equipment
2. Where the solvent entering the dry-cleaning equipment is preheated using the latent heat of the solvent vapor passing from the still to the condenser
3. Where steam distribution pipe work is lagged with a suitable material to the correct thickness, as outlined in BS5422:1990 or Fuel Efficiency Booklet 8, table 16
4. Where the system uses preset automatic controls as opposed to manual controls
5. Where flash steam from the condensate return system is collected and directed back to the boiler feed tank
6. Where the boiler used to produce steam has efficiency the same as, or greater than, 85% (gross)

0–2

Continued

Points

E17 Lifts

One credit is awarded where evidence provided demonstrates that the assessed developments passenger and/or goods lifts match motor output to passenger demand and returns excess energy to the grid or to meet other on-site demand.

0–1

E18 Escalators and traveling walkways

One credit is awarded where evidence provided demonstrates that escalators avoid unnecessary operation when there are no, or only a few passengers; thereby minimizing energy consumption.

0–1

E19 Energy management

Up to three credits are awarded where evidence provided demonstrates that the assessment stakeholder has achieved accreditation under the Carbon Trust's Energy Efficiency Accreditation Scheme OR where the retail organization is not accredited under the scheme, two credits are available where evidence provided demonstrates good practice in terms of energy management, monitoring and targeting.

0–3

TRANSPORT SECTION CREDITS   0–16
T1 Provision of public transport

Up to four credits are awarded based on the proximity of the development to a public transport access node with a good service frequency. Determined by using the BREEAM table.

0–4

T5 Cyclist facilities

First credit: Where evidence is provided to demonstrate that there are covered, secure and well-lit cycle racks for staff and customer use as follows:

Customers Covered and secure cycle racks equal to 5% of the total number of customer car parking spaces (excluding disabled spaces and mother and baby spaces where provided). This is subject to providing a minimum of 10 cycle racks. Developments providing at least 50 customer cycle racks will comply regardless of the number of parking spaces.

Staff Covered and secure cycle racks equal to 10% of the total number of staff employed within the development during any one shift.

Second credit: Where, in addition to the above, information is provided to demonstrate that there is adequate provision of at least two of the following:

1. Changing facilities and lockers for staff use
2. Showers for staff use
3. Drying space for wet clothes for staff use

0–2

T6 Pedestrian and cycle safety

First credit:

Where evidence provided demonstrates that there are dedicated cycle lanes leading from site entrances to on-site cyclist facilities

Second credit:

Where evidence is provided to demonstrate that pedestrian routes form a direct route onto and off the site

0–2

Points

T7 Travel survey
First credit:
Where evidence is provided to demonstrate that a travel survey has been carried out to determine the travel patterns of the building users who work at and commute to the retail development
Second credit:
Where evidence is provided to demonstrate that a travel survey has been carried out to determine the travel patterns of customers, visitors and deliveries to the retail development

0–2

T8 Travel plan
One credit is awarded where evidence is provided to demonstrate that a travel plan has been developed and tailored to the specific needs of the users of the assessed development.

0–1

T10 Travel information space
Two credits are awarded where evidence is provided to demonstrate that there is a dedicated space within the development for the provision of up-to-date public transport information.

0–2

T11 Local quality partnerships
First credit: Where evidence provided demonstrates that the retailer or landlord is an active member partner in a Local Freight Quality Partnership
Second credit: Where evidence provided demonstrates that the assessment stakeholder is an active member partner in a Local Quality Bus Partnership (QBP) or other public transport quality partnership

0–2

T13 Remote purchase of goods and services
One credit is awarded where evidence is provided to demonstrate that customers can purchase goods or services without the need to travel to the retail development.

0–1

WATER SECTION CREDITS   **0–14**

W1 Water Consumption
Up to three credits are awarded where evidence provided demonstrates that sanitary facilities are designed to minimize the consumption of potable water as follows:

One credit
Building developed before 2000:
Where all toilets have an effective flush volume of six liters (1.6 gal) or less
Buildings developed post 2000:
Where all toilets have a dual-flush cistern with a six-liter main flushing capacity and reduced flush volume of four liters (1.1 gal). In both cases, there must be instructions on the appropriate operation of the flushing device provided on the cistern, or nearby for a group of cisterns.

Two credits
Buildings developed before 2000:
Where all toilets have a dual-flush cistern with a six-liter main flushing capacity and reduced flush volume of four liters, plus instructions on the appropriate operation of the flushing device provided on the cistern, or nearby for a group of cisterns.

Continued

Points

Buildings developed post-2000:
Where all toilets have a dual-flush cistern with four-liter main flushing capacity and reduced flushing capacity of two liters (0.5 gal) or where all toilets have a vacuum-flush system or they are waterless. In both cases, there must be instructions on the appropriate operation of the flushing device provided on the cistern, or nearby for a group of cisterns.
One credit
Where, of the following, the two that offer the greatest possible reduction in water consumption are installed:
1. All taps are one or a combination of the following types: timed turnoff push taps, electronic sensor taps, spray taps, aerating taps.
2. All showers, where specified, have a nominal flow rate the same as or less than nine liters (2.4 gal) per minute at 1.5 bar pressure.
3. All urinals are either infrared proximity detection with controls on each individual urinal (so the urinal only flushes after its use) or waterless.

0–3

W2 Water meter
One credit is awarded where evidence is provided to demonstrate that a water meter with a pulsed output will be installed on the mains supply to each building.

0–1

W3 Major leak detection
One credit is awarded where evidence provided demonstrates that a leak detection system is installed.

0–1

W4 Sanitary supply shutoff
One credit is awarded where evidence provided demonstrates that proximity detection shutoff is provided to the water supply to all urinals and toilets.

0–1

W5 Water recycling
Two credits are awarded where evidence provided demonstrates the specification of systems that collect, store, and where necessary, treat rainwater or graywater for toilet and urinal flushing purposes.

0–2

W6 Irrigation systems
One credit is awarded where evidence provided demonstrates that low-water irrigation systems are specified/installed, or where planting and landscaping is irrigated via rainwater or reclaimed water.

0–1

W7 Water recirculation: vehicle wash
Up to two credits are awarded where evidence is provided to demonstrate that vehicle-washing facilities include a water reclaim system.

0–2

W8 Maintenance of sanitary fittings and controls
One credit is awarded where evidence is provided to demonstrate that there are established and operational maintenance procedures covering all sanitary fittings.

0–1

Points

W9 Water consumption monitoring

Two credits are awarded where evidence is provided to demonstrate that water consumption monitoring is carried out, targets for reductions are in place and there is evidence of a historical downward trend in water consumption for the development.

0–2

MATERIALS & WASTE SECTION CREDITS

0–21

MW1 Materials Specification – Major building elements

Up to four credits are awarded where evidence provided demonstrates that the following major building elements specified have an "A rating," as defined in the Green Guide to Specification. One credit for each of the following:
1. Roof
2. External wall
3. Windows
4. Upper floors

0–4

MW2 Hard landscaping and boundary protection

One credit is awarded where at least 80% of the combined area of external hard landscaping and boundary protection specifications achieve an A rating, as defined by the Green Guide to Specification.

0–1

MW4 Low-impact paints and varnishes

One credit is awarded where evidence provided demonstrates that paints and varnishes used for internal decoration and durability have a low environmental impact, i.e., they achieve a Green Guide A rating or they have a European Eco-label.

0–1

MW5 Reuse of building façade

One credit is awarded where at least 50% of the total façade (by area) is reused and at least 80% of the reused façade (by mass) comprises in-situ reused material.

0–1

MW6 Reuse of building structure

One credit is awarded where evidence provided demonstrates that a design reuses at least 80% of an existing primary structure and for part refurbishment and part new build, the volume of the reused structure comprises at least 50% of the final structure's volume.

0–1

MW7 Recycled aggregates

One credit is awarded where significant use of crushed aggregate, crushed masonry or alternative aggregates (manufactured from recycled materials) is specified for "high-grade" aggregate uses (such as the building structure, ground slabs, roads, etc.).

0–1

MW8 Responsible sourcing of materials

Up to three credits are awarded where materials used in structural and nonstructural elements are responsibly sourced. For timber product, this requires third-party certification to show that the timber has come from a sustainably managed source (or reused timber). For nontimber products, this requires the materials have EMS certification at either the process stage or the process and extraction phases.

0–3

Continued

MW10 Designing for robustness
One credit is awarded where protection is given to vulnerable parts of the building such as areas exposed to high pedestrian traffic, vehicular and trolley movements.

0–1

MW13 Storage of retailer recyclable waste
One credit is awarded where evidence provided demonstrates that there are dedicated facilities for the separation and storage of retail-generated recyclable waste materials.

0–1

MW14 Storage of household recyclable waste
One credit is awarded where evidence provided demonstrates that there is or will be provision for recycling storage facilities on-site, for the collection of customers' household recyclable wastes.

0–1

MW15 Storage of customer recyclable waste
One credit is awarded where evidence provided demonstrates that there are separate (but grouped) bins for the collection of customers' recyclable materials in the retail development.

0–1

MW16 Compactor/Baler
One credit is awarded where evidence provided demonstrates that either a compactor or baler is provided for compacting/baling waste generated on-site; a water outlet is provided for cleaning; and the development achieves the BREEAM credit for storage of retailer recyclable waste (MW13).

0–1

MW17 Composting
One credit is awarded where evidence provided demonstrates there is either a composting vessel on site for organic waste and adequate storage for organic material or there is a dedicated space for organic waste to be stored prior to removal and composting at an alternative site.

0–1

MW18 Waste minimization
First credit: Waste Policy and strategy
Where evidence provided demonstrates that there is a company policy addressing recycling and waste management and minimization, and a site-specific waste management strategy has been developed
Second credit: Waste Monitoring
Where, in addition to a waste policy and strategy, evidence provided demonstrates that there are adequate waste collection/storage facilities and that waste monitoring is carried out on a regular basis
Third credit: Waste Auditing
Where, in addition to a waste policy and waste monitoring, evidence provided demonstrates that a waste audit will be carried out at least once a year

0–3

Points

| LAND USE AND ECOLOGY SECTION CREDITS | 0–10 |

LE1 Reuse of land

One credit is awarded where evidence provided demonstrates at least 75% of the proposed development's footprint is on an area of land, which has previously been developed or used for industrial purposes in the last 50 years.

0–1

LE2 Contaminated land

One credit is awarded where evidence provided demonstrates that the land used for the new development has, prior to development, been defined as contaminated, and where adequate remedial steps have been taken to decontaminate the site prior to construction.

0–1

LE3 Ecological value of site and protection of ecological features

One credit is awarded where evidence provided demonstrates that the construction zone is defined as land of low ecological value, and all existing features of ecological value on the surrounding site and boundary area will be fully protected from damage during site preparation and construction work.

0–1

LE4 Mitigating ecological impact

Credits are awarded based upon the degree of negative impact the new development has on the site's existing ecology. In a formal BREEAM assessment, the ecological impact of the development is calculated based on the area of habitat and number of floral species displaced, using BREEAM's ecological value calculator. As a guide, the following can be used to estimate the likely number of credits:

No credits can be awarded where the new development will displace a significant majority of the existing site's ecological habitat types and areas.

One credit

Where a majority of the existing site's ecological habitat types and areas are not displaced as a result of the new development

Two credits

Where either the development displaces none of the existing site's ecological habitat types and areas or where there is no (or very limited) existing site ecology; for example, the new development is a refurbishment or it is on contaminated land or brownfield land that has been derelict/unoccupied for less than one year

0–2

LE5 Enhancing site ecology

First credit:

Where evidence provided demonstrates that the design team (or client) has:

1. Appointed a professional to advise and report on enhancing and protecting the ecological value of the site, and

2. Implemented the professional's recommendations for general enhancement and protection for site ecology

Continued

Points

Additional credits:
One credit:
Where evidence is provided to demonstrate a positive increase in the ecological value of the site of up to (but not including) six species, or
Two credits:
Where evidence is provided to demonstrate a positive increase in the ecological value of the site of six species or greater

0–3

LE6 Long-term impact on biodiversity

One credit where the mandatory requirements and at least two of the additional requirements have been achieved
Two credits where the mandatory requirements and at least four of the additional requirements have been achieved

Mandatory Requirements:
A suitably qualified ecologist must confirm in writing that:
1. All relevant U.K. and EU legislation relating to protection and enhancement of ecology has been, or will be, complied with during the design and construction process
2. An appropriate management plan is produced covering at least the first five years after project completion. This should include details of the scope of the management plan
3. Key responsibilities, and with whom these responsibilities lie, e.g., owner, landlord, occupier, FM, other

Additional Requirements:
1. A "Biodiversity Champion" has been nominated
2. Site work force trained in how to protect site ecology during the project
3. Record and monitor actions taken to protect biodiversity during construction
4. Creation of a new ecologically valuable habitat, appropriate to the local area
5. Site works programmed to minimize disturbance to wildlife
6. Where actions taken to protect/enhance biodiversity take full account of the UK Biodiversity Action Plan (UK BAP) and use local biodiversity experts

0–2

POLLUTION SECTION CREDITS   0–20

P1 Refrigerant GWP—Building services

One credit is awarded where evidence provided demonstrates the use of refrigerants with a global-warming potential (GWP) of less than five or where there are no refrigerants specified for use in building services.

0–1

P2 Preventing refrigerant leaks

First credit:
Where evidence provided demonstrates that refrigerant leaks can be detected or where there are no refrigerants specified for use in the building or development
Second credit:
Where evidence provided demonstrates that the provision of automatic refrigerant pump down is made to a heat exchanger (or dedicated storage tanks) with isolation valves or where there are no refrigerants specified for the development

0–2

Points

P3 Refrigerant GWP – Cold storage
One credit is awarded where evidence provided demonstrates the use of refrigerants with a GWP of less than five within cold storage systems.

0–1

P4 Insulant ODP and GWP
One credit is awarded where evidence provided demonstrates that the specification of insulating materials avoids the use of substances with a global-warming potential (GWP) of five or more in either manufacture or composition.

0–1

P5 Insulant ODP and GWP – Cold storage
One credit is awarded where evidence provided demonstrates that the specification of insulating materials avoids the use of substances with a GWP of five or more in either manufacture or composition.

0–1

P6 NOx emissions from heating source
Up to three credits available depending on the dry NOx emissions from delivered space heating energy as follows:
One credit where dry NOx emissions are equal to 100 mg/kWh (at 0% excess oxygen);
Two credits where dry NOx emissions are equal to 70 mg/kWh (at 0% excess oxygen);
Three credits where dry NOx emissions are equal to 40 mg/kWh (at 0% excess oxygen).

0–3

P7 Flood risk
Two credits can be awarded where evidence provided demonstrates that the assessed development is located in a zone defined as having a low annual probability of flooding, or
One credit can be awarded where evidence provided demonstrates that the assessed development is located in a zone defined as having a medium annual probability of flooding and the ground level of the building, car parking and access is at least 600mm (26.6 in) above the design flood level for the site's location.
One credit can be awarded where evidence provided demonstrates that Sustainable Urban Drainage techniques are specified to minimize the risk of localized flooding, resulting from a loss of flood storage on site through development

0–3

P8 Minimizing watercourse pollution
One credit can be awarded where evidence provided demonstrates that on-site treatment such as oil separators/interceptors or filtration have been installed for areas at risk from pollution, i.e., vehicle maneuvering areas, car parks, waste disposal facilities, delivery facilities or plant areas.

0–1

P9 Pollution prevention
One credit is awarded where evidence provided demonstrates adequate guidelines and plans are in place for minimizing and dealing with pollution-related incidents.

0–1

Continued

Points

P11 Renewable and low-emission energy
First Credit:
Once credits can be awarded where evidence provided demonstrates that a feasibility study considering renewable and low-emission energy has been carried out and the results implemented.
Additional Credits:
One additional credit can be awarded where the first credit is achieved and where evidence provided demonstrates that at least 10% of total energy demand for the building/development is supplied from local renewable or low-emission energy sources.
Two additional credits can be awarded where the first credit is achieved and where evidence provided demonstrates that at least 15% of total energy demand for the building/development is supplied from local renewable or low-emission energy sources.

0–3

P12 Reduction of nightime light pollution
One credit is awarded where evidence provided demonstrates that the external lighting design is in compliance with the guidance in the Institution of Lighting Engineers (ILE) Guidance notes for the reduction of obtrusive light, 2005.

0–1

P13 Noise attenuation
One credit is awarded where evidence provided demonstrates that sources of noise from the development do not give rise to the likelihood of complaints from existing noise sensitive premises, amenity or wildlife areas that are within the locality of the site.

0–1

P14 Kitchen wastewater filtration
One credit is awarded where evidence provided demonstrates that food oils are separated from wastewater prior to discharge to the local sewer.

0–1

Indicative BREEAM Rating Range
Pass	23–47%
Good	43–57%
Very Good	53–67%
Excellent	> 65%

BREEAM scoring is based on a percentage, which is scaled by factoring a slightly different weight to the raw point score.

When analyzing the score in raw-point form, it is practically impossible to achieve 100 percent. Point credits earned in one area may make credits in another area more difficult to achieve. Trained BREEAM assessors use documentary evidence to award credits. Building Research Establishment cautions that non-assessors are likely to overestimate a building's performance because they may lack the knowledge about the measurement methods and the simplification of the weighting system that BREEAM uses. However, in all BREEAM systems, BREEAM assesses buildings against a set of criteria that results in an overall score, which will fall within a band providing either a pass, good, very good or excellent rating.

SCALED BREEAM SCORING

Scoring system: fail 0–24; Pass 25–40; Good 40–55; Very Good 55–70; Excellent 70–100

BREEAM Category	Number of Credits	Value/Credit	Maximum Score
Management	9	1.67	15
Health and well-being	15	1.00	15
Energy	17	0.83	14
Transport	13	0.83	11
Water consumption	6	0.83	5
Materials	11	0.91	10
Land use	2	1.50	3
Ecology	8	1.50	12
Pollution	11	1.36	15
Total			**100**

Source: BREEAM

GLOBAL REPORTING INITIATIVE

Another organization seeking to become the authority for standards in comparing levels of sustainability from company to company is the Amsterdam, Netherlands-based Global Reporting Initiative (GRI), which incorporates principles of environmental and social performance.

GRI's model combines reporting standards of an economic, environmental and social nature for organizations to demonstrate to their stakeholders how the organization performs in comparison to its peers. GRI hopes that someday building owners and managers will use its reporting guidelines universally throughout the world and that it becomes as common a practice as financial reporting is today.

Toward that goal, GRI developed Sustainability Reporting guidelines that encompass nongreen building issues under the sustainability umbrella. The areas of disclosure go beyond the typical issues dealing with energy and the environment.

These areas mostly relate to social responsibility, such as economics, social contribution, labor practices and decent working conditions, human rights, society, and product responsibility.

The key environmental sustainability areas covered by GRI are similar to the LEED and BREEAM models, but GRI categorizes them differently. GRI calls for

eight basic environmental aspects and one catchall aspect titled "overall." The eight aspects are:

1. Materials
2. Energy
3. Water
4. Biodiversity
5. Emissions, effluents and waste
6. Products and services
7. Compliance
8. Transport

One must keep in mind that unlike LEED and BREEAM, whose criteria is geared for buildings of various types, the GRI Sustainability Reporting is designed for all types of organizations, which may or may not involve buildings. Many public companies, some of which are large retail companies, report through GRI.

GRI'S CRITERIA FOR ENVIRONMENTAL PERFORMANCE

Materials
This includes materials used by weight or volume and the percentage of materials that are recycled.

Energy
This includes direct and indirect energy consumption by source, energy conservation and efficiency initiatives, and the use of renewable energy.

Water
This includes sources of water consumed and how these sources are affected, and the percentage and total volume of water that is recycled or reused.

Biodiversity
This includes the location and amount of land owned, leased or managed in, next to, or near protected areas; how activities, products and services affect biodiversity and protected areas, habitats restored or protected; how biodiversity is managed and to what extent are endangered species affected.

Emissions, Effluents and Waste
This includes direct and indirect greenhouse gas emissions, emissions of ozone-depleting substances, water discharge by quality and destination, types of waste and disposal methods, amounts of spills that affect the environment, quantity of transported, imported, exported, or

treated hazardous waste; identity, size, protected status, and biodiversity value of water bodies and related habitats affected by water discharges and runoff.

Products and Services

This includes initiatives and results to mitigate environmental impact of products and services, and percentage of products sold and their packaging materials that are reclaimed.

Compliance with Regulations

This includes monetary sanctions and fines assessed for noncompliance with environmental laws and regulations.

Transport

This includes significant environmental impact of transporting products, goods and materials used by the organization, and transporting members of its workforce.

GLOBAL COMPANIES USE GRI

AEON reports its sustainability program through GRI, which anyone can access on GRI's Web site. AEON is a conglomerate that runs shopping centers, general merchandise stores, drugstores, supermarkets and specialty stores including Talbot's and Laura Ashley.

The Chiba, Japan-based AEON Mall Company, Ltd. currently has an aggressive expansion plan in place around the world. The Japanese developer's main emphasis is China and Southeast Asia. By 2020, AEON's expansion will rank it among the largest shopping center companies in the world.

AEON (also spelled ÆON) has adopted a forest policy to ensure that all new shopping centers it builds are well landscaped with carbon-absorbing trees. AEON has involved more than 50,000 people planting six million trees with the goal of absorbing 1,600 tons (1,450 metric tons) of carbon dioxide by 2010.

Other retailers reporting through GRI are Boots Group, C&A, Carrefour SA, Gap, Hennes & Mauritz AB, Kingfisher plc, Marks and Spencer plc, McDonald's Corporation, Metro AG, Office Depot, Otto GmbH & Co KG, Pinault-Printemps La Redoute SA, Safeway plc, Seven-Eleven Japan Co Ltd., Staples Inc., Starbucks Corporation, Target Corporation, Tesco plc and The Body Shop International plc.

In addition to AEON, some real estate companies that manage shopping centers and report through GRI are Canary Wharf Group plc, Hammerson plc, Land Securities Group plc (the largest real estate company in the United Kingdom), Lend Lease Corporation Ltd., Sonae Sierra, and Swire Properties Limited.

For more information on GRI and its Sustainability Reporting guidelines, visit http://www.globalreporting.org/Home.

The European Union promulgates the EU Building Program for commercial buildings, highlighting energy efficiencies over similar nongreen buildings.

Organizations are regularly surfacing in different countries competing for the certification of choice when it comes to buildings seeking the "green seal of approval."

The German Sustainable Building Council (GeSBC) seeks to be the authority in Germany. German buildings also use a standard called PassivHaus, which highlights a residential building's efforts dealing with energy efficiency and matters that send fewer pollutants into the atmosphere. The term PassivHaus refers to a specific construction standard for residential buildings and seeks energy savings of 90 percent compared to existing housing.

Italy and Germany sometimes use CasaClima/KlimaHaus, which has similar energy-related components as PassivHaus and covers other areas of green building

Sonae Sierra, a global developer and manager of shopping centers based in Lisbon, Portugal, established individual Corporate Responsibility (CR) Working Groups to manage each of the company's critical corporate social responsibility areas, make recommendations to Sierra's CR Steering Committee and implement tactics. Individuals at different management levels from across the Sierra organization make up each of the groups, all of whom take responsibility for driving performance in each area.

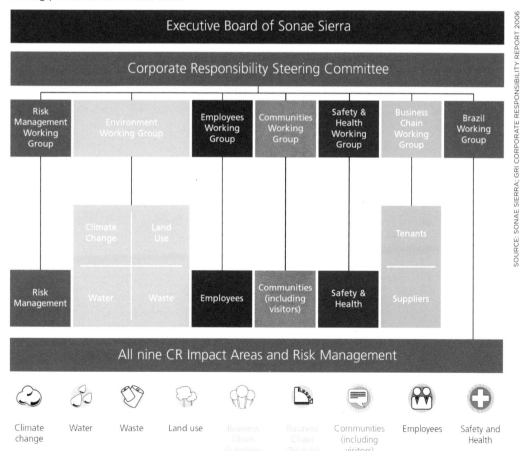

SOURCE: SONAE SIERRA; GRI CORPORATE RESPONSIBILITY REPORT 2006

designs, promising that a KlimaHaus building is energy conscious, comfortable, environmentally friendly, health conscious, economically profitable, free of construction damage and enhances property values.

LOCAL RATING SOURCES

The choice for learning about green building practices and to obtain third-party certification or rating is now quite extensive. In Texas, Austin Energy offers the Austin Energy Green Building rating system. Along with that comes consulting, resources and education to help lower energy costs, design a more sustainable building and promote interior health and safety. (See case studies on Chipotle and H-E-B in Chapter 9.)

Utility companies typically design programs for a homeowner or a building professional seeking to rate a project, but since the service is usually free, it is worth staying current on local green building issues by seeking input from utility companies.

Austin Energy is a community-owned electric utility company operated as a department of the City of Austin. Additional information is available at http://www. austinenergy.com/ including the Excel file depicting the Commercial Green Building Rating Tool that can be downloaded for no charge. Follow these directions from the home page: *Home > Energy Efficiency > Programs > Green Building > Programs > Commercial Program > Commercial Green Building Rating Tool*

AUSTIN ENERGY GREEN BUILDING
(AEGB Commercial Program)

Scoring system:
Point Requirements for Star Ratings

★	Basic requirements
★★	30–36 points
★★★	37–43 points
★★★★	44–58 points
★★★★★	59 or more points

Basic Requirements

1	**Building Systems Commissioning (Cx)**	1. Design intent 2. Document in CD 3. Cx plan 4. Verification 5. O&M documentation & training 6. Cx report.	Req'd

Continued

2	**Storm Water Runoff & Water Quality Control**	Meet current city drainage and water quality standards and ordinances for the project site watershed.	Req'd
3	**Roofing to Reduce Heat Island**	1. Use Energy Star qualified roof for 90% (min.) of roof area* *or* 2. Vegetated roofing for 50% (min.) of roof area* *or* 3. Combination of the two for 75% (min.) of roof area*. *roof area over conditioned space only	Req'd
4	**Building Energy Use Efficiency**	Exceed current City of Austin Building Lighting and Envelope requirements by 15% each or exceed code building performance model by 15%.	Req'd
5	**Building Water Use Reduction**	Reduce planned indoor potable water consumption below the baseline (EPAct) by at least 15%. Ref: Water Use Reduction Calculator	Req'd
6	**Low VOC Interior Paints and Coatings**	Meet or exceed Green Seal GS-11, GC-03 for Paints and SCAQMD Rule 1113 for Coatings.	Req'd
7	**Storage and Collection of Recyclables**	Provide appropriately sized, easily accessible area dedicated to the separation, collection and storage of materials for recycling, including at minimum, the top two (four for multifamily >100 units) identified recyclable waste stream items.	Req'd
8	**Construction Waste Management**	Recycle or salvage at least 50% by weight nonhazardous construction demolition waste excluding excavated soil & stone. Ref: Const. Waste Calculator	Req'd

Team

1	**Integrated Project Design Team & Sustainable Goals**	1. Choose team members early in design phase. 2. Document sustainability goals. 3. Hold sustainability team meetings during each phase of design through construction to track progress. 4. Include sustainability goals in specifications. 5. Incorporate sustainability features, proposed certification into preconstruction meeting.	1

1

	Site		
1a	**Site Selection— Environmental Sensitivity**	Site is not located in the Drinking Water Protected Zone. Site is not a greenfield.	2
1b	**Site Selection— Desired Development Area**	Site located within the Urban Watershed Desired Development Zone.	4
2	**Diverse, Walkable Communities**	Building(s) connects with neighboring properties with pedestrian and/or bicycle-only paths (shading preferred) that are separate from vehicular traffic. Project includes or is located within ½-mile walking distance of residences and at least 10 Basic Services, which are accessible via a safe route intended for use by pedestrians that does not require crossing a road more than 5 lanes wide or 35 miles per hour.	1
3	**Brownfield Redevelopment**	Rehabilitate contaminated site.	1
4	**Site Characteristics Study**	Document existing site characteristics; map all potential natural hazards (including traffic and pollution sources). Plan to maintain or restore existing site features. Site building to minimize impact and to utilize natural characteristics.	1
5a	**Transportation Alternatives— Public Transportation**	Locate building within ¼-mile of at least two bus stops or within ½-mile of a rail stop (or future rail stop with proposed completion within five years).	1
5b	**Transportation Alternatives— Bicycle Use**	Bicycle securing areas and shower/changing facilities for 10% or more of the building occupants. One bicycle parking space per rider, one shower per eight riders, temporary lockers. Safe routing on property.	1
5c	**Transportation Alternatives— Parking Capacity**	Parking does not exceed minimum local zoning requirements. Preferred parking for carpools for 5% (min.) of building occupants.	1

Continued

6a	**Site Development—Protect or Restore Open Areas**	Limit disturbance to 40 ft beyond building perimeter; 10 ft beyond walkways, patios, surface parking; 15 ft beyond roadways & utility trenches; 25 feet beyond any pervious areas that require additional staging. Previously developed sites: At least 50% of the post-development open area (site area minus building footprint) is vegetated using native/adapted plants. Vegetated roof areas may be included in open area calculations, if plants meet the definition of native/adapted.	1
6b	**Site Development—Maximize Vegetated Open Area**	Provide vegetated open area* equal to 20% of the project site area. *May include vegetated roof areas, if plants are meet the definition of native/adapted.	1
7a	**Additional Heat Island Reduction—Site**	1. 50% of site hardscape any combination of: Vegetative open-grid paving (at least 50% pervious), paving materials with SRI 29 min., vegetative shading planted over non-roof impervious surfaces within 5 years, or 2. Locate 50% of parking underground or in structured parking with a roof SRI 29 min.	1
7b	**Additional Heat Island Reduction—Roofing**	1. High albedo roof with a solar reflectance ≥ 75% (<2:12 pitch), ≥ 45% (≥2:12 pitch) for 90% of roof area, or 2. Vegetative roof for 50% of roof area, or 3. Combination high albedo/vegetative for 75% of roof area.	1
8	**Light Pollution Reduction**	Exterior lighting meets COA Code-Chpt.25-2, E, Art. 2.5; IESNA RP-33 Light Trespass; and Illuminance levels at specific facilities.	1
9	**Integrated Pest Management (IPM)**	Implement IPM plan to minimize environmental impact and use least toxic practices for site and building management.	1
10	**Outdoor Environmental Quality**	Shaded seating for minimum of 10% of building occupants.	1

	Energy		
1a	**Additional Energy Use Efficiency 25%**	Exceed current code building by 25% or better using the ASHRAE 90.1-2001 App. G Performance Rating Method.	2
1b	**Additional Energy Use Efficiency 30%**	Exceed current code building by 30% or better using the ASHRAE 90.1-2001 App. G Performance Rating Method.	2
1c	**Additional Energy Use Efficiency 35%**	Exceed current code building by 35% or better using the ASHRAE 90.1-2001 App. G Performance Rating Method.	2
1d	**Additional Energy Use Efficiency 40%**	Exceed current code building by 40% or better using the ASHRAE 90.1-2001 App. G Performance Rating Method.	2
1e	**Additional Energy Use Efficiency 45%**	Exceed current code building by 45% or better using the ASHRAE 90.1-2001 App. G Performance Rating Method.	2
1f	**Additional Energy Use Efficiency 50%**	Exceed current code building by 50% or better using the ASHRAE 90.1-2001 App. G Performance Rating Method.	2
2	**Green Energy**	10-year GreenChoice® commercial agreement for 100% of building's electricity use. If GreenChoice® unavailable, 2-year contract for Texas or Green-e certified National RECs for 100% of building's annual electricity use.	1
3a	**Renewables 2%**	On-site renewable energy system for 2% of energy needs.	1
3b	**Renewables 5%**	On-site renewable energy system for 5% of energy needs.	1
4	**Additional Commissioning (Cx)**	1. Cx agent design review < 50% CD's. 2. Demonstrate bldg. systems operate in accordance w/ design intent. 3. Demonstrate bldg. structure & envelope performance in accordance w/design intent. 4. Seasonal re-Cx through warranty period. 5. Cx report	1

Continued

| 5 | **District Cooling** | Tie into Austin's district cooling and heating loop for all HVAC energy needs. | 1 |

| | | | **17** |

	Water		
1a	**Irrigation Water Reduction 50%**	Use high-efficiency irrigation, rainwater catchment, and/or climate-appropriate plant materials. Reduce by 50% over baseline. Ref: Irrigation Water Use Reduction Calculator	1
1b	**Irrigation Water Reduction 75%**	Reduce by 75% over baseline. Ref: Water Use Reduction Calculator	1
1c	**Irrigation Water Reduction 100%**	Reduce by 100% over baseline. Ref: Water Use Reduction Calculator	1
2a	**Indoor Potable Water Use Reduction 25%**	Use low-flow fixtures or zero-water-use fixtures. Reduce by 25% over baseline. Ref: Water Use Reduction Calculator	1
2b	**Indoor Potable Water Use Reduction 35%**	Reduce by 35% over baseline. Ref: Water Use Reduction Calculator	1
2c	**Indoor Potable Water Use Reduction 45%**	Reduce by 45% over baseline. Ref: Water Use Reduction Calculator	1
2d	**Indoor Potable Water Use Reduction 55%**	Reduce by 55% over baseline. Ref: Water Use Reduction Calculator	1
3	**Stormwater Management**	Manage by infiltration 25% of the water quality volume (WQV) for sites ≥ 50% existing IC or 50% of the WQV for sites < 50% existing IC. Ref. ECM 1.6.7	1

	Indoor Environmental Quality (IEQ)		
1	**Indoor Air Quality Monitoring**	Install permanent carbon dioxide monitoring system that provides feedback in a useable form to make adjustments for ventilation system. Commission all systems to the preferred parameters for optimal performance.	1
2	**Indoor Chemical & Pollutant Sources**	Identify and ventilate areas of point source pollutants (i.e. copy machines, print shops, janitors closets, labs) 1. Provide ventilation directly to the outside of the building. 2. Construct a full height deck to deck partition or a hard-lid ceiling enclosure between these areas and occupied spaces. 3. Operate at negative pressure relative to surrounding areas under all operating conditions by testing.	1
3	**Daylighting**	Provide adequate daylighting and integrate daylighting systems with electric lighting systems and controls.	1
4	**Views to Outside**	Glazing systems and interior partitions allow for a minimum of 75% of regularly occupied spaces a view of vision glazing (between 2'-6" and 7'-6" above finish floor) and a view of the outdoors.	1
5	**Thermal Comfort**	Install mechanical systems (thermal, ventilation and dehumidification) and monitoring system so ensure optimal parameter for thermal comfort for all operating conditions according to ASHRAE 55-2004.	1
6	**Individual Controllability**	Install and commission systems for individual occupant controllability for thermal comfort for 75% of the occupants.	1
7a	**Low-Emitting Materials - Adhesives and Sealants**	All installed sealants and adhesives meet South Coast Air Quality Management District (SCAQMD) standards. Ref: Low VOC Calculator	1

Continued

7b	**Low-Emitting Materials— Flooring Systems**	All flooring systems meet IEQ 7a reqmts. All installed carpet meets CRI Green Label Plus min. standard. All carpet pads meet CRI Green Label min. std. All resilient flooring is FloorScore certified. Ref: Low VOC Calculator	1
7c	**Low-Emitting Materials— Composite Wood**	All installed composite wood has no added urea-formaldehyde. Ref: Low VOC Calculator	1
7d	**Low-Emitting Materials— Insulation**	All installed insulation (excluding piping) contains no added urea-formaldehyde. Ref: Low VOC Calculator	1
8	**Moisture Prevention**	1. No vinyl wall coverings or vapor barriers for surface treatments on interior of exterior wall (also include in tenant agreements.) 2. Install building envelope drainage plane systems, including flashing and overhang systems. 3. Document building will be pressurized.	1
9	**Acoustic Quality**	1. Define appropriate background sound levels, reverberaton decay times, speech intelligibility, & sound isolation. Identify spaces where impact noises are likely & address potential problems. 2. Mechanical & duct systems designed to meet guideline RC,NC or NCB of ASHRAE Applications Design Guidelines for HVAC Sound & Vibration Control Chpt. 3. Appropriate vibration isolation for mounted equipment. 4. Select non-"tonal" equipment. 5. Specify surface finishes and/or masking systems to provide appropriate sound intelligibility & privacy. 6. Specify partitions, ceilings, floor/ceiling assemblies, building layouts, & vestibules to provide adequate sound isolation between spaces. 7. Mitigate intermittent noise sources, e.g., footfall & loading dock noise.	.1
10	**Outdoor Pollutant Sources**	Entrances, operable windows, and fresh air intakes shall be located a minimum 30 feet away from designated smoking areas & air intakes shall meet the min. separation distance requirements of ASHRAE STD. 62.1-2004, Table 5-1. Install signage designating smoking and no-smoking areas. Install entryway systems (grills, grates, mats) at least 6 feet long. Mitigate air-borne contaminates from outdoor air pollutant sources.	1

11	**Construction Indoor Air Quality**	Implement SMACNA Guidelines for Occupied Buildings Under Construction, or similar plan. Plan should include key areas of IAQ protection: Scheduling, Source Control, HVAC Protection, Pathway Interruption and Housekeeping.	1
			14
	Materials and Resources		
1	**Additional Construction Waste Management**	Recycle or Salvage at least 75% by weight of construction demolition and land-clearing debris. Ref: Const. Waste Calculator	1
2a	**Building Reuse —Envelope and Structure 40%**	Incorporate at least 40% (surface area) of existing building envelope and structure. Ref: Bldg. Reuse Calculator	1
2aa	**Building Reuse —Envelope and Structure 80%**	Incorporate at least 80% (surface area) of existing building envelope and structure. Ref: Bldg. Reuse Calculator	1
2b	**Building Reuse —Interior Non-structural Elements**	Incorporate at least 50% (surface area) of interior nonstructural elements. Ref: Bldg. Reuse Calculator	1
3a	**Salvaged Materials 5%**	Use salvaged or refurbished materials for 5% (dollar value) of project building materials. Ref: Bldg. Materials Calculator	1
3b	**Salvaged Materials 10%**	Use salvaged or refurbished materials for 10% (dollar value) of project building materials. Ref: Bldg. Materials Calculator	1
4a	**Recycled Content 10%**	Use Recycle Content materials for 10% (dollar value) of project building materials. Recycled Content = 100% post-consumer + 50% post-industrial Ref: Bldg. Materials Calculator	1
4b	**Recycled Content 20%**	20% (dollar value) of project building materials have Recycled Content. Ref: Bldg. Materials Calculator	1

Continued

5a	**Texas Sourced Materials 30%**	Building materials and products extracted or manufactured regionally within Texas for at least: 30% (dollar value) of project building materials. Ref: Bldg. Materials Calculator	1
5b	**Texas Sourced Materials 50%**	50% (dollar value) of project building materials meet requirements above. Ref: Bldg. Materials Calculator	1
6	**Certified Wood**	Use Certified Wood (FSC) for at least 50% (dollar value) of project wood-based materials. Ref: Certified Wood Calculator	1
	Low VOC Paints, Coatings, Adhesives, Sealants	Exterior paints meet Green Seal standards; exterior sealants, coatings, and adhesives meet SCAQMD standards for 100% (dollar value) of these material costs. Ref: Low VOC Calculator	1
	Total Points—Materials & Resources		**12**

	Education		
1	**Educational Outreach**	Provide at least 2 services to include: comprehensive signage, case study, and/or outreach program (ex.: guided tours).	1
	Total Points—Education		**1**

	Innovation		
1	_____		1
2	_____		1
3	_____		1
4	_____		1
5	_____		1
	Total Points—Innovation		**5**

| | **Total Points—Voluntary Measures** | | **77** |

Source: Austin Energy

HOW SYSTEMS COMPARE

Two sources worth noting are the U.S. EPA Web site tools and resources for measuring building performance and the ASHRAE 90.1 standard. ASHRAE 90.1 evaluates the energy demands and costs of the heating, cooling, lighting, and other systems of a building design. It then compares these costs to base building design that meets ASHRAE 90.1 requirements.

The EPA rating system provides a unique value for a facility in a specific location with specific programmatic requirements relative to other buildings regionally or across the United States, and takes into consideration top-performing buildings with the Energy Star rating.

For tools and resources library of the U.S. EPA and Energy Star ratings, visit http://www.energystar.gov/. For updated information on ASHRAE 90.1 resources and standards, visit: http://www.ashrae.org/technology/page/548.

Some organizations helping to set standards use a customized sustainable development approach, creating plans and designs to address specific development site opportunities and community environmental challenges.

"The Natural Step, a green consulting firm, advocates this nonprescriptive approach, as does Arup, a major planning and design consulting firm that has had success developing custom goals and strategies per site," said Loweth. In doing so, many strategies used by Arup support LEED, BREEAM and other organizations, including sustainability legislation and codes that affect specific buildings.

Arup provides engineering, design, planning, project management and consulting services for buildings, and in the 2000s has made inroads on sustainability compliance guidelines. Arup does business in the Americas, Australia, Asia, Europe and the Middle East but continues to expand its network. The Natural Step is a Swedish-based nonprofit advisory and research organization that can help companies make strategic decisions toward social and environmental sustainability.

These types of organizations can be directed to determine strategies based upon company or project-specific sustainability performance goals. When comparing the pros and cons of the assessment tools available, you will find a common thread among the various systems—BREEAM, Green Globes, LEED and others. There is much more agreement than disagreement regarding what constitutes best energy and environmental practices.

Green building best practices have become universal. Building environmental experts concur on what to do and what to avoid during the design stage, the construction phase and the ongoing building operations. This level of consensus is positive for all involved in the building industry.

PHOTO: MELAVER INC.

ABERCORN COMMON

Hybrid Vehicle Parking Only

Another Property Developed by 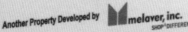 melaver, inc.
SHOP^ADIFFERENCE

Melaver Inc. developer of Abercorn Common was the first LEED-certified shopping center in the United States.

Chapter 9

How Retailers Are Responding

ANITA **R**ODDICK, **AN** activist and entrepreneur, launched a retail concept in the 1970s that ultimately caused her to be branded the Queen of Green. She got together with a medical herbalist and created a few concoctions for the skin after seeing Polynesian women rubbing cocoa butter on their skin during her travels to the Far East. "Their skin was like velvet," Roddick remarked, clarifying how she came up with the idea for what later became a worldwide retail chain of cosmetics.

BODY SHOP'S ECO-FRIENDLY APPROACH

Roddick opened her first cosmetic and health-oriented Body Shop in Brighton, England, on March 27, 1976, at a time when the only customary corporate responsibility was to pay bills and accumulate a hefty bottom line. Her inventory mainly consisted of 15 of her own branded creams and potions, most of them made with cocoa butter and other natural ingredients. Her store carried them in various sizes to give the appearance of having abundant stock-keeping units (SKUs).

Roddick personally dispensed these products in Brighton from her modest store. She also inspired her regular customers to recycle by offering to refill their used plastic bottles with another dosage of cosmetics. Her idea for recycling these small bottles with handwritten labels arose out of the necessity to save on purchasing containers, but the most conscientious consumers appreciated this environmentally friendly approach, one that also lowered the Body Shop's costs, resulting in a savings Roddick passed on to her customers.

Roddick was also among the first retailers to tout natural and organic, cruelty-free skin care cosmetics that were not tested on animals and that contained ingredients

imported from poorer countries. She extolled the importance of ethics in business through social responsibility standards.

What was initially a niche concern for Roddick eventually became a mainstream movement known as "sustainability in retailing." Roddick built her *retailgreen* business on a corporate eco-consciousness philosophy and later sold its franchises, company stores and the sustainable retail image to L'Oreal, which now owns and operates 2,200 stores around the world. The rest, as they say, is history. This business pioneer, the daughter of Jewish-Italian immigrant parents, with a cause célèbre, transformed the worldwide skin care industry and influenced other forms of retailing.

Roddick did so by selling the virtues of the products she carried, some made from ingredients imported from poorer countries such as aloe vera from Guatemala, rich moisturizers and soap fragrances from Ghana and Brazil, and marula oil from the mainly arid southwest African country of Namibia.

Her timing was impeccable. Her nature-based cosmetics, such as oil for moisturizing and conditioning crushed from the grapefruit-size brazil nuts gathered in a responsible manner by Xingu Indians from South America's huge, endangered Amazon rainforest, coincided with the environmentalist movement of the late 1970s and 1980s.

Anita Roddick personally guaranteed the local tribe a 10-year over-market price for the brazil nut harvest, and had the Body Shop build a co-op processing plant in Altamira, Brazil, with an eye toward sustainable harvest of Amazonia, as the Amazon rainforest is known. Amazonia is one of the world's most important natural resources in the fight against climate change.

PHOTO: MATT TILGHMAN © 2008 ISTOCK INTERNATIONAL INC.

The dense vegetation in the Amazon—prevented from seasonal defoliation by its tropical climate—continuously recycles carbon dioxide into oxygen. The Amazon rainforest was nicknamed the "lungs of our planet" because it produces about a fifth of Earth's oxygen, a fact that Roddick recognized as important to every living creature.

The late businesswoman Dame Anita Roddick, DBE (Dame Commander of

Above: Vast tracts of virgin forest in the Brazilian states of Matto Grosso and Para are being destroyed illegally and turned into farmland for cultivating soya beans. Far right: The Amazon rainforest was nicknamed the "lungs of our planet" because it produces about a fifth of Earth's oxygen.

ANITA RODDICK
1942–2007

PHOTO: BRAZIL2 © 2008 ISTOCK

the Order of the British Empire) proved to the world of retailing during her life-time, as well as after her death in 2007, that there was money to be made from caring about social causes and the environment. Her selling message was radical. It was not about the customer but about the customer's care. She would say, "Buy this mascara; it could change someone else's life." Even today, the Body Shop reminds its customers, "With every piece of marula oil enriched make-up you choose, you're helping women in Namibia improve their lives and the lives of their children." Moreover, improving people's lives starts with preserving the environment. Protect our Planet is an ongoing Body Shop campaign—one that promotes both sustainability and bottom-line profits.

INVESTING IN GREEN

Many green tactics are associated with investment costs that offer a payback to retailers that can be easily quantified. Beyond the obvious monetary return-on-investment (ROI) models, retailers have begun to qualify the residual payback in public relations capital, as the retailer is perceived as being willing to do its part for society and future generations of customers. Sustainability is becoming mainstream for the largest retail chains.

Nearly two-thirds of the largest U.S. retailers said their retail chains are actively involved in sustainable practices, according to a survey of chief financial officers conducted by BDO Seidman, LLP.

However, 83 percent expressed some involvement in green practices.

Among the retailers involved in green initiatives, 34 percent are modifying their operation to implement green tactics internally, but that is the only thing these retailers are doing. An additional 9 percent of retailers with a green agenda are strictly focused on carrying green products, while 57 percent are doing both.

The desire to burnish their corporate image influenced about two-thirds of the retailers to institute sustainable programs, according to the study. Financial incentives accounted for only 15 percent of the reason to go greener, while 10 percent cited zoning regulations or government mandates as the reason to implement green programs.

For retailers, the shift to green is not

PHOTOS: R. E. MILIAN

The Body Shop posts its corporate social responsibility slogans inside the stores and by the showcase windows for browsers to see. Today, the Body Shop shown here at the Toronto Eaton Centre in Toronto, Canada, continues to promote the principles promulgated by the founder, Dame Anita Roddick, DBE, and sell the cosmetics that customers want.

easy, as it is often difficult to quantify the payback. The shift usually starts as an unwavering commitment of a CEO who believes that sustainability is the company's duty. That CEO is often one who places great value on stakeholder goodwill.

Some consumer-oriented companies have pursued a green agenda by adding products or instituting green practices. Others, such as L'Oreal, did it by acquisition, as was the case with the Body Shop. Through acquisition, a company can buy a green reputation along with the business.

Many retailers are searching for new, natural green products or are expanding those lines, prompting takeovers of natural and organic consumer product companies.

Following the Body Shop acquisition, two large acquisitions in the natural and organic segment of the cosmetics industry included Colgate-Palmolive's buyout of 86 percent of Tom's of Maine in 2006 and the bleach manufacturer Clorox's acquisition of natural personal care company Burt's Bees in 2007. Today, Burt's Bees continues on a double-digit growth path.

Colgate-Palmolive is now learning new, sustainable operating techniques from Tom's of Maine. For example, Tom's of Maine offsets all its energy use to run its manufacturing plant in Kennebunk, Maine, with wind power, and it rewards its employees up to US$4,000 in benefits for buying a hybrid car for their personal use.

Sustainability is not new at Tom's of Maine. The firm has been operating with strict environmental policies for decades. Its green practices include using products that are biodegradable, avoiding animal testing, donating 10 percent of its profits to charitable organizations, using soy-based ink in all printing, recycling and reusing as much as possible of everything, and even performing green audits on its suppliers.

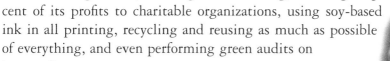

Capitalizing on a consumer trend for natural and organic products, Colgate-Palmolive bought Tom's of Maine (founders Kate and Tom Chappell holding a plaque they received from Taking Action for Animals for not using animals in testing their products).

PHOTO: ©TOM'S OF MAINE

In 2007, Wal-Mart began to carry Tom's of Maine products, partially because of the influence of Colgate-Palmolive and because of the popularity of its green products. Before Tom and Kate Chappell, the founders of Tom's of Maine, struck the deal, they started to pay close attention to their new client, the world's largest retailer.

The Chappells said that Wal-Mart was turning the tide on sustainability and was demanding the same of all its suppliers. Fortunately for the Chappells, they were already doing everything right to preserve the environment. "One of our central beliefs is that Tom's of Maine can be financially successful while behaving in a socially responsible and environmentally sensitive manner," said Tom Chappell.

BED BATH & BEYOND'S SHAREHOLDERS

Retailers are not only facing pressure to respond to the green movement because of the regulatory climate or because of public interest. Shareholders are also urging action. A shareholder proposal placed the issue of sustainability squarely on a proxy for shareholders to vote on during the 2006 and 2007 annual meetings of Bed Bath & Beyond shareholders.

It was not that the U.S. retailer, which operates three retail chains comprising 900 stores, was not doing enough to be green. The shareholder group that put sustainability on the ballot simply wanted proof of carbon disclosure and a detailed report on what Bed Bath & Beyond was doing to make its operation sustainable.

Company documents ultimately showed that Bed Bath & Beyond does indeed have a host of programs that address the consumption of natural resources and help prevent climate change.

In 2007, the retailer opened a pilot store where it is testing different forms of skylights, automatic dimmers, solar faucets that use ambient lights to turn water on and off and other techniques, without much fanfare or publicity. Management said it is learning as much as possible about which systems are efficient enough to roll out nationwide across the chain.

During the past three years, Bed Bath & Beyond implemented a capital plan for new and renovated Bed Bath & Beyond stores, Christmas Tree Shops and Harmon Stores to upgrade their lighting systems and equipment in order to reduce energy consumption.

Beginning in 2005, the retailer switched to environmentally friendly HVAC equipment that uses non-CFC refrigerant in place of the R-22 refrigerant that contributes to the depletion of Earth's ozone layer. According to the EPA, U.S. chemical manufacturers will only be able to produce the R-22 refrigerant after 2010 for equipment manufactured before 2010. After 2020, R-22 will not be manufactured at all.

Yet Bed Bath & Beyond did not wait to be mandated by law. It began to implement these changes on new and replacement equipment as soon as it recognized the danger to Earth's atmosphere.

PHOTO: R. E. MILIAN

A shareholder proposal placed sustainability on a proxy for shareholders to vote on during the annual meeting of Bed Bath & Beyond shareholders in 2006 and 2007. The operator of name-sake stores, as well as Christmas Tree Shops and Harmon's Stores, opposed the proposal but it is nevertheless maintaining an aggressive sustainability program. Above are two adjacent store concepts in Paramus, New Jersey.

Solar power has become a hot topic for the New Jersey-based retail chain. Bed Bath & Beyond has plans for solar arrays on four of its New Jersey facilities. The company estimates that the combined solar arrays amount to a reduction of about 109,500 barrels of crude oil over a 30-year period and lessen carbon-dioxide emissions by 38 million pounds (17.2 million metric tons)

This is equivalent to providing electricity to 1,700 average American homes for 30 years. Other well-known retailers across the United States and other parts of the world have also begun to design, build and operate greener stores.

ECO OPTIONS AT THE HOME DEPOT

The Home Depot started a green program in 1990. It has since expanded it to new areas and continues to help reduce GHG emissions worldwide by promoting energy-efficient solutions to the public. The world's largest home improvement chain is positioning itself as the retailer that will help its customers reduce their environmental footprint.

With 2,221 retail stores in all 50 states, the District of Columbia, Puerto Rico, the U.S. Virgin Islands, 10 Canadian provinces, Mexico and China ringing up more than US$80 billion in annual retail sales, The Home Depot is conducting a makeover of its image with a marketing campaign to push its Eco Options product line.

Eco Options point-of-purchase (POP) signs educate The Home Depot customers about the choices they can make when purchasing products from major appliances to lightbulbs. The program also teaches them to save energy and reduce their carbon footprint.

By 2007, The Home Depot had classified more than 3,000 products as Eco Options due to their energy efficiency, sustainable forestry, healthy home, clean air or water conservation. These products usually have less of an impact on the environment than competing products. The company predicts the Eco Options line will consist of 6,000 stockkeeping units and account for 12 percent of its sales by 2009.

The Eco Options products range from all-natural insect repellents and cellulose insulation to front-loading washing machines and certified wood. "They are very popular with customers," said Sue Bush, a nine-year veteran of the Paramus, New Jersey, home improvement store who proudly sports nearly a dozen employee service pins on her bright orange apron.

"The Home Depot is dedicated to sustainability and to helping our customers choose projects and products that have less of an impact on the environment," explained Ron Jarvis, senior vice president of environmental innovation at The Home Depot, in a prepared statement in July 2007.

To promote the Eco Options concept, The Home Depot created a special educational and interactive microsite—linked from its regular Web site—for consumers to obtain answers to help them reduce their environmental footprint. "The new Eco Options microsite makes it easy for homeowners to identify ways they can personally make an impact on the environment and on their wallets," explained Jarvis.

A microsite, also called "minisite" or a "weblet," refers to an individual Web page or cluster of pages that function as an auxiliary supplement to a primary Web site. The Home Depot is also applying some of the Eco Options principles to its real estate and store operations. Some of The Home Depot's newest stores feature sustainable architectural elements that help them operate more efficiently. Examples of those stores include The Home Depot operations in New York City, the Park Royal store in Vancouver, British Columbia, and the store in Greenfield, Massachusetts.

The company is trying to develop flexible store designs that can be adapted into sustainable, urban, previously developed sites rather than on greenfield land. This requires its real estate department to alter store designs to achieve the targeted environmental benefits.

In 2004, the fast-expanding retailer built more than half of its new stores on existing sites, a key component of the LEED sustainable site criteria.

The Home Depot is trying to lessen impermeable surfaces around its new store sites by building more landscaped islands, leaving as many existing trees as possible and reducing the size of paved surface whenever appropriate rather than substituting the traditional asphalt surfaces with permeable pavement.

PHOTOS: THE HOME DEPOT USA INC.

One of the most cost-saving measures and GHG-reducing programs that The Home Depot has undertaken for its stores involves energy efficiency. Through a number of initiatives implemented at all stores, the retailer reduced energy consumption per square foot by 12 percent in 2004 compared with 2000.

Beginning in 1999, a construction task force of the company's internal environmental council worked to integrate energy-efficient specifications into its revamped store design. One important change to The Home Depot's new store design was the use of energy-efficient T5 lighting, which replaced the previous high-bay halides with clear plastic domes around the bulbs.

The Home Depot and many other retailers operating in high-bay industrial spaces and other big-box retail buildings

The Home Depot labels appropriate merchandise with the Eco Options logo to inform consumers about environmentally friendly products. The interactive microsite http://www.homedepot.com/ecooptions/ educates customers about The Home Depot's Eco Options products and suggests projects that help to improve the environment. The Web page titled Energy Efficient explains about Energy Star ratings, solar lighting and programmable thermostats. It also offers product suggestions and gives visitors a tool for calculating savings on cooling and heating costs.

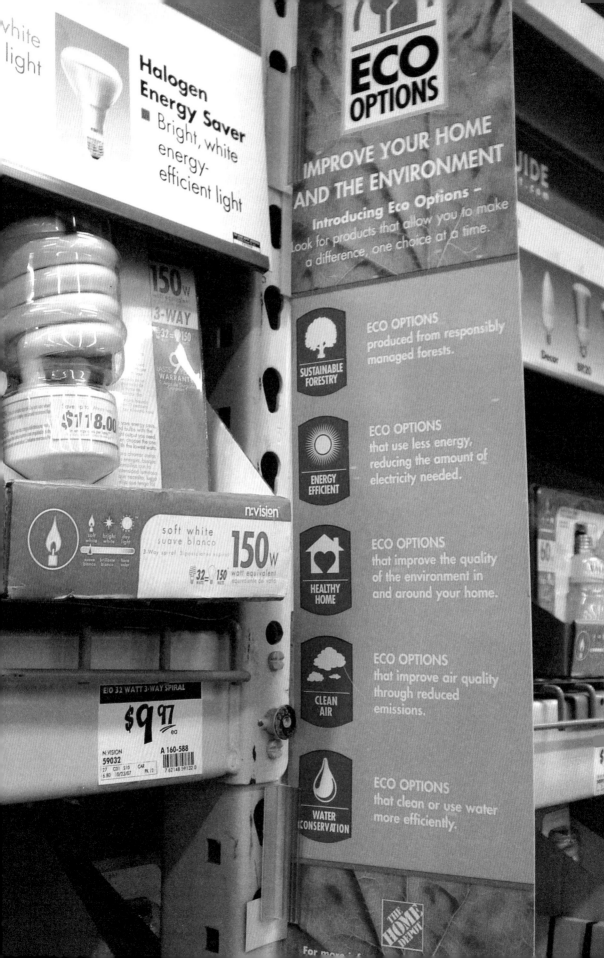

Halogen Energy Saver
■ Bright, white energy-efficient light

white light

ECO OPTIONS

IMPROVE YOUR HOME AND THE ENVIRONMENT

Introducing Eco Options –
Look for products that allow you to make a difference, one choice at a time.

SUSTAINABLE FORESTRY
ECO OPTIONS produced from responsibly managed forests.

ENERGY EFFICIENT
ECO OPTIONS that use less energy, reducing the amount of electricity needed.

HEALTHY HOME
ECO OPTIONS that improve the quality of the environment in and around your home.

CLEAN AIR
ECO OPTIONS that improve air quality through reduced emissions.

WATER CONSERVATION
ECO OPTIONS that clean or use water more efficiently.

150W 3-WAY
32 = 150

Save up to $18.00

n:vision

soft white
suave blanco
3-Way spiral 3-posiciones espiral

150W
watt equivalent
equivalente del vatio
32 = 150

EIO 32 WATT 3-WAY SPIRAL

$9 97 ea

N.VISION
59032
77 C01 S10
6.80 10/23/07
CAR
Pk.12
A 160-588
7 62148 59132 0

Decor   BR20

$3.97

THE HOME DEPOT

For more i

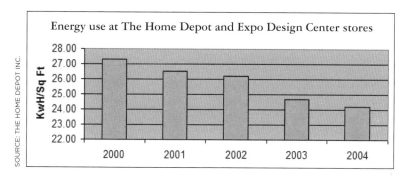

Energy use at The Home Depot and Expo Design Center stores

SOURCE: THE HOME DEPOT INC.

All The Home Depot stores in Canada, Mexico and the United States and all Expo Design Center stores reduced energy consumption by an average of 12 percent per square foot from 2000 to 2004.

PHOTO: R. E. MILIAN

The Home Depot in Royal Palm, Florida, lessens impermeable surfaces around the store site with landscaped islands, natural palm trees and a retaining pond.

are replacing high-intensity discharge (HID) fixtures, such as mercury vapor and metal halide lamps as well as the standard one-inch T12 fluorescent fixtures with T5 High Output (T5HO) fluorescent fixtures.

The T5HO is a 5/8-inch tubular fluorescent lamp, available from 24 watts to 80 watts. Typical T5HOs produce 5,000 lumens, nearly double that of standard T8 lamps, and more than double that of standard T-12 fluorescent linear lamps. This lamp has other advantages over other types of fluorescent lamps including cost effectiveness, good color rendition and high-energy efficiency.

Moreover, the installation and maintenance cost of the store's lighting system can be radically reduced with T5HO luminaires because only half the number of lamps are required and because of added performance gains by using single-lamp cross-section fixtures.

In large open-area applications, such as big-box stores, the number of lamps required may be as low as 40 percent of those required with conventional T8 lamps.

Peter Ngai, PE, FIES, LC, a vice president of engineering for the Berkeley, California-based Peerless Lighting, compared the lighting performance of T8, T5 and T5HO luminaires. He used wattage, lumens-divided-by-watt efficacy, op-

timal ambient operating temperature, and warm-up time as the objective criteria for his evaluation.

"Generally speaking, for indirect lighting applications, T5HO is the most desirable light source due to its small size and high-lumen package, which enable luminaire designers to create superior optical distributions with minimal loss in efficiency," concluded Ngai during a presentation he made in New York at the 2003 LightFair International. The LightFair International Trade Show and Conference is North America's largest annual convention dedicated to architectural and commercial trade lighting.

Many retailers using T12 lighting systems in the 1980s in their stores switched to T8s in the late 1990s. In the 2000s, the common switches have been from T12s to T8s, T5HOs, or high-efficiency HIDs.

According to the U.S. Department of Energy's Federal Energy Management Program, the system wattage reduction resulting from replacing existing fixtures with the lower-wattage T5HOs offers significant energy savings. Further reductions can be achieved with various types of lighting controls like multilevel switchers, motion sensors, occupancy sensors and photosensors.

Photosensors are electronic control devices that automatically adjust lighting output levels based on the amount of natural light detected. These lighting control devices enable building operators to control the lighting environment automatically by either dimming or raising the light levels and by switching them on and off.

Lighting is only one—albeit the most important—energy-saving feature of The Home Depot new store design. Other sustainable specs include entrance vestibules to prevent the air conditioning or heating from escaping and well-insulated reflective roof membranes with rooflines that are four feet (1.2 m) lower than those of the less efficient older stores.

PHOTO: R. E. MILIAN

In addition to The Home Depot, many other retailers, such as Harmon Discount Health & Beauty stores (pictured above in Westwood, New Jersey), are replacing the standard one-inch T12 fluorescent fixtures with T5 High Output (T5HO) fluorescent fixtures as pictured above.

The Home Depot achieved an average of 34 percent in energy savings in stores built in 2003 and later compared to older stores. On stores renovated since 2003, the retailer reconfigured the HVAC systems to optimize efficiencies, converted the storefront signs to using light-emitting diodes (LED) lighting, and implemented an efficient low-watt bulb program in all lighting displays. The company also installed horizontal lumber doors that open in stages based on the size of the load, to control the amount of air that escapes when the door is open.

Recognizing the retailer's efforts in energy efficiency, EPA gave the Energy Star Retail Partner of the Year Award to The Home Depot in 2006 and again in 2007.

Fortune magazine also named The Home Depot the Number 1 Most Admired Specialty Retailer every year between 1993 and 2006 (except in 2004), partly because of its record on environmental and community responsibility, which was one of eight ranking criteria.

In 2005, *Canadian Geographic* magazine gave The Home Depot the Canadian Environment Award gold medal prize in the Climate Change category for its Mow Down Pollution program; and the City of Toronto, Ontario, presented the retail giant with the Toronto Green Award of Excellence in Market Transformation.

The Home Depot is a voting member of the USGBC Retail Committee, which is working on an application guide for retailers to use when pursuing LEED certification for their store buildings. The Home Depot also instituted sustainability programs to encourage suppliers to preserve the environment.

The home improvement big-box retailer sells more Forest Stewardship Council (FSC) wood—and has converted more vendors to FSC wood harvesting—than any other retailer in America.

Certified wood assures the buyer that it came from non-endangered forests that have been managed and harvested under strict guidelines, and are monitored by a third party. Some FSC-certified timber can be traced through its entire journey from stump to shelf.

Since the late 1990s, The Home Depot, Lowe's, Staples and about 400 other companies made a commitment to phase out products originating from endangered forests.

In fact, The Home Depot has flatly stated it will not purchase uncertified wood products sourced from a list of the world's 10 most threatened and most biologically significant forest eco-regions as identified by the World Wildlife Fund (WWF) in February 2001, such as Brazil's Amazon, which our atmosphere relies on to absorb 70 billion tons (63.5 billion metric tons) of carbon a year.

According to the WWF, the cutting of trees and unsustainable management of forests lead to the loss of nearly 36 million acres of natural forests each year, an area larger than the state of New York.

In 2006, The Home Depot teamed up with the Conservation Fund to offset carbon emissions through reforestation. It cooperated with the United Nations on its Plant a Billion Trees program.

DUKE UNIVERSITY'S SMART HOME

The Home Depot also helped develop a live laboratory for students to collaborate on advancing technology related to green buildings. The project, The Home Depot Smart Home, is a 6,000-square foot (560 sq m) experimental residential dormitory operated by Duke University's Pratt School of Engineering.

The facility functions as the technology research lab of the Duke Smart Home program, a student research endeavor dedicated to exploring energy efficiency and environmentally sustainable smart buildings.

The Home Depot Smart Home project involves Duke undergraduate students from different academic disciplines such as computer science, environmental science, civil and environmental engineering, electrical and computer engineering, materials science, mechanical engineering and biomedical engineering.

The Home Depot Smart Home living and working lab gives Duke University an opportunity to conduct research that it can use to apply for patents and write research papers for others to learn about smart buildings.

The Home Depot helped develop The Home Depot Smart Home for students, a laboratory at Duke University's Pratt School of Engineering, to collaborate on advancing technology related to green buildings. Visible in this photo are photovoltaic panels in the front of the house. The panels transform sunlight into electricity to power lights in the dorm and to power a large aluminum-harvesting and storing rainwater system that irrigates the property and provides nonpotable (not for drinking) water for toilet flushing and washing clothes. The prototype home is located on Duke's main campus at Durham, North Carolina.

PHOTO: DUKE UNIVERSITY PRATT SCHOOL OF ENGINEERING DUKE SMART HOME PROGRAM

LOWE'S FORAY INTO GREEN TERRITORY

Late in 2001, The Home Depot's chief competitor, Lowe's Companies, agreed to let Southern California Edison (SCE) put its Rancho Cucamonga, California, store design under the microscope. SCE worked with Lowe's to identify energy efficiency opportunities for new Lowe's home improvement warehouse stores that the rapidly expanding chain was planning in future years.

Recognizing the growing trend of big-box stores, SCE wanted to ensure that these stores incorporate efficiencies in their store design. The Rosemead, California-based SCE, a unit of Edison International, is the largest electric utility in California, serving more than 13 million

residents in a 50,000-square-mile (129,500 sq km) area of central, coastal and Southern California (excluding the city of Los Angeles and a few other cities).

The energy simulation study that SCE's consultants performed at Lowe's investigated the energy benefits of selected design alternatives, including possibly integrating high-efficiency lighting systems, daylighting strategies, and efficient HVAC units.

To test efficient alternatives incorporated into proven store layouts, upgrades were made to the standard prototypical Lowe's store, with two significant changes to help lower the internal loads. Workers redesigned new lighting power density and cut back on the amount of electric lighting used during daylight hours by adding photoelectric controls. The upgrade called for ample skylights to be added to provide natural lighting in the store. The skylights were placed above shopping aisles but spaced carefully throughout the roof so as not to conflict with the packaged HVAC rooftop units.

These units were replaced with new high-efficiency constant volume package rooftop units with EER ratings of 11.0 or higher. For optimum control, an energy management system was added to the new prototype design to reduce the building's electric demand when appropriate.

The study analyzed the standard Lowe's store wall construction and vulnerable points within the building envelope design. The building envelope is the interface between the interior of a building and the exterior. The building envelope, or "skin," consists of structural elements and materials and finishes that enclose the store building, separating the store's climate-controlled interior from the unprotected hot or cold weather outside.

This envelope includes the walls, doors, windows, roof and floor surfaces. Building envelopes must balance requirements for ventilation and daylight while providing thermal and moisture protection. Envelope design is usually a major factor in determining the amount of energy a building will use during operation, but this is not necessarily so with big-box retail stores like Lowe's.

Typically, the standard building envelope insulation in big-box stores is adequate in the summer because internal loads are taxed by heat produced from ambient lighting, display lighting and occupant loads, all of which compete with the air-conditioning loads within the building interior.

Engineers conducting the study determined that Lowe's would not achieve significant enough efficiencies by changing the traditional store building envelope design.

When the SCE released the study in 2002, Lowe's agreed with the report's conclusions that stated that the greatest opportunity for energy savings would come from placing skylights above aisles in the store's high rack areas. These would be supplemented with automatic photoelectric controls to turn off energy-efficient electric lights when interior daylight levels are ample.

This combination reduces both lighting loads (the number one user of energy at large stores) and cooling loads (the number two user), since reduced electric lighting increases cooling capacity.

When the study was completed, Lowe's benefitted by having a plan it could easily adapt to its new prototype rollout. SCE in turn could share energy-saving tips from the study with other big-box retailers to help reduce the energy consumption of large stores in California.

When SCE released the findings of the Lowe's study in 2002, sustainable building design seemed unreachable for shopping centers and retail stores. By 2006, the Lowe's store located at 6400 Brodie Lane in southwest Austin had achieved the prestigious LEED Gold rating certification.

In addition, the Austin Energy Green Building Program recognized the Lowe's southwest Austin store for its environmentally focused and energy-friendly store design and awarded it the 4-Star Commercial Green Building rating.

The civil engineering design and coordination of the site components helped the 160,000-square-foot (14,900 sq m) megastore store achieve full compliance with the stringent criteria set forth by Travis County, the City of Austin, the LEED Gold and the Austin Energy Green Building Program.

Lowe's environmentally friendly design and construction practices in southwest Austin include:

- Indoor water savings in excess of 47 percent
- Energy savings in excess of 50 percent
- Rainwater collection system that eliminates the use of potable water for landscape irrigation and reduces the use of potable water in the garden center

PHOTO: R. E. MILIAN

Lowe's Companies has been rapidly expanding, and in the process is trying various green building tactics such as the Lowe's megastore in southwest Austin that received the LEED Gold certification recognizing a host of sustainable practices. Pictured above is the Lowe's store in Paterson, New Jersey, which opened in 2007 with many of the energy-saving features tested at the southwest Austin store.

- Using local, low-emitting materials with high recycled content

- Having more than 90 percent of construction waste diverted from the landfill

- Commitment to purchase green power (energy produced by renewable sources) for half of the store's electricity needs

The Lowe's store in southwest Austin is the first large-format retail store to receive a LEED Gold certification and ranks among the highest of LEED-rated projects in the state of Texas

"This store is a visible example of our commitment to be a good steward of the environment not only in Austin, but as we look at responsible construction practices across the country," said Michael Chenard, Lowe's director of environmental affairs, in a press release.

Lowe's—along with JCPenney, Limited Brands, Meijer, Office Depot and Wal-Mart—earned the Environmental Excellence Award from EPA's SmartWay Transport Partnership in 2007. The EPA recognized the retailers for their leadership in conserving energy and lowering GHG emissions from their transportation and freight delivery system.

EPA cited some of Lowe's accomplishments in connection with this award:

- Increased shipping by rail

- Increased its use of SmartWay carriers to 62 from only four since Lowe's first joined SmartWay in 2004

- Increased use of full trailers, reducing approximately 36,000 truck loads and reducing highway mileage by over 25 million miles (40 million km)

- Increased drop and hook use from 43 percent in 2004 to 83 percent in 2006

- Increased intermodal shipping by over 4,000 shipments in 2007

- Instituted a more efficient process for inbound and outbound freight deliveries

- Increased efficiency of truckload shipments allowing more products to be shipped on fewer trailers

"By 2010, we plan to transport ninety percent of our shipments by SmartWay Transport Partners," said Steve Palmer, Lowe's vice president of transportation, in an official statement on November 6, 2007.

Lowe's was one of 34 companies and organizations to receive the Environmental Excellence Award. The awards were announced at the annual conference of the Council of Supply Chain Management Professionals in Philadelphia, Pennsylvania.

EPA estimates that with full industry participation by 2012, the SmartWay program will achieve annual fuel savings nationwide of 3.3 to 6.6 billion gallons (12.5 to 25 billion liters) of diesel fuel, eliminating 33 to 66 million metric tons (36.4 to 73.8 million tons) of carbon-dioxide emissions and up to 200,000 tons (181,400

metric tons) of nitrogen oxide emissions. More information on SmartWay is available from the EPA at http://www.epa.gov/smartway.

Lowe's sustainable practices date back to the early 2000s. In 2003, Lowe's installed its first solar electric system at its West Hills store in Los Angeles, California. At the time, it was one of the largest commercial solar rooftop electric systems in the United States and the largest at any U.S. retail store. The 370-kilowatt solar system generates enough electricity during the daytime to power more than 370 homes.

The PowerLight solar generation system covers 37,500 square feet (3,485 sq m) of rooftop at Lowe's store in West Hills and features 2,535 solar roof tiles made from Shell Solar modules. The Shell modules, manufactured in the United States, were chosen for their reliability and performance.

The rooftop system features a lightweight photovoltaic roofing assembly that delivers solar electricity to the building while protecting the roof from the damaging effects of the weather and ultraviolet radiation. The tiles also help insulate the building, reducing heating and cooling requirements.

Mooresville, North Carolina-based Lowe's Companies Inc. operates more than 1,450 home improvement stores in 49 U.S. states and several stores in Canada through a subsidiary, Toronto-based Lowe's Companies Canada ULC.

WAL-MART'S CARBON FOOTPRINT DIET

The world's largest retailer has been reducing its carbon footprint for quite some time. The big-box chain—best known for the ubiquitous Wal-Mart general merchandising stores, neighborhood markets, Wal-Mart Supercenters and Sam's Club—has a gigantic environmental footprint from its vast store operations in Argentina, Brazil, Canada, China, Costa Rica, El Salvador, Guatemala, Honduras, Japan, Mexico, Nicaragua, Puerto Rico, the United Kingdom and the United States.

Wal-Mart's long-term program, instated long before sustainability became a green building enthusiast's buzzword, now includes daylight harvesting through automated photosensors and skylights, white reflective cool roofing, heat reclaim, high-efficiency HVAC units (EER rating between 11 and 13), centralized energy management system monitoring, active dehumidification and exterior signage powered by energy-efficient LED lamps.

According to Charles R. Zimmerman, PE, vice president of prototype and new format development at Wal-Mart Stores Inc., the retail giant is the world's second-largest user of energy after the U.S. government. As a result, energy conservation has become an essential part of Wal-Mart's overall cost reduction strategy.

Don A. Moseley, PE, Wal-Mart's director of sustainable facilities, says that Wal-Mart has learned a great deal by observing energy conservation techniques the company implemented at stores built in the early 1990s, which includes the operations at Lawrence, Kansas; Moore, Oklahoma; and the City of Industry, California. "If it weren't for those early experiments, Wal-Mart wouldn't be as advanced today in sustainable practices," said Moseley.

With assistance from engineers representing a utility company, several architects and consultants, Wal-Mart began experimenting in the 1990s with daylight harvesting and other important green-building concepts. For example, at the 131,000-square-foot (12,170 sq m) City of Industry, California Supercenter, Southern California Edison utility company monitored the environmental features of the store for possible application to other building uses.

According to the Rosslyn, Virginia-based Lighting Controls Association (LCA), affiliated with the National Electrical Manufacturers Association (NEMA), Wal-Mart installed three different types of skylights and watched how each of them performed. Novar Controls Corporation provided photocontrols. Luminaires came from Thomas Industries Inc./Day-Brite.

Wal-Mart hired architects Dru Meadows, RA, and Charles Bell of BSW International of Tulsa, Oklahoma, to oversee the City of Industry store design project. Nancy Clanton, PE, of Clanton & Associates in Boulder, Colorado, helped design the lighting scheme. Gregg Ander, AIA, and Carlos Haiad from Southern California Edison of San Dimas, California, conducted several efficiency and sustainability studies during the installations and monitored results. Gregory Franta, FAIA, of

PHOTOS: R. E. MILIAN

Before Wal-Mart opened its first experimental stores, it had been harvesting daylight for years. Photo at top shows a Supercenter in Royal Palm, Florida, with the lights off because it is using the daylight from the skylights on the roof. At lower left, photosensors automatically activate the fluorescent lights at dusk at the Supercenter in Kissimmee, Florida, as the devices detect little light entering the store from the skylights. Late at night when stock clerks begin stocking the refrigerated cases at the Supercenter in Monroe, New York (lower photo), the daylight harvesting system sets the store's lighting according to Wal-Mart's specifications, a more comfortable lower lighting level that is appropriate for the biological clock that regulates human circadian rhythms.

PHOTOS: R. E. MILIAN

An older Wal-Mart in the Village of Airmont, New York, (top) has energy-efficient T5HO fluorescent lighting but does not have skylights to harvest daylight. Left and above, the Supercenter in White Plains, New York, also used T5HO fluorescent lamps, but because of the multilevel aspect of the site, daylight harvesting with skylights is not possible.

ENSAR Group Inc., based in Boulder, Colorado, acted as daylighting consultant, and Jack Vest, III, PE, with Consulting Engineers of Tulsa, Oklahoma, functioned as the electrical engineer. Engineers from Wal-Mart's Bentonville, Arkansas, oversaw the entire project, carefully evaluating successes and failures every step of the way.

The plan they implemented at the City of Industry store became the 1990s foundation of Wal-Mart's now famous green store innovations, heralded all over the

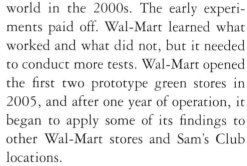

world in the 2000s. The early experiments paid off. Wal-Mart learned what worked and what did not, but it needed to conduct more tests. Wal-Mart opened the first two prototype green stores in 2005, and after one year of operation, it began to apply some of its findings to other Wal-Mart stores and Sam's Club locations.

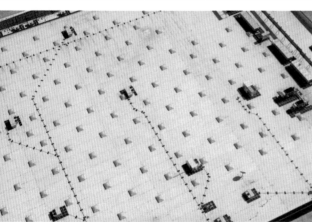

Both prototype stores, one in Aurora, Colorado, and one in McKinney, Texas, offer customers Wal-Mart's complete line of products and services. The store design from the customer's perspective is quite similar to other Wal-Mart stores, but the company has set in place new environmental technologies designed to highly reduce initial construction and operational waste, to use recycled and renewable materials, and to optimize water and electricity usage.

Top: Wal-Mart used a different ceiling at its experimental Supercenter in Aurora, Colorado, compared to its typical Supercenters. This one is pitched to allow clerestory windows to harvest daylight, seen at the right of this photograph. Middle: Wal-Mart's experimental green store in McKinney, Texas, has a white reflective roof and a grid of skylights to help the store harvest daylight. Photocells regulate the store lighting system at hundreds of Wal-Mart energy-efficient stores. Lighting is synchronized with efficient skylights to minimize power consumption and improve daylighting. Lower: The efficient skylights (pictured at Wal-Mart's McKinney, Texas Supercenter) are made of two-layer polycarbonate sheets designed for all Wal-Mart stores to meet its own specifications. The skylights shield against harmful ultraviolet rays while admitting most of the visible light and preventing heat loss at night.

PHOTO COURTESY OF PAMELA LIPPE, e4 inc.

PHOTO COURTESY WAL-MART STORES INC.

Gauging from the potential of this limited rollout, Wal-Mart opened a third store in the St. Louis, Missouri, market, taking the tactics of sustainable design and operation to new heights.

To save water, Wal-Mart's prototype stores installed drought-tolerant landscaping and irrigate with a drip system that sends water directly to the roots of the plants, minimizing water lost to evaporation and runoff—an effect that occurs with conventional sprinkler systems.

The stores also utilize a series of energy-efficient tactics to produce heat, such as regenerating heat from the refrigeration racks, using radiant floor heating and burning waste-recycled cooking and motor oil to heat water. The McKinney, Texas, experimental store, located in the Sunbelt, where sunshine is plentiful, uses solar power to help meet its energy needs. The Aurora store also does, which gives the retailer a comparison of results.

However, Wal-Mart is not yet convinced the solar systems work as well as they should, and so more experiments are underway. The electric meters on the solar installations at the McKinney store, initially experienced problems, causing faulty readings. Spring and summer months in Aurora were the most successful for solar power generation.

PHOTOS COURTESY OF PAMELA LIPPE, e4 inc.

The wind turbines at first experienced mechanical issues but continue to hold promise for future application. Moseley, a Wal-Mart veteran engineer since 1989, monitors all aspects of these prototype stores for possible implementation of successful sustainable techniques that Wal-Mart can roll out across the entire chain. One such technique at these two stores involves planting native grasses and trees to reduce water needed for irrigation. The test has proven the merit to extend this practice to all stores.

Waterless urinals installed in the men's restrooms in the prototype stores were designed to save one to three gallons (3.8 to 11.4 liters) of water per use. They have also proven valuable for rollout across the chain.

Small countertop photovoltaic panels charge batteries used to power the restroom sink sensors. The sensors activate the flow of water without using electricity when customers place their hands beneath the faucet. Based on the success of these

Above: Wal-Mart uses solar-powered signs at its experimental Supercenter in Aurora, Colorado. Below: Signs at the Wal-Mart Supercenter in Aurora, Colorado, inform customers how its heat reclaim system uses otherwise wasted heat to melt snow, warming the paving surface near handicap parking spaces and crosswalks.

systems, Wal-Mart will install water-conserving sinks at all new and remodeled stores.

LED TECHNOLOGY

One of the most substantial discoveries involves LEDs, which resulted in Wal-Mart rolling out this type of lighting for various uses to all new and renovated stores in 2007 and beyond. The Wal-Mart LED system was designed by Lumination (formerly GELcore), a subsidiary of General Electric.

LEDs, which Wal-Mart used to light exterior building signage and its freezer and jewelry cases, produce more lumens per watt than incandescent bulbs and last much longer. Some types of LEDs have a lifespan of up to 100,000 hours, which is double the life of the best fluorescent bulb and can last twenty times longer than the best incandescent bulb.

"The lifespan of LED lights is projected to be at least ten years beyond conventional lighting. This significantly reduces the need to manufacture and dispose of fluorescent lamps, which need to be replaced on average every two years," said Moseley.

Wal-Mart projects US$2.6 million in energy savings annually through the replacement of fluorescent lamps in 500 U.S. stores with LED.

"LED technology, when combined with motion detection, can provide over 70 percent more energy-efficient operation than fluorescent illumination," Moseley said.

Wal-Mart is also using LEDs and low mercury lamps as a replacement for incandescent lightbulbs in some applications. "Wal-Mart utilizes 'low mercury' lamps throughout its stores and clubs," said Moseley. These bulbs are considered nonhazardous material and can be disposed of in any landfill. Moseley said that Wal-Mart has chosen to recycle these lamps anyway.

In 2007, it became standard for Wal-Mart to use LED lights in freezer cases in its newly constructed stores and clubs.

PHOTO: R. E. MILIAN

Wal-Mart is now using LEDs to light exterior signs economically and to save on relamping at the Wal-Mart Supercenter in Kissimmee, Florida (right). Unlike neon, LEDs do not result in lumen depreciation or color shift over their long lives. About two years after Wal-Mart first began experimenting with LEDs, it had retrofitted most exterior signs with LEDs.

A major benefit to using LEDs in freezer cases is that the lighting is more uniformly distributed than with fluorescent bulbs, thus appearing brighter to customers.

Fluorescent lighting is no longer considered ideal in freezer cases now that LEDs have become a popular alternative. The cold temperatures tend to affect the mercury vapor pressure in fluorescent lighting and reduce lamp life and lamp output.

In addition, fluorescent lamps produce some radiant heat, robbing cool temperatures from the freezer and refrigerated cases. LED lights produce much less heat and contain no mercury.

Zimmerman is responsible for one of about a dozen networks at Wal-Mart that focuses on sustainability, mainly energy management and reduction of carbon dioxide emissions.

Other Wal-Mart networks concentrate on a wide array of sustainability areas, such as recycling, water conservation, and sourcing organic foods and sustainable consumable merchandise.

Zimmerman insists on a centralized system for energy management for his roughly 4,000 Wal-Mart and Sam's Club stores in the United States and Canada.

Wal-Mart closely watches all stores to make sure store personnel comply with the company's energy efficiency standards. The retailer does this by operating a centralized energy management system that controls all its Wal-Mart and Sam's Clubs in North America.

The centralized Wal-Mart energy management system controls the temperature in all North American stores and tracks energy usage by store 24 hours a day in 15-minute increments, outputting data by kilowatt-hour consumed.

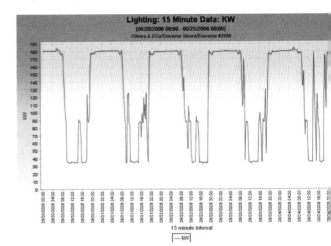

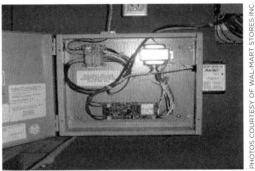

Wal-Mart's daylight harvesting system, showing a graph with fluctuations in energy use. The smart daylighting system uses photocontrols to regulate lighting levels, adjusting for natural light entering through a grid of skylights above store aisles, and dims or brightens fluorescents to maintain the optimum level of light while using the minimum amount of energy.

One kilowatt-hour is the energy that one 100-watt bulb uses during ten hours and typically retails between US$0.11 and US$0.36 in the United States.

In reviewing printout reports that resemble electrocardiogram ribbons, Zimmerman ensures minimum energy spikes, those for which many utility companies charge higher rates.

Wal-Mart now uses a photometric (photocells) system to regulate store lighting levels. The lighting system is synchronized with efficient skylights spread in wells linearly throughout the roof of the store. As the sun moves higher in the sky at about 10:00 A.M., Wal-Mart's software regulates the amount of lumens emitted, and the light dims to save energy. The effect is invisible to the customer. The lighting eventually turns off to optimize energy savings on a clear day, letting the skylights assume its daylighting role.

When clouds pass overhead, the Wal-Mart lighting sensors brighten the lights gradually so that the same level of brightness remains consistent throughout the day.

These efficient skylights are made of two-layer polycarbonate sheets designed for Wal-Mart to its own specifications. The skylights shield against harmful ultraviolet rays while admitting most of the visible light and preventing heat loss at night.

According to Zimmerman, Wal-Mart uses skylights with three layers of polycarbonate sheets in northern climates to prevent heat loss. Zimmerman also notes that there is quick payback for this type of daylight harvesting system. It can save enormous amounts of energy. He projects an annual savings of US$100,000 per store and a cost to install and operate the daylight harvesting system at US$200,000. It is roughly a two-year payback.

"Over ninety-five percent of newly constructed Wal-Mart Supercenters and Sam's Clubs include a daylight harvesting system," said Moseley. "By integrating dimmable T8 fluorescent lamps, electronic dimming ballasts and computer controlled daylight sensors with the skylights, Wal-Mart takes full advantage of natural daylight when available," Moseley added.

Moseley said that by using these specific lamps, the reduction of energy is approximately 15 to 20 percent compared to using the older systems, T12 fluorescents or HID—the three main types of high-intensity discharge lamps: mercury vapor, metal halide and sodium.

As of autumn 2007, Wal-Mart had approximately 2,000 Supercenters in the United States with daylight harvesting in place (over 334 million square feet [31 million sq m]), Moseley said. Additionally, there were more than 450 Wal-Mart general merchandise stores, neighborhood markets, and Sam's Clubs contributing another 60 million square feet (5.8 million sq m) of space where Wal-Mart harvested daylight.

Don A. Moseley, PE, Wal-Mart's director of sustainable facilities and a veteran professional engineer with Wal-Mart since 1989, monitors all aspects of the prototypical high-efficiency Wal-Mart stores for possible implementation across the entire chain.

PHOTO: R. E. MILIAN

In this Wal-Mart Supercenter in Royal Palm, Florida—typical of other U.S. Wal-Mart Supercenters—sensors turn off T8 fluorescent luminaires when bright daylight filters through the skylights. On cloudy days, photo sensors dim but do not completely turn off Wal-Mart's fluorescent lighting in order to give the appearance to customers that lighting levels are consistent and the differences are barely noticeable. The T5HO luminaires that Wal-Mart used in the prototype stores are slightly more efficient than T8s, but T5HOs do not respond to dimming as well as T8s, which dim perfectly from full capacity to total darkness. T5HO luminaires will dim to 35 percent of capacity. They then tend to shut off abruptly, which is noticeable to customers.

PHOTO: R. E. MILIAN

Wal-Mart's home office personnel refer any temperature-related problems—whether in the stores' refrigerated units or the selling areas—to contractors to correct, sometimes before store management is even aware of the problem.

If a freezer door remains open for more than 45 minutes, the system sends a signal to the central office to make the energy watchdogs aware.

"Wal-Mart installs occupancy sensors in most nonsales areas in its newly constructed stores," said Moseley. "These areas include but are not limited to restrooms, break rooms and offices." These sensors detect activity in a room and automatically turn off the lights when the space is unoccupied, Moseley said.

After a year and a half of studying the 2005 prototype stores, in 2007 Wal-Mart opened three high-efficiency Supercenters in various climates to test adaptability for the rapidly expanding chain. The Highland Village, Texas, store is in a hot climate. The other two are further north, one in Kansas City, Missouri, and the other one in the heart of the U.S. Midwest, Rockton, Illinois.

The high-efficiency Supercenter in Highland Village, Texas, a 192,000-square-foot (17,800 sq m) store, is catering to the health- and climate-conscious consumer trend by offering organic foods, a bicycle shop and a green efficient store design. The full-service bicycle shop even employs bicycle mechanics on the premises.

The Highland Village store, which opened in November 2007, uses 20 percent less energy than similar-sized Supercenters. It features integrated heating, cooling and refrigeration systems,

Wal-Mart's prototype Supercenter in McKinney, Texas (middle), was among the first commercial LED installations of this magnitude in U.S. retail, rolling out in 2005. Wal-Mart enclosed the deli and dairy sections with doors. The motion sensor-driven lights in the store's refrigerated cases automatically turn off when not in use for a few seconds just to save a bit of energy, and then quickly turn back on when a customer approaches. The savings add up. LED lights have a longer lifespan than fluorescent bulbs. They produce less heat, use significantly less energy than typical grocery case lighting and are virtually maintenance free (LED bulbs are to the left of the merchandise in the top photo). These high-efficient stores consume 20 to 25 percent less energy on average than the typical Supercenter. Although all Supercenters are energy-efficient by comparison to most big-box stores, they do not incorporate all the energy-saving measures of Wal-Mart's prototypical high-efficient Supercenters. An example is the open deli case in the Supercenter in Kissimmee, Florida (bottom left), where the cooling escapes, akin to leaving your refrigerator door wide open.

PHOTO COURTESY OF WAL-MART STORES INC.

PHOTO: R. E. MILIAN

and lighting innovations using daylight from the grid of skylights to conserve energy.

Deborah Weinswig, a retail analyst for New York City-based Citigroup, toured the Highland Village store with Wal-Mart vice president and regional general manager, John Murphy, and she was pleasantly surprised with the store's environmental innovations and adaptability to the upscale suburban neighborhood, which includes recreational bicycle trails.

"We were very impressed with the new Wal-Mart Supercenter in Highland Village, Texas, which had a more upscale feel and design than the typical Supercenter," said Weinswig, in a Citigroup analyst report.

Receiving approval from the City of Highland Village to build the store was not easy, but the store's sustainable aspects and Wal-Mart's willingness to preserve a 150-year-old tree and a bike path in the back of the store became a big plus with public officials and the community in this community-minded Denton County suburb.

The company also built a wall to buffer the bikers from motor vehicles, recognizing that adding certain amenities and being eco-friendly help Wal-Mart gain acceptance in communities across the world.

A month before the Highland Village store opened, Zimmerman spoke at the ICSC World Summit in Cape Town, South Africa, and announced the high-efficiency store concept to an impressed audience. He said, however, that sustainability is nothing new at Wal-Mart.

"We have been concentrating on saving energy long before it was called sustainability," Zimmerman told an audience of 1,500 shopping center and retail executives gathered from around the world to learn about Wal-Mart's initiatives.

HIGH-EFFICIENCY STORE—SECOND GENERATION

Wal-Mart dubbed the three high-efficiency Supercenters as HE.1 (high-efficiency 1) stores in 2007 because it has since switched to HE.2 models in 2008 to take store efficiency to new levels. The Rockton HE.1 store included many features from the original 2005 experiments:

- Many floors are made of integrally colored concrete instead of carpet or tile, reducing the need for certain harsh chemical cleaning products
- All baseboards and chair rails are made of recycled plastic
- Restroom sinks use sensor-activated, low-flow faucets. The low-flow faucets reduce water flow by 84 percent, while the sensors save approximately 20 percent in water usage over similar, manually operated systems
- To achieve a 20 percent overall energy reduction, the Rockton store uses a 100 percent integrated water-source-format heating, cooling and refrigeration system, where water is harnessed to heat and cool the building

- Energy-saving, motion-activated LEDs in refrigerator and freezer cases are expected to create a 2 to 3 percent energy reduction

- A state-of-the-art Munters Dehumidification system is expected to increase overall store energy efficiency by roughly 2 percent

Wal-Mart likes to keep the temperature inside all its stores in the summer at 75°F (24°C). "We use an active dehumidification system that dries the air so that the customer stays comfortable and the thermostat can be kept higher," said Zimmerman.

Zimmerman explained that many other building operators unwittingly crank up air conditioning, which consumes a great deal of energy, mostly to remove humidity. That is the most expensive way to take the humidity out of interior air.

Contrary to popular belief, traditional air-conditioning systems do not necessarily reduce the relative humidity of the supplied air, particularly in humid settings such as restaurants and supermarkets. When the air is cooled, the relative humidity often increases instead of decreasing, as is generally the case when cooling dry space. This results in a humid indoor climate, which in turn leads to discomfort—and even to mold and bacteria growth.

The new third-generation Munters Humidity Control Unit (HCU) that Wal-Mart employed in its high-efficiency stores allows for separate controls of temperature and humidity, with a high success rate.

The Wal-Mart system saves energy by cooling the air to the target temperature and uses supplemental humidity controls to dry the air for ambient comfort. This keeps the temperature slightly higher, at 75°F, but feeling just as comfortable.

The first HE.2 Wal-Mart energy-smart store opened in January 2008 in the Village of Romeoville, Illinois, and the company immediately set out to open three more HE.2 Supercenters in 2008.

Much of the improvement in HE.2 energy efficiency comes from a new secondary refrigeration loop combined with an advanced water-source heating, cooling and refrigeration system.

Wal-Mart tested the technology in its experimental stores and now uses a nonrefrigerant-based solution to cool refrigerated and freezer cases, resulting in a 90 percent reduction in refrigerant. It was the first time in the United States that building operators paired secondary loop technology with a water-source heating, cooling and refrigeration system to a large scale.

Saving operating costs gives the large discounter an enormous competitive advantage, which Wal-Mart chief executive officer H. Lee Scott delineates through his widely publicized philosophy: Everyday low costs equal everyday low prices.

"There is no conflict between our business model of everyday low costs and everyday low prices and being a more sustainable business," said Scott.

Zimmerman said he traveled to various countries to analyze energy use and costs at Wal-Mart stores, and he found that the most energy-efficient stores are the ones in the United States.

In the United States, Wal-Mart has grown organically and therefore has designed those stores to meet its own set of proven criteria. In other countries, Wal-Mart's market entry has been through acquisition of other chains.

Energy savings in countries other than the United States often mean savings that are more substantial because for the most part the cost of electricity is higher. According to a 2006 International Energy Agency report, electricity costs to industry vary tremendously by country. Electricity costs in the United States are among the lowest at approximately US$0.06 per kilowatt-hour, along with Norway at US$0.06 and France at US$0.05.

At the other end of the spectrum, electricity costs to businesses in Italy run about US$0.24 per kilowatt-hour, US$0.15 in Ireland, US$0.13 in the United Kingdom, US$0.13 in Hungary, the Slovak Republic and Austria and US$0.12 in Japan.

Wal-Mart's Sustainability 360 campaign extends to the product it carries, helping Wal-Mart customers reduce their environmental footprint.

The upside for Wal-Mart operating in multiple countries is that the higher the cost, the faster the payback becomes for investing in energy-efficient equipment. In countries where costs are high, implementing energy-saving measures is that much more lucrative.

Wal-Mart's consumption by kilowatt hour per square foot varies from a high of 57 kWh per square foot in the United Kingdom to a low of 27 kWh per square foot in the United States and Mexico. Wal-Mart China stores consume about 28 kWh per square foot, Japan and Argentina about 34 kWh per square foot and Puerto Rico about 48 kWh per square foot.

Based on the positive results of Wal-Mart's experiments, the world's largest retail chain is implementing a program called Sustainability 360 across all its stores. Among the host of initiatives, Wal-Mart is requiring many of its suppliers to use renewable energy in manufacturing and distributing their products and has set a goal to reduce the bulk of merchandise packaging the chain stocks in its stores by 5 percent by 2013.

The packing reduction initiative alone is expected to remove 213,000 trucks from the road, saving about 324,000 tons (294,928 metric tons) of coal and 67 million gallons (254 million liters) of diesel fuel per year.

The pilot involves seven product categories, and if successful according to Wal-Mart's standards, the world's largest retail chain will roll out similar programs throughout its entire supply chain. Wal-Mart made this a goal because of the success of a previous experiment. Wal-Mart worked with one of its toy suppliers to reduce packaging on 16 merchandise items. The result: 230 fewer shipping containers, saving 356 barrels of oil and 1,300 trees.

Wal-Mart is also phasing out products and packaging containing the toxic polyvinyl chloride (PVC) plastic, commonly known as vinyl. Sears Holdings (Sears and Kmart) and Target are also working to reduce and phase out PVC in products and

packaging as well as encouraging vendors to label their PVC-free merchandise.

In 2007, the Carbon Disclosure Project (CDP), a not-for-profit group, and Wal-Mart formed a partnership to measure the amount of energy (and resulting carbon footprint) used to assemble and transport products throughout Wal-Mart's supply chain including procurement, manufacturing and distribution process.

In public disclosures, Wal-Mart projects that its prototype stores will be between 25 and 30 percent more energy efficient and produce about one-third less global-warming emissions over the next three years.

Wal-Mart spends about US$500 million annually in sustainable systems and technologies. As the retailer implements these systems at all existing Wal-Mart stores, Sam's Clubs and distribution centers across the world between 2006 and 2012, Wal-Mart predicts a 20 percent reduction in greenhouse gas emissions—a substantial reduction considering its colossal carbon footprint.

Zimmerman told the ICSC audience in Cape Town, "Reducing Wal-Mart's carbon footprint and GHG emissions is our responsibility." To prove this philosophy, Wal-Mart shares its findings with other retailers, competitors and government in an open book fashion, Zimmerman explained to the ICSC delegates.

SHARING BEST PRACTICES

One meeting in which Wal-Mart and other retail executives got together to share green building practices took place on December 5, 2007, prior to the start of the ICSC CenterBuild Conference held in Phoenix, Arizona, for the design-build industry.

The meeting primarily included senior store design and construction managers for Wal-Mart, Kohl's Corporation, The Home Depot, Target Corporation, Limited Brands, Belk Department Store, Macy's Inc., JCPenney Company, Dillard's Inc., Nordstrom Inc. and others.

"We shared best practices regarding sustainability design applications like efficient lighting systems," said Bryan Novak, CDP, senior national director of site and building construction for Wal-Mart, while stressing Wal-Mart's commitment to share sustainability best practices with other retailers.

Raymond Silverstein, CDP, senior vice president of strategic store operations, store design and construction at Limited Brands, agreed about the importance of retailers meeting with their peers to talk about best practices and shared learning on sustainable store design and construction. "Everybody is grappling with similar issues," said Silverstein.

The group discussed the efforts by various retailers to go green, especially in new store construction, the techniques that each company is employing to educate in-house staff on green building tactics and what was the word out on the street about the progress of the USGBC on new retail LEED standards then still under review.

Silverstein is confident that retailers have been making great progress in imple-

PHOTO: R. E. MILIAN

Retailers met on January 17, 2008, at ICSC headquarters in New York to share best practices in green store design, construction and operations. Standing L–R: Jeffrey Bowen, director of technical operations (Dillard's Inc.); Thomas J. Connolly, SCLS, divisional vice president (Walgreens); Charles P. Stilley, president, real estate (AMC Realty Inc., a unit of AMC Entertainment Inc.); and Gary J. Nay, vice president, real estate (Macy's Inc.). Sitting L–R: Robert S. Jordahl, senior vice president, store planning and construction (Belk Inc.); Don A. Moseley, PE, director of sustainable facilities (Wal-Mart Stores Inc.); Ray Silverstein, CDP, AIA, senior vice president, store design and construction (Limited Brands); David Rayner, vice president, real estate (Ulta Inc.); and Gayle Aertker, senior vice president, real estate and development (Dollar General Corporation).

menting their retail green agendas. "Retailers in general are ahead of the curve," said Silverstein. "We need to get our suppliers and vendors up to speed quickly," he said, referring to the need for design and construction contractors to be attuned to sustainable practices in order to help retailers keep up the pace of their green building efforts.

Richard P. O'Leary, CDP, vice president and director of construction services for the JCPenney Company, agrees about information sharing. "Sharing of information encourages others to change design standards by sharing steps to success," said O'Leary.

TARGET'S BULLS-EYE POINTS GREEN

Experimenting with sustainable techniques for large big-box stores is not the sole purview of Wal-Mart, the largest retail chain in the world. Its rival competitor, Target Corporation, is also way out front in the sustainability arena, although more low-key about its progress.

Target is combating the urban heat island (UHI) effect in the third-largest metropolitan area in the United States by creating green roofs on four of its Chicago-area stores, in the heart of the U.S. Midwest region. UHI is common in metropolitan cities, such as Chicago and New York, that tend to be significantly warmer than their surroundings and could ultimately affect generally rising global temperatures. UHI is not the same as global warming because the effect heats Earth's ambient air in urban areas rather than the atmosphere that covers Earth, but it does contribute toward warmer temperatures in general.

Two methods for buildings to counteract the negative heat island effect is by using white or reflective materials on horizontal surfaces, such as parking lots and roofs, and by planting vegetation on roof containers irrigated by graywater, ground-

water or well water. Vegetation or bodies of water absorb CO_2 and release cooling moisture into the atmosphere. However, large areas of black asphalt surfaces used for parking, driving and roofs absorb solar energy and retain heat. These structures also reflect, store and release heat into the air after the sun goes down.

Dark surfaces have the opposite effect of water and vegetation. They warm the surface of the planet rather than cool it. They have a low albedo whereas trees and light-colored surfaces have a high albedo. Albedo refers to the ability of a surface to reflect rather than absorb solar radiation. White rooftops can reflect up to 65 percent of the

PHOTO COURTESY OF WESTON SOLUTIONS INC.

Target's "green roof" in Chicago, Illinois, counteracts the urban heat island (UHI) temperature warming effect with its white reflective roof and with oxygen-generating vegetation on roof receptacles irrigated by groundwater. It also keeps the building envelope better insulated, which saves on heating and cooling costs.

sun's radiant heat, providing a cooling effect. Green roofs also reflect light but have the added benefit of minimizing stormwater runoff and filtering CO_2 from the air.

Conventional roofs on Target's Chicago stores have been turned into green roofs by adding drought-resistant vegetation planted in flats made of recycled plastic, which are then placed on a filter fabric set directly on top of the roof membrane surface. The plants require minimal maintenance.

"Up to half of the roof space has the green roof at these stores," David A. Luick, Target Corporation's manager for strategic development initiatives, told an audience of ICSC members on October 17, 2007, at the ICSC Fall Conference held in New Orleans, Louisiana.

"Advantages of the green roof include reducing heat island [effect] and stormwater management, but it creates a perfect storm for pigeons flying over the parapet walls and littering the sidewalks below," added Luick, explaining unintended consequences of green designs.

To a layperson, the roofs of these stores look like Target's nursery department facing the downtown Chicago skyline, but it is instead an example of a socially responsible retailer doing its part to conserve the environment and demonstrate its receptiveness to Chicago's commitment to sustainability.

The green roofs at these Target stores are only one of the company's initiatives toward promoting sustainability. Like Wal-Mart, Target is experimenting with technology to build and run green stores at its McKinley Park and Peterson Avenue locations in Chicago and one store in Allen Park, Michigan.

These stores integrate tactics such as using ozone-friendly HVAC and refrigeration equipment, irrigating landscaping efficiently, locating in urban areas near public transportation, monitoring for optimum energy and water performance, ensuring low levels of CO_2 and using low-emitting building materials, such as paints and carpet.

"We're unique because we own so many of our projects," said Luick. When Target sets out to design and operate green stores, it has the resources and ability to make an impact with its massive real estate portfolio that consists of land and buildings under ownership for about 85 percent of its stores, 24 distribution centers and the corporate headquarters.

The company is unwavering in its commitment. "Sustainability has been part of our fabric for years," said Luick, explaining that sustainability is not a passing fad for the Minneapolis, Minnesota–based retailer whose brand image bulls-eye design is widely recognizable, even when appearing by itself. "We see it as stewardship instead of sustainability."

Stewardship of the environment involves Target generating its own green power. The retailer purchased from Oklahoma Gas & Electric the maximum amount of electricity generated by wind power to power its Oklahoma stores.

In California, the retailer entered into a multi-year energy supply contract with Minnesota Methane that began in July 2006 and runs through 2009 to purchase renewable energy from a Minnesota Methane plant located in the Los Angeles Basin.

The renewable energy from this contract accounts for 14 percent of Target's Direct Access energy purchases.

Target, the fifth-largest retailer by sales volume in the United States behind Wal-Mart, The Home Depot, Kroger and Costco, participated in the Energy Conservation Incentive program offered by Southern California Edison in 2005. Target's architects and engineers designed a roof for the Fontana, California, store that uses hundreds of Solatube skylights to harness solar energy. With this system, a rooftop skylight directs sunlight and diffuses it into an acrylic lens located in the store's ceiling.

During June (the period offering the most amount of sunlight), the skylights provide as much as 100 percent of the store's sales floor lighting needs for six hours a day. In December (the shortest sunlight period), the maximum output is 75 percent of sales floor lighting needs for four hours a day.

In 2005, Target took advantage of California's grant programs to harvest solar power at two other stores in Los Angeles and one store in El Cajon in San Diego. The photovoltaic panels located on the roof of these stores are generating 20 percent of the stores' year-round electricity needs.

The company estimates greenhouse gas reductions from the three stores of 15,000 tons (13,600 metric tons) of carbon dioxide annually. Based on the initial test and ongoing state incentives for renewable energy, Target retrofitted 14 additional Target stores in California with the solar panel systems in 2007.

Target is just one of many retail companies installing photovoltaics in California. Because with the state's rebate program combined with federal tax credits, a retailer can recover between 50 and 60 percent of the cost of installing a solar power system at a big-box stores or distribution centers.

In using electricity generated by burning fossil fuel, Target Corporation also remains committed to operating in an efficient manner, which helps to reduce greenhouse gases and cut energy costs. All Target stores use energy-efficient lighting and HVAC equipment, as well as building control systems that help manage energy consumption. The stores also employ refrigeration antisweat heater controls to help reduce energy use while maintaining proper operation of the equipment. The company is installing LED instead of neon for all exterior signage in new and renovated stores, which results in an 80 percent energy savings and reduced maintenance costs, as LED lasts much longer than neon.

An integrated centralized energy management system monitored at Target headquarters controls lighting, refrigeration equipment, and heating and cooling systems in all stores. Similar to Wal-Mart's system, alarms notify operators of deficiency in store comfort. The stockrooms are all equipped with motion sensors to turn off lighting when not in use.

Target was among the first retailers to install T8 fluorescent lamps and electronic ballasts when they were introduced in 1992. The retailer has started changing its three-lamp lighting fixtures to a two-lamp fixture and projects 22 percent in energy savings without compromising lighting levels in the stores.

Recycling is an important aspect of green building design and being community

minded means sending less waste to burden landfills. Target has cut waste by more than 70 percent through innovative reuse and recycling programs that won awards from the U.S. EPA in 2003 and 2004. "Part of Target's DNA is our commitment to the community, and certainly that ties into the environment as well," said Amy von Walter, a spokeswoman for the company.

For Target, being community minded means to do the right thing for both Target and the community, and logic must prevail when expanding. Target documents its commitment to sustainability by posting dozens of green initiatives on its Web site, and many new Target stores show evidence of Target's progress. However, some municipalities want more. They are enacting tough green-building ordinances that some retailers, such as Target, cannot accept.

"Anecdotally, we have seen ordinances that are draconian," said Luick. "In one community in California, they told us to put in a Target store that has to meet platinum LEED standards. 'We won't give you a CO [certificate of occupancy] until you get LEED certification,' they said. It's an oxymoron because by LEED standards, you have to be open a year [before the USGBC will LEED-certify the store]," said Luick.

Luick's comments serve as a wake-up call for city planners and elected officials to exercise patience as large retail chains move closer toward green building practices. It will not happen overnight. Retailers will do what makes sense to them, and Target is no exception. "The key is: Where does it fit in from a financial equation? From an environmental equation?" asked Luick rhetorically.

U.K. RETAIL: JOHN LEWIS PARTNERSHIP

In the United Kingdom, two of the companies most committed to sustainable retailing are John Lewis Partnership and Marks & Spencer plc.

John Lewis Partnership (JLP) unveiled an aggressive plan to upgrade existing John Lewis department stores and Waitrose supermarkets to comply with an internal set of sustainable criteria that John Lewis has set for itself. JLP also plans to build new greener stores.

John Lewis's criteria clearly define the level of green standards to make its stores healthy and comfortable for customers and employees. It also sets standards for operating efficiently at lower costs and minimizing the impact of the operation of the stores on the environment. The plan has five fundamental components:

1. Strategic: provides support for sustainable demand by stakeholders

2. Feasibility: determines if a store can be built to support the need and considers how developers and contractors can help to achieve sustainable goals

3. Planning and design: answers what a store will look like, how it will function and sets a level of performance

4. Construction: determines how to build a store and coordinates with suppliers and subcontractors

5. Operation and maintenance: describes how a store will be used and how to monitor performance

The John Lewis Partnership plan goes beyond environmental sustainability. It also focuses on corporate social responsibility and uses various external models as guidelines. Among them are the BREEAM Retail Guide to Specifications, the Construction Industry Research and Information Association (CIRIA) Sustainable Construction Procurement, the Commission for Architecture and the Built Environment (CABE), and several others.

MARKS & SPENCER TO BE CARBON NEUTRAL

Marks & Spencer plc—or "M&S" as customers call it—has also teamed up with BREEAM and others for its sustainability measuring stick. The London-based retailer has 520 stores in the United Kingdom and 240 stores in 34 countries of which 219 are franchises. M&S promotes its sustainability program in a campaign called Plan A.

Plan A is a five-year, 100-point plan to tackle issues of sustainability and corporate social responsibility (CSR)

M&S trained 1,500 employees to give nutrition advice to customers, hoping customers and employees will choose healthier lifestyles through the healthy food M&S offers with clear labeling. Lower right is a Simply Food store at Flyover, Hammersmith, London, operated by BP Retail UK and Marks & Spencer at BP Connect gasoline stations. Lower left, M&S encourages its customers to recycle hangers as part of its Plan A program.

PHOTOS: M&S

around the world. Like Wal-Mart, M&S is working with its customers and suppliers to combat climate change, to reduce waste and to safeguard the world's natural resources.

Additionally, Plan A incorporates some CSR goals such as trading ethically to improve the lives of workers that supply the products M&S retails and building a healthier generation through its offering of natural, organic and pesticide-free food products. M&S trained 1,500 employees to give nutrition advice to customers and now promotes a line of products—from energy-saving compact fluorescent lightbulbs to composters—under the *green home* banner.

Plan A also calls for a reduction of food that M&S transports by energy-guzzling airplanes. To alert customers, M&S uses an airplane symbol on the packages of food transported by air.

M&S claims that the strategy behind Plan A is based on what the customer wants M&S to do and because it is the right thing to do. M&S ads boast that it has a Plan A because the company believes it is now the only way to do business. The retail chain calls it "Plan A" because there is no Plan B.

M&S integrates Plan A across all retail stores and its Web site. On its Web site it offers a footprint calculator developed by World Wildlife Fund (WWF), a global science-based organization working in 90 countries on issues ranging from the survival of species to climate change. The Web site claims that M&S customers can measure their carbon emissions in just five minutes and offers tips on how to reduce them.

M&S is researching alternatives into clothing disposal, which could entail donating clothing to the poor, composting them or recycling them. M&S also encourages its customers to recycle and does so itself in every manner possible.

An aggressive store renovation plan is a priority for M&S because it can help the chain run more energy-efficient stores and reduce carbon dioxide emissions. Plan A objectives call for sourcing renewable energy and sustainable materials and for proper waste management techniques.

In 2007, the first of a new breed of green stores opened using a new low-energy infrastructure. According to Niall Trafford, executive of store design and specification at Marks & Spencer, the chain is committed to improving the efficiencies of the existing store portfolio to meet M&S's target of becoming carbon neutral by 2012.

Trafford expects that the remodeled store at Bournemouth will use one-quarter less energy and emit about half of the CO_2 per year compared to other M&S stores. Work is underway for the stores at Glasgow Pollok and Galashiels to become green stores as well.

In addition to becoming a zero-carbon emitter by 2012, M&S plans to send no waste to landfills, expand its sustainable sourcing program, become the model for ethical trading and promote standards for customers and employees to live a healthier lifestyle.

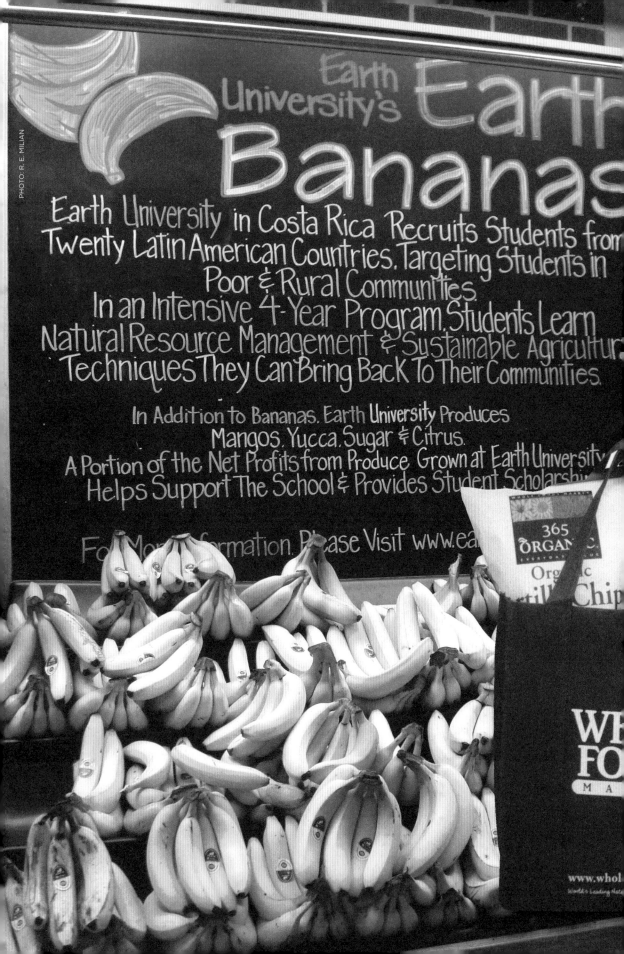

WHOLE FOODS MARKET IS LEED SILVER

Whole Foods Market, one of the leading natural and organic foods supermarket chains, opened its first green store in 2004 in a Casto Lifestyle Properties' mixed-use development in downtown Sarasota, Florida. A year later, the 36,000-square-foot (3,340 sq m), full-service supermarket received the LEED Silver certification from the U.S. Green Building Council.

In spring 2005, a second Whole Foods Market (in Austin, Texas) opened and was later certified as sustainable. This 80,000-square-foot (7,430 sq m) Whole Foods building was rated under the LEED Commercial Interiors pilot project.

This Austin flagship green store, located just blocks from where Whole Foods Market began as a small neighborhood grocer in 1980, is at the corner of Sixth Street and Lamar Boulevard.

PHOTO COURTESY OF WHOLE FOODS MARKETS INC.

The store is the largest Whole Foods store in the chain, which has 270 locations in the United Kingdom and the United States. The LEED-certified store anchors Austin's Market District, sometimes referred to as Sixth and Lamar, which has become downtown Austin's dominant retail destination and includes a development by Schlosser Development Corporation.

Whole Foods is known for selling organically grown fruits and vegetables and its natural meats from animals that have been raised on a 100 percent vegetarian diet—free of added hormones, steroids and antibiotics. The Sarasota store is further underscoring that wholesome corporate image through its sustainability design concepts.

PHOTO: R. E. MILIAN

The Austin store features a water treatment system designed to capture two-thirds of the roof water for cleaning purposes. It recycles materials; uses nontoxic, environmentally friendly public artwork; has a highly reflective white, energy-saving roof system; has installed skylights to bring daylight indoors; and runs high-performance, energy-saving mechanical and electrical systems.

Today, Whole Foods Market uses 100 percent green power. The retail chain is now on EPA's National Top 25 List. Since 2004, EPA has rec-

PHOTO COURTESY OF MACERICH

Top right: Whole Foods Market in a sustainable site in Austin, Texas, downtown Market district is LEED certified. Left page: Whole Foods Markets buys bananas from a supplier in Costa Rica that uses students from 20 Latin American countries and teaches the students sustainable agricultural techniques they can take back to their own countries. This compelling display at the Princeton, New Jersey, store informs customers. Lower right: Whole Foods Market in Princeton.

ognized Whole Foods Market every year with a Green Power Leadership Award for its commitment to purchasing green power.

In 2007, Whole Foods Market increased its green power purchasing to include more than 509 million kilowatt-hours of wind-based renewable energy credits. This was enough renewable energy to offset 100 percent of the electricity used in all of its stores, facilities, bake houses, distribution centers, regional offices and global headquarters in the United States and Canada. Whole Foods Market was the only large retail company to offset 100 percent of its electricity use with renewable energy credits.

In 2006, the company purchased 509 million kilowatt-hours (kWh) of green power consisting mostly of biogas, solar and wind power. Austin Energy, Community Energy, On-site Generation, PNM and Renewable Choice Energy supplied Whole Foods with the green power.

Whole Foods has been using solar energy since 2004. The chain hired SunEdison, LLC—headquartered in Beltsville, Maryland—to install equipment at various stores. The equipment consists of multiple roof mount systems ranging from 50 kW to 245 kW per store, which the retail chain buys at rates that are competitive with conventionally produced electricity. SunEdison is North America's largest solar energy services provider, marketing renewable energy to a broad base of commercial, municipal and utility customers at or below the prevailing retail utility rates. Lee Kane, Whole Foods environmental coordinator, was pleased with SunEdison's service and the ease of using solar power. "Installing solar could not be more user-friendly," said Kane.

Whole Foods began the sustainable construction of a 77,000-square-foot (7,150 sq m) store in Vornado Realty Trust's Bergen Town Center (formerly Bergen Mall) in Paramus, New Jersey. Developing green construction methods, selecting green building materials and building some stores to LEED certification standards are among Whole Foods Market's green building priorities for all its new stores.

The company has not registered the Bergen County location for LEED review, although it is demanding high-performance, Earth-friendly construction methods and recycling or reusing construction materials. These construction techniques

Whole Foods Market in White Plains, New York, caters to an upscale health- and sustainability-focused customer.

PHOTOS: R. E. MILIAN

PHOTO: R. E. MILIAN

In 2007, Whole Foods Market began the sustainable construction of a 77,000-square-foot (7,150 sq m) store at Vornado Realty Trust's Bergen Town Center in Paramus, New Jersey. Developing green construction methods, selecting green building materials and recycling construction waste are among Whole Foods Market's green building priorities for the Bergen County location. Whole Foods Market site work, pictured above, depicts how the contractor is reusing construction and demolition (C&D) materials generated at the construction site. The waste materials are are pulverized and reused as shown in this photo. The scrap materials are quite valuable, but they lose their value if the construction crew operating heavy equipment commingles the material. The costs savings and environmental benefits of recycling can be significant for retailers building big-box stores. Recycling concrete and asphalt pavement saves energy by decreased consumption of natural resources, such as mining crushed stone or extracting and refining petroleum. Recycling or reusing these materials also keeps debris out of landfills and saves purchasing fill material or soil amendments to prepare the site.

are part of Whole Foods Market's overall plan to build and operate greener stores. The food retailer made a commitment to purchase renewable energy as part of a portfolio approach to reducing the company's carbon footprint, which also includes:

- Fueling trucks with biodiesel at four of the company's nine distribution centers
- Composting food waste at stores and facilities
- Recycling plastics, glass and aluminum at stores
- Selling canvas and reusable shopping bags
- Offering a bag refund to encourage shoppers to reuse bags
- Offering compostable food packaging for prepared foods

PHOTOS: R. E. MILIAN

In a survey of American consumers, Aveda made it to the top ten Image-Power Green Brands. Aveda burnishes its green image with ads such as the in-store signs seen in this photo of the Aveda store at the Fashion Show mall in Las Vegas in 2008, which claims Aveda is the first beauty company using 100 percent wind power in manufacturing its products. The top photo is of the Aveda storefront at West-field Garden State Plaza in Paramus, New Jersey.

TRADER JOE'S PRIVATE GREEN LABEL

Trader Joe's now ranks among the top 10 green brands of private labels sold by retailers across the world. Others include Whole Foods, Wild Oats, IKEA, Body Shop and Aveda, according to the 2007 ImagePower Green Brands survey, conducted by WPP's Landor Associates, Penn, Schoen & Berland Associates and Cohn & Wolfe.

Survey respondents equated green- and organic-branded products as being better quality, justifying a premium price at retail.

Even nonusers surveyed were more likely to use green brands in the future and to consider them the next time they made a purchase simply because of reputation, as these nonusers perceived them to be healthier and superior to nongreen products.

Trader Joe's takes a stance on genetically modified food. All products in Trader Joe's private label have been sourced from non-genetically modified ingredients since the company resolved to do so in 2001.

Trader Joe's surveyed its customers at the beginning of this century and determined that, given a choice, its customers prefer to eat foods and beverages made without the use of genetically engineered ingredients. This discovery set the chain on a path to "green up" its operation at a time when the grocery business was in competitive flux, either trying to reduce costs to compete with SuperTarget and Wal-Mart Supercenters or to move upscale to compete with the organic and prepared gourmet food segment.

If Trader Joe's buyers note a big-selling item containing ingredients that could potentially be derived from genetically engineered crops, they will approach their suppliers to produce the products by replacing nonorganic ingredients with greener alternatives.

PUBLIX IS WISE ON GREEN

Publix joins the organic specialists and other mainstream supermarkets in making its stores a little greener. The upscale grocer is building environmentally friendly stores to qualify for LEED certification. "Publix GreenWise Market was created to meet the needs of our customers who are seeking a healthier lifestyle for their families without sacrificing the occasional indulgence," said Maria Brous, a spokeswoman for the Lakeland, Florida–based

PHOTOS: R. E. MILIAN

Ever wonder what it means when a product is labeled **ORGANIC?**

Well, it refers to the way they are grown and processed. Organic food is grown without using most conventional pesticides, herbicides, or commercial fertilizers. Organic food cannot be irradiated or genetically engineered. Organic farms strive to conserve soil and water to enhance environmental quality for future generations.

Trader Joe's prides itself on selling fresh and organic products as part of its green image to avoid ingredients derived from genetically engineered crops.

chain, in a Publix Asset Management Company official statement in September 2007. "We recognize that our customers have become more food and environmentally savvy and want to explore these options in one convenient location."

Publix generates more than US$23 billion in annual sales and owns 914 stores in Alabama, Florida, Georgia, South Carolina and Tennessee. The company launched the GreenWise product line in 1999, and based on how the products are selling, it built a green store that concentrates almost entirely on organic products under the Green-Wise brand. The move is part of a trend in the retail industry similar to The Home Depot's Eco Options that labels natural and eco-friendly products to achieve easy recognition and to gain instant consumer acceptance.

TRADER JOE'S

The crown jewel of this effort is a Publix GreenWise specialty store that Publix opened in the Legacy Place Shopping Center in Palm Beach Gardens, Florida, in 2007 to compete for the healthy-minded food customer. The new store is less than five minutes from the king of organics, Whole Foods Market.

The first step in making the new prototype Legacy Place store into a truly retail green store was to seek and achieve certification by Quality Certification Services (QCS). QCS started as the certification program of Florida Certified Organic Growers and Consumers, certifying organic farming, livestock-raising ranches, product processing, packing and handling operations, and certifying retailers such as the Publix Supermarket in Dacula, Georgia, and Wild Oats Market in Boulder, Colorado. QCS offers United States Department of Agriculture (USDA) ISO Guide 65- and USDA National Organic Program-accredited certification options.

Publix then applied for LEED certification for Legacy Place because of the green building tactics it employed, such as reducing energy consumption by utilizing skylights throughout the store and using photocontrols, a light-sensing system that monitors daylight entering into the store to adjust fluorescent lighting. To keep the store insulated, GreenWise Market has a

The white reflective roof on the new Publix GreenWise Market in Palm Beach Gardens stands out prominently as an integral element of a sustainable green building. Other features that can be evidenced from the photo are daylight harvesting with a grid of skylights, high-efficiency HVAC rooftop units and extensive use of high-level windows glazed with SageGlass.

PHOTO COURTESY OF SIKON CONSTRUCTION CORPORATION

highly reflective roof with a soy-based coating that helps to diminish air-conditioning loads.

Energy-efficient, cool LED lighting is used in the store's refrigerated cases, coolers and freezers. Secondary coolant systems and refrigerants throughout the store mitigate ozone-depleting gas emissions.

The store is working with Florida Atlantic University on a composting effort that uses food scraps such as external lettuce leaves and coffee grounds for making rich soil instead of sending them as waste to a landfill. The architect for the store specified renewable material in the store design, some as obvious as bamboo sales fixtures.

SIKON Construction Corporation in Deerfield Beach, Florida, was the general contractor entrusted with following rigorous LEED standards in building the 45,000-square-foot (41,180 sq m) Publix GreenWise Market. SIKON assigned its Green Team, led by R. E. "Ed" McWhorter, president, and Dale E. Scott, CDP, senior vice president, to ensure that all prerequisites of LEED were met for the new GreenWise Market during the critical construction phase.

Scott explained that dozens of green features were incorporated into the GreenWise store, citing high SageGlass windows and curtain walls that elegantly and efficiently control daylight while maintaining a view and connection to the outdoors. "SageGlass functions similar to gradient lens sunglasses," said Scott. The glass is energy efficient and eliminates uncomfortable heat gain, even on the brightest and hottest days in South Florida.

GreenWise carries more than 100 take-home prepared-meal options, offering its customers an alternative to upscale restaurant dining in the convenience of their homes. The market has more than 3,000 higher-margin natural and organic food products not currently available at mainstream Publix stores, reminiscent of health pledges commonly found at Whole Foods Markets, Wild Oats Markets and Trader Joe's.

Walking down the aisles of the prototype GreenWise Market, customers are flanked by private-labeled and national-branded products boasting healthy promises such as "100% organic," "USDA Certified Organic," "made with organic ingredients," "naturally grown," "preservative free," "no artificial sweeteners," "all-natural," "earth friendly," "vegan" and "vegetarian."

Publix GreenWise Market introduced a new color-coded shelf tag system to help customers understand the various levels of organic origins of the products it sells. A brown tag with the USDA Organic logo indicates a 95 to 100 percent organic product. A brown tag with the phrase "Made with Organic Ingredients" indicates the product contains 70 to 94 percent organic ingredients and a white tag indicates a conventional supermarket item.

Publix Super Markets Inc. leases 770 stores from shopping center property owners and owns 80-plus stores and open-air shopping centers. Following the success of the first GreenWise location in Palm Beach Gardens, Publix is rolling out the GreenWise concept in Boca Raton, Coral Springs, Tampa and Vero Beach.

H-E-B HAS GREEN BRAGGING RIGHTS

For more than 100 years, the H.E. Butt Grocery Company (now simply known as H-E-B) has been trying to make the right decisions to prevail as the dominant grocer, serving millions of customers in more than 150 communities throughout Texas and Mexico.

The innovative food retailer, known for its fresh food, quality products, convenient services and a commitment to environmental responsibility and sustainability, knew that such a market position could only be preserved through proven leadership in energy and environmental design of its store buildings.

H-E-B had one tough choice to make in developing its experimental green store #28 in Austin, Texas: go with LEED or go with local. It chose the latter. On May 9, 2006, the Austin #28 store, located in the Escarpment Village Shopping Center on West Slaughter Lane, was awarded the 4-Star Green Building Rating from Austin Energy, and with that came the local notoriety for being green that H-E-B was seeking.

PHOTOS: AUSTIN ENERGY GREEN BUILDING CASE STUDY

Green sustainable practices are paramount in the food business. The 93,000-square-foot (8,640 sq m) H-E-B grocery and drugstore is the crown jewel of the 60-acre site and is surrounded by environmental wonders, including a coffee shop with an 8,000-square-foot (740 sq m) green roof with solar cells, visible to those driving by. In fact, the site is covered by environmental contracts between the City of Austin and the developer to maintain the area bordering the Barton Springs Edwards Aquifer Recharge Zone as natural as possible.

Above: This interior view shows posters being used by H-E-B to inform customers about H-E-B's strategy to go green. Below: Exterior of H-E-B sustainable store at the Escarpment Village Shopping Center in Austin, Texas.

The task for preserving the natural environment that surrounds the area fell to Sheila Morales, an architect by trade and a LEED-accredited professional working directly for H-E-B's in-house planning and design team. Morales took the Austin Energy Green Building Rating questionnaire with the Microsoft Excel calculators and carefully analyzed each area of sustainability to determine what would be appropriate for H-E-B and the Barton Springs Edwards Aquifer Zone. With Morales's conclusions, her team understood that green goals were required to be incorporated into the project from the outset.

Two important elements involved the value in rating points assigned by the Austin Energy committee and defining possible rebates from the utility company. Austin Energy rebated over US$55,000 for high efficiencies achieved for the installation of the HVAC system, for the use of reflective roofing, and for efficient lighting.

Morales used in-house building commissioning to assure that all building systems were properly designed, installed and functioning per the design intent. Basic building commissioning is typically a mandatory requirement for Austin Energy's GreenChoice, LEED and other similar green building certification systems involving commercial buildings.

In new construction and renovation projects, commissioning should be considered a prerequisite incorporated into the construction documents and include:

- Engaging a commissioning team independent from the party responsible for construction
- Reviewing design intent and design documentation
- Developing and carrying out the commissioning process
- Verifying documentation and installation, functional performance, training, operation and maintenance
- Completing a commissioning report
- Take follow-up actions to bring any deficiencies up to design standards

With a positive commissioning report in place, Morales submitted the results to Austin Energy. H-E-B's submission package reveals innovation in green design and practices that merit Store #28 being singled out in a case study. These include:

- Minimal site disturbance to 40 feet beyond building perimeter
- Stormwater management plan addressed both rate and quality of stormwater runoff from the site
- Stormwater collected, filtered and reintroduced to the aquifer
- About one-third of impervious cover on the H-E-B site is shaded
- Native and adapted plants combined with high-efficiency irrigation controllers reduce water consumption
- Low-flow fixtures including aerated faucets and target spray valves
- H-E-B has become the fourth-largest subscriber of Austin Energy's Green-Choice program
- Energy performance 45 percent better than if built only to code
- High-efficiency HVAC system

- Lighting design calculated at 61 percent more efficient than code
- Sensors regulate artificial lights as daylighting from skylights, and clerestory windows shed natural light
- About 58 percent of the materials used to construct the building were manufactured in Texas, and 66 percent were manufactured within 500 miles of the site
- Approximately 32 percent of building materials were previously recycled content
- Almost 80 percent of construction waste (127 tons [115 metric tons]) diverted from landfills
- No·added urea-formaldehyde in composite wood or insulation materials
- Low-VOC adhesives, sealants and flooring materials
- CO_2 monitoring inside building
- Installed a 92 percent reflective single-ply roofing, which exceeded Energy Star roof requirements
- Waste heat reclaimed from the refrigeration compressor is transferred to heat water, which offsets water heating fuel requirements by 65 to 75 percent
- No HCFCs or CFCs used in the HVAC and refrigeration equipment
- Sanitation chemicals automatically measured and dispensed to ensure safety
- An energy management system continuously controls and monitors refrigeration, HVAC and lighting systems
- In-store education program teaches employees and customers about H-E-B's environmental strategies
- H-E-B donates perishable products to the Capitol Area Food Bank two to three times a week

According to the rating submission, H-E-B paid about 18 percent above typical store premiums for architectural and engineering (A/E) fees. However, the green building cost premium was less than 1 percent above what would have typically been paid for a similar size store.

The submission package explains that all the extra costs were recovered within the first 18 months from rebates, building commissioning savings, GreenChoice power savings and electric use savings.

H-E-B now has an extensive sustainability upgrade that it is rolling out to all stores in the chain.

SAFEWAY STEADFAST ON GREEN

When Safeway closed an old store in downtown Portland, Oregon, and opened a 47,000-square-foot (4,550 sq m) store on October 8, 2003, the U.S.-based retailer crossed into sustainable territory.

The new store building is part of a mixed-use project that has apartments located above it and an underground, two-level parking garage, known as the Museum Place development—a sustainable building that LEED certified for its environmentally responsible design and construction.

The store achieved a 17 percent reduction in energy use with innovations of that time that included daylight harvesting, high-tech monitors for refrigeration cases and a heat recovery system that uses the heat generated by the electrical and refrigeration equipment to warm the building.

While many grocery stores back their merchandise display cases against the sides of the walls, limiting the amount of window space, the Museum Place Safeway has 300 linear feet (91m) of windows on three sides to allow natural lighting into the store, lessening the need to use artificial lighting.

Safeway's Nancy Harp helped design the Museum Place Safeway store with GBD Architects of Portland and strived to earn LEED points for several tactics that were employed. Since then, Safeway Inc. has placed its sustainable program on a fast track and is now among the most progressive companies with a retail green agenda. Safeway set an internal policy, the Greenhouse Gas Reduction Initiative, which it designed to manage the chain's carbon footprint, address climate change and reduce air pollution.

Safeway adopted its formal program in 2006 to comply with California's AB-32 legislation and then discovered all the benefits a comprehensive green program can bring. From the outset, Safeway joined the Chicago Climate Exchange (CCX) and the California Climate Action Registry (CCAR), and worked closely with the U.S. EPA to reduce its carbon footprint.

The retailer also concentrated on training its employees with consistent, ongoing, continuously updated employee communication and education programs regarding GHG emissions, environmental stewardship and the company's efforts to reduce its carbon footprint.

Safeway titled their efforts the Power to Save employee education initiative, which consists of 10 energy-saving tips for store employees.

To reinforce its commitment, management plays energy-saving strategies via video in a continuous loop in employee breakrooms and supports the communication with newsletters.

The company reduced energy consumption by opening stores that are more efficient than the typical, older Safeway stores and began using new technology, such as no-heat freezer doors, to reduce electricity use. In September 2007, Safeway installed solar panels at its 55,000-square-foot (5,100 sq m) retail facility in Dublin,

California, during a renovation project to supplement an efficient wind-powered energy installation that the store already used.

Now the fourth-largest retail purchaser of renewable power, Safeway Inc. is powering its first 23 California stores with solar energy. Solar equipment installed at locations through 2008 will produce approximately 7,500-megawatt-hours of electricity per year, which is enough to generate one-fifth of the average power usage for those stores and almost half of the power that those stores require for peak-hour operation.

Safeway's initial 23-store solar program rollout is only the beginning of Safeway's pilot program, which will prevent 10.4 million pounds (4,700 metric tons) of carbon dioxide from being emitted into the atmosphere. This amount is equal to removing 1,000 cars from the road annually or planting 4,000 acres of evergreen trees. As Safeway becomes more experienced with solar power, it will address its remaining stores and augment the stores' electricity requirements with more renewable power.

Safeway has been using environmentally friendly wind energy from wind turbine generators since 2005. The retailer ranks among the largest retail purchasers of wind energy, buying enough wind energy chainwide to power all of its 300 fuel stations and more than 50 stores.

In the mid-2000s, Safeway purchased a minimum 87,000 megawatts of wind energy annually and powers all of its fuel-filling stations entirely by renewable wind energy. Wind power is sourced from various wind power harnessing plants across the United States, including the San Gorgonio Pass near Palm Springs, California; the Montezuma Hills, Rio Vista area of California; a site near Lamar and Springfield, Colorado; the Edgeley/Kulm project in North Dakota; one site near Kennewick, Washington; Waymart, Pennsylvania; and Custer County, Oklahoma.

The retailer plans to purchase 87 million KWs of renewable wind energy in 2008. Its annual purchase prevents 55,000 tons (49,895 metric tons) of carbon dioxide emissions, roughly equivalent to planting 45,000 acres of trees to absorb that amount of carbon dioxide.

In the transport area, Safeway converted its distribution fleets in California and Arizona to biodiesel. The company now uses 550 trucks in California and 79 in Arizona that operate on B20 biodiesel, a blend of 20 percent biodiesel (made from 100 percent virgin soybean oil) and 80 percent petroleum diesel. B20 biodiesel reduces sulfur, carbon monoxide, hydrocarbon and particulate emissions.

The retail chain estimated that this program saved more than US$17.8 million in 2006 due to technology and conservation measures such as:

- Adopting a five-minute idle policy that keeps drivers from running trucks unnecessarily during loading and unloading

- Using automatic systems to keep tires inflated at levels that maximize efficiency

- Switching to large-capacity trailers to limit the number of trips to each store
- Using tractors with an aerodynamic profile
- Running route optimization software to determine the most efficient delivery route
- Having drivers shift gears more effectively to maximize engine performance

Based on the success of this initial test, in 2008 Safeway changed the remainder of its fleet of more than 1,000 trucks in the United States to run on a cleaner-burning blend of traditional diesel and biodiesel fuel, derived from vegetable oils or animal fat instead of petroleum. Safeway estimated that the switch from conventional fuel to green fuel would help reduce its annual carbon dioxide emissions by 37,500 tons (34,019 metric tons). This is equal to removing 7,500 cars from the roads per year.

Safeway has long been a leader in recycling at its stores and distribution centers, and in 2006, the retail grocery chain recycled more than one-half million tons (453,592 metric tons) of cardboard, plastics and compostable material.

If all the waste that Safeway diverted from landfills in 2006 by recycling responsibly were compacted as dense as soil over a football field, the stack would reach 190 feet (57.9 meters) high and cover roughly 385,000 cubic yards (294,354 cubic meters). This program constitutes smart recycling because it reduces the cost of waste hauling and disposal as well as complies with environmentally sustainable practices.

In California, each Safeway store diverts more than 85 percent of its total solid waste from landfill disposal, which is well above the state-mandated goal of 50 percent.

Safeway's well-managed and documented recycling program consists of:

- 316,041 tons (286,700 metric tons) of corrugated cardboard collected and baled for sale to cardboard brokers for recycling into other fiber products
- 8,920 tons (8,100 metric tons) of plastics (excluding beverage bottles returned for deposit under state recycling programs) collected and baled for sale to brokers for recycling into mixed plastic products such as parking lot bumpers and plastic lumber products
- 87,949 tons (79,800 metric tons) of compostable materials, such as produce trimmings, unsalable produce and bakery products, and waxed boxes sent to a composting site to turn into soil amendment
- 70,320 tons (63,800 metric tons) of food waste (such as bread, dairy products, cooking oil, fat and bone from store meat recycled into animal feed), supplements and biodiesel fuel
- 18,395 tons (16,700 metric tons) of miscellaneous materials including aluminum and other metals, paper, wood, batteries, oil, refrigerant and paper bags

TESCO'S FRESH & EASY GREEN IMAGE

Tesco plc, the U.K.'s top grocer, with more than 20 percent market share—operating 3,250 stores in 12 countries in Europe and Asia—is rolling out small grocery stores on the U.S. West Coast, stressing a few advantages over its competitors.

Compelling low pricing, running-in-and-out convenience, a focus on fresh and being environmentally oriented are among the attributes this global retailer has devised to capture customers in the United States to do their grocery shopping at its new Fresh & Easy Neighborhood Market concept.

Tesco intends to offer customers a faster, easier shopping experience while still providing fresh produce, meat, fish and a selection of fresh, prepared meals—hence the name Fresh & Easy.

These neighborhood markets are smaller than the typical supermarket, roughly between 10,000 and 14,000 square feet (930 and 1,300 sq m), with inventory consisting of about 3,500 SKUs, slightly less than half (45 percent) being fresh&easy private label brands.

Some retail real estate landlords are helping Tesco expand because they believe the concept is catching on with American consumers. "Tesco is truly on the cutting edge of operating grocery chains with fresh&easy private brands that feature no artificial colors or flavors, no added trans fats and only using preservatives when absolutely necessary," said Paul Loubet, Regency Centers vice president of investments.

Loubet made his complimentary comments when he announced the new 14,000-square-foot (1,300 sq m) Fresh & Easy store planned to open in 2009 at Jefferson Square, a shopping center that Regency is building to LEED Core and Shell standards in California's Coachella Valley at La Quinta.

Citing the first group of stores that it began opening in the last two months of 2007 in Arizona, California and Nevada, Tesco informed the U.S. public

Fresh & Easy Neighborhood Market, a new grocery chain rapidly expanding on the United States West Coast, has made it a priority to reduce its impact on the environment.

Neighborhood Market

that the new Fresh & Easy stores aim to reduce their impact on the environment. Among the key green features of the Fresh & Easy Neighborhood Market are:

- Installed a 500,000-square-foot (46,500 sq m) roof-mounted solar harvesting system on its Riverside, California, distribution center
- Along with Safeway Inc. and Target Corporation, Tesco is now a member of the California Climate Action Registry, California's only official voluntary registry for GHG emissions, set up to help companies and organizations with operations in California to establish GHG emissions baselines against which any future GHG emission reduction mandates may be applied. Visit: http://www.climateregistry.org
- Offers customer recycling and recycles or reuses all its display and shipping materials
- Reserved parking spaces at its stores for employees and customers with hybrid vehicles and bikes
- Uses LED lighting in freezer cases and exterior signs
- Installed night shades on refrigerated cases to keep cool air from escaping
- Installed secondary-loop systems on refrigerated cases to capture and reuse cool air
- Uses skylights to harvest daylighting in new stores by dimming artificial lights, as the skylights bring in more natural light
- Added extra insulation to save on energy for heating and cooling
- Does not sell tobacco products
- Purchased transport trucks that significantly reduce noise
- Does not use or sell Styrofoam and only sells energy-efficient lightbulbs in its stores—no incandescent bulbs are allowed
- Is now part of the LEED pilot volume certification program

The portfolio volume program is geared toward helping companies integrate the LEED green building rating system into multiple new and existing buildings. The USGBC is working with several participants in the pilot program to develop both appropriate submittal documentation for volume certification and the necessary quality control tools to help integrate LEED standards into the design, construction and operations practices of participating organizations.

Starbucks approached the USGBC in 2001 to seek volume certification of its prototype green store design, according to Jim Hanna, Starbucks' environmental affairs manager. The coffee retail chain has hoped that the portfolio program would streamline the documentation and certification process by recognizing standardized and consistently delivered performance throughout its portfolio of new or existing stores.

Fresh & Easy joined Stop & Shop, Giant Food, Starbucks, Bank of America and other retail chains to track environmental performance and seek volume certification of their retail buildings from the USGBC.

"Fresh & Easy has made it a priority to reduce its impact on the environment in every neighborhood in which we operate," said Simon Uwins, chief marketing officer of Fresh & Easy, making a commitment to the American public. "From solar panels to recycling, we're doing everything we can to reduce emissions, use energy efficiently and be environmentally responsible in all facilities and operations."

Fresh & Easy estimates its typical store uses about 30 percent less energy than a typical grocery store, or 940,000 pounds (426 metric tons) less carbon dioxide emissions per store per year. This is equivalent to taking 92 passenger vehicles off the road for one year. The company has also committed to build LEED-certified buildings, recycle or reuse all shipping and display materials, and use environmentally friendly semitrailer trucks to transport food.

Fresh & Easy trucks use less diesel fuel to power the trucks and to cool the products they transport. These trucks are equipped with such modern energy-efficient technologies as hybrid refrigeration, automatic refrigeration, electrical standby, and engine shutoff systems.

STOP & SHOP AT A GREEN STORE

Stop & Shop strives for its supermarkets, mostly located in the wintery U.S. Northeast, to use 40 percent less energy than other area supermarkets. The stores' energy-efficient attributes include daylight harvesting; T5 fluorescent lighting systems with dimmable ballasts and occupancy sensors controlled by state-of-the-art energy management systems; refrigeration systems with high-efficiency fan motors; high solar gain; low-energy glass coatings to block the heat, not the light, and white reflective reinforced thermoplastic polyolefin (TPO) roofing membrane. The TPO membrane reduces air-conditioning needs by about 96,000 BTUs for each store per year.

The environmentally friendly Stop & Shop Supermarket Company based in Quincy, Massachusetts, with 388 stores in Connecticut, Maine, Massachusetts, New Hampshire, New Jersey, New York and Rhode Island, opened its first EPA Energy Star certified store in Southbury, Connecticut, in 2005.

EPA assigns the Energy Star label to buildings that display superior energy efficiency, using about 35 percent less energy than average buildings. Stop & Shop, along with its sister company Giant, based in Landover, Maryland, has set a goal to achieve the Energy Star designation for its entire portfolio of stores.

The Southbury store has many energy-efficient attributes, which has reduced the electrical load by 28 percent compared to similar stores built before 2001. Among the features Stop & Shop implemented in the Southbury store are:

- Skylights over the sales floor that provide natural light during the day and allow for the highly efficient T5 fluorescent lighting system to be dimmed automatically by a state-of-the-art energy management system

- Store backrooms and office areas equipped with occupancy sensors to turn the lights off when unoccupied

- High-efficiency fan motors in the refrigeration systems with variable-speed compressors, low-energy glass doors and non-ozone-depleting refrigerant

- Heat reclaimed from the refrigeration system and utilized to heat the sales floor, the water used in the restrooms and for meal preparation

- Well-insulated roof with a white reflective surface to reduce the cooling capacity required to condition the store in the summer months and minimize the urban heat island (UHI) effect

Stop & Shop began rolling out low-energy stores with the 2001 opening of the Stop & Shop Superstore in Foxboro, Massachusetts. By the end of 2007, the company had opened 94 stores that include many of the concepts first tested in the Foxboro store, which has become the standard Stop & Shop store design.

Because of their energy-saving efforts, the Stop & Shop Supermarket Company and its sister company, Giant Food, were selected by the USGBC in November 2007 to participate in the portfolio program pilot for LEED volume certification for existing buildings.

On February 7, 2008, the sister chains achieved their goal when EPA announced that Stop & Shop and Giant Food were the only supermarket chains that EPA awarded the coveted 2007 Energy Star Leaders recognition. Featured is a Giant Food store in Hyattsville, Maryland.

PHOTO: R. E. MILIAN

"Our acceptance into this pilot recognizes Stop & Shop and Giant's strong environmental leadership and innovation, and our early commitment to and success in developing and operating green and energy efficient stores," said José Alvarez, president and chief executive officer for Stop & Shop and Giant Food, on November 6, 2007.

"We have many standardized environmentally responsible programs and systems in our stores, such as water conservation, recycling and solid waste management," said Jihad Rizkallah, vice president of design and engineering for Stop & Shop and Giant.

Stop & Shop stores recycle plastic shopping bags and shrink/pallet wrap. The retailer sends this material to a recycling vendor to make composite decking, also known as synthetic lumber.

Stop & Shop and Giant recycled more than 1,500 tons (1,360 metric tons) of plastics, more than 2,500 tons (2,270 metric tons) of expired perishables through various organics recycling programs and more than 100,000 tons (90,700 metric tons) of cardboard in 2006.

To top off its eco-friendly program, Stop & Shop even purchased Sterling Planet's Green-e certified renewable energy to match 100 percent of its electricity use at its Kennebunk, Maine, store, which opened on June 15, 2007. Sterling Planet supplied 2.7 million kilowatt hours of renewable energy to the company in 2008. The intent of this purchase was to avoid nearly four million pounds (1,814 metric tons) of carbon dioxide pollution in 2008, the test pilot year.

Stop & Shop's purchase is in the form of Renewable Energy Certificates (RECs)—also known as green certificates, green tags or tradable renewable certificates. RECs represent the environmental attributes of the power produced from wind, solar and other renewable energy projects. They are sold separately from commodity electricity companies. Customers can buy RECs whether or not they have access to green power, through their local utility or a competitive electricity supplier.

The Stop & Shop Supermarket Company and Giant Food combined employ more than 82,000 and operate 575 stores in the Northeast.

CIRCUIT CITY RECYCLES BATTERIES

Circuit City Stores Inc., a leading specialty retailer of consumer electronics with 627 big-box stores in the United States and more than 950 retail stores in Canada, is trying to get its customers to go green. Circuit City teamed up with the Rechargeable Battery Recycling Corporation (RBRC)—a nonprofit, public service organization dedicated to recycling used and no longer working rechargeable batteries and old cell phones—on a joint program that integrates RBRC's recycling program, Call2Recycle, with its vast network of store locations.

Circuit City is helping to recycle used rechargeable batteries commonly found in cordless electronic products such as cordless phones, laptop computers, PDAs, digital cameras and cell phones.

The program is part of the rechargeable power industry's commitment to conserve natural resources and to prevent cell phones and rechargeable batteries from entering the solid waste stream. RBRC recycles nickel-cadmium (Ni-Cd), nickel-metal hydride (Ni-MH), lithium-ion (Li-ion) and small sealed lead-acid (SSLA) batteries.

Rechargeable batteries, such as Ni-Cd or SSLA batteries, contain toxic heavy metals such as cadmium, mercury and lead, and it is against the law in the United States and other countries to dispose of them with normal waste.

These heavy metals present no threat to human health or the environment while the batteries are being used as intended. However, they can cause serious harm if they are discarded with ordinary household or workplace waste, according to the U.S. EPA.

Approximately 73 percent of municipal solid waste is either land filled (covered with soil) or incinerated. Neither of these methods is suited for the disposal of rechargeable batteries. In landfills, heavy metals from rechargeable batteries have the potential to leach slowly into the soil, groundwater and surface water.

A spokesperson for EPA said that these heavy metals could enter the air, if incinerated, through smokestack emissions, which would then concentrate in the ash produced by combustion. When the incinerator ash is discarded, the heavy metals in the ash can cause havoc to the environment.

The Circuit City/RBRC program makes recycling of rechargeable batteries and cell phones accessible and convenient for residents near the vast Circuit City network of stores in the United States. Consumers are now conveniently dropping off these used items in RBRC collection boxes located in all Circuit City stores.

To gain high profile and to convey the dangers in discarding these rechargeable batteries in household waste, RBRC spokesman Richard Karn is now appearing in public service ads. Karn is most recognized as the nice-guy handyman "Al Borland" from the American television sitcom *Home Improvement*.

PHOTO: R. E. MILIAN

PHOTO COURTESY OF RBRC

Top: Rechargeable Battery Recycling Corporation (RBRC) spokesperson Richard Karn showcases cell phones and batteries that customers can now recycle at Circuit City stores. Karn is most recognized as "Al" from the American television sitcom, *Home Improvement*. Circuit City's Call-2Recycle program at all U.S. stores in 158 markets, including this store in Paramus, New Jersey, has made it easy for customers to recycle used rechargeable batteries commonly found in cordless electronic products such as cordless phones, laptop computers, PDAs, digital cameras and cell phones.

BEST BUY LOWERS THERMOSTAT

Best Buy, headquartered in Richfield, Minnesota, sells consumer electronics, home office products, entertainment software, appliances and related services through more than 1,200 retail stores in the United States, Canada, China and Mexico.

Starting in 2008, Best Buy intends to build only eco-friendly stores. According to Brenda Mathison, Best Buy's director of environmental affairs, the company created a prototype design in conjunction with the USGBC that has a combination of energy-efficient lighting, rainwater recycling, recycled building materials, a high-efficiency HVAC system and use of daylighting to harvest natural daylight.

All of Best Buy's existing U.S. stores are already controlled by a central energy management system for lighting, heating and cooling equipment. These systems reduced Best Buy's annual electric use by approximately 85 million kilowatts in 2007, enough to power about 9,000 U.S. homes for one year.

Best Buy feels that a large portion of the energy used in its stores results from HVAC and that most customers and employees in the stores would not likely notice if the store temperature increased or decreased by one degree.

As a result, Best Buy is considering instituting a one-degree (higher in the summer, lower in the winter) change. Best Buy figures that a one-degree difference in its thermostats would save over 11 million-kilowatt hours of energy and close to US$1 million annually in energy costs for its U.S. stores alone.

Adjusting a thermostat by one degree is simple, but how do retailers plan their new stores' energy requirement for heating and cooling?

In order to plan energy for a new store, it is important to understand the cost of energy relative to the outside temperature. It is preferable to establish a degree day factor that would allow a retail company to determine energy requirements for its store building heating and, to a lesser extent, for building cooling.

PHOTOS: R. E. MILIAN

Top: This Best Buy store, built in the late 1990s, is unable to harvest daylight with skylights because it is in a ground-level location that is part of the enclosed, multilevel Pyramid Companies-owned Palisades Center in West Nyack, New York. Older, high bay energy-wasting metal halide, high-pressure sodium or mercury vapor lighting can be improved for energy consumed, color rendition and efficiency at big-box stores. Retailers can cut wattage by more than half and cut kilowatt hours by more than 75 percent in older stores by replacing the lighting system with high-performance metal halide (MH) or fluorescents, such as T8s and T5HO luminaires. Lower photo: In 2007, Best Buy opened a 34,000-square-foot store (3,150 sq m) in the Toronto Eaton Centre. The store is located in a mixed-use development in Toronto, Canada, employing many green features and was designed by Zeidler Partnership Architects and Queen's Quay Architects International. One unique energy-saving feature is green, renewable deep-lake cold water energy from Lake Ontario, used to cool the store through a deal its landlord, Cadillac Fairview Corporation, worked out with the utility company, Enwave.

The factor can be applied to all fuels, district heating and electric heating consumed to determine the straight-line relation between gas used and the extent to which the daily mean outside temperature falls below 65°F (18°C). The degree day relates to the mean average of the daily maximum and minimum outside temperatures, then subtracted from 65°F.

Lighting is another high-energy user for all retail applications. Best Buy also plans to retrofit its U.S. stores with ceramic metal halide lights dimmable by zone to reduce lighting costs by 20 percent.

In 2007, Best Buy Company Inc. filed a corporate social responsibility report in which it revealed many of its social responsibility initiatives, including green measures. The report follows the G3 guidelines provided by the Global Reporting Initiative (GRI).

One of the areas covered in the report was recycling. In 2007, Best Buy recycled 64,752 tons (58,700 metric tons) of cardboard, 1,492 tons (1,350 metric tons) of plastic, 27,270 tons (20,200 metric tons) of pallets, 5,025 tons (4,560 metric tons) of metal, 15,000 tons (13,600 metric tons) of consumer electronics and 27,500 tons (24,950 metric tons) of appliances.

Best Buy became a founding member of EPA's Plug-In to eCycling program. In 2006, the retailer joined other members, and they combined to recycle more than 17,000 tons (15,400 metric tons) of e-waste. The company rolled out a prepaid mail-in cell phone recycling program at more than 730 participating Best Buy stores across the United States. Additionally, Best Buy contributes US$1 to the Boys and Girls Clubs of America for each phone it receives.

Store employees at Best Buy have agreed to minimize waste. The TV Wrap, a reusable, padded wrap for flat-panel televisions, reduced the amount of packaging delivered to customers' homes by 80 percent in fiscal 2007. The boxes and foam used in packaging of the television are recycled through the stores.

RECREATIONAL EQUIPMENT HAS SILVER LINING

Many stores are following suit on sustainability, and the number of interested retailers is growing. For example, Recreational Equipment Inc. (REI), a national retail cooperative selling outdoor gear and clothing, received the LEED Silver rating in 2006 for its 29,335-square-foot (2,725 sq m), two-level store in the Soffer Organization's SouthSide Works in Pittsburgh, Pennsylvania.

LEED certification was not a first for this environmentally conscious retailer. This store's certification followed REI's LEED Gold certification for its Portland, Oregon, store, which had become the first retail store in the United States to receive the Gold designation in 2004.

According to Maury Zimring, environmental services consultant and former LEED program coordinator for the USGBC, the savings from the sustainable practices that REI incorporated into the LEED Silver-rated Pittsburgh SouthSide Works location were:

- Water use reduction by 32.4 percent

- Energy Star equipment employed for equipment and appliances for 91 percent by rated power

- 100 percent of the electricity comes from renewable sources

- 92.53 percent of construction, demolition and packaging debris was diverted to uses other than a landfill

- Recycled content comprised 16.1 percent of the total value of the materials

- Minimum daylight factor of two percent in 94.34 percent of all spaces within the store

STARBUCKS' PROTOTYPE STORE DESIGN

In 2005, Starbucks opened its first green store in Hillsboro, Oregon, and the company is hoping to roll out a green store design for its feverish expansion that includes low-environmental-impact building materials and practices, and energy- and water-efficient equipment.

The Hillsboro store received the LEED Gold rating in commercial interiors. Among the sustainable features are extensive use of daylighting; reduced-flow water fixtures; energy-efficient appliances, lighting and fixtures; abundant use of recycled and renewable building materials; and paints and flooring that are low in toxic emissions. For example, Starbucks installed Eco-Terr flooring tiles made from 70 percent postconsumer recycled content and 10 percent postindustrial recycled content.

Starbucks operates 6,566 stores and franchises 3,729 stores in the United States, and sustainability has now become a company-wide agenda, as green measures are being implemented at all of its locations worldwide. Outside the United States, the coffee retailer operates in 41 countries with 1,613 company-operated stores, and 2,488 joint venture and licensed stores.

Starbucks developed an environmental footprint analysis that assessed solid waste generation, recycling and the stores' consumption of energy and water. It is also using a system comparable to the LEED green building design to test a number of environmental performance improvement initiatives at many of its store locations. Reducing GHG emissions and conserving energy are a top priority.

Starbucks is already at the number 10 spot on the U.S. EPA National Top 25 List for stores purchasing green power. It purchased 20 percent of its total energy (185 million kilowatt-hours) from 3 Degrees, a supplier of wind-generated electricity.

The company also promotes sustainability to its customers in a number of ways, including inviting customers to visit the stores and pick up free coffee grounds to use as an element of composting in their homes. In 2007, Starbucks teamed up with Global Green USA on the Planet Green Game, an interactive, educational online

game that educates participants about global warming and suggests how people can minimize their carbon footprints.

The Starbucks Coffee Company's affinity for green buildings goes beyond its store locations. The Starbucks Center, the world headquarters for Starbucks in Seattle, Washington, is now the largest and oldest building in the United States (constructed in 1912) to earn the LEED Gold certification for existing buildings, according to Seattle developer Nitze-Stagen & Company.

Sustainable building features at the Center include renewable energy for about 31 percent of the property's electricity, efficient lighting, waterless urinals and recycling. Starbucks encourages employees to use alternative transportation, offering storage and changing rooms for bicyclists, and convenient parking for employees who use flex fuel cars and other alternative energy vehicles.

Starbucks Center is a mixed-use property consisting of 300,000 square feet (27,900 sq m) of retail plus office, warehouse and industrial space, totaling 2.1 million square feet (195,000 sq m) on 17 acres of urban land. Nitze-Stagen is the managing agent.

THE PANTRY AND UNIVERSITY OF FLORIDA TEAM UP

In 2006, The Pantry Inc., an independently operated convenience store chain in the southeastern United States, opened the first convenience store in Gainesville, Florida, to have achieved the LEED certification. The store's design was developed in conjunction with academics from the nearby University of Florida.

The 5,150-square-foot (480 sq m) store has five Kangaroo-brand gasoline dispensers and two diesel fuel lanes. It also features a charging station to "pump" energy for electrical vehicles.

GIANT EAGLE'S GREEN SUPERMARKET

Pittsburgh, Pennsylvania-based Giant Eagle supermarket chain—achieving annual sales of US$5.5 billion—also has had a sustainability strategy for several years. The Giant Eagle store (not to be confused with Royal Ahold's Giant Food) in Zaremba's Brunswick Town Center near Cleveland, Ohio, achieved the LEED certification in 2004.

Its numerous initiatives included rooftop HVAC units that use 417A refrigerant, a heat-reflecting roof, filtration of stormwater into an adjacent marshland, display cabinets made of recycled strawboard and recycled gypsum wallboard.

The 72,256-square-foot (6,713 sq m) Giant Eagle supermarket in Zaremba's Brunswick Town Center near Cleveland, Ohio, achieved the LEED certification in 2004. The green store design includes the store's white thermoplastic-polyolefin-membrane roof, which prevents heat island effect, and rooftop HVAC units that use 417A refrigerant and are equipped with modulating outside air dampers that

PHOTO COURTESY OF MCG ARCHITECTURE

The Giant Eagle store in Zaremba's Brunswick Town Center near Cleveland, Ohio, achieved the LEED certification in 2004.

automatically adjust between air-conditioning and outside air ventilation. Carbon dioxide sensors monitor the number of occupants in the store and send a signal to the dampers to regulate airflow. The project architect was MCG Architecture.

THE KROGER COMPANY CONSUMES LESS

Kroger, like other supermarket chains today, is striving to be greener, and it is making significant progress to reduce energy consumption of its stores, warehouses and truck fleet.

Many of its stores have undergone renovations to reduce their energy usage. Kroger is in the process of replacing lighting at most of its stores with energy-efficient lamps. Whenever possible, Kroger also plans to take advantage of daylight-harvesting systems, which adjust the amount of artificial lighting to compensate for natural light entering from skylights. Another major move is the upgrade of the stores' refrigerated cases, using "smart motors," which are more efficient.

Since 2000, Kroger has reduced energy consumption by over 20 percent, which is about 1.3 billion kilowatt-hours, according to Kroger disclosures.

CHIPOTLE'S SUSTAINABLE FOOD WITH INTEGRITY

Chipotle Mexican Grill Inc., the fast-food, burrito restaurant chain that wants people to think of its more than 670 restaurants as providers of food with integrity, is trying to influence public opinion with outdoor and other forms of advertising touting sustainable food.

In Phoenix, Arizona, an outdoor billboard larger than the nearby restaurant's storefront informs potential customers that the meat Chipotle serves is raised with

care, not chemicals. Chipotle is a leading restaurant provider of naturally raised meat—beef, pork and chicken—from naturally, humanely bred animals fed a vegetarian diet and not given antibiotics, added hormones or growth stimulants.

"We are changing the way the world thinks about and eats fast food," said Steve Ells, founder, chairman and CEO of Chipotle. Ells says the chain's Food With Integrity slogan is helping to build awareness and increase demand for sustainably raised foods among customers: "We are educating our customers about the tastes and benefits of eating fresh, naturally raised foods."

When Chipotle opens a new restaurant in Gurnee Mills, located midway between Chicago, Illinois, and Milwaukee, Wisconsin, it plans to erect a 60-foot (18.3 m) wind turbine that will let people know from a mile away that this unit of the popular chain is greener than anyone ever imagined. The six-kilowatt wind turbine to be built on an outlot parcel across from the outlet mall near Chipotle will help power the restaurant.

In Phoenix, Arizona, an outdoor billboard larger than the nearby restaurant's storefront informs potential customers about the merits of sustainable food. In top left photo, customers wait in line, on a typical Friday afternoon in January 2008, at Chipotle on East Thomas Road in Phoenix, to purchase beef, pork or chicken made from naturally, humanely raised animals that are fed a vegetarian diet free of antibiotics and hormones.

PHOTOS: R. E. MILIAN

The architect, Jon P. Buerg, AIA, LEED AP, of Wilkus Architects in Eden Prairie, Minnesota, explained the virtues of the restaurant's turbine to the Village of Gurnee planners when he requested a zoning variance in August 2007. He said Chipotle is committed to the environment and plans to pursue LEED certification for the restaurant building.

Chipotle is working to make lighting and ventilation systems energy efficient, as well as incorporating other environmentally friendly initiatives such as harvesting rainwater for irrigation, according to the minutes from the hearing.

Buerg said that restaurants in general are not energy efficient, and he feels that a wind turbine is a good aesthetic fit for the location and will help the restaurant generate its own clean, renewable electricity.

Buerg expects the giant turbine to generate adequate electricity to meet the restaurant's needs, and Chipotle will sell any power it does not use to Commonwealth Edison (ComEd), the electric utility company serving Northern Illinois.

Sustainability is not new for the restaurant chain named for the dried, mesquite-smoked jalapeno pepper. Chipotle typically incorporates regionally sourced building materials into their restaurant design and uses interior finishes made from recycled material such as stainless steel, galvanized steel and corrugated metal.

PHOTO: AUSTIN ENERGY GREEN BUILDING CASE STUDY

When Chipotle wanted to make its restaurants more sustainable, it turned to Austin Energy to learn about green building practices, which the fast-food chain implemented in the above sustainable site in downtown Austin, Texas. Building green is just one extension of the philosophy of Chipotle's founder and CEO, Steve Ells, put forward in a program he calls "Food With Integrity." Chipotle features foods that are nutritious, in season, unprocessed, family farmed, sustainable, naturally raised, hormone free, organic and delicious.

Each restaurant is somewhat different, but all seem to convey a level of quality from the architectural features to the tasty but spicy food trimmings. In Austin, Texas, Chipotle redeveloped a ground-level corner location in the downtown historic Eugene Bremond building at 801 Congress Avenue. There, Chipotle implemented a construction waste management program that reused 100 cubic yards (76.5 cubic meters) of material, diverting it from ending up at a landfill.

Glavan Fehér Architects, working with Scott L. Shippey, director of design for Chipotle Mexican Grill, specified restoring the original floor tile and incorporated some of the classic building's features.

Chipotle also added various energy-saving techniques such as using motion sensors in the restrooms and inside the walk-in cooler and new high-efficiency HVAC and water heating equipment—both exceeding energy code requirements by 15 percent and 20 percent, respectively.

Chipotle chose to pursue a local green building rating for the sustainable Austin location. Upon completion of the Congress Avenue restaurant in 2004,

Chipotle became the first restaurant in Austin to earn the 4-Star Green Building rating from Austin Energy's Green Building Program (see Chapter 8). For example, Chipotle used LED lighting on exterior signage, employed daylighting techniques to reduce interior artificial lights and brightened up the interior.

The following sustainable features helped Chipotle's Austin restaurant earn the prestigious rating, according to the project submission, which now forms a notable case study for others to learn about green building design:

- Redeveloped existing urban commercial location
- Installed recirculation water system with a tankless water heater, which reduces the amount of time that it takes to heat the water from about two minutes to 10 seconds
- Highly efficient HVAC system
- Participates in Austin Energy's GreenChoice Program
- Maintains the building cooler by using awnings
- Reduced waste by separating salvageable materials during demolition and re-using exterior windows, storefront and doors
- Recycled during construction to divert an estimated 100 cubic yards (76.5 cubic meters) from landfills
- Restored original tile floor instead of replacing it
- Used low-maintenance finishes including stainless steel, galvanized steel and corrugated metal, which are durable, have recycled content and have a long life cycle
- Used dedicated in-store recycling area
- Used nontoxic cleaning supplies
- Reduce noise pollution with insulated air conditioning
- Maintained positive pressure indoors at 200 cubic feet (5.7 cubic meters) per minute (cfm) to reduce infiltration
- Water-based sealant used to reduce VOCs
- All finishes (except wall paint) prepared off-site to lessen VOC levels and minimize airborne VOC particles after the materials were installed in the restaurant

With the Congress Avenue restaurant complete and operating successfully, Chipotle executives are eyeing a national certification that makes allowances for retail use rather than the standard commercial real estate criteria that does not recognize the energy demands for bright lighting, cooking and refrigeration equipment as well as water consumption traditionally associated with retail and restaurant uses. Shippey joined Ben Packard of Starbucks and David Luick of Target Corporation on the

Retail Committee of the USGBC to help come up with a LEED system that better addresses a retailer's green building criteria.

Chipotle has already entered one project (1401 Wynkoop Street in Denver, Colorado) in the LEED for Retail pilot program seeking LEED certification.

As restaurants such as Chipotle become creative in green building design, there is no limit as to how the green message will be delivered next. For Chipotle, it is the refillable gift card—one that does not end up in a landfill when the card's value reaches zero. Unlike petroleum-based plastic, the Chipotle gift card is made of corn plastic, a natural material that is fully biodegradable.

Denver, Colorado–based Chipotle operates urban storefronts, shopping center end caps, pads and freestanding buildings. Restaurants, ranging between 1,000 and 2,800 square feet (93 and 260 sq m), typically have patio seating and serve alcoholic beverages.

GOLDEN ARCHES TURNING GREEN

In Savannah, Georgia, the freestanding Abercorn Common McDonald's restaurant, which opened in 2005, is among the 70 percent of fast-food behemoth McDonald's 30,000 restaurants worldwide that are all owned and operated by franchisees such as Gary Dodd.

Dodd's fast-food restaurant boasts the familiar golden arches and has similar friendly counter and seating as other McDonald's restaurants. Dodd's employees wear the golden arches logo aprons as they serve packaged Big Macs, cheeseburgers, fries, McNuggets, chicken nuggets and basic salads to customers waiting in line, much the same as in other typical McDonald's. However, Dodd's McDonald's stands out from the rest in efficiency and its carbon footprint.

Dodd worked with Melaver Inc., the developer of the LEED-certified Abercorn Common, and Mooresville, North Carolina–based Adams + Associates Architecture to blend the franchisor's prototypical building specifications with the green building standards that the developer applied to the rest of the community center.

The persistent design-build approach earned the Abercorn Common McDonald's the Gold LEED Core and Shell designation in 2006. The McDonald's restaurant site—converted into a low carbon footprint building made of recycled and local materials—became the fast-food giant's first LEED-sustainable restaurant in the world. The Oak Brook, Illinois–based chain serves 52 million customers in more than 118 countries every day.

David Anderson of Adams + Associates Architecture designed the sustainable McDonald's interior to achieve 75 percent daylight from 1,008 square feet (94 sq m) of windows and clerestory glass.

The restaurant's solar orientation maximized north light entering into the restaurant and minimized radiant heat that would have occurred to a greater extent had the building been situated differently on the site. This strategy helps McDonald's save electricity for lighting, and with other energy-saving measures employed at this

location—such as circulating fresh air by demand control ventilation—this green building is between 20 and 30 percent more energy efficient than the typical McDonald's unit of comparable size.

Bike racks and preferred parking for hybrid vehicles encourage trips that do not rely on gas-guzzling motor vehicles. The restaurant's outlot also has pervious surface parking pavement to help prevent stormwater runoff.

Stormwater can collect debris, chemicals, dirt and other pollutants as it flows into a storm sewer system or directly into a lake, stream, river or wetland. Contaminated water entering a storm sewer system is eventually discharged untreated into water bodies used for drinking water. Impervious surfaces such as driveways, sidewalks and paved asphalt streets prevent stormwater runoff from naturally soaking into the ground.

The restaurant famous for its golden arches sports a reflective white roof that helps to keep the building cooler in the summer and reduce the urban heat island (UHI) effect.

To ensure LEED certification from the outset of construction, Anderson specified numerous local and regional building materials such as concrete, steel and gypsum board to construct the McDonald's. This helped to reduce fuel costs to transport material to the site had it originated many miles away.

Anderson said that 85 percent of the construction material he specified for the restaurant had been previously recycled, which avoided overtaxing landfills, and at least half the wood the contractors used to build the restaurant came from sustainably managed forests.

The multinational chain has a green agenda that goes beyond Savannah. Bob Langert, McDonald's vice president of corporate and social responsibility, said that the restaurant chain emphasizes recycling through the packaging they offer at all the restaurants.

Cups, bags, napkins and wrapping paper for the food it prepares are made from 45 to 100 percent recycled material. McDonald's even changed the packaging of its famous Big Mac, removing a mere one-quarter inch of the back flap, thereby saving three million pounds of packaging a year, according to Langert. McDonald's also recycles all of the boxes used to ship food and material to the restaurants as well as recycling the oil they use for frying and cooking.

McDonald's uses the Global Reporting Initiative (GRI) Draft G3 guidelines for its CSR reporting. In those reports, the company revealed its practices to preserve the environment right down to the heart of the food supply chain.

Beef production has various negative effects on natural resources. For example, raising cattle requires large quantities of water, and animal waste from feedlots washes nitrogen and impurities into rivers and streams during heavy rainstorms. This runoff can also transport antibiotics and hormones to water streams.

Another negative effect of beef product is the methane greenhouse gas emitted from animal waste, which can contribute to climate change.

McDonald's is pressing suppliers to create lagoons to collect runoff from feedlots and to use the wastewater to fertilize agricultural crops. Some of the suppliers'

feedlots are beginning to cover the lagoons to trap methane gas emissions. One of McDonald's slaughterhouses even installed a methane-fueled generator to convert animal waste into electricity and to fuel other equipment.

Working with Conservation International, the fast-food chain also established sustainability guidelines for fisheries worldwide and has implemented a number of tactics to help preserve the environment.

Among McDonald's ongoing sustainability goals are promoting water efficiency, eliminating the release of waste into water, limiting the emission of harmful by-products into the atmosphere, using ecologically sustainable renewable resources, minimizing waste, maximizing recycling, ensuring proper handling and disposal of solid waste, maintaining soil health and conserving energy.

KOHL'S TAPS SOLAR POWER

Kohl's Department Stores is in the process of converting 64 of 80 stores in California (and three in Wisconsin) to partly using solar power. Kohl's operates 929 stores in 47 states and Kohl's is seeking approvals to convert stores to solar power in Arizona, Colorado, Connecticut, New Jersey and Oregon.

Kohl's drive for converting to green power raised its rankings on the EPA National Top 25 List of all companies and on the Top 10 Retail List of the largest green power purchasers. In 2007, Kohl's became one of 17 organizations in the United States to be recognized by EPA with the Green Power Leadership Award for being the number two retail purchaser of renewable energy.

In 2006, Kohl's purchased more than 201 million kWh of green power, which is electricity generated from renewable resources such as solar, wind, geothermal, biogas, biomass and low-impact hydro. Green power made up 20 percent of Kohl's total energy purchase.

Beltsville, Maryland–based SunEdison will install and regulate the solar power systems at Kohl's and resend the surplus electricity to the power grid for distribution to other customers. Kohl's did not incur costs for the installation.

Kohl's (as well as Safeway, Best Buy and Macy's) selected California for the solar experiment because the state has plenty of sunshine and a generous incentive program to encourage solar energy use. SunEdison has also worked with Wal-Mart, Staples, Whole Foods and Macy's.

In the first year of operation, the solar panels installed on the roofs of the Kohl's stores are expected to generate enough clean energy to offset more than 28 million pounds (12,700 metric tons) of carbon dioxide.

Based on the U.S. average emissions rates, EPA estimates that Kohl's green power purchase is equivalent to avoiding the CO_2 emissions of about 23,000 automobiles each year, or is the amount of electricity capable of supplying power to more than 12,000 average American homes annually.

Sustainability is catching on. For Kohl's it is no different. On the heels of its solar rollout and EPA recognition, Kohl's wants to extend its environmental stewardship

by pursuing sustainable building certification on more than 80 new store locations opening in 2008 and 2009.

Kohl's will measure its sustainable building practices in accordance with the LEED Green Building Rating System. The retailer will pursue the certification in as many as 28 U.S. states beginning with store openings in autumn 2008 and continue through 2009.

"Kohl's is committed to being environmentally responsible, which was first evidenced through our extensive solar rollout and green power purchases and is now being further extended by the use of green construction methods and LEED certification," said Ken Bonning, executive vice president of logistics for Kohl's.

Kohl's will add to the new stores such practices as low-flow toilets, high-efficiency heating and cooling systems, and recycled and locally sourced building materials. The new stores will include sophisticated energy management systems, which have centralized control systems and occupancy sensor lighting for stockrooms, breakrooms and management offices.

All new roof installations will be Energy Star rated. Additional features include irrigation controls, localized water heaters, and high-efficiency lighting, heating and cooling as well as ongoing recycling of cardboard boxes, hangers and packaging at all stores and distribution centers.

In 2006, Kohl's recycled more than 100,000 tons (90,700 metric tons) of cardboard, plastic and packaging, 89,000 pounds (40 metric tons) of cans, glass and aluminum, and 180 million hangers.

SUN POWER: NO RAIN IN MACY'S PARADE

Macy's had a solar power system installed in its Westminster, California, store and has begun to expand the program to 28 California stores. Half of the stores are in Southern California.

SunPower Corporation designed the renewable energy system. The Silicone Valley–based manufacturer will be installing photovoltaic equipment at other Macy's stores to augment the power Macy's purchases from local utility companies. SunPower is a manufacturer of high-efficiency solar cells, solar panels and solar systems.

Macy's will buy the solar power systems from SunPower for 11 stores, and purchase just the solar-generated electricity for the remaining 17 stores under an innovative agreement called "SunPower Access."

At the end of the 10-year solar services agreement, the 800-plus department store chain's options include renewing the agreement as is, transferring the equipment to new store locations or buying the systems.

Julie Blunden, SunPower's vice president of public policy, said that SunPower could have entered into an agreement with Macy's that covered more stores and had a longer timetable if it were not for the federal tax credit expiring in 2008.

"Because the current tax credit only goes through the end of this year, some customers are only contracting for projects that can be completed by the end of the

Above are two Macy's stores in sunny climates. At left is the Macy's furniture store at Macerich's Scottsdale Fashion Square (Scottsdale, Arizona), and at right is Macy's at Taubman Centers' Mall at Wellington Green (Wellington, Florida). Neither of these stores generates solar power, unlike Macy's 28 stores in California. This example demonstrates that retailers are willing to install renewable energy systems, given adequate assistance from government. In January 2006, the California Public Utilities Commission adopted the California Solar Initiative to offer more than US$3 billion in incentives for solar energy projects, and many retailers responded to the call. Adding a federal incentive for renewable energy installation and utility companies' incentives to the state's inducement, Macy's easily justified moving into the solar arena. Arizona and Florida fell behind the race to become less dependent on fossil fuels. Those states have financial incentives for renewable energy installations in commercial buildings but do not match those of California.

year," said Blunden in January 2008. "California incentives played a big part in the stores that received solar in 2007 by allowing the investment to meet our financial hurdles," said Gary J. Nay, vice president, real estate for Macy's Inc.

As more combined incentives become available for retailers from the federal government, state government and utility companies, Macy's and other leading retailers will likely step up their solar initiatives outside of California. Meanwhile, California—to a great extent, and Hawaii and New Jersey to a lesser extent—is where the action is as far as solar power.

"We are working on plans to include generating solar power for a new store to open in Elk Grove, California in 2009," Nay said. "We are investigating the possibility of solar at City North opening in Phoenix in 2009 but no others in Arizona."

When all of the initial equipment is installed and operational, Macy's program will have a total of 8.9 megawatts of solar power at its California stores. The 294-kilowatt system at the Westminster Macy's store generates about 586,000 kilowatt-hours of solar electricity per year, which could offset more than 11 million pounds (five metric tons) of carbon dioxide emissions over the 30-year lifetime of the system. This GHG reduction amounts to planting about 53 acres of trees or removing 37 cars from the roads per year.

The energy management program for Macy's in California also combines solar power with other energy efficiencies. According to Tom Cole, vice chair for Macy's Inc., energy efficiency upgrades—including high-efficiency lighting, new HVAC systems and energy management systems—will reduce consumption at the California pilot stores from utility companies by about 40 percent, which almost doubles the impact of the solar power.

Macy's anticipates the offset from the solar and other energy savings to be in the range of 24 million kilowatt hours of energy consumption annually. This would

reduce Macy's carbon footprint by more than 195 million pounds (88,450 metric tons) of CO_2 emissions over the anticipated life cycle of the systems. This amount equates to removing 1,144 cars per year from the streets of California.

In addition to solar power, Macy's has a range of sustainable practices for associates to follow. Macy's hired outside experts to conduct annual environmental audits to ensure that its facilities comply with local, state and federal environmental laws. Several measures that Macy's implemented in 2007 and 2008 besides solar power generation include:

- Purchase and use of recycled materials
- Routinely monitor and regulate indoor air quality
- Maintain policies to ensure compliance with environmental laws
- Use of ozone-depleting substances
- Employ strict procedures for the storage, handling and disposal of hazardous waste

SUSTAINABILITY MATTERS EVERY DAY AT JCPENNEY

"Be careful of the spare moments of life. You will find that a great opportunity is locked up in them," said James Cash Penney in August 1919. The words of wisdom from the founder of America's century-old national department store chain could apply to many principles, but he probably did not realize his remarks also would someday relate to the way Myron E. "Mike" Ullman III, JCPenney's current chairman and chief executive officer, is driving Penney's operations to combat climate change.

The JCPenney Company cares about the environment and is taking a series of measures to prove it. For one, it reports on its carbon footprint annually through the Carbon Disclosure Project and explains what it is doing to reduce it.

One of JCPenney's initiatives chain-wide is recycling. Penney has collected and recycled cardboard boxes and packaging at its stores and distribution facilities for

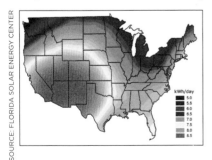

SOURCE: FLORIDA SOLAR ENERGY CENTER

This image comes from a study that the Florida Solar Energy Center conducted on the performance of 2-kW photovoltaic (PV) systems installed on highly efficient homes across the United States. The image illustrates the regions that offer the most potential for harnessing solar energy, with the Southwest desert having the greatest solar resource in the continental United States. Regions with the most solar output offer the most cost-effective location for using solar energy, notwithstanding financial incentives that hasten the investment payback.
To view the complete study, visit: http://www.fsec.ucf.edu/en/publications/html/FSEC-PF-380-04/

more than 30 years. In 2006, the retailer recycled more than 95,000 tons (86,200 metric tons) of cardboard, and 12,000 tons (10,900 metric tons) of plastic hangers and other plastic.

JCPenney is now testing reusable shopping bags that not only help reduce the reliance on throwaway plastic bags but can also support afterschool programs, which is one of JCPenney's traditional charitable cause. Net proceeds from sales of these bags, introduced in 2007 at 75 stores in the San Diego, Miami, Minneapolis, Seattle and Austin districts, were donated to the JCPenney Afterschool Fund to provide children in need with access to life-enriching afterschool programs.

During the first half of the 2000s, JCPenney, now selling more than US$20 billion in merchandise, invested more than US$75 million to install energy-efficient EMS technology, including lighting retrofits, high-efficiency lighting, occupancy-based control of lighting, efficiency control of vending equipment, variable speed drive control of fans and pumps, and high-efficiency HVAC equipment.

In 2006, these efforts resulted in year-over-year elimination of close to 31,000 tons (28,100 metric tons) of greenhouse gas emissions by reducing energy use across all stores, even as operating hours in Penney stores increased by 5 percent and net store square footage increased 2.3 percent. As a result, Penney reduced energy consumption by 2 percent in stores and by 3 percent across its distribution centers.

Now JCPenney wants to take it one step further. Penney is looking to reduce consumption, both the cost and the resulting emissions. One way to do this is by installing new equipment and systems. The other is through an education and awareness program. Penney wants its employees (about 150,000) to be more energy thrifty, both at home and at work, and uses the EPA's Energy Star program to help generate awareness.

Since EPA launched its Energy Star program in 1992, it says Americans have saved US$14 billion in electricity and cut GHG emissions equal to those generated by 25 million vehicles.

Penney's long-term capital plan calls for installing new EMS systems or upgrading existing HVAC and lighting control systems in 800 stores by 2008. A third-party energy monitoring system will be installed in all stores. The system will be centralized, as the one used by Wal-Mart and Target. It will set schedules, points, alarms and trends as well as regulate consumption and help identify problems.

Penney is now concentrating on four key areas to reduce energy consumption: educational awareness training, retrofitting lighting for more efficiency, upgrading HVAC systems and working within proven EPA programs to reduce fuel emissions relating to merchandise delivery.

An aggressive new store construction program has begun. Penney opened its first green store in October 2007 at The Shops at Northfield Stapleton, Forest City Enterprises Inc.'s LEED-certified, mixed-use development located in northeast Denver, Colorado.

In a September 2007 press statement, Michael Dastugue, senior vice president and director of property development for JCPenney, said the company conducted a top-to-bottom review of its store construction process and equipment to determine where the Penney Company could operate more efficiently. The sustainable pilot store in Denver was the result of those findings.

According to Paul Freddo, JCPenney vice president of real estate and a member of the executive committee of ICSC's board of trustees, Penney executives are monitoring the performance of the pilot store's new sustainable building features with an eye toward incorporating the proven tactics into the design of its new and renovated stores going forward.

Among the innovations that JCPenney implemented in the 104,000-square-foot (9,660 sq m) Denver location are:

- Recycled exterior brick from the waste petroleum byproducts firing process
- Recycled ceiling tiles
- Carpet by Shaw made from 100 percent recycled material
- Most construction waste materials such as concrete, metal and drywall were separated during the construction phase and recycled, which diverted them from ending up in a landfill
- Exterior construction and landscaping materials sourced regionally or locally to minimize carbon dioxide emissions from trucking
- Low-wattage LED lighting in exterior signs
- Occupancy sensors that turn off lights in store offices, restrooms, dressing rooms and stockrooms to save energy when not in use
- Low volatile organic compound (VOC) paints, adhesives and sealants
- Low-consumption plumbing fixtures
- High-efficiency Energy Star-rated washers and dryers in the hairstyling salon and on-demand water heaters

The new JCPenney pilot store has substantial sustainable features. However, most of the 50 stores that JCPenney built and opened in 2007 use high-efficiency HVAC systems, solar-reflective R20-rated insulating reflective white roof membrane by Stevens EP and high-efficiency lighting, like the pilot green store.

To ensure the store buildings are constructed and operated for peak efficiency, the JCPenney real estate department hires certified commissioning agents and charges them with the task of making the stores meet high standards of sustainability.

"Our company's philosophy is Every Day Matters, and that point of view extends to our concern for the environment, which we know is shared by our customers and

reflected in their shopping decisions," said Jim Thomas, vice president and director of corporate social responsibility at JCPenney.

Thomas said the new Denver store is a testing ground for new eco-friendly building features to be included in new stores in coming years.

The department store retailer, operating 1,067 stores in the United States and Puerto Rico, has embarked on an aggressive effort to have 800 JCPenney stores equipped with a new Energy Management System (EMS).

Much like Wal-Mart, Penney's EMS will allow it to remotely monitor the stores' electrical and mechanical systems; schedule the operation of lighting, electrical and HVAC equipment; and regulate store comfort and optimize energy efficiency system-wide by eliminating wasted energy.

Between 2001 and 2006, JCPenney spent more than US$75 million to install EMS technology, lighting retrofits and high-efficiency HVAC systems in many of its stores. By 2006, these initiatives eliminated 31,000 tons (28,100 metric tons) of GHG emissions per year by reducing energy use across all stores despite net store square footage increasing during the chain's expansion.

This type of achievement earned Penney a notable environmental distinction. The U.S. EPA named the JCPenney Company the 2007 Energy Star Partner of the Year for outstanding energy management and reductions in greenhouse gas emissions. In October 2007 JCPenney became the first operator of retail buildings to earn the Energy Star label for superior energy efficiency and environmental performance.

EPA also recognized JCPenney in October 2007 with the SmartWay Transport Partnership partners' special achievement award for contributing to reduce the environmental impacts of the freight sector. The SmartWay Excellence Awards honor organizations that integrate innovative strategies and technologies into their business operations, resulting in reduced energy consumption and GHG emissions.

JCPenney increased the number of SmartWay Carriers by more than 20 percent in 2007. Since joining the program, JCPenney has increased the number of SmartWay carriers from 28 to 46.

To raise awareness about the SmartWay program and get its drivers to buy into its importance, Penney distributed a quarterly survey to its delivery drivers. The surveys covered a broad range of operational topics, such as how to improve the company's loading and unloading procedures and other practices that can lower energy use and help the environment.

JCPenney's recycling program also merits kudos for the retailer, as it has been collecting and recycling cardboard boxes and packaging at its stores and distribution facilities for more than 30 years. In 2006 alone, the Penney Company recycled more than 95,000 tons of cardboard (86,200 metric tons), 8,000 tons (7,260 metric tons) of plastic hangers, 4,700 tons (4,260 metric tons) of other plastics, 9,000 fluorescent lamps and 32 tons (29 metric tons) of lighting fixture ballasts.

Penney chairman Mike Ullman said that Penney's goal is to be a leader in per-

formance and execution within the retail industry. Green building design is among many of Penney's initiatives to reduce costs and help preserve the environment.

Compared to similar stores in the United States, the JCPenney stores collectively spend about US$250,000 less per year on energy and avoid emitting three million pounds (1,360 metric tons) of carbon dioxide per year, said representatives of the EPA. This is equal to the greenhouse gas emissions from a power plant that uses coal fuel to generate electricity for 200 homes.

"JCPenney is once again demonstrating that what is best for the environment can be best for your wallet," said Bob Meyers, principal deputy assistant administrator for EPA's Office of Air and Radiation.

Of almost five million commercial buildings in the United States, retail buildings consume the most energy and are responsible for the second-largest percentage of greenhouse gas emissions, EPA noted.

The four Energy Star JCPenney stores recognized by EPA are all in the state of Washington and are located in South Hills Mall in Puyallup, Vancouver Mall in Vancouver, Bellevue Square in Bellevue and Cascade Mall in Burlington. On average, the four Penney stores use about 35 percent less energy—in turn, generating less CO_2—than typical retail stores of similar size in Washington, according to the EPA.

Retail buildings eligible to earn the EPA Energy Star label include department stores, discount stores, hypermarkets/supercenters, warehouse clubs, drugstores, dollar stores, hardware/home improvement centers, apparel and hard-line specialty shops.

Penney's green building profile raised a few notches when its prototype green store opened in Denver's LEED-certified Shops at Northfield Stapleton. According to O'Leary, JCPenney cosponsored an EPA bus tour to promote energy efficiency, which stopped at the Northfield Stapleton store during the grand opening festivities in October 2007. (See Chapter 13.)

Following the successful launch of the Denver green store, JCPenney is pursuing LEED certification for two more green stores. One is an 116,585-square-foot (103,734 sq m) store, anchoring the Village at Fairview. Fairview is a Collin County suburb of the Dallas, Texas, Metroplex located near the Penney headquarters.

This store is located in a dense development of The MGHerring Group, which features about one million square feet (92,900 sq m) of retail, entertainment and dining, and is adjacent to a hotel and convention center.

Other anchors of the open-air lifestyle center include Dillard's, Barnes & Noble Booksellers, the Container Store, the Village Roadshow eight-screen theater and Macy's. Densification is a sustainable tactic and this mixed-use development, which also includes residential units and office space, sets the example.

The second green JCPenney store is a 105,300-square-foot (9,780 sq m) store, opening in 2009. It is located at the Stamko Development Company's Centre at La Quinta, California.

LIMITED BRANDS ENVIRONMENTAL POLICY

Limited Brands considers its corporate culture to be values-led, and as such is integrating the protection and preservation of global resources into its everyday business practices. The retail giant keeps a pledge prominently displayed on the company Web site for all stakeholders to see that the company is committed to sustainable, responsible and sensible environmental behavior.

The pledge states that management at Limited Brands believes that effective management begins with the thoughtful procurement of supplies, equipment and merchandise, and carries on through to its daily business operations reaching all the way to the customer. Limited Brands has interwoven sustainability throughout every step of its operation and has made a full commitment to:

- Minimize waste generation and maximize recycling
- Conserve energy and preserve natural resources
- Promote the increased use of recycled content paper
- Select and partner with environmentally responsible suppliers
- Forge relationships with environmental agencies and nongovernmental organizations
- Hold management accountable for its environmental stewardship efforts

Limited Brands conducted an environmental footprint assessment to quantify its GHG emissions company-wide and to create goals for reducing its environmental impact.

The short- and long-term goals extended to the retailer's store operations as well as its infrastructure.

By 2011, Limited Brands plans to replace all existing T12 linear fluorescent lighting fixtures in its Ohio, New York and New Mexico distribution centers with lamps that are more efficient. Once completed, the retrofit will reduce annual energy consumption by about 15 million kWh and reduce emissions of carbon dioxide by 8,640 metric tons (9,520 tons).

The company has also vowed to intensify its conservation efforts at its specialty stores, which include Victoria's Secret, Bath & Body Works, Express, Limited, White Barn Candle Company and Henri Bendel, and to reduce GHG emissions in shipping merchandise to its 3,700 store locations in two areas:

1. **TRANSPORTATION:** The retail chain switched 30 percent of inbound freight from truck to rail and significantly reduced diesel fuel consumption and emissions in 2006, which caused it to triple the program in 2007. This resulted in savings of 175,000 gallons (662,450 liters) of diesel fuel and reduced emissions of carbon dioxide by roughly 2,000 tons (1,820 metric tons). The company also utilized highly efficient trailer stacking techniques to optimize the use of

trailer space, reducing the number of trucks and the amount of energy required to transport merchandise.

2. **STORE LIGHTING:** Numerous energy efficiency projects resulted in significant savings and emissions reductions. Starting in 2002, Limited Brands began a systematic program to replace lighting in store remodel projects with more efficient lighting technology. The company was able to reduce energy consumption by more than 25 percent in its older stores. One lighting retrofit project at approximately 834 stores, scheduled for completion in 2008, replaced lighting fixtures with lower wattage, higher-efficiency compact fluorescent lamps (CFLs) to reduce annual energy consumption by about 40 million kWh and cut emissions of carbon dioxide by almost 33,000 tons (30,000 metric tons).

PHOTOS: R. E. MILIAN

An added benefit of replacing less efficient bulbs with compact fluorescent lamps is that the newer lighting generates less heat, which reduces the amount of air-conditioning needed to cool the stores.

Limited Brands is also replacing all store HVAC rooftop units with more efficient ones. Between 2007 and 2009, Limited Brands expects to replace 270 units and estimates it will reduce annual energy consumption by 1.3 million kWh and reduce emissions by 842 tons (764 metric tons) of carbon dioxide.

Raymond "Ray" Silverstein, CDP, senior vice president of strategic store operations, store design and construction at Limited Brands, said the company is considering every opportunity for energy savings, looking at products and technology that can help reduce energy consumption without minimizing light levels and comfort at the stores. "We're substituting LED on store signs and shelf [display] lighting," said Silverstein. "All of our lighting has been redesigned—totally—over the past two years," said Silverstein in December 2007.

Reusing and recycling are part of Limited Brands' overall sustainability program. The Columbus, Ohio–based retailer has agreed to increase the amount of recycled paper used in its Victoria's Secret catalogs and to increase the environmental standards it requires from papermakers cutting the forests that stretch across northern Canada. Limited Brands mails 350 million Victoria's Secret catalogs every year to sell intimate apparel products.

The retailer's catalogs will use either 10 percent recycled paper, postconsumer waste (PCW) paper or 10 percent new

Limited Brands plans to replace the existing lighting at The Limited stores (top photo located at General Growth Properties Woodbridge Center in Woodbridge, New Jersey) with luminaires that are more efficient. Limited Brands' Victoria's Secret will use at least 10 percent recycled or FSC paper for 350 million catalogs to promote its intimate apparel and beauty brands. Pictured below is the Victoria's Secret store at The Forum Shops at Caesars in Las Vegas, Nevada, developed and managed by Simon Property Group.

paper from sources certified by the Forest Stewardship Council (FSC) as paper pulp that originated in sustainably managed forests. Toward that goal, the public company printed its annual report and proxy statement on PCW paper.

As part of the retail chain's environmental platform, Limited Brands is committed to:

- Minimize waste generation and maximize recycling
- Conserve energy and preserve natural resources
- Promote the increased use of recycled paper
- Work with environmentally responsible suppliers
- Partner with environmental agencies and nongovernmental organizations
- Become accountable for environmental stewardship efforts
- Reduce energy consumption in 3,500+ stores and facilities by increasing the lighting efficiency
- Reduce the amount of waste that is sent to landfills and increase the amount that is recycled

Limited Brands adopted the 3Rs: reduce, reuse and recycle. Working with suppliers and vendors, the retailer has been reducing the amount of paper, packaging materials and other natural resources used in its business operations with great success. The trendy apparel and beauty supplies chain recycled more than 9,000 tons (8,165 metric tons) of paper and cardboard in 2007 and about 75 percent of all materials in the distribution centers.

Bath & Body Works, a concept of Limited Brands, sells naturally made products.

In 2005 alone, Limited Brands recycled:

- 8,200 tons (7,440 metric tons) of corrugate and office paper
- 280,000 pounds (127 metric tons) of alcohol-containing products, rather than disposing the material as hazardous waste
- 54,000 pounds (24 metric tons) of metal
- 478,000 pounds (217 metric tons) of plastic
- 3,350 tons (1.5 metric tons) of wood from pallets
- 54,000 pounds of computers and other electronics
- 178,000 pounds (81 metric tons) of glass

EPA also recognized Limited Brands with an honorable mention in the "very large business" category. The award was for noteworthy accomplishments in waste

reduction, given at the 2006 WasteWise and National Partnership for Environmental Priorities Annual Conference held in Arlington, Virginia.

"From our perspective, sustainability, environmental awareness and sensitivity make good business sense," said Silverstein. "It's good for the community and good for our brands."

IN-DEPTH ANALYSIS LED GAP TO SET POLICY

Gap Inc. used environmental consultancy firms CH2M HILL and SustainAbility to help it conduct an analysis of its entire operation. The extensive study examined the environmental challenges that the global retail company faces and analyzed the potential impact to its business.

Gap Inc. operates Gap, Banana Republic, Old Navy and Piperlime brand names in more than 3,100 stores in the United States, the United Kingdom, Canada, France, Ireland, Japan and the Middle East.

The huge size of this global retailer compelled the consultants to segregate the areas over which Gap can have the most control and influence, based on the level of societal concern for each area. Upon reviewing the results of the study, Gap executives concluded that the greatest positive impact could be made within their store and facility construction and the ongoing operation of Gap stores, including packaging.

However, Gap executives felt that the company has considerable influence over raw material and textile production, garment production and transportation of goods, and as such has begun to develop programs to tackle those areas.

Armed with that type of information, Gap prepared a business plan to help it become greener and reduce its environmental footprint.

The result was Gap adopting an environmental strategy that focuses on three key areas:

1. Energy conservation

2. Cotton/sustainable design

3. Output/waste reduction

In 2003, the retailer joined the EPA's Climate Leaders program, a voluntary partnership between industry and government that encourages companies to develop long-term strategies to reduce greenhouse gas emissions. Gap set aggressive energy-use reduction goals by May 2005, pledging to reduce GHG emissions by 11 percent per square foot from 2003 to 2008 at its U.S. stores.

In a key action to help achieve energy efficiencies, Gap installed a computerized energy management system (EMS) in about 40 percent of its U.S. stores. The system monitors the performance of the lighting, heating, ventilation and air-conditioning systems in the larger, programmed stores, resulting in energy cuts at U.S. stores in 2006 by 8.7 percent compared to its benchmark 2003 year.

PHOTO: R. E. MILIAN

Gap also began switching from traditional fluorescent lamps to low-mercury fluorescent lamps as the old ones burn out throughout its stores, offices and distribution centers. This will save energy and help reduce the amount of toxic waste that ends up in landfills or incinerators.

When Gap focused on energy and monitoring of targeted areas, savings began almost immediately when in 2004, energy consumption at U.S. stores averaged 29.21 kWh per square foot. In 2005, the average declined to 28.38 kWh per square foot, and in 2006, the average fell again, this time to 27.34 kWh per square foot.

At its eight distribution centers throughout the world, the company reduced energy consumption by:

- Resetting thermostats (78°F [25.5°C]) in the summer and 66°F [18.9°C] in the winter)
- Replacing standard light fixtures with energy-efficient ones
- Reducing or eliminating unnecessary lighting
- Installing automatic controls for shutting off conveyor systems
- Installing computerized building management systems to monitor and control energy use at its three largest U.S. distribution campuses (Fresno, California; Gallatin, Tennessee; and Fishkill, New York)

In addition, Gap is installing a one-megawatt (MW) solar power system at its West Coast distribution center in Fresno, California. The system will generate

approximately 1.9 million kilowatt-hours (kWh) annually, which is equivalent to the electricity required to power approximately 350 U.S. homes.

MMA Renewable Ventures LLC, a subsidiary of Municipal Mortgage & Equity LLC, financed the system and will own and operate it for Gap. Under the terms of a long-term power purchase agreement, Gap Inc. will buy predictably priced power from MMA Renewable Ventures for the next 20 years, shielding the retailer from rising energy costs and helping it use renewable energy.

MMA combined technology with 3 Phases Energy and SunPower to develop and install the system, which has more than 5,000 photovoltaic panels on a mounted track designed to harness solar radiation.

The San Francisco Bay Area Council recognized Gap as a Regional Transportation Initiative Employer for the wide range of employee transportation options it offers at its headquarter offices in San Francisco and San Bruno, California. Those

Gap Inc. adopted an environmental strategy that focuses on energy conservation, cotton/sustainable design and output/waste reduction. Featured at left is Gap's Times Square location in New York City that was retrofitted in an existing building facade. Gap Inc. installed a computerized energy management system (EMS) in about 40 percent of Gap's U.S. stores, including the Kissimmee, Florida, location featured above. The system enables Gap to monitor the performance of lighting and HVAC systems.

options included shuttling 7,000 passengers per month, encouraging car pools and providing designated parking and locker rooms with showers to promote the use of bicycles by employees.

Gap's buyers have also been purchasing fabrics made of materials that are more environmentally friendly. For example, Banana Republic carried a skirt made of a hemp/silk blend. Hemp is a natural fiber that requires few pesticides and fertilizers to grow, thus helping to reduce the harmful impact on soil. Gap also joined the Better Cotton Initiative in 2005 to promote environmentally, socially and economically sustainable cotton cultivation practices globally. World Wildlife Fund (WWF) helped launch the Better Cotton Initiative.

Gap has begun to carry organic cotton, which is grown without the use of synthetic pesticides and fertilizers. Gap stores sell men's T-shirts and tanks made with 100 percent organic cotton.

The apparel chain is also doing its share of reusing and recycling paper, packaging material and waste. One of the first things Gap did in 2006 was to notify all its suppliers that its preference is to use paper with recycled fiber content, unbleached and made with chlorine-free pulp. By 2008, much of the paper and corrugate Gap was purchasing had a minimum postconsumer content of 15 percent, and postconsumer content is as high as 68 percent. Unlike Limited Brands, Gap does not publish thick, glossy catalogs, but its Old Navy circulars that are inserted in newspapers use 80 percent postconsumer paper.

Gap also made a deal with Parallel Products, a national recovery center in Kentucky, to convert waste perfume (a hazardous substance) into ethanol, a renewable automobile fuel additive.

PHOTO COURTESY OF GAP INC.

Gap has begun to carry organic cotton, which is grown without the use of synthetic pesticides and fertilizers. BabyGap stores sell an organic collection that includes bodysuits for US$19.50 and organic wrap velour hoodies (featured above) for US$34.50. The organic collection is made with 100 percent organic cotton.

MODELL'S SPORTING GOODS UPGRADES HVAC

Between 2005 and 2006, Modell's Sporting Goods installed a new system that monitors the heating, ventilation and air-conditioning (HVAC) system of 133 of its big-box sporting goods stores. Maximum Performance Group (MPG), the maker of the eMAC system that Modell's installed to work with its existing HVAC equipment, predicts that Modell's will realize US$840,000 in energy savings. This is based on the mean cost of US$0.12 per kilowatt-hour of electricity in the Northeast. Modell's stores are located in 11 states from Virginia to New Hampshire and in the District of Columbia.

MPG projected Modell's will save 7.4 million kilowatt-hours a year (an estimated 17 percent energy savings). The 117-year-old family-owned retail chain serviced by the Northeast power transmission grid—where power plants primarily burn carbon fuel (oil, coal and gas)—will remove 4,700 tons (4,260 metric tons) of carbon dioxide emissions from the atmosphere.

Not only was this program successful in cutting energy costs and giving Modell's environmental bragging rights, but it also came with incentive dollars that the New York State Energy Research and Development Authority contributed to Modell's capital expenditure for the upgrade to its 27 stores located in New York State.

MPG's parent company, Lime Energy, also installed 350 rooftop eMAC monitoring and controlling devices on the HVAC systems at 50 retail stores owned by P.C. Richard & Son, a U.S. family-owned electronics retail chain operating large stores in New York and New Jersey.

After five years of operation, Lime Energy estimates that P.C. Richard & Son saved more than US$700,000 a year in energy costs. Lime Energy estimated that the reduction in electric power achieved by this electronics chain would have been sufficient to power 324 households for one year and would have released 2,786 tons (2,527 metric tons) of carbon dioxide into the atmosphere.

Modell's near Times Square in New York City (above) is among 133 sporting goods superstores that will save 7.4 million kilowatt-hours a year (an estimated 17 percent energy savings) and will remove 4,700 tons (4,260 metric tons) of carbon dioxide emissions from the atmosphere due to the chain's sustainability upgrades.

IKEA SHRINKS ENVIRONMENTAL FOOTPRINT

Anders Dahlvig, president of the world's largest home furnishings retailer, the IKEA Group, says that it is not easy for a company the size of IKEA to be successful with social and environmental work. Such efforts take a dedicated organization with clear goals, strategies, timetables and responsibilities. Above all, it requires a vision to create a better everyday life for its many stakeholders.

"We realize that we are only [at] the beginning, and we have a long way to go before our work is a natural, integrated part of our day-to-day business," Dahlvig admits. Yet IKEA stands out among many retailers in promulgating corporate social responsibility and documenting its practices to help preserve the environment.

Like Wal-Mart and other mass merchants that rely on low retail prices to attract large masses of consumers, IKEA has always tried to do more with less. Even before it was popular or required, to save on costs, IKEA had been using its resources in an economical way.

According to the large home furnishings and furniture big-box retailer, the three cornerstones of its environmental work are:

1. Cost consciousness and resource efficiency result in less usage of raw material and in less waste and discharges.

2. The extensive use of wood, which is a recyclable, biodegradable and renewable material, is excellent from an environmental point of view.

3. Training and engaging coworkers to work with environmental issues is paramount.

According to Dahlvig, IKEA has for years tried to save on raw material, energy and other resources. "As a consequence, we often also reduce waste and discharges," Dahlvig said.

IKEA develops its own branded products or works closely with suppliers in outsourcing merchandise and is able to take all aspects of a product's life into consideration.

By considering the amount and types of raw materials as well as how the product performs, this global retailer has been able to put its environmental influence on a large amount of products to minimize environmental impact.

A large proportion of the raw material IKEA uses for making home and office furnishings is wood and wooden fiber extracted from trees, bamboo, straw, hemp, cottonseed, sugarcane and other plant-based sources. Wood can be renewable, recyclable, biodegradable and environmentally responsible if it originates in well-managed forests.

Like The Home Depot, Lowe's Companies and other responsible large purchasers of wood products, IKEA makes sure that the solid wood products it sources directly or indirectly are certified and that they do not originate in ecologically critical intact forest landscapes, such as Burma and Brazil.

The IKEA lightbulb—using only seven watts of power—is a more environmentally friendly alternative to an incandescent bulb. It has 10 times longer life and consumes up to 80 percent less energy per the output of lumens. The brass-and-nickel-plated bulb with a dome made of glass and silicone—designed and made by IKEA of Sweden—has an enormous life approximating 10,000 hours. Compact fluorescent lamps (CFLs) contain mercury and cannot be disposed with regular waste. When these bulbs finally reach the end of their life cycle, U.S. IKEA stores will gladly take them back from customers, even though under U.S. federal hazardous waste laws, lamp users are responsible for complying with disposal requirements. IKEA properly disposes them to keep the mercury inside the CFLs from seeping into the environment. For more tips on spent fluorescent and high-intensity discharge lamp recycling, visit http://www.lamprecycle.org, a service of the U.S. National Electrical Manufacturers Association. At the IKEA store in Dubai Festival City in the United Arab Emirates (right), IKEA has abolished plastic bags in response to a local newspaper campaign, and it is discouraging the use of paper sacks it carries by promoting its reusable blue bags for sale at Dh6 ($US 1.67).

PHOTO: R. E. MILIAN

Recycling generally refers to several possibilities for retailers. It sometimes refers to how a retailer recycles waste produced by its operation or how it purchases recycled products for its stores to sell.

Like other major retailers such as Whole Foods, Safeway, A&P and Publix, IKEA is selling IKEA logo bags for US$0.59, which are made of recycled material that customers can reuse when going shopping. However, to better compel its customers to "think green," the Swedish retailer is now charging for plastic throwaway bags that they once gave away free.

Called the "Bag the plastic bag" program, IKEA charges five cents for plastic bags, and in the United States, it is donating the income to American Forests, a nonprofit conservation group. IKEA's aim is to help curtail the amount of plastic shopping bags that Americans pick up at stores, using them once and then tossing them out.

Stores in the United States distribute more than 100 billion plastic bags each year, according to research conducted by IKEA. The average U.S. family of four uses 1,460 plastic shopping bags every year, which can take up to 1,000 years to naturally decompose in the environment. It is this type of research and environmental pressures, which retailers like the IKEA Group are experiencing today, that are compelling retail chains all over the world to take remedial action.

According to the IKEA worldwide director of sustainability, Thomas Bergmark, for three years IKEA has issued an annual social and environmental report on its Web site with supplemental communiqués in the IKEA catalogs and customer club magazines. "This campaign is to be more aggressive and more transparent in these issues," Bergmark told *Grist* magazine in February 2007.

IKEA is involved in several strategies to cut fossil fuel consumption. One proposed strategy involves stores that would produce their own renewable energy, such as solar, wind, biomass or geothermal, for heating and cooling. According to Bergmark, IKEA is considering building these energy-generating systems in new stores, but the company is still analyzing the feasibility of retrofitting existing stores.

In cases where the retailer does not deem retrofits as feasible, IKEA is looking into compensating in other ways, such as purchasing carbon credits or by sending excess energy produced at other stores back into the grid to minimize its overall carbon footprint, said Bergmark.

Bergmark expects that as much as 60 percent of all energy IKEA consumes in 2009 will come from renewable sources, and by that date, he expects the retailer will function 15 percent more energy efficient than in 2006. However, IKEA faces several challenges because of its business model. Sustainability practices stress sourcing from local or regional suppliers to minimize the environmental impact from the transport of goods, such as carbon fuel emissions.

Yet IKEA stores in North America depend on imports from Europe and Asia for much of their merchandise. However, Bergmark says that as IKEA continues to expand in North America, the possibilities for local sourcing will increase.

PHOTO: R. E. MILIAN

In the interim, IKEA is looking at such options as reducing the size of merchandise packaging and using trucks powered with biofuels to lessen the environmental impact of transporting the merchandise to its stores.

WALGREENS GOES GREEN

The century-old Walgreen Company is implementing a number of green strategies at its stores throughout the United States. The largest U.S. retail pharmacy chain teamed up with ImaginIt Inc., a Denver-based provider of solar electricity service, to install solar electric systems in 96 stores and at two distribution centers in California.

The new systems will generate more than 13.8 million kilowatt-hours per year. The solar roof panels at those stores will supplement between 20 and 50 percent of Walgreens' consumption of electricity, previously generated at utility plants by burning fossil fuels.

PHOTO: R. E. MILIAN

Walgreens anticipates it would take more than 22 million gallons (83.3 million liters) of natural gas a year to produce the electricity it is now generating with photovoltaic (solar) cells. That is comparable to planting more than 5 million tree seedlings that, when fully grown, would ultimately absorb through photosynthesis the amount of carbon dioxide power plants supplying these stores would have otherwise emitted each year by burning fossil fuels.

According to Dana Ione Green, Esq., senior vice president and general counsel of Walgreens, the retail company engages in activity to reduce carbon emissions, and she cited the retailer's installations of solar electric systems and its partnership with the EPA's Energy Star as examples.

Above: Walgreens is among many retailers attempting to satisfy consumers by featuring popular organic green products. Left: A water retention pond collects rainwater in a reservoir bordering a Walgreens store located in a community center in West Palm Beach, Florida.

Walgreens also has a company-wide recycling program to prevent paper, lamps, glass, lightbulbs, batteries, ink cartridges, Polyolefin shrink-wrap film and cardboard from ending up in landfills.

Its fleet of tractor trucks uses ultralow sulphur diesel (ULSD). Walgreens' light-duty trucks use biogasoline or flex fuel (E-85). At its Deerfield, Illinois, headquarters, Walgreens instituted a ride-share program and established a shuttle service to nearby mass transit stations for employees and visitors.

In April 2007, Walgreens opened a 12,000-square-foot (1,115 sq m) store in the five-level Broadway Crossings in Seattle, Washington, a sustainable building that has two levels of underground parking below the store and 44 subsidized housing units on four levels above it. The green building incorporated more than 50 sustainable features including windows and recycled low-VOC carpets that meet environmental standards.

OFFICE DEPOT: BUY GREEN, BE GREEN, SELL GREEN

Office Depot Inc. released its Corporate Citizenship Report in 2007 outlining each area of its environmental strategy to become a greener retailer by buying and selling green products and by improving the way it operates its stores.

The global supplier of office products and services sells more than US$15 billion to consumers and businesses of all sizes. Through its three business units of the North American Retail Division, the North American Business Solutions Division and the International Division, Office Depot is doing all it can to polish its green image around the world. The retailer's increasing environmental vision to *buy green, be green and sell green* stretches across all aspects of its operations.

Buy Green: The retail giant is one of the world's largest resellers of paper and because of that, it can help prevent abuse to forests. In 2004, Office Depot formed the Forest & Biodiversity Conservation Alliance to ensure that its suppliers source forest fiber from companies that follow sustainable forestry practices.

Be Green: The Fortune 150 retail company with a global presence has instituted various initiatives such as investing US$20 million in energy system upgrades, upgrading inefficient HVAC equipment, retrofitting lighting and investing in renewable energy.

Sell Green: Office Depot identified more than 3,000 products with environmental attributes. To inform customers, the retailer produced a catalog of green products, tips and solutions, and posted it on its microsite: http://www.officedepot.com/promo.do?file=/guides/buygreen/buygreen.jsp.

SOURCE: OFFICE DEPOT

Office Depot launched a microsite linked to its main site featuring green products, tips and solutions.

After many years of recycling waste, the retail chain has been enhancing its green image since it launched a recycling service for computers and other home electronic equipment at its 1,100 stores in North America. Office Depot rolled out the program throughout the United States and Canada in 2007 after collecting 108,000 pounds (49 metric tons) of electronic hardware in a 100-store test during the previous year.

Office Depot saved about 1.25 million gallons (4.73 million liters) of fuel in 2006 by using intermodal transportation such as combining ships, railroads and trucks instead of strictly using over-the-road transportation.

The company also converted its fleet of delivery trucks to the Sprinter vehicle, which is 40 percent more fuel efficient than the box truck, and it switched to all-battery-operated forklifts at its U.S. distribution centers.

It is now considering using plastic shipping pallets as an alternative to wood pallets. The chain projects to save money and reduce fuel consumption by gaining space on trucks and in trailers from stacking plastic pallets.

The Office Depot sells to customers in 43 countries throughout North America, Europe, Asia and Latin America, either through wholly owned entities, majority-

owned entities or other ventures covering 36 countries, or through alliances in an additional eight countries.

In Europe, where Office Depot has fewer stores than in North America and more of a distribution-based business model, it has targeted its efforts toward building greener corporate offices and warehouses. Office Depot is developing greener buildings in Europe that include technologies such as:

- Central lighting controls for warehouses with daylight sensing, timing modules and movement sensors to ensure lighting is used only when necessary

- Air exchange systems that cool buildings overnight using natural air circulation

- Heating systems based on biofuels such as scrap wood chips

In a report to the Carbon Disclosure Project, Office Depot executives said they recognize that weather-related events linked to greenhouse gases, such as droughts, hurricanes and floods, bring a range of operational risks that can dramatically affect the ability of a company to operate.

In 2005, several hurricanes, including Katrina, forced Office Depot to close its South Florida headquarters for one week, and it took several weeks for operations to normalize at the global retail company. Following this calamity, Office Depot reported in 2006 that the company had developed various efforts to reduce greenhouse gas emissions. Office Depot

- Began calculating GHG emissions in the largest countries where the office supply store operates, including the United States, Canada, United Kingdom, Ireland, Germany and the Benelux (Belgium, Netherlands and Luxembourg monarchies)

- Reduced absolute GHG emissions by 10.1 percent across its North American facilities between 2005 and 2006, notwithstanding a 4.5 percent increase in total square footage of facilities, and saved 65.9 million kilowatts of electricity

- Began reporting to Carbon Disclosure Project

- Joined the U.S. EPA Climate Leaders program

- Joined the Business Roundtable's Climate Resolve program

- Joined the U.S. EPA Green Power partnership to purchase renewable energy equal to 12 percent of total electricity consumption

By reducing kilowatt-hours, Office Depot significantly exceeded its savings target of US$4.3 million and saved US$6.2 million in costs in 2006 alone.

Office Depot also retrofitted in 2006 more than 400 stores in North America with energy-efficient T5 fluorescent lamps and added T5 coverage across the chain's

entire North American footprint of over 1,200-plus stores. The office supply chain also added 350 pieces of high-efficiency HVAC equipment in North America.

Office Depot installed new light sensors in 750 stores in North America at employee breakrooms, restrooms and management offices that automatically shut off lights when these rooms are not occupied.

In February 2008, Office Depot celebrated the groundbreaking of its first Office Depot *green store* on Anderson Lane in Austin, Texas. The store is part of the volume certification portfolio program, a pilot program the USGBC formed to help retail chains achieve LEED certification at numerous locations and to facilitate the certification process for retailer's prototype designs.

The new Anderson store has many energy-efficient features including T5 lighting, skylights, high-efficiency HVAC units and insulation, enhanced energy management system, state-of-the-art temperature controls, and a reflective roof.

"By becoming the first office supply retailer to 'build green' using the LEED volume certification program, we are once again setting a precedent for others in our industry to follow," said Yalmaz Siddiqui, environmental strategy advisor for Office Depot.

The company is upgrading its energy management system at 700 additional stores in the United States and Canada. This system tracks energy usage and trends from a central location and sets temperatures much the same way as the JCPenney and Wal-Mart systems do. The system will also identify and notify Office Depot's "energy police" about energy-use anomalies such as lights left on overnight, malfunctioning HVAC units and doors left open that allow heating or cooling to escape.

The retailer is also getting the word out to its customers about how they can contribute to improving the environment. In educating the public, Office Depot demonstrates the icons to watch out for when shopping for merchandise—at Office Depot and other retailers—to help them shrink their environmental footprint.

The Office Depot store on Hollywood Boulevard in Hollywood, Florida, pictured here, which opened in February 2008, features many energy-savings techniques including T5 narrow-diameter fluorescent light tubes that are roughly three to four times more efficient than standard fluorescent bulbs of similar wattage. During the same month, Office Depot began building its prototype green store in Austin, Texas (not pictured here), and employed the same T5 lighting technology but has added skylights, a bicycle rack, designated parking for hybrid vehicles, and other sustainable features that the Hollywood store does not have.

PHOTOS: R. E. MILIAN

Office Depot attained an average of 33 percent post-consumer recycled content for cutsheet paper used in its North American corporate operations.

Office Depot also reduced absolute greenhouse gas emissions from North American facilities by 10 percent, even though it increased square footage of facilities by 4.5 percent in 2007.

In 2007, the company published its fourth *Green Book* catalog, in six countries and in five languages. The catalog featured 3,000 environmentally preferable products with hundreds of tips and ideas for achieving a "greener office."

In 2004 and 2005, the company recycled 20,000 tons (18,140 metric tons) of corrugated cardboard, recognizing that an office supply retailer impacts forest resources where paper products originate. As such, the Florida-based company relies on independent auditing and verification of Office Depot's paper suppliers and on the management practices and forest certification programs of the forest operations from which they source the wood fibers. Preference is given to suppliers that source

Office Depot is informing customers how they can improve the environment by demonstrating which icons to look for when shopping for merchandise that will help diminish shoppers' environmental footprints. Each of the icons begins with the prefix "re," such as recycled paper, and stresses that recycled content is still the most common environmental attribute.

IMAGE COURTESY OF OFFICE DEPOT

PHOTO COURTESY OF OFFICE DEPOT

Carl "Chuck" Rubin, president of North American retail for Office Depot, launches the company's tech recycling service photo operation. Rubin has a long record of accomplishment in leading retail enterprises, previously as a partner of Accenture (where he functioned as a retail consultant) and as a merchandiser and store manager for Federated Department Stores (now Macy's Inc.). Office Depot published *The Green Book,* a catalog featuring more than 3,000 green products it sells.

their materials from forestlands that are certified by an independent third party as sustainable.

Office Depot's senior management files its profile disclosure on the Global Reporting Initiative. Management acknowledges that an increasing reliance on independent verification strengthens the company's public commitment to environmental stewardship and the responsible, transparent and accountable approach to implementing the retailer's stated environmental policies.

Office Depot's progress in sustainability since 2004 is consistent with many large retailers. These retailers are testing various green tactics and learning what works and what does not. They are realizing that many conservation tactics actually save money besides helping to preserve the environment.

This exercise will lead to large-scale rollout of green operating systems that will become standard retail practices in the 2010s.

Office Depot in Royal Palm, Florida. The South Florida chain has a green strategy to save energy and improve the environment.

PHOTO: R. E. MILIAN

Chapter 10

Can Green Measures Boost Sales?

S USTAINABLE TACTICS SUCH as daylighting reduce store-operating costs. That much we know. But can they also increase retail sales? David Green thinks so. In fact, he swears by it. "My feeling is that productivity, which can be measured more easily and reliably in office or classroom situations, serves as a proxy for impacts to be expected in retail environments," said Green, AIA, LEED AP, a principal at Los Angeles, California-based Altoon + Porter Architects.

Overwhelmingly, studies show that improvements in indoor environmental quality are associated with increased productivity, increased sales, decreased absenteeism and improved health and comfort, according to Green. He points to several human productivity studies conducted by Heschong Mahone Group Inc. (HMG), documenting the effects of daylighting on building occupants.

In one study, HMG analyzed test score results for more than 21,000 students from three U.S. primary education school districts in California, Colorado and Washington. The California-based building energy efficiency consulting firm concluded that introducing natural light in an indoor environment has as much positive effect on the productivity of students in schools as it does for occupants in office buildings and retail stores.

When combining ventilation and outdoor view with daylight and other aspects of positive indoor environmental quality, the impact on human performance is astonishing. One HMG research paper showed that in one year, the students in classrooms with the most daylighting in the Capistrano Unified School District (Orange County, California) progressed 20 percent faster on math exams and 26 percent faster on reading tests.

Many retailers, concerned about saving energy and money, have instituted daylight harvesting programs during new store construction and store remodeling only to discover that skylighting has also had a positive effect on sales.

PHOTO: R. E. MILIAN

BJ's Wholesale Club in Edison, New Jersey, boosts sales with natural daylight by augmenting skylights with two types of overhead lighting, metal halide lamps and T-8 lamps with electronic ballasts. Natural lighting helps lift customers' spirits, particularly during short winter days in northern New Jersey. As pictured above, at night, high bay, high-performance metal halide (MH) lamps light up the store, as the sun sets at right. The Edison warehouse club opened in 1991. It does not harvest daylight in the traditional sense like Wal-Mart and Costco do because all of BJ's lamps remain on during the day instead of dimming with photosensors. In addition, the skylights were not appropriately distributed for optimum daylighting. The lamps are controlled by a central EMS at BJ's headquarters in Natick, Massachusetts, that dims the lights after closing to about half of capacity until the next morning. BJ's electricity savings came when the company converted the overhead lights in all stores in 2002 from 400-watt metal halide lamps to 350-watt metal-halide lamps with pulse-start ballasts.

Studies conducted for (and by) retailers show that products appear more vibrant under daylight. Skin tones seem more natural. Home furnishings look cozier and inviting. Plants appear healthy and attractive. Food looks tasty and fresh.

Natural light even helps customers choose apparel and clothing accessories, since it reveals the "true" colors of these products. However, the most compelling factor for using natural light in a retail built environment is that it may also improve the browsers' attitudinal propensity for shopping.

All these reasons have compelled retailers from home-improvement warehouse stores like Lowe's Companies to mass merchants like Wal-Mart to use extensive skylights and photocontrols to help boost sales, cut costs and reduce GHG emissions.

"Daylighting is one of the significant elements of good indoor environmental quality along with glare control, noise control, increased ventilation effectiveness, thermal control, humidity control and indoor pollution control," said retail design expert David Green.

A 1999 HMG study examined sales levels at 108 nearly identical retail stores of a well-known chain, two-thirds of which had skylights and one-third that did not, finding that sales were as much as 40 percent higher in daylit retail environments.

CUSTOMERS RESPOND TO DAYLIGHTING

Most of us conduct our lives indoors. We spend lots of time at home, working in an office, shopping inside stores, visiting with business professionals in their offices, dining at restaurants and taking part in recreational indoor activities, such as going

PHOTOS: R. E. MILIAN

The BJ's Wholesale Club in Paramus, New Jersey, (top left and below) in bright daylight, uses skylights in a similar manner as the BJ's club in Edison, New Jersey. The metal halide lamps do not turn off during the day because the skylights simply do not have the coverage for full day-light harvesting. The Paramus location opened in 1999. The Home Depot store in North Bergen, New Jersey (top middle), which opened in 2007, uses skylights to brighten the store while keeping its fluorescent lights on similar to BJ's Wholesale Club. This practice does not allow BJ's or The Home Depot to harvest daylight in the same manner that Costco and Wal-Mart do. The DSW big-box shoe store in Paramus, New Jersey (top right), features high bay halides in the evening, to create the appearance that the store is bright, although no natural light is entering through the vast diffused skylights over the sales floor. Daylighting is an effective way for this leading U.S. branded footwear specialty retailer, which operates 255 stores in 36 states, to boost retail sales while helping to brighten the customers' day. DSW Inc. is headquartered in Columbus, Ohio.

to the movies, visiting museums and attending sporting events. All of this diminishes our exposure to natural daylight.

There are many reasons why customers respond better during the day under natural light. Today we have scientific proof that supports the positive effect that natural lighting has on human behavior, mood and attitude. We experience the world through our senses—touch, smell, taste, hearing and vision—but because our eyes contain 70 percent of our sense receptors, our vision largely determines how we feel about our surroundings, and our vision picks up only what is exposed to light. That light passes through our pupils and into the retina, where receptor cells interpret whether sunlight or shadows make up the surroundings. These cells then send a signal to the pineal gland of the brain.

The gland reacts by producing the highest levels of melatonin in pitch dark, gradually decreasing production to the lowest levels in the brightest sunlight. Humans and many animals interpret the variation of melatonin in the bloodstream as the body's circadian rhythm, or biological clock, inducing drowsiness during the high-melatonin cycle. The biological clock affects our moods and our performance and attempts to put us on a daily cycle of alertness and tiredness.

It appears that daylight is the necessary ingredient, keeping the melatonin cycle in our bodies in sequence with the outside world. Humans function better when melatonin levels are high at night and low in the day.

This is another reason why green building experts suggest minimizing light pollution at night and encouraging daylighting indoors during the day.

In high latitudes, the daily cycle of light is further aggravated by the annual cycle of the seasons, with the long days of summer followed by the short days of winter. Observers believe that this cycle has a negative effect on moods and well-being during winter months.

One in ten persons in colder climates suffers from seasonal affective disorder (SAD), a form of depression characterized by seasonality, depressed moods, decreased libido, decreased energy, a tendency to sleep too much and a general feeling of tiredness. There are even reports that SAD causes unwarranted weight gain from increased appetite and a craving for sweets. With the arrival of spring, energy returns to persons afflicted with SAD, and some weight loss might occur.

According to a Mill Hill Essay by Michael A. Ferenczi published in 1997 by the National Institute for Medical Research, a large number of studies demonstrate the efficacy of light therapy in treating the symptoms of SAD. Ferenczi noted that exposure to natural daylight helps in alleviating the symptoms of SAD, but modern urban lifestyles do not lend themselves to sufficient daylight exposure. We often spend most of our daytime hours indoors in the semidarkness of poor artificial lighting.

A study of adults living in San Diego, California, showed that on average, Californians between forty and sixty years old spend less than one hour per day in daylight, according to Ferenczi.

Dr. Ian Arnold, MD, CCFP, agrees with Ferenczi, noting that symptoms of SAD, such as fatigue, lack of energy, decreased motivation, depressed mood, carbohydrate

craving and weight gain beginning when daylight savings time ends—from the Tropic of Cancer to the Arctic Circle and from the Tropic of Capricorn to the Antarctic Circle—are caused by a lack of daylight.

Retailers that understand the physiological effects of indoor environmental quality—daylighting and melatonin production cycles, sound and acoustic comfort, thermal comfort relating to temperature, humidity level and air velocity, and other elements of indoor air quality—are poised to maximize retail sales simply by making the best use of customer comfort.

"It is not easy to isolate and measure the separate effects of these various indoor environmental qualities each on their own," said Green. "Further, in retail situations there are many more possible factors affecting retail sales."

EFFECTS OF DAYLIGHTING ON RETAIL SALES

In 1999 and again in 2003, HMG conducted extensive surveys of a large, undisclosed retail chain for Pacific Gas & Electric (PG&E) Company and the California Energy Commission (CEC). To gain the full support of this prominent chain, which is usually protective of internal competitive information, HMG, PG&E and CEC promised anonymity.

At the conclusion of both studies, HMG presented evidence that this national chain was experiencing up to 40 percent higher sales in its California stores, primarily daylit by diffusing high-illumination skylights and supported by automatic control of electric artificial lights, compared to similar nondaylit stores using only artificial lighting.

According to Lisa Heschong, a licensed architect and a principal of HMG who directed and authored both studies, all other things being equal, an average nonskylit store in the chain would likely generate between 31 and 49 percent higher sales with the addition of skylights. "This was found with ninety-nine percent statistical reference," noted the report's executive summary.

To ensure reliability, HMG used statistical models with up to 50 explanatory variables between 1999 and 2001. Heschong examined the relationship between average monthly sales levels and the presence of daylight in the stores, while carefully controlling such variables as size and age of the stores, amount of parking, demographics, the competitive climate, and other store characteristics and performance matrices.

According to Heschong, the CEC commissioned a study of another retail chain in an entirely different retail sector to see if the original findings would hold. However, this second chain had much more variables from store to store, whether or not the store used daylighting.

The retailer for the second study had a greater range of daylighting and climatic conditions than the first study participant, which had a standardized store and daylight design. The second retail chain sampling was smaller, 73 versus 108, and there was a much greater variation in the basic store plan and layout than the first chain

surveyed. Nevertheless, Heschong found that increased hours of daylight per store were strongly associated with increased sales in the second sampling but at much smaller relative percentages than the previous study.

The most significant variance in the second group of stores was parking adequacy. Daylit stores that had smaller-than-average surface parking lots experienced lower sales compared to nondaylit stores with ample parking, while stores with average or ample parking that also used daylighting experienced higher sales than nondaylit stores. As both the amount of daylight inside the store and parking availability increased, so did sales, according to Heschong.

Average sales for the second chain's daylit stores ranged from zero to 6 percent higher with a maximum of about 40 percent higher than nondaylit stores. The most productive daylit stores studied in this second chain were consistent with the first chain, previously surveyed twice. The daylit stores of this second chain also had a slightly higher number of transactions per month.

The study for the second chain also analyzed energy efficiency and cost savings related to daylight harvesting. Heschong estimated average whole building energy savings for the daylit stores using a combination of skylights with photocontrols at US$0.24 per square foot (US$2.58 per sq m) based on a 2000–2003 vintage lighting design that is not highly efficient. She projected a potential of up to US$0.66 per square foot (US$7.10 per sq m) in savings if the stores were to switch to a state-of-the art design, using 2003 retail electricity rates. Today's rates are higher, thus the savings are greater.

Most important, the study for the second chain concluded that the profit from increased sales associated with daylighting was worth at least 19 times more than the energy savings using the most conservative of estimates, but more likely these profits could be 45 to 100 times more than the energy savings.

The complete studies along with specifications about lighting and photocontrols are available for download at http://www.h-m-g.com/Default.htm.

Daylighting and photocontrols are not new. Daylighting strategies using skylights have been the company standard for Costco Wholesale Corporation since 1985. Costco's skylights are very similar to Wal-Mart's skylights. Costco typically uses rectangular four-feet-by-eight-feet (1.2 by 2.4 m) skylights made by Bristolite Skylights, headquartered in Santa Ana, California. These skylights cover about 4 percent of the roof area, evenly distributed over the aisles below. The ceilings are typically 25 feet high (7.6 m), which helps to spread the natural light evenly throughout the surface of the warehouse store. The skylights are made of acrylic-clad fiberglass, which increases transmission of natural light with minimum heat gain.

Costco uses only one photosensor, manufactured by Day Light Controls of Redmond, Washington, to turn on the high intensity discharge (HID) bright white 400-watt metal halide luminaires manufactured by Venture Lighting, headquartered in Solon, Ohio. The photosensor sits on top of one of the skylights and triggers the daylighting system to turn on or off the electric lights. In both cases, one-third

of the lights come on (or off), and then later another third follows. One-third of the lighting always remains on during store hours so that obvious changes in lighting do not distract the customers. A centrally located EMS controls all of it.

Heschong, whose energy-efficiency company also developed the SkyCalc skylighting design software, offers several recommendations for big-box retailers wishing to design optimum skylight/daylight harvesting systems:

- Use skylights with maximum light transmission, a moderate U-factor and diffusing qualities to prevent glare from sunspots or hotspots on the merchandise

- Use automatic photocells to dim or turn off lights when interior daylight levels reach optimum illumination

- Paint the ceilings white regardless of whether the ceiling is finished or open; all structural elements should be white; light-colored flooring also helps

- Distribute skylights uniformly by spacing them apart less than 1.5 times the ceiling height

David Green recommends that shopping malls take a cue from retailers such as Wal-Mart and Costco to design a system that harvests daylight to optimize energy and create a pleasant surrounding for customers. "In retail centers, harvesting daylight while rejecting heat energy [through the use of Low-E glazing] keeps the lights turned off during the day and lowers the cooling load," said Green, who believes that lighting is one of the most important architectural features in a retail environment.

"Lighting is a central issue in retail, and daylighting is having particular importance in the overall appeal and comfort of a retail environment," Green said, adding that lighting is also essential to energy conservation strategies in retail buildings.

PHOTOS: R. E. MILIAN

Daylight harvesting, also called daylighting, is not a new concept. Costco Wholesale Corporation has been using daylighting since 1985. It is amazing that more retailers do not take advantage of this technology.

Since it opened in 1992, the Costco Wholesale membership warehouse in Nanuet, New York, has been equipped with light fixtures that use 400-watt metal halide lamps from Venture Lighting in combination with photocontrols and skylights for daylight harvesting of natural sunlight. Studies on daylight harvesting, a lighting strategy designed to lower energy bills for big-box retailers, show that consumers prefer shopping in stores that bathe aisles with natural light to accurately render colors and brighten up the indoor atmosphere.

Pictured is the interior of the Nanuet Costco, depicting the metal halide lights at dusk automatically becoming brighter as the skylights give off less natural light. These 400-watt metal halides—formerly state-of-the-art technology—may no longer be the most ideal for daylight harvesting. This standard probe start metal halide lamp system has 100 mean lumens per watt (LPW) with a life of 20,000+ hours; 40,000 initial lumens, 26,000 mean lumens.

Costco's lighting supplier, Venture Lighting (affiliated with Advanced Lighting Technologies Inc. with a facility in India), based in Solon, Ohio, instead recommends for big-box daylight harvesting a 450-watt e-Lamp Uni-Form pulse start metal halide system with Opti-Wave electronic ballasts in a constant lumen situation. This system has 99 mean LPW with a life of 20,000+ hours, which is similar to the Nanuet Costco lamps but has 46,000 initial lumens and 39,000 mean lumens, much brighter than the one that Costco Nanuet purchases from Venture Lighting. The 450-watt system that Venture Lighting recommends has continuous dimming of 100 percent down to 50 percent of rated lamp power. That system has the dimming capability built in with a control interface for continuous dimming, sensor dimming or daylight harvesting controls.

Hybrid lighting designs allow bright sunlight to provide up to 100 percent of illumination during midday, when energy costs are highest. Most utility companies charge by the watts consumed plus a demand charge for peak usage. Continuously dimmable lighting saves energy under these conditions. When clouds roll in or nighttime falls, power is automatically increased continuously to maintain nearly constant light levels.

According to Venture Lighting, the type of lamp incorporated with daylight harvesting is critical. The lamp's light quality should blend well with natural light and provide good color rendering and contrast. Venture Lighting's recommended Uni-Form pulse start metal halide e-Lamp produces both a bright white light that blends with natural light and a consistent color quality that accurately renders colors of products, the retailer's logos, in-store signs and other objects. The e-Lamps combine with Opti-Wave high frequency electronic ballasts to create dimmable metal halide lighting to capitalize on daylight harvesting.

The Issaquah, Washington-based Costco Wholesale Corporation, with annual sales of US$64.4 billion, is the fourth-largest retailer in the United States and the eighth largest in the world. It operates 529 warehouses, including 389 in the United States and Puerto Rico, 75 in Canada, 19 in the United Kingdom, five in Korea, five in Taiwan, six in Japan and 30 in Mexico.

Chapter 11

Shopping Centers Go Green

WHAT CAN SHOPPING centers do to go green? Many of them are proving the value of sustainable green practices, but not everyone is exactly aware of what green means.

The green building movement continues to gain momentum. Yet people often think only of government office buildings, schools and libraries as green buildings. Retail buildings do not necessarily come to mind as having resource-efficient construction, renovation and operation. Shopping centers are often perceived as not being at the forefront of the green building movement, and this is simply not true.

The line between good building practices that have existed for years and green building design, more recently touted by environmentalists, is sometimes blurred because both stress efficiencies in buildings. Efficiency has always been a priority for shopping center owners when purchasing equipment and installing building systems.

Not only are there opportunities to upgrade to energy-saving equipment at existing properties, but there are less obvious solutions, too. These can take the form of modifying operations practices. "Significant impact can be made with simple changes such as shifting a night cleaning schedule to early morning daylight hours to reduce use of artificial lighting," said Brian F. Griffin, vice president of national operations for General Growth Properties.

OPERATIONAL EFFICIENCIES AT CBL

For decades, shopping centers have utilized a number of sustainability tactics that include minimizing contaminants indoors, energy management systems, water-tolerant landscaping, cardboard recycling and other waste management practices, to name a few. But years ago, such tactics were not known as sustainability.

CBL & Associates Properties addresses the issue of sustainability. "We spend company-wide between US$50 million and US$70 million a year to upgrade operating systems and equipment that reach the end of their life cycle," said Thomas W. Guerra, SCSM, director of operations at CBL & Associates Properties Inc. He added that most of these upgrades focus on state-of-the-art sustainable designs that have efficiencies built in to save on ongoing operating costs and reduce energy consumption.

These include replacing site lighting with quick-start smart ballasts that are even more energy saving than the standard metal halides CBL is replacing, upgrading HVAC central plants and rooftop units to more efficient Energy Star-rated models and changing out dark roofs with a "cool roof" that is white, reflective and better insulates the building envelope. With a head start in these areas, shopping center designers, construction professionals and property managers are moving closer to sustainable design and operation.

However, the road to sustainability is long, and the course is a learning process. Many developers want to cautiously travel that road, particularly when undertaking new developments.

"We are still exploring the best way to implement green best practices in our new development projects and our existing portfolio," said Jim Williamson, senior project manager of development at CBL. CBL is nevertheless making great progress by developing new projects that are environmentally friendly, and the experienced developer is hiring LEED-accredited architects to do it.

CBL developed a magnificent 1.3 million-square-feet (120,775 sq m), open-air mixed-use complex in Pearland, Texas (just south of Houston), comprising retail shops, department stores, hotel, housing and a special events center. The project is centered on a central park for community activities. It promotes sustainable living by offering a live-work-shop-play environment, a trendy concept consistent with its autumn 2008 opening.

This type of project is considered to be on a sustainable site because driving, which is associated with GHG emissions, can be minimized by having many uses integrated in an urban setting. The new Pearland Town Center offers a unique lifestyle and shopping experience. It features canopies, trellises, awnings and colonnades framing the façade of the storefronts.

CBL incorporated a warm, inviting pedestrian environment highlighted by tree-lined boulevards, curbside parking, lush landscaping, a decorative water feature, a community events pavilion and walking paths.

"Of our many development projects underway throughout the country, Pearland Town Center is the most ambitious and exciting we have ever designed," said Stephen Lebovitz, president of CBL. Lebovitz hired Omniplan to design and supervise implementation of Pearland's unique architectural design elements.

Omniplan is one of the most committed architectural companies on sustainable design in the United States. It incorporates sustainability as a routine design element, not an added service. Almost half of Omniplan's professional staff is LEED-accredited professionals, including the principals.

While not all projects that Omniplan designs seek LEED certification, the architectural firm still sets an equivalent LEED Silver level of sustainability as a minimum goal for every project it works on.

"We believe that through a truly integrated design process, this level of sustainable design does not have to cost more, and in fact, we believe that it can cost less and will certainly cost less to operate," said Cari K. Walls, LEED AP, director of business development for Omniplan.

As a word of caution, sustainability in retail development should not be seen as a destination—a final resting place—but rather as a journey toward greener, more sustainable and efficient buildings.

Sustainability of shopping centers at the highest level, such as LEED Platinum, is rarely feasible today because the buildings have dozens of independently operated retailers, restaurants and other uses. Additionally, electrical loads in retail buildings are more demanding.

In these vibrant retail settings attracting tens of thousands of patrons per week, much of the energy demand to power the high levels of lighting needed to display merchandise and refrigerate perishables comes from electricity generated by burning fossil fuel at the regional utility company rather than renewable solar and wind power sources. But even that is changing.

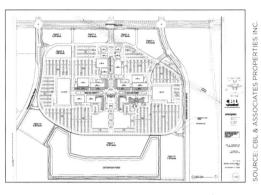

SOURCE: CBL & ASSOCIATES PROPERTIES INC.

CBL & Associates hired Omniplan to design Pearland Town Center near Houston, Texas, a chic lifestyle-oriented 2008 mixed-use project in a sustainable urbanlike, walkable site. The 1.3-million-square-foot (120,775 sq m) development includes 300 residential units, a 110-room Courtyard by Marriott hotel, 50,000 square feet (4,650 sq m) of office and 750,000 square feet (69,700 sq m) of upscale retail, which includes Chico's, White House/Black Market, Ann Taylor Loft, Coldwater Creek, Brooks Brothers Country Club, Victoria's Secret, Hollister, Macy's, Dillard's and Barnes & Noble.

Omniplan designed the project to meet LEED standards of sustainability, but the developer has not applied for LEED certification. According to Omniplan, this level of sustainable design does not have to cost more, and may even cost less, but will certainly cost less to operate: a benefit CBL and its tenants will reap.

REGENCY GETS GREENER ALL THE TIME

Executives at Regency Centers Corporation, a Florida-based real estate investment trust with 447 grocery-anchored community shopping centers and single-tenant properties, believe that for shopping centers to become truly green buildings, the retailers and other stakeholders have to work in unison from the earliest phases of design right through the construction phase.

To prove this, Regency placed a scorecard on the construction site of the 67,226-square-foot (6,245 sq m) Shops of Santa Barbara in California. Contractors working for the City of Santa Barbara, Regency (the developer responsible for the construction of the open-air shopping center), and the major

retailers—Circuit City and Whole Foods—made entries of sustainable practices employed during construction onto the scorecard.

The scorecard served several purposes. It helped stakeholders learn the parts each of them played toward achieving a sustainable development. It documented the contractors' collective sustainable practices and served as a tool to apply for LEED certification upon completion of the project.

Shops of Santa Barbara
Hitchcock Way & State Street
Santa Barbara, California 93105

SOURCE: REGENCY CENTERS CORPORATION

While building the Shops of Santa Barbara to LEED standards, Regency Centers placed a scorecard on the construction site for contractors working for the City of Santa Barbara, Regency (the developer responsible for the construction of the open-air shopping center) and the major retailers (Circuit City and Whole Foods) to make entries of sustainable practices employed during construction.

Regency and the USGBC closely worked to assemble the collection of this data to determine the feasibility of using this system in other projects that involve many ownership entities and multiple general contractors, such as in the construction of retail properties and mixed-use projects.

The Shops on Main, a lifestyle and town center Regency is developing in Schererville, Indiana, is the second project (after Santa Barbara) that Regency is pursuing for LEED core and shell certification. "The reasons Regency has chosen to move in the direction of sustainability are several," said Mary Lou Fiala, Regency's president and chief operating officer and the ICSC chairman from 2008 to 2009.

"First, it's pretty clear that our shopping centers impact the environment, particularly our developments. Second, in most cases we are a long-term owner and operator of the centers we develop," she said. "As such, we saw an opportunity to be better stewards within the communities we serve, while at the same time offering space that is more attractive to our tenants."

Fiala's retail experience has helped her focus on what makes retailers successful. Before joining Regency, Fiala served as a retail expert for Security Capital Global Strategic Group after almost two decades of retail merchandising and management experience with Burdines, Macy's and Henri Bendel.

Regency anticipates that tenant demand for sustainable shopping centers will increase significantly over the next few years because of public demand and as retailers begin to recognize that sustainable centers provide significantly lower operating costs, according to Fiala.

"By making substantial commitments to sustainability, Regency seeks to be better neighbors locally, while again demonstrating first mover leadership within the entire shopping center industry," Fiala said.

Regency's tenants seem supportive of this strategy. More than 75 percent of Regency's portfolio is leased to U.S. national and regional retailers—many of which

have their own green programs, such as Bed Bath & Beyond, CVS/Pharmacy, JCPenney, Kroger, Lowe's Companies, Office Depot, Publix GreenWise Market, Safeway, Starbucks, Target, Trader Joe's, Wegmans Food Market and Whole Foods Market.

Regency's move toward sustainability came about rather quickly, proving that large and small shopping center development and operating companies can do likewise using similarly clear vision and focus.

In October 2006, Regency assembled a team of open-minded company executives and outside consultants to explore the feasibility of embarking on a sustainable program laying emphasis on green building practices.

The first step of this green task force was to assess every area of Regency's business model to determine the practicality of incorporating and supporting sustainable building and operating practices and LEED certification.

"Knocking down the preconceived notions is one of the biggest hurdles for people to overcome in taking their companies toward a direction of sustainability," said Scott Wilson, vice president, construction for Regency Centers. Wilson, who became a believer during the process, led the Regency task force that recommended the LEED-focused development program.

"I had preconceived notions. When I put them aside and learned what reality is, I found out it is not as expensive or as complicated," said Wilson.

A few months later, Regency was already developing two new shopping centers using many LEED standards. By November, the community center developer announced a full-fledged program outlining goals for sustainable features to be added to properties throughout its development pipeline.

Regency named its program Greengenuity, and its sustainability measures are now included as standard practice for all new and existing centers.

Regency plans to pursue the LEED certification for 20 percent of its projects starting in 2008, 40 percent of projects starting in 2009 and 60 percent of projects starting in 2010.

Regency's chief investment officer, Brian Smith, said that management expects that basic steps to achieve the LEED minimum level will be a nominal addition to the total cost of the project. Some practices will be implemented at no extra cost to baseline since Regency plans to substitute these enhancements as part of new development construction, as part of renovation upgrades or in replacing equipment at the end of its life cycle.

In new developments, Greengenuity baseline measures include smart irrigation and planting native foliage, low-flow plumbing fixtures, low VOC paints and adhesives, high-efficiency HVAC, efficient lighting for reduced energy consumption and green housekeeping cleaning products.

In existing centers, the Greengenuity baseline measures will be incorporated along with new capital expenditure guidelines. When replacement of the existing elements becomes necessary, features such items as white reflective roofs, native plants and eco-friendly parking lot lighting will be installed.

The Regency tenant buildout criteria were revised to guide the tenants as they build out their space, including suggestions for efficient lights; low VOC paints and adhesives; and other green design-build practices and products.

Regency already has in-house recycling programs, sustainable design criteria for new offices, purchasing policies emphasizing recycled content and a campaign to reduce printing, according to Brian Smith.

"It is quite interesting how Regency's query into sustainability or green building, as we first referred to it, evolved," Fiala explained. "At first, it was simply an investigation into whether we should incorporate green elements into the construction of our new centers. Within the first couple of months of digging into it, it became very apparent to us that the sustainability movement was bigger than just that.

"If we were truly intending to embrace the essence of this movement, then we had to ensure that it reached to the core of our culture and affected the way we do business in every aspect of our operations: developments, operating centers and our business operations," she explained.

"Becoming a sustainable owner and LEED developer is not only the right thing to do, it's something we're committed to," said Martin "Hap" Stein Jr., Regency's chairman and chief executive officer.

"We have made that commitment, and to us, anything less is simply greenwash," Fiala added.

Creative, decisive ways of making retail buildings green as Regency is doing are surfacing all over the world, each with its own set of criteria and level of accomplishments.

WESTERN EUROPE'S SUSTAINABLE DEVELOPMENT

In Western Europe, many countries follow the National Sustainable Development Strategy promulgated by the United Nations, and shopping centers have been frequently developed as green buildings for years.

Land Securities, a real estate investment trust (REIT) in the United Kingdom, has developed a consistent environmental management policy across its portfolio, which it uses to guide its new developments, renovations and operation of its shopping centers.

Among Land Securities' green building tactics are a strict recycling policy, using graywater to irrigate the turf of its shopping centers and using all Forest Stewardship Council (FSC)-certified wood in its construction projects.

The FSC forest certification program and the Programme for the Endorsement of Forest Certification (PEFC) are international forest certification systems that promote responsible harvesting of the world's forest resources to meet the needs of present and future generations.

FSC alone has certified more than 220 million acres of forests in 82 countries as sustainable wood that is properly harvested and systematically replenished.

Earth's forests are vital to reducing GHGs and helping to cool the atmosphere as trees release moisture, produce oxygen and remove carbon dioxide from the air. Trees are also helpful in many other ways. Trees add beauty, provide shade and last beyond a human lifetime.

When harvesting trees for their valuable wood and wood byproduct resources, one must consider replacing trees and the 20 to 30 years it will take to grow these trees to maturity for harvesting.

Western European shopping centers are so much on the forefront of the sustainable building movement that the British Council of Shopping Centres launched a Web site in 2007 to share useful sustainability practices in the United Kingdom. The Web site covers industry research, publications, news reports and links to regulations that mandate U.K. green building standards. Some of these regulations include energy-saving requirements coming from the European Commission in Brussels.

SONAE SIERRA VOTED MOST SUSTAINABLE

Sonae Sierra, a leading global company that builds, owns and manages 47 shopping centers in Brazil, Germany, Greece, Italy, Portugal, Romania and Spain—comprising 17.2 million square feet (1.6 million sq. m.) of retail—has held a leadership position in environmental and corporate responsibility for years.

"In today's world, to be a business leader, you have to be an environmental leader," Dr. Elsa Rodrigues Monteiro, head of institutional relations, environment and communications for Sonae Sierra, told an audience of retailers and retail property executives at the ICSC World Summit in Cape Town, South Africa, in October 2007.

In her role at Sierra, Dr. Monteiro tracks recycling rates, energy consumption and water consumption by country for the developer. Between 2002 and 2007, the company reduced energy use by 25 percent, she explained, emphasizing that Sierra now installs environmental management systems (EMS), which are in accordance with ISO Standard 14001:2004, in all new developments. Since 2004, an additional 10 operating properties have been upgraded to the same standard.

Lloyd's Register Quality Assurance (LRQA) recognized Sierra's efforts for meeting the state-of-the-art ISO 14001:2004. LRQA is a prestigious member of the Lloyd's Register Group. The London, U.K.–based nonprofit is the world's first classification society providing impartial certification since 1760. Sonae Sierra was the first shopping center developer to be awarded this environmental certification.

ISO 14001:2004 is now accepted universally and is highly regarded in Europe for EMS excellence. It has become one of the most reputable environmental standards in the world, advocated by government officials and environmentalists.

PHOTOS COURTESY OF SONAE SIERRA

Sonae Sierra changed the operation of the chillers at ViaCatarina in Oporto, Portugal's second-largest city and capital of the country's north. The efficiency was greatly improved:
Investment: US$29,240
Reduced energy use: 300,000 KWh per year
Cost savings: US$29,000 per year
Carbon emission avoided: 159 tons (144 metric tons) per year

Sonae Sierra retrofitted the parking garage lighting at Centro Colombo in Lisbon, Portugal.
Investment: US$182,800
Reduced energy use: 400,830 KWh per year
Cost savings: US$34,810 per year
Carbon emission avoided: 200 tons (181 metric tons) per year

José Quintela and Promontório, the architect for Sonae Sierra, specified using geodrains at Centro Vasco da Gama in Lisbon, Portugal, to remove groundwater and prevent flooding.
Investment: US$14,600
Reduced water use: 190,674 cubic feet (5,399 cubic meters) per year
Cost savings: US$14,900 per year

ISO 14001 requires establishing an environmental policy and calls for evaluating certain aspects of a company's products, activities and services that affect the environment and suggests that measurable targets should be set to implement programs. ISO 14001 also provides a measuring system to evaluate the achievement of objectives and suggests corrective action.

Sonae Sierra, with a total gross leasable area (GLA) of more than 19.4 million square feet (1.8 million sq m), is developing an additional 5.4 million square feet (501,700 sq m) in 13 more projects in Brazil, Germany, Greece, Portugal, Romania and Spain. Sonae Sierra had two of its shopping and leisure centers in Portugal, the Centro Colombo in Lisbon and NorteShopping in Matosinhos, EMS certified as ISO

PHOTO COURTESY OF SONAE SIERRA

Shopping and entertainment center RioSul Shopping, in Seixal, Portugal, an innovative development owned equally by Sonae Sierra and RockSpring, has achieved substantial savings by installing a new HVAC central plant system. The coefficient of performance (COP) for the chiller is 6.8. José Quintela da Fonseca/LaGuarda & Low is the project architect.

Ownership invested US$485,500 on this HVAC upgrade. It saved 2,024 MWh per year in energy usage, achieved a reduction in operating expenses by US$216,700 per year and prevented 1,020 tons (925 metric tons) of GHG emissions per year.

14001. Other Sierra centers followed, and the well-respected leading retail developer is now applying that system to all of its centers.

Sonae Sierra makes its sustainable agenda widely known by voluntarily completing an annual sustainability report based on standards established by the Global Reporting Initiative (GRI). This report covers the company's activities pertaining to economy, labor practices, society and other areas, including environmental performance.

Additionally, Sonae Sierra tracks the level of social responsibility in various key areas, which enables it to self-declare compliance of GRI Guidelines to a level of C+. An affiliate of Deloitte Touche Tohmatsu independently verifies Sonae Sierra's report, and Sierra makes the report available to all its stakeholders for comment.

Sonae Sierra calls this report "Corporate Responsibility (CR)" and gives a detailed breakdown on its strategy for dealing with a multitude of subjects by country in which it operates shopping centers. These include areas of operation that impact climate change, waste management, recycling, land use, business chain (segregating it by its suppliers and its tenants), the communities surrounding each center, the center's employees, and issues of health, safety and water conservation

For example, Sonae Sierra boasts one of the most thorough initiatives involving water conservation and an effort to avoid water contamination. These include:

1. Water-efficient designs, rainwater harvesting, use of graywater recycling, water-efficient sanitary equipment (such as spray taps and low-flush toilets) and use of non-water-intensive plant species in landscaped areas, as well as specifying efficient drip irrigation systems

2. Reduced impact of pollution on local water supplies; use of filter drains to prevent pollution from rainwater runoff; porous paving in parking areas; wastewater separation in the drainage system; wastewater pretreatment equipment including oil separators and hydrocarbons separators; measures to avoid the risk of water pollution from construction activities; and during property operations phase, regularly analyze the contamination level of shopping center discharges to sewers, streams and other water runoff bodies

Water consumption monitoring, audit and implementation of recommendations at two of Sonae Sierra's shopping centers helped achieve substantial savings in water use and on costs of water and sewer charges.

	Centro Colombo	NorteShopping
Total investment	US$36,550	US$51,200
Reduced water use per cubic foot	1,917,330	1,105,000
(per cubic meter)	(54,293)	(31,290)
Reduced water use by percentage	35.0%	21.4%
Cost savings	US$96,350	US$23,800

Source: Sonae Sierra

The overall approach that Sonae Sierra undertook in 2006 helped earn the company the ICSC Europe ReSource Award in 2007. ICSC created this award to help distinguish a developer, a project, a manager or a tenant in the shopping and leisure center sector that makes a long-term commitment to sustainable development.

TURNING GREEN INTO GOLD

Ronald A. Altoon, CDP, FAIA, partner-for-design at Los Angeles, California–based Altoon+Porter Architects, has been one of the shopping center industry's most tireless and ardent proselytizers for the sustainability movement.

From the lectern of the ICSC University of Shopping Centers at the University of Pennsylvania's Wharton School in Philadelphia to the podium of ICSC's Center-Build Conference in Phoenix, Arizona, Altoon has been advocating the merits of green building design with the passion of a televangelist preaching from his pulpit.

Altoon argued for sustainable design during the late 1990s and for most of the 2000s, finally defying the pundits who believed that the retail green building movement would be a short-lived trend that would soon blow over.

"The fact that we're here doing this plenary session in South Africa is indicative of how far we've come in recognizing sustainability," Altoon said while moderating a panel at the ICSC World Summit in South Africa on October 3, 2007, entitled "Turning Green into Gold." Altoon praised ICSC and his panel for helping to bring sustainability into the industry's forefront.

Altoon reviewed key green building concepts that his company had designed for new retail developments and redevelopments in different parts of the world. Among the developments he presented, Altoon described the sustainable design features his team instituted at Botany Town Centre in southeast Auckland, New Zealand, a development of AMP Capital Shopping Centres.

He also explained the green building program his group designed for the Queen Ka'ahumanu Center (located in Maui, Hawaii) while working in concert with the developer, General Growth Properties. The creative design for the superregional center features a partially opened Teflon-coated fiberglass roof that gives the look and feel of an enclosed shopping mall. The roof shelters patrons from the rain and from Maui's hot sun but allows light and the tropical island air to flow through the building.

Botany Town Centre, a development of AMP Capital Shopping Centres, in southeast Auckland, New Zealand, is one of the largest retail developments in the country. The following sustainable tactics were achieved in the redevelopment:

- Developed mixed use (office, retail, entertainment, dining, civic space) in a densely urban area and connected with the community

- Open-air design, no air-conditioning

- Promoted alternative transportation by integrating public transportation access, bus stations and taxi stands relocated on the site, connected to future light rail; provided bicycle storage, showers, lockers and changing rooms

- Protected natural habitat and maximized open space
- Used proper stormwater design, achieving quantity and quality control
- Used water-efficient, locally sourced landscape materials indigenous to the area and added water conservation features
- Minimized urban heat island effect and light pollution
- Used ozone-friendly refrigerants
- Optimized energy performance and increased ventilation
- Organized storage and collection of recyclables achieving 10 percent of recycled content
- Diverted 75 percent of construction waste from landfill
- Sourced 20 percent of construction materials that were extracted, processed and manufactured regionally
- Used certified wood
- Controlled pollution from construction activity
- Used low-emitting materials, such as carpets, adhesive, sealants, paints and coating
- Achieved daylight from 75 percent of spaces and views
- Used a LEED-accredited professional

Altoon pointed out that as the developing world attains wealth and population continues to grow, the citizens of these developing countries will want the material goods we have been accustomed to having, such as cell phones and air-conditioning. This will increase the world's carbon footprint, he said, and he challenged the shopping center

PHOTOS COURTESY OF ALTOON+PORTER ARCHITECTS

Top right: The conservatory that Altoon+Porter Architects designed for Botany Town Centre is an attractive architectural feature but functions as an energy-saving structure. The design conveys heat as it naturally rises, which stratifies at the highest level. This design allows for greater use of an economizer cycle to occur at the air-handling unit (AHU), which maintains free cooling for most of the year to reduce energy use. Vents at the cupola (the top third-tier roof extension) and the operable clerestory windows (at the middle second-tier roof extension) allow for natural ventilation.

DESIGN DRAWING COURTESY OF ALTOON+PORTER ARCHITECTS

Middle and bottom right: Queen Ka'ahumanu Center in Kahului, Maui, Hawaii, managed by General Growth Properties Inc., used these sustainable design elements:
- Developed in densely urban area and connected with the community
- Reused existing building and expanded vertically; maintained 75 percent of existing walls, floors and roof
- Controlled pollution from construction activity
- Diverted 75 percent of construction waste from landfill
- Promoted alternative transportation by integrating public transportation access and parking capacity for commuters
- Used water-efficient landscape and added water conservation features
- Used on-site geothermal renewable energy
- Increased ventilation; no air-conditioning in common areas
- Achieved daylight from 75 percent of spaces and offered views of exterior
- Organized storage and collection of recyclables

PHOTOS COURTESY OF ALTOON+PORTER ARCHITECTS

industry to take immediate action to integrate sustainable design and operation into retail properties.

"The issue is to turn good design into good business," said the committed architect. To paraphrase the words of Jonas Salk [developer of the polio vaccine], and relate it to sustainability, 'our greatest responsibility is to be good ancestors' to our grandchildren."

LESSONS FROM OFFICE AND RESIDENTIAL

U.S. shopping center companies are adopting green practices that have been considered standard for years in Europe. They are quickly advancing by assigning a senior executive to ensure sustainable practices are enforced in development, renovations and building operation.

Some real estate companies that develop a combination of office, residential and retail may have a head start because of their green building work in other real estate asset classes.

Chicago, Illinois–based Joseph Freed & Associates has an aggressive sustainability program in place at its residential communities and is already adapting some of the techniques it employs in residential buildings to its retail properties.

The Cleveland, Ohio–based Forest City Enterprises is another fully integrated real estate development company that extends green building practices to retail from ideas that arise in its other divisions. Likewise, Jacoby Development focused on sustainability as the cornerstone of the master plan for redeveloping an abandoned brownfield in Midtown Atlanta.

SIMON'S CARBON DISCLOSURE

The publicly traded member of the Standard & Poor's 500, Simon Property Group Inc., began disclosing its carbon dioxide emissions in the early 2000s. It joined the Carbon Disclosure Project (CDP), an independent, not-for-profit group that monitors carbon footprints of large companies such as Simon.

The Carbon Disclosure Project tracks about 2,400 public companies around the world, noting current and projected GHG reduction goals for investors to access. Advocates for this type of disclosure maintain that climate change is a business risk, meaning it can potentially affect the bottom line. As such, they say that these investors should factor this variable into their pricing model for trading a company's stock.

Some investors do and some do not, but for those that do, many public companies are now publishing extensive information about their environmental footprint.

The largest shopping center company in the United States launched a program to reduce carbon emissions in 2004 and appointed George Caraghiaur to oversee it as the company's vice president of energy services. Caraghiaur retained Ameresco Energy Services Company to evaluate the use of energy by Simon's 380 shopping centers in the United States and suggest ways to reduce consumption through such initiatives as HVAC, lighting, maintenance equipment and vehicles—all of which also emit CO_2.

The good news for Simon shareholders is that CO_2 reductions also came with cost savings that either went directly to increase the company's funds from operations or reduced its tenants' occupancy costs—depending on lease forms (fixed CAM or pro rata).

Between 2004 and 2007, Simon reduced its electricity usage by more than 10 percent each year compared to the previous year without affecting comfort, safety or reliability. This reduction represented an annual cost savings of more than US$11 million. This confirmed the importance for Simon to maintain a focus on best operating practices, management reporting and cost-effective investments in energy efficiency to control usage.

Caraghiaur took it one step further. He hired a subsidiary energy provider of the Con Edison Company to conduct an energy audit of the centers in the U.S. Northeast in order to learn how to make more energy cuts, something he sees as a win-win proposal.

"Every kilowatt-hour we don't use is a kilowatt-hour we don't have to pay for. Moreover, it's a kilowatt-hour that does not have to be produced by a power plant," said Caraghiaur. "In other words, energy efficiency is good for the bottom line and for the environment."

Recognizing the importance of energy savings for real estate users, the National Association of Real Estate Investment Trusts (NAREIT) joined forces with EPA and awarded Simon the Light Gold Award in 2005, 2006 and 2007, a prize that honors companies that have demonstrated superior and sustained energy use practices.

Some of the practices that Simon employed were commonsense tactics to control energy costs without affecting comfort, safety or reliability. Caraghiaur and Simon property managers started by examining operating practices, and together they implemented low-cost/no-cost procedures throughout the portfolio, such as:

- Minimizing energy use in vacant spaces
- Keeping tight control over hours of operation for all lighting systems in the common area, parking lots and back-of-the-house areas
- Zoning lighting systems to gain better control of them and minimize waste
- Monitoring lease violations that increase energy costs for the landlord
- Optimizing start/stop of all HVAC systems to meet cooling requirements while minimizing costs
- Adjusting temperature set points to minimize HVAC costs while meeting comfort requirements
- Using outside air to cool the property when outside air temperature and humidity make it possible to do so
- Minimizing energy use through proper use of energy control systems

GENERAL GROWTH CONSERVES AND RECYCLES

Energy-efficient design is a standard emphasized in General Growth Properties' developments and renovations. This includes incorporating systems that reduce electrical consumption, using the most efficient HVAC equipment, designing and

installing energy management systems, using daylighting to reduce artificial lighting needs, having well-insulated white roofs to reflect instead of absorb the sun's radiant heat and specifying appropriate shading devices to reduce heat load.

The company conducted a thorough review of its operations system-wide to ensure that sustainability best practices were being implemented across the board. The results were very favorable. According to Lisa Loweth, vice president of sustainability for General Growth Properties, the company implemented these energy conservation programs in 2007:

- Investment in energy management systems

- Energy Star–rated HVAC equipment

- Cool white roofing specification

- Lighting retrofit

- Central plant upgrades

- Managed seasonal temperature set points and timing

- Diligent maintenance of equipment to ensure optimum efficiency

- Minimal operation of temperature, exhaust and lighting equipment beyond operating hours

- Adjusted automatic door timing

- Use of photocells to control back-of-the-house lighting

- Adjusted cleaning schedules to maximize use of daylight

- Staged equipment operation

- Load shedding/demand control to reduce peak consumption

- Controlling seasonal equipment and year-round equipment

The Chicago, Illinois–based REIT did not stop at energy conservation. General Growth has been stepping up its sustainability program in many other ways, one of which is recycling. In December 2006, ICSC and EPA recognized General Growth Properties with the Outstanding Shopping Center Owner Award during ICSC's CenterBuild Conference in Phoenix, Arizona.

ICSC and EPA created the America's Marketplace Recycles Awards program to recognize outstanding efforts by the shopping center industry to conserve resources, recycle materials and purchase recycled content products.

The program recognizes companies as well as individual shopping centers that excel in recycling because shopping centers and their retailers generate a tremendous amount of materials that can be recycled, such as corrugated cardboard, paper, glass, plastic, metals, food waste, landscape trimmings and shipping pallets.

Not only did General Growth take the big prize, but five of its shopping malls in the Dallas-Fort Worth, Texas Metroplex also took home the Most Innovative Recycling Program Award: Hulen Mall (Fort Worth), Vista Ridge Mall (Lewisville), Parks at Arlington (Arlington), Town East Mall (Mesquite) and Collin Creek Mall (Plano).

General Growth's recycling and reuse programs divert more than 25,000 tons (22,700 metric tons) of recyclable material from landfills annually. They include:

- Cardboard recycling
- Technology equipment recycling
- Lightbulb recycling
- Battery recycling
- Cooking grease recycling
- Parking lot reconstruction specification of minimum 15 percent recycled asphalt product (RAP), often ground on site
- Donate old store fixtures to Habitat for Humanity ReStore
- Reusable temporary barricade program

General Growth also tested a green shopper engagement program at Highland Mall in Austin, Texas, in 2007 called E-Cycling. This program diverted 133 tons (121 metric tons) of electronics equipment to recycling facilities.

Recycling is important for various reasons. It helps to reduce landfill gas emissions from decaying matter as well as reduce natural resources and energy needed to manufacture new products.

ICSC president and chief executive officer, Michael P. Kercheval said, "This awards program continues to provide both EPA and ICSC the opportunity not only to highlight those shopping centers and retailers that are leading the way regarding recycling, but has given us another avenue to get the word out about the importance of recycling and supporting green initiatives."

In addition to energy conservation, recycling and green cleaning programs, General Growth is also carefully evaluating new technologies, specifications and practices. "We are testing hybrid security vehicles at 20 properties," said Loweth. Due to the frequent braking and slow speeds typical of operating these vehicles, hybrids are constantly recharged through braking, thus reducing fuel use.

Many municipalities' health departments have not yet approved the use of waterless urinals, which use a liquid chemical seal to trap and flush urine without using water to wash it out.

Manufacturers claim waterless urinals are perfectly sanitary and pose no odor problem. The waterless urinals connect to the sewage system but do not draw fresh water. Instead, the conventional water-filled urinal drain has a floating chemical layer, which forms a barrier that prevents sewer vapors from escaping.

UNIQUE CARTRIDGE DESIGN REQUIRES NO ADDITION OF SEALANT BETWEEN CHANGES

ILLUSTRATION COURTESY OF FALCON WATERFREE TECHNOLOGIES LLC

DIAGRAMS ILLUSTRATE HOW LIQUID SEALANT FLOATS ON WATER...   **...AND HOW URINE PASSES THROUGH IT, BECOMING...**   **...SECURELY ISOLATED FROM THE RESTROOM, WHILE PROCEEDING TO THE DRAIN**

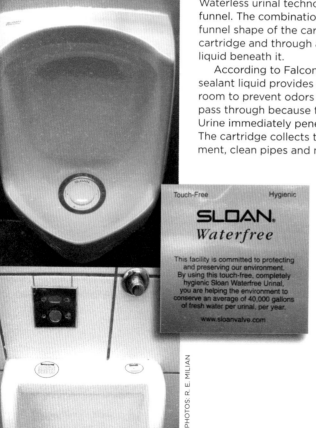

PHOTOS: R. E. MILIAN

Touch-Free   Hygienic

SLOAN.
Waterfree

This facility is committed to protecting and preserving our environment. By using this touch-free, completely hygienic Sloan Waterfree Urinal, you are helping the environment to conserve an average of 40,000 gallons of fresh water per urinal, per year.

www.sloanvalve.com

Waterless urinal technology involves a cartridge shaped to act as a funnel. The combination of nonstick, nonporous materials and the funnel shape of the cartridge ensures that all urine passes into the cartridge and through a unique sealant liquid that floats on top of the liquid beneath it.

According to Falcon Waterfree Technologies, this fresh-smelling sealant liquid provides an airtight barrier between urine and the restroom to prevent odors from escaping the drain, but it allows urine to pass through because the sealant liquid is lighter than water and urine. Urine immediately penetrates the sealant liquid and flows to the drain. The cartridge collects the uric sediment, leaving an odor-free environment, clean pipes and no water waste.

Falcon claims that the only maintenance required is routine cleaning of the fixture and an easy change of the cartridge, performed approximately three or four times per year.

A replaceable and biodegradable, liquid-sealed cartridge in the Sloan Waterfree Urinal (pictured middle left photo) filters waste so liquids enter the drain and sediments are collected for disposal when the cartridge is replaced after 6,000 to 7,000 uses. The cartridge also features a sealing ring to provide an airtight barrier between the cartridge and the housing.

The cartridge also features a sealing ring to provide an airtight barrier between the cartridge and the housing.

General Growth Properties retrofitted all urinals (pictured lower left at White Marsh Mall in Baltimore, Maryland, in 2008) with Waterless Eco Urinals manufactured by Ecotech Water LLC.

According to Falcon Waterfree Technologies, a supplier of waterless urinals, this fresh-smelling chemical layer acts as an airtight sealant barrier between urine and the restroom to prevent odors from escaping the drain below. However, this liquid allows the urine to pass through it because it is lighter than water.

Pleas from General Growth local property managers for water conservation at the municipal and county level have influenced changes to building and health codes that had not previously considered this modern technology to allow use of this water-saving fixture. This cleared the way for General Growth to place a bulk order, and in 2008, it was systematically installing waterless urinals in the men's restrooms at about 100 of its properties.

Compared to conventional urinals, waterless urinals can save from one to three gallons (3.8 to 11.3 liters) of water per use. One urinal at a busy commercial establishment can conserve up to 45,000 gallons (170,350 liters) of water a year by eliminating flushing.

General Growth management anticipates conserving more than 35 million gallons (132 million liters) of water annually after these urinals are installed, and other shopping center companies are experiencing similar success replacing flush urinals with waterless urinals. Forest City Enterprises installed waterless no-flush urinals at the Mall at Robinson in Pittsburgh, Pennsylvania. Jon Ratner of Forest City said the initial investment was US$6,600 plus US$6,300 in installation costs. Ratner figured his payback period to be roughly three months per urinal considering a savings of US$43,205 in water and sewage plus US$1,458 in annual maintenance savings.

General Growth encourages other green initiatives and safety practices in the upkeep of its properties. The company requires its cleaning service contractors to use Green Seal certified cleaning products. Green Seal is an independent nonprofit organization that certifies environmentally friendly products and services.

General Growth is committed to using cleaning products that are environmentally friendly, according to Julie Jones, SCMD, SCSM, General Growth's senior vice president of management, capital deployment and national operations. These include Green Seal products that are biodegradable, low in volatile organic compounds, low in aquatic and human toxicity and free of such things as ammonia, phosphates and reproductive toxins.

General Growth is also undertaking green practices in other areas of operations. In 2007, General Growth Properties used LED lights on a Christmas tree at its Westlake Center in Seattle. Its success led the firm to require all Christmas decorations to exclusively employ LED lights, beginning with the 2008 holiday season. "The LEDs really have potential," said Loweth.

MACERICH'S STRATEGIC ENERGY PLANNING

A Strategic Energy Planning (SEP) program for a shopping center goes beyond energy management systems and energy audits to increase energy efficiency. To the Santa Monica, California–based Macerich Company, SEP is an integrated, compre-

hensive process that is planned and implemented company-wide for optimum efficiencies and operational sustainability in all its retail facilities.

The LEED-accredited professional, Jeffrey M. Bedell, CEM, CPP, heads up Macerich's SEP program and has responsibilities for energy management at all 73 large regional malls that the real estate investment trust owns and manages in the United States.

According to Bedell, it is critical for those looking for long-term risk mitigation and cost control to consider all options. These include energy efficiency, alternative and renewable energy generation, energy management controls, load management, facility operations controls, energy and equipment procurement, and sustainable development or redevelopment.

For the SEP program to succeed, Bedell says that a commitment from a high-level executive is necessary to assess, invest, implement, monitor and adjust the program when necessary. This type of commitment helps to achieve the project's long-term goals by preventing well-thought-out plans from becoming derailed too early in the implementation phase.

A thorough financial pro forma is a necessary part of this process, to justify investments that will achieve a lucrative payback. Bedell recommends preparing a life cycle assessment of equipment upgrades and a ten-year pro forma to gauge the performance in terms of costs and savings resulting from the SEP program. As markets, technologies and facility use changes occur, the plan must have flexibility built into it to be able to adjust it, at least on an annual basis.

The Macerich Strategic Energy Plan focuses on five key strategies for implementation to save energy, reduce operating costs, maintain a proper course and minimize impact to the environment:

1. New construction, redevelopment/renovation

- High-efficiency design standards
- Continuous building commissioning process
- Energy-efficient equipment purchasing policies
- Allocate proper operations and maintenance (O&M) budgets
- Use of LEED or equivalent system when possible
- Implement new technologies

2. Deferred maintenance/operations

- Address current backlog
- Prevent additional backlog
- Establish minimum operational requirements
- Set benchmarks
- Reinvest operating savings

3. Energy-efficiency strategies and projects

- Central production systems
- Distribution systems
- Building systems
- Energy communication, controls and energy management system (EMS) at a building level

4. Commodity procurement/supply-side opportunities

- Commodity procurement
- Management of emerging markets
- Energy redistribution at properties
- Identification, prioritization and tracking by regions, states and property

5. Energy management planning

- Energy monitoring and control system (EMCS)
- Utility- and building-level submetering
- Energy information systems (EIS)
- Operational decision making
- Daily operation and maintenance
- Integration of EMCS and supply-side market conditions
- Measurement and verification (M&V)

According to Bedell, a properly implemented SEP plan should have the following steps:

1. Establish baseline

Typically, a one- to three-year average of facility usage, demand and cost for all utilities should be factored into the model. This should include a disaggregation of energy use for the facility to define current energy usage. For example, do not place too much emphasis on lighting efficiency if only 5 percent of total energy consumed is devoted to lighting.

2. Property assessment

A detailed conditional assessment of equipment and infrastructure is necessary to create the plan.

3. Growth and system degradation

It is important to anticipate the property's growth in terms of energy use over the next ten years; factor in a decrease in efficiencies for aging systems and infrastructure that the plan anticipates will remain in place for the duration.

4. Escalation and inflation rates

The financial experts should be included in the formulation of this model to ensure an accurate pro forma that takes financial factors into consideration that will likely influence costs over time.

5. Establish the "business as usual" forecast

One alternative scenario in the pro forma should project financial impact if the organization were to do nothing beyond operating the systems with further energy management systems invested. This provides a comparison throughout the ten-year period, not only the starting point.

6. Determine appropriate strategies and tactics

Prepare a detailed plan that contemplates each of the strategies and tactical plans to be implemented in the proper order over time. Major areas to focus on for most properties are:

- Plan for development, redevelopment or expansion that involves major construction. This will result in a new set of circumstances that should influence efficiencies.

- Focus on operations and building commissioning to maximize the efficiency of the systems and equipment already in place.

- Replace or modify end use equipment to reduce energy consumption or demand.

- Consider commodity/supply-side systems after implementing efficiencies; procurement systems often lead to further energy savings.

- Plan your energy management on a long-term basis. This is an essential process using an energy information system to integrate, optimize, monitor and continually adjust the facility to achieve long-term results.

7. Develop a detailed scope of work

Consider all costs in your assessment including development, design, engineering, metering and contingencies. Remember to take advantage of grants and incentives available to reduce the overall cost.

8. Develop a financial pro forma

It should be based on an assessment of life cycle of costs and benefits, not a snapshot in time, which is typically done to consider payback of individual projects. A proper pro forma allows sound financial decision making based on market parameters projected over time. Use financial tools such as cash flow projections, return on investment (ROI) and net present value (NPV) when considering investing on multiple equipment and systems to reduce energy costs, rather than using a simple payback analysis.

9. Conduct a sensitivity analysis

Prepare a pro forma sensitivity analysis of the effect on profitability of a comprehensive strategic energy-planning program based on engineering and cost estimates and on the savings derived from implementing all systems over time. Run sensitivities to your pro forma for pricing and savings, using various scenarios such as one at 10 percent and two at 15 percent above and below what you anticipate. This will help you understand the inherent risks in the projects and provide options for mitigating those potential risks.

To ensure comparison of strategy within the Macerich portfolio, Bedell suggests that each strategy be detailed as follows:

- **Strategy overview** (introduces the strategy and the general approach that has been taken in the assessment of the strategy)
- **Property assessment** (considers present situation and conditions relative to the strategy)
- **Strategy benefits and impacts** (outlines the expected financial and qualitative benefits the property would realize by implementing the strategy)

By implementing the tactical recommendations within the five stated strategies, Macerich is able to address the aging and deteriorating condition of its energy infrastructure and to afford it a means to evaluate financial results.

Macerich also has many green building programs for new developments, redevelopments and existing centers. One project, Santa Monica Place in California, will de-mall the current structure in an "adap-

RENDERING COURTESY OF OMNIPLAN

Santa Monica Place opened in 1980. Less than three decades later, Macerich is razing parts of this Southern California 557,000-square-foot (51,750 sq m) mall to transform it into an outdoor shopping wonder in order to better connect the project with shoppers on the adjacent Third Street Promenade. Omniplan, working in association with The Jerde Partnership of Los Angeles, is adding many green building features as part of the redevelopment.

tive reuse" of the property to create an open-air shopping district that will become a natural extension of the Third Street Promenade. Macerich will incorporate a series of green building practices in that project as well as in another redevelopment known as The Oaks.

Located in Ventura County, California, The Oaks is undergoing a multiphase renovation and expansion that includes an interior renovation, the addition of an open-air specialty venue with upscale shops, a multiscreen cinema, freestanding restaurants, a new Nordstrom department store, a multilevel parking structure and a new food court with indoor and outdoor seating.

During the demolition of the restoration project, Macerich created an on-site recycling program to grind and store construction material such as brick, stone, concrete and other debris to reuse sustainably as base material.

"We have an operations protocol, which we've updated with a heightened focus on green initiatives," said Kenneth M. Gillett, SCSM, senior vice president, property management—West for the Macerich Company and chairman of ICSC's Certified Shopping Center Manager (CSM) Admissions and Governing Committee.

Another Macerich project, the Village at Corte Madera (California), received high acclaim for stepping up its recycling program, which is more important than ever before. Solid waste per person in the United States is currently 4.4 pounds (2 kg) compared to 2.7 pounds (1.2 kg) in 1972. Recycling prevents overtaxing landfills and wasting materials and resources.

Prior to August 2007, the Village at Corte Madera only recycled cardboard. Kathleen B. Lovold, senior property manager of the open-air upscale shopping center in Marin County, stepped up the company's efforts by urging both retailers and customers to recycle paper, plastic, metal and glass as well.

"We launched the new program with a recycling kickoff breakfast for our retailers, attended by nearly half of our retailers," said Lovold. She said that the merchants were supportive of the center's initiative even though it added a few extra steps in their closing and trash procedures.

The property worked with the waste disposal vendors International Environmental Management and Mill Valley

Top: Kathleen B. Lovold, senior property manager of the Village at Corte Madera (standing), convinces merchants to step up their recycling efforts from only cardboard to all materials, at a recycling kickoff breakfast meeting in August 2007. Middle: Special recycling receptacles were strategically placed around the property to encourage customers to recycle. Bottom: Recognizing how important stakeholders are, Macerich informs them about its sustainability practices through its "Happenings" newsletter, which it distributes to merchants, employees, community leaders and other stakeholders.

Refuse Service. Both companies sent representatives to the merchant breakfast and answered retail-specific questions about the new recycling service available three times a week.

Mill Valley Refuse Service provided each of the four shopping center buildings with recycling bins that are stored outside the retailers' back doors, aligned with their cardboard recycling bins. The property provided the containers in the common areas for the shoppers' convenience.

There was no added cost to step up the recycling efforts, and the stakeholders now feel a sense of accomplishment in doing their part for the environment.

Macerich lets their stakeholders know how important they are in its "Happenings" newsletter, which it distributes to merchants, employees, community leaders and other stakeholders.

FORMER BROWNFIELD: ATLANTIC STATION

Brian M. Leary spent most of his time while attending Georgia Tech's College of Architecture harboring a dream. He dreamed of one day creating a master plan that would become a successful national model for environmentally sensitive smart growth and new urbanism. He envisioned a revolutionary development that would buck six decades of U.S. suburban trends and rival the urban designs of Europe's finest cities.

To Leary, Atlanta was a place in which people drove to get somewhere that they could walk to, and he did not like to drive or take the bus, as he often did while growing up. So determined was this young man to fulfill his dream that he concentrated his undergraduate degree in architecture, his master's degree in city planning, and he focused on transportation and land development while in graduate school at Georgia Tech.

He even surprised his professors with a thesis outlining a redevelopment plan for a defunct and neglected Atlantic Steel property north of downtown Atlanta that would provide a national model for smart growth and brownfield remediation through the creation of a 24-hour, live-work-shop-play community.

Brian Leary planned and executed the green building mixed-use project in Midtown Atlanta known as Atlantic Station. The redeveloped brownfield opened on October 21, 2005.

The title of Leary's master's thesis was "Atlantic Station: A place to live, work and play."

Leary's big break to realize his dream came when he presented his thesis to another urban visionary—James "Jim" Jacoby, chairman and chief executive of Jacoby Development. Jacoby bought into Leary's concept, and Leary joined him in 1997 as vice president of design and development for Atlantic Station LLC, using the name from his school thesis to coin the name of the gargantuan development that now ranks among the largest and most difficult developments ever assembled in Atlanta.

Remediating brownfields had been tried, but it required plenty of capital and a willing market for the redeveloped site. Jacoby joined forces with AIG Global Real Estate Investment Corporation to source the capital.

Atlanta had been experiencing a boom and suburban land was cheap, so the supporting factors were not favorable for an urban infill project like Atlantic Station. The Atlanta metropolitan area kept expanding outward with residential and commercial development having no end in sight.

However, Leary and Jacoby kept their eyes on the goal. Leary negotiated with the U.S. EPA and received the necessary support to make Atlantic Station and the new Seventeenth Street multimodal bridge the first Project XL and transportation control measure of its kind in the United States. The Seventeenth Street Bridge over the Downtown Connector has reconnected Midtown with the west side of Atlanta.

Project XL, which stands for Environmental Excellence and Leadership, is an EPA program designed to test innovative ways to achieve better and more cost-effective public health and environmental protection. The rest, as they say, is history. Leary's dream of urbanization and environmental design had finally become a reality.

Atlantic Station is a model for smart growth and sustainable development. The remediated brownfield, now a mixed-use project in Midtown Atlanta, has retail, office, hotel and multifamily housing for 10,000 residents. Dillard's department store, Target and Regal 16-screen Cineplex are among its retail anchors.

PHOTO COURTESY OF JOHN WILLIAMS, ATLANTIC STATION

Atlantic Station, codeveloped by AIG Global Real Estate Investment and Jacoby Development Inc., is today a 138-acre (56-hectare) brownfield mixed-use redevelopment in Atlanta's Midtown business district. It exemplifies green building design, smart growth and sustainable development.

Atlantic Station was named after the once-polluted century-old Atlantic Steel Mill. It is located at the nexus of the two busiest highways in Georgia, Interstates 75 and 85.

The massive environmental reclamation of the deserted steel mill site took two years to complete. In addition to the commercial success of Atlantic Station, the project has implemented various notable examples of green development in sustainable sites with creative green building design and ongoing sustainable operations practices. Among the initiatives Atlantic Station incorporated into the redevelopment are:

- Removing 9,000 loads (165,000 tons [149,700 metric tons]) of contaminated soil and materials from the site in the remediation phase

- Pulverizing 132,000 cubic yards (100,921 cubic meters) of concrete building foundations and 164,000 cubic yards (125,387 cubic meters) of granite, and reusing as backfill to level the building site, which saved on trucking, dumping and using up resources for raw material

- Creating an aesthetically pleasing one-acre pond to function as a stormwater detention facility that reduces peak runoff from postdevelopment conditions to equal or lower than predevelopment conditions

- Installing an interception system on the site to collect groundwater and to monitor and treat intercepted groundwater prior to discharging to the municipal sewer system

- Planting 2,800 new trees on the property and in surrounding neighborhoods

- Installing an air quality monitoring program (in conjunction with EPA) consisting of site design criteria and transportation performance targets that encourage alternatives to single-occupancy vehicle trips

- Using Firestone and Sika Sarnafil reflective roofing systems to minimize urban heat island (UHI) effect and alleviate indoor temperatures

- Adding an HVAC system that operates more than 25 percent more efficiently than traditional systems using a two-mile-long (3.22 kilometers) network of 36-inch (91 cm) pipes to deliver chilled water from a 50,000-square-foot (4,650 sq m) central cooling plant to office, residential and retail buildings

- Planning to build a cooling plant by Energy Solutions, a subsidiary of Southern Company, expected to reduce the project's electricity load by 15 to 20 percent

- Having the 171 Seventeenth Street building certified as the first LEED Silver for a Core & Shell high-rise office building in Georgia

- Building a new 130-foot-wide (40 m) multimodal bridge on Seventeenth Street to enhance transportation flow and encourage bicycle traffic

- Densifying the site with a mix of businesses, retail facilities and residences (on average less than 1,500 feet [457 m] apart) to encourage pedestrian traffic and a live-work-shop-play environment where transportation by motor vehicle for working, shopping or recreation is not necessary, which eliminates thousands of tons of GHG emissions

- Facilitating frequent shuttle service using clean-fueled, rubber tire transit shuttle system that circulates between the nearby Metropolitan Atlanta Rapid Transit Authority (MARTA) station and the project

- Providing electric car charging stations and priority parking for electric vehicles

- Offering a car-share program using electric vehicles, specially designated parking for car pools and guaranteed rides

- Planning shared parking among retail and office uses including the use of metered streetside parking and parking structure beneath the retail

- Using nonstandard street lane widths, nonstandard block size and larger turning radii to allow vehicles to turn into and out of driveways to prevent them from encroaching upon oncoming traffic and to favor pedestrian activity

- Having pedestrian-friendly sidewalks on all surface streets

When Jacoby and Leary eventually complete the master development plan in the 2010s, Atlantic Station will have more than 15 million square feet (1.4 million sq m) of retail, office and hotel space, and multifamily housing for 10,000 residents, as well as 11 acres (4.45 hectares) of public parks.

The vast 138 acres (56 hectares) of Atlantic Station will contain enough residential and commercial activity to act as a new urban magnet north of Atlanta's downtown, fulfilling Leary's original dream.

FAIRLANE GREEN

In the United States, Archon Group LP, the real estate subsidiary of Goldman Sachs, collaborated with Ford Land, Ford Motor Company's real estate and development subsidiary, to develop a site known as Fairlane Green in Allen Park, Michigan. It consists of 243 acres (98.3 hectares) comprising the former Clay Mine, a reclaimed industrial landfill. It is not far from Fairlane, southeastern Michigan's 2,360-acre master-planned community developed by Ford Land.

The acquisition by Archon from Ford Land took on a creative condominium ownership structure. Today, Ford owns the landfill below the land surface and as such retains maintenance obligations and environmental liability. Archon owns the land surface, the building structures now constructed (other than the 11 acres [4.5 hectares] it sold to Target for its store) and the air rights.

When the entire Fairlane Green development is eventually completed, two-thirds of the 243-acre (98.3-hectare) site will be green, meaning planted natural landscaped areas not covered by buildings, parking or roads. Typically, retail and existing infrastructures cover about 10,000 square feet (930 sq m) per acre (0.4 hectare). Fairlane Green is less dense, at about 4,000 square feet (370 sq m) per acre.

The first phase includes 105 acres (42.5 hectares), of which only 60 acres (24.3 hectares) are buildable to promote green space. The crown of the development is the 405,000-square-foot (37,600 sq m) Fairlane Green, a multi big-box–anchored power center opened in autumn 2006. The center successfully achieved the LEED Gold for Core and Shell certification for sustainable design and construction.

The project received US$30 million in tax increment financing (TIF) from the Michigan Department of Environmental Quality and the City of Allen Park to reimburse for substantial costs associated with remediation of wasteland and then building on the former landfill.

TIF is a tool used in the United States and other parts of the world to borrow from future gains in taxes to finance the current improvements that will help generate those tax gains.

Fairlane Green's TIF-subsidized costs included site work to reduce settlement, protect the landfill cap, reinforce slopes and install utilities. Grant Trigger of Honigman Miller Schwartz and Cohn LLP structured the condominium concept and helped secure the TIF.

Dallas, Texas–based O'Brien & Associates Architecture designed Phase I of Fairlane Green. VCC, also of Dallas, took on the vertical construction. JM Olson of

The first phase of Fairlane Green in Allen Park, Michigan, achieved the LEED Gold for Core and Shell certification for its sustainability efforts. The power center, now open for business, boasts several of the most popular multi-big-box retailers, including Barnes & Noble, Bed Bath & Beyond, Famous Footwear, Longhorn Steakhouse, Michaels, Old Navy, On the Border, Pier 1 Imports, Target, T.J. Maxx and World Market. Below: The master plan rendering of Fairlane Green adds needed retail while promoting parklike green spaces.

PHOTOS COURTESY OF ARCHON GROUP LP

St. Clair Shores, Michigan, did the site work construction. NTH Consultants took charge of the geotechnical engineering, and Atwell-Hicks handled the civil engineering.

Fairlane Green is not alone. The list of shopping centers in North America that are achieving their sustainable building goals is growing. These centers are either converting to green practices by implementing substantial green building tactics (such as the superregional Yorkdale Shopping Centre) or by receiving the coveted LEED certification from the USGBC (such as the open-air community center Abercorn Common and the mixed-use project Northfield at Stapleton).

ABERCORN COMMON: FIRST LEED CENTER

PHOTOS: MELAVER INC.

The 169,000-square-foot (15,700 sq m) Abercorn Common in Savannah, Georgia, ranks among the greenest of community shopping centers. It was the first LEED-certified shopping center in the United States and was actually certified under the LEED office Core and Shell program because at the time LEED had no standards for retail. The center first opened in 1968—then known as Abercorn Plaza—as part of the original commercial area on Savannah's Southside.

In 2004, it underwent a US$30-million redevelopment that emphasized environmental efficiencies as a key goal along with a re-tenanting and renovation to maximize the property's potential.

The first sustainability tactics were implemented during the demolition and construction phases by recycling 85 percent of the debris and installing environmentally friendly equipment.

The 169,000-square-foot (15,700 sq m) Abercorn Common in Savannah, Georgia, is a LEED-certified shopping center. Abercorn Common looks simply like a nice, modern community center to the unsuspecting eyes, but it is more than that. It is an example of green building design, construction and operation, one of the innovators of the shopping center industry in the 2000s.

Old-fashioned bricks were dismantled from the fascia and reinstalled as floor pavers. For community tie-in, these pavers were engraved with names of residents and businesses as part of a charity benefit.

The redeveloped center has become a positive influence on the environmentally conscious local consumer. There are front-end parking spaces reserved for hybrid model cars and signs that remind customers of the center's commitment to sustainable operation.

Water is now captured from the roof and parking lot and is diverted to a cistern that collects five million gallons (18,900 liters) of water a year. The water is treated and reused for irrigation purposes.

The green practices employed by this community center are numerous. A white reflective roof, water-saving plumbing in sinks and toilets in addition to using waterless urinals, low-VOC paints and sealants, and other techniques have earned the center its LEED Silver certification.

Abercorn Common buildings also now have HVAC systems that are 30 percent more energy efficient than typical retail buildings. Melaver Inc., the developer of Abercorn Common, persuaded some of the center's retailers—such as Michael's—to seek LEED certification, then reached a milestone when the center's McDonald's restaurant franchise achieved the Gold LEED green building certification. (See Chapter 9.)

The redevelopment of Abercorn Common has turned it into a shopping destination that is attractive and modern while maintaining the unique old charm of Savannah. The public has been receptive to the greening of Abercorn Common. "As people are becoming more aware [of the positive aspects of sustainability], they are looking for those features in their everyday life," said Roman L. Stankus, AIA, LEED AP. Stankus is vice president of Atlanta, Georgia–based Ozell Stankus Associates Architects, the project architect for Abercorn. Common.

WESTFIELD

When executives for the Green Building Council-Australia (GBCA) decided to adapt its popular rating system for offices to retail, the first place they went to was the Westfield Towers in Sydney, Australia, to meet with Westfield officials. That is because Westfield is one of the world's leading development companies of shopping centers and dominates the Australian shopping center industry.

The Westfield Group is an internally managed, vertically integrated owner of shopping centers, undertaking development, design, construction, asset management, property management, leasing and marketing activities. It has investment interests in 120 shopping centers in four countries, with a total value in excess of US$53 billion.

Now Westfield is working with the GBCA to develop a Green Star rating tool for the sustainable design of shopping centers. Westfield began a retrofit program in 2007 to improve lighting in its shopping centers while at the same time conserve energy, reduce GHGs and achieve cost savings.

By spring 2008, this program had already been completed in eleven centers on the U.S. West Coast, and twelve centers on the U.S. East Coast were undergoing

PHOTOS: R. E. MILIAN

similar improvements. Westfield expects these measures in the United States alone to save about 30 million kWh of electricity per year.

The total cost of the current program, after taking into account rebates from utility provider incentive programs, is US$4.6 million. Westfield will achieve significant savings by reducing the energy costs at those 23 centers by US$2.6 million per year, therefore recouping the cost in less than two years and realizing further ongoing cost savings in future years.

In Australia, Westfield developed a trial sustainable business management program within the International Food Court of Sydney Central Plaza. Westfield management works with food court retailers to reduce their environmental impact. Westfield measured the success of the program by conducting audits on the food court tenants' water and energy usage—now tracking at a 10 percent savings—transport, waste management and business management. Based on the success at Central Plaza, Westfield plans to roll out the program to other centers.

Westfield joined a consortium of shopping center companies to hire an independent consultant in the United Kingdom to conduct environmental benchmarking for its U.K. shopping centers. The group involved 130 other shopping centers across Europe that are seeking to establish best practices in Europe by sharing costs and consumption figures.

The study focused on the centers' impact on energy and climate change, water use, resource depletion and waste management against its peers. The report highlights ways in which the European shopping center industry can improve environmental management and sustainability, and gives the participating centers a useful tool for individual centers to benchmark their current performance against their peers and identify areas for improvement.

Top: Parking lot light standards replaced less energy-efficient models at Westfield Garden State Plaza in Paramus, New Jersey's largest shopping center. Additionally, the food court lighting was upgraded and the mall's new parking structure was constructed with efficient metal halide lighting. (See above photos.) Lighting retrofits at Westfield Garden State Plaza (shown) and at 22 other Westfield shopping centers in the United States will account for US$2.6 million per year in energy savings. The global shopping center developer estimates a payback of less than two years after factoring in utility company rebates and other incentives.

YORKDALE SHOPPING CENTRE WINS ICSC AWARD

At the 2006 ICSC CenterBuild Conference, the ICSC International Design and Development Awards unveiled its first award for sustainable design. The award went to Yorkdale Shopping Centre of Toronto, Ontario, Canada.

ICSC International Design and Development Awards jury discuss the sustainable design features of Yorkdale Shopping Center at the ICSC World Summit in Cape Town, South Africa in 2007. L-R: Ian F. Thomas CDP, chairman of Vancouver, British Columbia–based Thomas Consultants Inc., Ronald A. Altoon, CDP, FAIA, partner-for-design at Los Angeles, California–based Altoon+Porter Architects, Arcadio Gil Pujol, CSM, CMD, CDP, managing director of Madrid, Spain–based LaSBA, S.A., Gordon T. Greeby, Jr., CDP, PE, president of Lake Bluff, Illinois–based The Greeby Companies and Kathleen M. Nelson, ICSC past chairman and president of New York–based KMN Associates Inc.

PHOTO COURTESY OF OXFORD PROPERTIES GROUP

ICSC awarded Yorkdale Shopping Center in Toronto, Ontario, Canada, the International Design and Development Awards for sustainable design in 2006.

The international judges for ICSC, inspired by the developer's initiatives for green practices, bestowed this award by consensus. Oxford Properties Group, an Ontario Municipal Employees Retirement System (OMERS) company, redeveloped the center.

Yorkdale's US$60-million expansion in 2005, on the former site of its Eaton's department store, increased the size of Yorkdale to more than 1.6 million square feet (148,650 sq m). It added H&M, Home Outfitters, Tommy Hilfiger, Old Navy and Zara as anchors in the converted vacant department store space. H&M, Old Navy and Zara used the 60-foot (18 m) department store shell to create their multilevel stores.

Yorkdale Shopping Centre is now marketing its sustainability efforts with a program called Greening Yorkdale. Although the project did not apply for LEED Canada certification, the project undertook many tactics outlined in LEED questionnaires, including the sustainable site being connected to a mass transit subway station and to regional and local bus lines.

The architect designed the new retail mall into the shell of the vacant Eaton's department store, as required in sustainable reuse of buildings. The general contractor for the project implemented a successful waste management program. This program segregated different forms of waste and construction debris, including metal, concrete, wood and gypsum, and directed the material for recycling. This greatly reduced the amount of waste directed to the landfill.

The contractor extracted substantial amounts of removed asphalt and granular subbase of demolished pavements and reused them as aggregate for the new concrete subbase. Contractors also removed and stockpiled selected luminaires from the gutted ex-Eaton space and reused them in various locations throughout the building.

The architects and contractors who selected materials achieved the requirement for using products within the LEED maximum distances from the project to minimize transport-related emissions. Products such as steel, which were locally available, constituted a good portion of the total material cost of the project.

The operational efficiencies include stormwater management, which they achieved in all roof drainage with controlled flow. Light pollution was minimized with all-new, exterior wall-mounted fixtures,. Light standards were added to the existing parking, promoting dark sky and lessening light pollution.

MMC International Architects, which worked on the Yorkdale expansion, specified only low-flow plumbing fixtures, electronic faucets and flush valves to reduce water use. On the expansion area, the architect used HVAC rooftop units with full outdoor air economizers to reduce mechanical cooling when outdoor air is cool and can adequately cool the space.

In the existing shopping center building, the renovation program reused the chiller as it already utilized non-CFC refrigerant. To remove the spring and winter cooling requirement from the chiller, the architect added a heat exchanger. Water flowing from the cooling tower and back into the chiller converts it to chilled water—using much less power—to cool the coils, where air handlers blow air that cools the center in the summertime.

The electrical systems were fully commissioned to ensure they met the standards set forth in the original redesign. Operation and maintenance manuals were reviewed for sustainability adequacy and completeness.

In an effort to minimize the use of energy, the engineers introduced a building automation system (BAS), which can turn off equipment during periods of low load and unoccupied conditions. To achieve the targeted energy reduction, LED fixtures and metal halide lamps were used. Emergency exit signs are LED-type with five watts per face.

"Yorkdale Shopping Centre has reduced its energy costs from US$1.2 million in 2002 to US$800,000 in 2004 through a number of initiatives," John T. Crane, CET, MIPE, RRFA, the operations manager for Yorkdale, told the audience at an ICSC conference in 2007 in New Orleans, Louisiana, where he participated on a panel on sustainability.

Yorkdale implemented two energy-savings lighting strategies as part of the renovation. The first is ambient daylight level control. Due to the high daylight levels in the mall, lighting contractors installed an indoor photocell connected to the lighting control system. When the natural light level exceeds a predescribed level, the lights in the mall automatically turn off. This indoor photocell has a backup.

The second lighting strategy involves occupancy monitoring. The system schedules light fixtures to be on only during customer-occupied periods and reduces the light levels during cleaning and times when the mall is closed to the public.

Daylight levels in the renovated portion of the mall exceed LEED minimum requirements. "In fact, ninety-five percent of Yorkdale's lights are not on during the daytime," Crane said, referring to the newly installed mall lighting system.

Each tenant has a dedicated HVAC unit. This results in better control so that there will be no overcooling to accommodate heavily loaded areas, requiring subsequent reheating of air for other less loaded zones.

The stunning 60-foot-high (18 m) glass skylight and clerestory atrium running 300 feet (91 m) in length, which was the first of its kind installed in Canada, also exceeded LEED requirements for bringing in natural light.

In the operations phase following the redevelopment, a program for segregating and recycling was instituted, which includes separating and marking waste bins to encourage recycling.

The ventilation during peak times, particularly during the busy Christmas shopping season, will be increased in proportion to occupancy loads to enhance IAQ. During this season, all the rooftop units will be in the economizer *free cooling* mode, and outdoor air will be progressively increased to reduce the thermal loading due to heavy customer footfall.

Included in the criteria for selecting materials was the minimization of off gassing. Control of pollutant sources entering from outside the building have been addressed with the provision of walk-off matting at all public entry points. Regarding indoor areas, such sources as custodial rooms and waste storage are fully enclosed and with separate ventilation.

Yorkdale used a LEED-accredited professional as part of the design and construction team, not necessarily to help apply for LEED Canada for new construction and major renovations certification but to guide the developer in achieving a high level of sustainability in undertaking the massive redevelopment.

SALZBURG'S EUROPARK RECOGNIZED

The ICSC International Design and Development Awards handed out its second award for sustainable design during the 2007 ICSC CenterBuild Conference to EUROPARK, a shopping center in Salzburg, Austria.

Magister Marcus Wild, chief executive officer for SES Spar European Shopping Centres, the developer and owner of EUROPARK, accepted the award in Phoenix,

Arizona, while accompanied by his colleagues, Magister Christoph Andexlinger and Doctor Felipa Fernandes.

In Austria, any building that undergoes a major redevelopment must bring the building in compliance with current standards of environmental compatibility, explained Fernandes. As a result, SES ordered a transformation that made the building ecofriendly by the time the expansion opened in October 2005.

PHOTOS COURTESY OF SES SPAR EUROPEAN SHOPPING CENTERS

EUROPARK in Salzburg, Austria, received the ICSC International Design and Development Award for Sustainable Design in 2007 for various practices including harnessing daylighting, having vents that let fresh air in during spring and autumn, and successful efforts to connect mass transit to the site.

Massimiliano Fuksas, the architect for the project, examined every environmentally relevant aspect of the redevelopment and instituted modern building technology measures to lessen the impact on the environment. These measures included remediating the expansion site that had been polluted by a bus manufacturer that previously occupied the site, adding access for mass transit, improving indoor air quality and even making the development more environmentally sound to prevent affecting several endangered fauna and flora species native to the region.

Four independently operated rooftop HVAC units were equipped with cold and hot efficiency monitors.

The temperature and ratio of incoming air was fully automated via several thermostats throughout the mall. Upper vents can be opened to introduce fresh air, and three decorative water fountains function as a humidification system during the winter months to allow moisture to be absorbed by ambient air for comfort.

All ventilation systems reuse various forms of heat retrieval (rotational heat transfer units) to warm the building interior. The Interspar hypermarket anchor store even reuses the exhaust heat that its refrigeration system gives off. The heat is used for cooking by means of a sophisticated heat transfer plate.

The architect came up with a design that resembles nature, using interior natural light, no right angles and many organic forms usually found in ancient cities, according to Wild. "EUROPARK Salzburg was built with the most human quality in place, with water, green areas and good natural light inside," said Wild.

The developer added a new entrance to underground parking on the east end of the project to reduce noise pollution and created plenty of opportunities for store employees and customers to use mass transit.

Before the 546,000-square-foot (50,725 sq m) EUROPARK was expanded, only one bus line serviced the project from the central business district, in 10-minute intervals. During the redevelopment, the developer worked with the city's department of transportation to provide access by electric buses (Line 1, Line 142) and built an S-Rail EUROPARK station. The latter was made possible through a financial contribution by the developer.

During ongoing operation, EUROPARK maintenance workers separate and divert for recycling all glass, plastic, Styrofoam polystyrene foam insulation, metal, bulky waste, paper and cardboard. They also store organic waste products in coolers to minimize odors.

Wild is attempting to follow his successfully sustainable milestone, EUROPARK, with a second green wonder shopping center he opened in April 2007, in the south of Villach, Austria—a city once known as Santicum, dating back to Roman times.

ATRIO'S GEOTHERMAL COOLING AND HEATING

Achammer-Tritthart & Partner Architects & Engineers (ATP) incorporated some innovative sustainable tactics into the Atrio Shopping Center that could make a green building enthusiast salivate.

The mechanical and electrical engineering team, working with the architect, developed an energy concept that converted the in situ concrete piles forming the foundation of the building into "energy piles," which harness geothermal energy stored underground.

A medium circulates inside these piles to take advantage of the steady ground temperature for heat exchange purposes. The system draws geothermal renewable energy from deep inside the earth core to heat and cool the Atrio retail complex through a concrete pile absorber that has a heating capacity of 7,200 kW and a cooling capacity of 6,800 kW.

Whereas the Atrio's heating and cooling system involving energy piles represents an innovative technology for retail use, it is neither a new smart building concept nor an industry first.

A similar (although much smaller) system was installed one year before at Columbus Center in Vienna consisting of 300 piles (less than half the amount of the

PHOTOS COURTESY OF SES SPAR EUROPEAN SHOPPING CENTRES AND ENERCRET

The concrete piles forming the foundation of the building were turned into "energy piles," harnessing the energy stored beneath the ground to cool and heat the Atrio Shopping Center in Villach, Austria.

In early summer, the Atrio employs "free cooling." The system pumps a medium inside the energy piles, which is cooled by the cold soil several feet below the surface and then pumped to the air-conditioning system. As soil temperature rises, a chiller assists the process. During the winter, thermal energy is extracted from deep inside the ground by means of a heat pump.

For environmental innovation, such as the energy piles being installed at Atrio Shopping Center in Villach, Austria (left), SES Spar European Shopping Centres was awarded the ICSC European ReSource Award for sustainability at the European Shopping Centre Awards ceremony held in Amsterdam, the Netherlands, in April 2008.

PHOTOS COURTESY OF SES SPAR EUROPEAN SHOPPING CENTRES AND ENERCRET

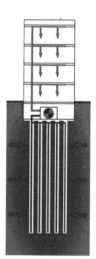

Winter
Aided by heat pumps, the energy piles heat the building and cool the soil.

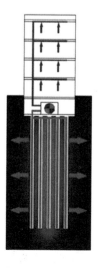

Summer
Aided by chillers, the energy piles cool the building and heat the soil. At lower temperatures, no chillers are required, resulting in "free cooling."

Atrio) and a diaphragm wall with a heating capacity of roughly 1,200 kW and a cooling capacity of 1,400 kW (about one-sixth the capacity of the Atrio).

According to EnerCret Nägele Energietechnik GmbH & Company (EnerCret), founded under a different name in 1982, there were about a dozen energy piles built every year in the mid-1980s, steadily increasing to less than one thousand new piles constructed annually through the remainder of the 20th century. In 2000, production shot up to 1,488 new energy piles and reached almost 5,000 systems built in 2004.

SES Spar used EnerCret technology to install energy-saving and cost-efficient pile foundations to heat and cool the largest shopping mall in the Alps-Adriatic region. EnerCret—short for energy and concrete—refers to generating energy with concrete pile structures.

The piles supply a thermal capacity of almost seven megawatts for cooling and 7.2 megawatts for heating. During the initial construction phase, workers erected 652 energy piles with an average length of 105 feet.

The total length of the tubes inside these piles if extended from end to end would reach almost 476,000 running feet (145,085 m). Atrio's energy piles are incorporated into almost all of the 800 foundation piles that support the building. The Atrio has nine heating circuit distributors and 1,176 absorber units. It also uses five chillers/heat pumps and one connection to the district heating.

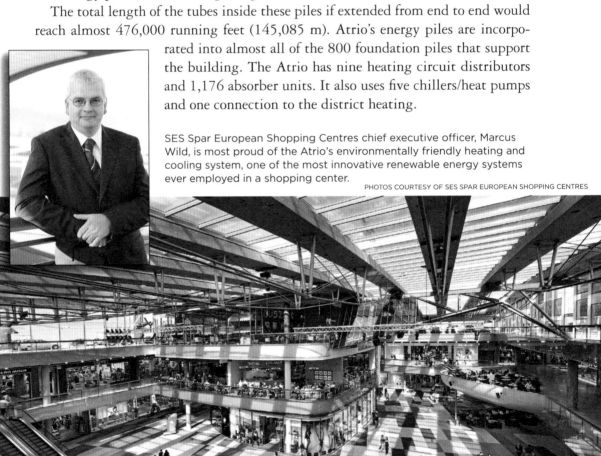

SES Spar European Shopping Centres chief executive officer, Marcus Wild, is most proud of the Atrio's environmentally friendly heating and cooling system, one of the most innovative renewable energy systems ever employed in a shopping center.

PHOTOS COURTESY OF SES SPAR EUROPEAN SHOPPING CENTRES

"They dug sixty meters (197 ft) deep below the surface to extract the optimum thermal energy to heat the center in the winter," said Marcus Wild.

Central Europe is ideal for harnessing thermal energy for cooling buildings, as ground temperature is about 55°F (13°C). EnerCret typically uses concrete structures such as piles, diaphragm walls, retaining walls and foundation slabs to absorb thermal energy from beneath the ground and from groundwater. The EnerCret system at the Atrio consists primarily of a 652-pile absorber used as a thermal conduit.

Fluid-filled pipe systems built inside the building's foundation elements absorb and transport the energy upward into the shopping center. According to EnerCret, pumping the cool liquid through the low-temperature heating system provides the Atrio up to 50 kW of cooling capacity for the building, using only one kW pump capacity. For each kilowatt of electricity consumed by the heat pump, up to four kW of thermal energy are produced as a bonus for the heating system.

"It's probably the most sustainable shopping center from a standpoint of energy efficiency using, for example, renewable energy as natural thermal water for heating," said Wild, referring to Atrio's use of the EnerCret technology.

This technology can be used in most buildings located throughout the world whether or not they are situated on land resting over a geothermal activity because not far beneath the surface, most land is cool enough to help cool a building.

Heat pumps make optimal use of low temperature levels of geothermal energy near the surface. Heat can be absorbed from the ground and used for space air heating and water heating. Running the process in the reverse direction provides cooling in the summer.

EnerCret contains the entire energy piles system within the building's foundation, unlike less efficient technology that requires extensive use of land surrounding the building to draw geothermal energy. Instead of creating heat within the building, as fossil fuel–fired furnaces do, the energy piles transfer heat from the ground into the building. The reverse takes place for cooling, as the heat is transferred from the building back into the ground.

The ground becomes a storage facility for excess energy by disposing the warmth during summer cooling, then later reusing it in the winter for heating and vice versa. Solar energy employed in combination with this technology can help store thermal energy underground in one season for use in the next, using virtually 100 percent clean green energy. Further carbon-free benefit can be achieved if a hydroelectric power station is employed to generate the electricity needed for this system.

Thermal energy is safe and has a long service life. This type of renewable power assures a consistent energy supply, as the energy source is underneath the shopping center and is self-regenerating.

The direct cooling method combining the use of a heat pump can reduce up to 80 percent of CO_2 emissions through savings in primary energy that would otherwise be used in a conventional central plant or rooftop unit HVAC system.

SES estimates that the Atrio has achieved an annual reduction of 853 tons (774 metric tons) of CO_2 emissions. According to EnerCret, the payback of the initial investment to install an energy pile system in energy savings is typically five years when undertaken as part of initial construction, as this system has to be installed at the time the building foundation is poured.

The Atrio's system is quite extensive, and the payback is longer. The return on Atrio's initial investment—including the frequency converters—should achieve full payback after eight years.

Reducing fossil fuel energy consumption is only one of many tactics that the Atrio employs. The center has an extensive system for reducing water consumption, minimizing light pollution and many other sustainable practices that SES incorporated into the design of the project.

SHOPS AT DON MILLS

Cadillac Fairview, one of the largest developers of retail and office space in Canada, is converting the one-half-century-old Don Mills Shopping Centre in Toronto into a more sustainable lifestyle, open-air center to maximize retail potential. The redevelopment will make it more energy efficient and reduce its carbon footprint.

Opening in spring 2009, the first phase consists of a retail lifestyle center. The second phase will include residential high-rises, likely to be LEED Canada–certified buildings that take advantage of the sustainable urban site, comprising office and retail conveniently located near mass transportation.

They detached 10,500 cubic yards (8,028 cubic meters) of old asphalt, pulverized it and reused it. They removed all steel and rebar from the demolished mall site and resold it for recycling purposes. The total material recycled amounted to 119,000 cubic yards (90,982 cubic meters), which means not having to truck out the demolished material to be dumped in a landfill and not having to purchase replacement material and truck it to the site, according to project architect Harry Pellow, FRAIC, principal of Pellow + Associates Architects Inc. in Toronto.

"This represents fourteen thousand truck trips [going and returning], which on an average of 20 kilometers [12.5 miles] per trip equates to two hundred eighty thousand kilometers [175,000 miles] that vehicles will not impact infrastructure, create wear and tear on city streets or create carbon emissions from fuel expended," said Pellow. "This is the equivalent of one hundred forty one-way trips [from Toronto] to Orlando, Florida."

Pellow specified other sustainable features for the Shops at Don Mills that will endure long after the contractors complete the construction:

- Sealants, paints and carpeting with low-emitting VOCs
- All double-glazed windows with spectrally selective low solar gain, low-E glass to reduce heat loss in the winter but also reduce heat gain in the summer

SOURCE: CADILLAC FAIRVIEW

PHOTO: R. E. MILIAN

PHOTO: R. E. MILIAN

Top inset: The master plan for the redeveloped Shops at Don Mills in Toronto, Ontario, Canada, includes lifestyle retailers, offices and residential buildings. It is designed as a planned urban community, with pedestrian-friendly sidewalks, a parklike atmosphere with large trees and a dedicated public square. Middle inset: Cadillac Fairview contractors crushed all concrete and brick material from the demolished Don Mills Shopping Centre and stacked it in a large mound to be later reused as base material for the Shops at Don Mills. Bottom inset: EllisDon construction workers segregated lumber, drywall, brick, mortar, concrete, shingles and other materials from the demolished Don Mills Shopping Centre. They pulverized each separate waste material in a portable grinder at the construction site and reused the waste as mulch, soil amendments and fill. On-site reuse of pulverized concrete (foreground) is an efficient and sustainable way of reusing construction waste that would otherwise be sent to the landfill.

Large photo: Cadillac Fairview CEO Peter Sharpe (left) inspects the construction site for the Shops at Don Mills in November 2007 with his development team, supervisors from general contractor EllisDon, and invited guests. The project opens in spring 2009 in a sustainable site in the north part of Toronto, creating a revitalized shopping destination. Subsequent phases include a 1,300-vehicle parking structure and residential units to promote a live-work-shop-play environment.

PHOTO: R. E. MILIAN

- Twenty energy-efficient, reflective light gray colored membrane roofs by Carlisle with Soprema moisture barriers and Thermoplastic Olefin (TPO); 45 reflective roofs with Accuplane tapered insulation that improves interior comfort and reduces energy costs by minimizing heat gain in the summer to reduce air-conditioning requirements and is well insulated to reduce heat loss in the winter; reflective properties will also reduce urban heat island (UHI) effect

- Low-flow plumbing fixtures and autoflushing valves to reduce use of potable water

- Abundant bike storage areas

- Special areas for recycling and collection of recycled waste

- Energy-efficient HVAC rooftop units by Lenox with economizers and refrigerants with POE 3 MA oil that does not use CFCs and HCFCs

- An energy management system fully commissioned to monitor the performance of each of the 20 buildings

- Energy-efficient, dark-sky, friendly exterior lighting system directed downward to minimize light pollution; extensive use of LED lighting in exterior and high and low switching to reduce power consumption

- All exterior and interior lighting controlled automatically by timers and/or sensors

- Considerable shade and weather protection using covered walkways and building canopies

- Abundant tree foliage with eight-to-ten-foot (2.4 to 3 m) rootballs, 25-foot (7.6 m) canopies (5- to 6-inch [12.7 to 15.2 cm] trunk caliper) to help absorb CO_2 and use of local plant material for water conservation

- Integrating pedestrian access to mass transit

The Toronto Green Development Standard helped guide the Shops at Don Mills, according to Anne S. Morash, vice president of development at Cadillac Fairview. The official City of Toronto green building standard contains performance targets and guidelines that relate to site and building design intended for the development to meet environmental sustainability. The standard integrates city guidelines with standards from LEED and Green Globes.

CADILLAC FAIRVIEW ON THE ROAD TO SUSTAINABILITY

The tactics employed at the Shops at Don Mills are just a few of Cadillac Fairview's standard green practices. The company is committed to implementing a system-wide environmental management system consistent with this policy and International Standard (ISO) 14001 to ensure, among other things, the training of employees to carry out their duties in compliance with all laws and regulations.

Cadillac Fairview shares environmental best practices with the operators of its various real estate asset classes. In 2007, the Building Owners and Managers Association (BOMA) awarded the Go Green Plus (Visez vert Plus) certification to Cadillac Fairview for its Toronto office portfolio, which includes the Toronto-Dominion Centre.

The award recognized that the Cadillac office division implemented environmental best practices in all aspects of building management and operation. This includes consumption of resources, waste reduction, recycling, sustainable building materials, indoor environmental quality and tenant awareness.

The Toronto-Dominion Centre comprises six high-rise buildings: the Toronto Dominion Bank Tower, Royal Trust Tower, Canadian Pacific Tower, TD Waterhouse Tower, Ernst & Young Tower and 95 Wellington West.

Enwave and the City of Toronto created the deep lake water-cooling system featured below. It is a form of clean, renewable, energy-efficient and sustainable energy that brings an alternative to conventional air-conditioning to the Toronto Eaton Centre and other Toronto buildings. A permanent layer of icy-cold water, 39.2°F (4°C), pumped from 90.8 yards (83 m) below the surface of Lake Ontario provides the naturally cold water.

Deep Lake Water Cooling System

1. Three intake pipes draw 4°C water from Lake Ontario at a depth of 83 meters. The water is then filtered and treated for the City's potable water supply.

2. At the ETS, the icy-cold water is used to cool Enwave's closed chilled water supply loop through 36 heat exchangers. The ETS is adjacent to the City of Toronto's John Street Pumping Station.

3. Chilled water can bypass the cooling plant and continue to the customer building. If necessary, water can be further chilled by two 4700-ton steam-driven centrifugal chillers.

4. Heat exchangers at the customer building cool the internal building loop, providing chilled water for the building cooling system.

5. Enwave chilled water loop extends to other buildings.

6. Chilled water is returned to the Enwave Energy Transfer Station to repeat the cycle.

CUSTOMER SITE

ENWAVE ENERGY TRANSFER STATION

SUPPLY

RETURN

DISTRIBUTION NETWORK TO CUSTOMERS

5. **CHILLED WATER SUPPLY TO OTHER CUSTOMERS**

6. **ENWAVE CLOSED COOLING LOOP**

3. **ENWAVE SIMCOE STREET COOLING PLANT**

LAKE ONTARIO

1. **ISLAND FILTRATION PLANT**

INTAKE PIPES

WATER TO CITY

Benefits:
- Uses 90% less electricity
- Reduces thermal discharge from power plants to the lake
- Reduces air pollution
- Reduces CO_2 emissions
- Eliminates ozone depleting CFCs
- Eliminates cooling towers and improves water efficiency

LEGEND
- CHILLER
- DIRECTION OF WATER FLOW
- HEAT EXCHANGER

COURTESY OF ENWAVE

PHOTO: R. E. MILIAN

The relatively small heat exchanger (pictured right) uses the coldness of deep Ontario Lake water to cool the air of the 129,000-square-foot (12,000 sq m) expansion of the Toronto Eaton Centre. The creative use of this renewable source of energy saved the developer from having to install expensive on-site mechanical chillers for air-conditioning that consume tremendous amounts of electricity and use harmful CFC refrigerants.

Cadillac Fairview has also kept up with new technology. The company adopted Enwave's deep water cooling in 2004 when Enwave first introduced the system. By using Enwave's Deep Lake Water Cooling (DLWC), Cadillac is able to take advantage of naturally occurring cold water from Lake Ontario as if it were chilled water from a central plant's chiller system. The lake feeds the coils that air handlers blow through, to produce air-conditioning for downtown office buildings in Toronto.

The DLWC project can produce enough cooling to service 18 million square feet (1.7 million sq m) of office space or roughly 100 office towers in Toronto. The cost of bringing the water to cool buildings is about US$195 million.

DLWC reduced energy usage at the Toronto-Dominion Centre by 12 million kilowatt-hours in 2006 (8.8 megawatts during the peak summer period). "We were the catalyst working with a private group to get deep lake water cooling brought into downtown [Toronto] commercial buildings," said Peter Sharpe, president and CEO of Cadillac Fairview Corporation Ltd.

In addition to Cadillac's Toronto-Dominion Centre, other members of the group that helped Enwave to bring cold energy from Lake Ontario included the Royal Bank Plaza, Metro Toronto Convention Centre and the Air Canada Centre.

Sharpe added that supporting Enwave's investment in this technology helped his company lock in favorable pricing for the economical system for 25 years. "This should result in big savings for our tenants," said Sharpe, who also served as Canadian divisional vice president for ICSC for six years.

As is customary in many parts of Europe, steam district heating generated by an Enwave centralized plant supplies heat to 130 buildings in downtown Toronto, rather than each building having to generate its own steam individually. These buildings include those owned by Cadillac. Buildings receive piped-in steam heat in a highly energy- and cost-efficient manner, similar to the way the Toronto-Dominion Centre gets its piped-in deep lake cold water.

Following the successful launch of DLWC at the TD Centre, Cadillac Fairview later incorporated renewable cold energy into another significant project it owns and operates, the Toronto Eaton Centre, one of the best-known mixed-use developments in the world.

The Toronto Eaton Centre was the first retail complex to install the deep lake cooling system, according to Michael Ricketts, director of operations for the Toronto Eaton Centre portfolio of Cadillac Fairview.

In 2007, Cadillac Fairview used DLWC for a substantial expansion of the Toronto Eaton Centre when the retail portion of the project was expanded to add Canadian Tire (85,000 square feet [7,900 sq m]), Best Buy (34,000 square feet [3,160 sq m]), additional small shop space (10,000 square feet [930 sq m]) and Ryerson University (210,000 square feet [19,500 sq m]).

Cadillac Fairview arranged with Enwave to bring in two pipes originating from Lake Ontario. The company directed one pipe to the expansion and the other to the office tower by Queen Street for a future retrofit there.

Unlike an expensive central plant comprising huge chillers and a cooling tower, DLWC runs through two relatively small heat exchangers powered by several pumps to harvest the naturally cooled water from the lake.

Ryerson University has its own system, and the Toronto Eaton Centre uses a different one for the rest of the expansion, according to Ricketts.

"The entire Enwave's system is only sixty thousand tons (54,430 metric tons), and we have available four hundred fifty tons (408 metric tons) of which we are currently only using about three hundred tons (270 metric tons)," said Ricketts. The Enwave system has the capacity for cooling 6,800 homes or the equivalent in office space that it is presently servicing.

Ricketts said the Toronto Eaton Centre needs the expansion area cooled year-round because most of it is below grade. The heat generated by the stores' ambient lighting keeps the interior warm even in Toronto's winters, with temperatures hovering slightly below freezing except in January, the coldest month, when temperatures dip further.

PHOTOS: R. E. MILIAN

A major environmentally responsible move, Toronto Eaton Centre replaced all 10 electrical transformers from old Federal Pioneer containing PCBs (left) to General Electric dry-type (right).

If DLWC had not been available for the Eaton Centre expansion, it would have had to use expensive on-site mechanical chillers for air-conditioning that consume tremendous amounts of electricity and perhaps use harmful CFC refrigerants.

"The expansion uses only the coldness from the lake water, not the actual water, to provide the air-conditioning," said Ricketts. "This cold lake water does not touch the water in the utility's closed chilled water supply loop because the water is the source of drinking water for all of Toronto." The process only uses the coldness through a heat-exchange process. Upon cooling the Toronto Eaton Centre expansion, Enwave returns the fresh water to the citizens of Toronto through the city's normal potable water system.

As part of the ongoing process to make the Toronto Eaton Centre more sustainable, in 2007 Ricketts replaced all 10 Federal Pioneer transformers that used polychlorinated biphenyls (PCBs) with environmentally safe General Electric dry-type transformers at a cost of US$1.7 million.

PCBs are organic compounds attached to biphenyl and are considered extremely hazardous. They were manufactured as cooling and insulating fluids for industrial transformers and capacitors.

In 1976, the U.S. Congress enacted the Toxic Substances Control Act, which strictly regulates the manufacture, use and disposal of PCBs as a dangerous human carcinogen, due to their high toxicity and the damage PCBs can cause if an electrical transformer containing PCBs explodes, catches on fire or emits PCBs into the building in any other manner.

Cancer-causing PCBs leaking in buildings can cause a horrendous environmental hazard and can render a building uninhabitable until a hazardous material cleanup is completed. In addition to causing cancer, PCB exposure can have adverse effects on human reproductive, immune and endocrine systems. PCBs can also result in neurological effects to exposed victims.

A leak can spread harmful PCBs through the building's HVAC system, and if particles are flushed away, they can enter the city's water system. Even people walking through the building can track these colorless or light yellow oily liquids or waxy solid particles that have no smell or taste on the bottoms of their shoes or on their clothing.

PCBs have entered the air, water and soil from the time they were manufactured, during their use and upon disposal. Some PCBs were released by accidental spills and leaks during their transport. Other PCB contaminations occurred from leaks or fires in products containing PCBs, such as old electrical transformers similar to the ones removed from the Toronto Eaton Centre. PCBs do not rapidly break down in the environment.

PHOTOS: R. E. MILIAN

In the early 1980s, Toronto Eaton Centre was one of the first shopping malls in the world to encourage its customers to separate food court waste for recycling. The compactor that Toronto Eaton Centre now uses allows maintenance workers at the retail and office facility to separate cardboard from shrinkwrap and plastic bags for recycling.

Cadillac Fairview is now sharing some of the green building best practices that property managers institute across the portfolio of properties. In September 2007, the company appointed a director to handle green initiatives at a national level, and he is now working with property managers and suppliers to spread the green practices at Cadillac Fairview properties that otherwise operate decentralized throughout Canada.

"Our green plan is centered on five groups: energy management, waste management and diversion, environmental considerations, procurement and communication," said Robert L. "Rob" Furlan, P.Eng., Cadillac Fairview's director of national green services and standards.

Shortly after Furlan's position was created, the company added a green cleaning procedure to its national cleaning con-

tract, specifying green supplies such as Environmental Choice, and LEED-acceptable Green Seal, Energy Star and EcoLogo standards.

EcoLogo products have been assessed for their environmental impacts from the moment the raw materials were acquired through to the manufacturing, transportation, distribution, use and disposal of the product. EcoLogo products underscore green efficiency relating to energy use, amount of recycled material, hazardous substances and water use. More information is available at http://www.environmentalchoice.com/.

Energy Star–qualified products help users save energy and money on utility bills, and reduce air pollution and GHG emissions without compromising versatility of high-performing products. More information is available at http://oee.nrcan.gc.ca/energystar/.

Meanwhile, Cadillac Fairview began negotiating a national contract for all properties to place bulk orders of compact fluorescent lamps (CFLs), insisting that the manufacturer provide the properties a means for collecting used CFLs for recycling and properly disposing of the bulbs because of their mercury content.

Furlan, licensed by the Canadian Council of Professional Engineers, is using his engineering knowledge to broaden green practices throughout Cadillac's portfolio. His office functions as an umbrella department to coordinate activities that involve sustainability such as development (for new and renovated properties), operations (for ongoing processes), human resources (for training and educating about sustainability) and marketing (to get the word out about sustainability).

Getting out the word is clearly a goal of many shopping center companies that implement green practices. "We do good things, but we don't let people know about them," said Furlan. "We need a very clear and targeted communication plan for the key stakeholders of our company such as the tenants and their customers."

One such program that Cadillac Fairview has been conducting every summer across all its properties is the Energy Conservation Program. To help prevent brownouts and prevent the energy companies from having to spend millions of dollars to increase the capacity of power plants to handle peak demands, Cadillac Fairview shopping centers voluntarily undertake a series of initiatives to reduce electricity consumption during peak demand times in the summer months. These include reducing mall nonessential lighting, turning up the thermostat by four degrees and shutting down escalators one-half hour after the malls close. This program is publicized to tenants and customers to get buy in and to generate goodwill.

NORTHFIELD AT STAPLETON IS A GREEN BUILDING

Forest City's open-air Northfield is located in the heart of Denver, Colorado, at Stapleton, a mixed-use, urban infill project at the former location of the Stapleton International Airport.

SuperTarget, Circuit City, Bass Pro Shops Outdoor World, an 18-screen Harkins Theatres, JCPenney and Macy's department store anchor Northfield. The 1.2-million-square-foot (111,500 sq m) project received the LEED for Core and Shell Silver

certification in 2006 for its Main Street town center sustainable design, an area overseen by Jon Ratner, director of sustainability for Forest City.

The project was recognized for implementing sustainable practices, including boosting energy efficiency, selecting eco-friendly building materials, employing sustainable construction techniques and communicating its ongoing commitment to water management and to indoor environmental quality.

The Colorado Department of Public Health and Environment awarded the Stapleton project a Silver Level Environmental Achievement Award. In addition, the U.S. Conference of Mayors chose Stapleton for its Award for Excellence by the Mayors' Business Council for demonstrating civic responsibility and corporate commitment to economic development, urban revitalization, workforce development, affordable housing, education reform and water conservation. The Northfield Stapleton project been widely accepted by elected officials, retailers and the community because of Forest City's innovation and courage. (See Chapters 4 and 13.)

The accolades for sustainability continue to pour in for Forest City's effort in pushing its sustainability agenda. But even for projects that were not initially built as green buildings, Forest City is taking action to implement a few green tactics.

THE MALL AT ROBINSON RECYCLES

For years, the trash compactors at Forest City's Mall at Robinson near the Pittsburgh International Airport collected an average of 65.6 tons (59.5 metric tons) of cardboard a month, crushed it along with trash and directed it into a landfill.

Those practices are in the past. Starting in 2005, recyclable cardboard that the retailers of the shopping center receive with merchandise deliveries is properly recycled, helping the environment and saving the shopping center landfill costs. In the first year, the mall diverted 788 tons (715 metric tons) of paper and cardboard from the landfill.

The recycling of cardboard conserves resources, protects the environment and can be a reliable source of profit for businesses that would otherwise have to pay for hauling and landfill use fees. Corrugated packaging is a US$17-billion a year industry in the United States. It accounts for the largest segment of the packaging industry, with more than 90 percent of all products shipped in corrugated boxes.

Cardboard recycling was among several initiatives the Mall at Robinson implemented after the shopping center management made an alliance with the green-minded community group known as Sustainable Pittsburgh.

The 501(c) (3) nonprofit organization influences decision-making entities in the Pittsburgh, Pennsylvania, region to integrate economic prosperity, social equity and environmental quality to area businesses such as the visible 872,000-square-foot (81,000 sq m) mall that attracts more than seven million shoppers a year.

Sustainable Pittsburgh commissioned a comprehensive Sustainability Assessment of the Mall at Robinson. The organization engaged a dozen other groups to assess opportunities and make integrated recommendations for the mall to increase revenues, cut costs, conserve resources and demonstrate community leadership.

Additional initiatives the mall took as a result include the use of green cleaning products, the addition of new features in the center's energy management system that turn off the lights after mall hours, a replacement of 3,653 lightbulbs to more efficient versions and the use of more eco-friendly construction materials. New measures to help wildlife habitat were also implemented. For example, mall volunteers installed bluebird houses in open land around the shopping center, a coordinated effort with the Wildlife Habitat Council.

MANCHESTER DESIGNER OUTLETS

Sustainability is also a focus at several factory outlet centers. Vanderbilt Equities Corporation, the developer of Manchester Designer Outlets, has instituted a number of green building tactics at its Southern Vermont shopping center in the United States.

Vanderbilt installed fire retardant–coated cotton insulation throughout the 20 buildings housing the designer outlet shops. The cotton insulation is made from apparel and other recycled cotton products. It has no formaldehyde or other chemical irritants that other forms of insulation have. It maintains its insulation qualities at extremely low temperatures, better than fiberglass.

The insulation varies in R-value, depending on its thickness. R-value describes the insulation properties of certain building insulation materials. The higher the R-value, the greater insulation. For single-level buildings with attics, which are used at many factory outlet buildings, R-values range from R-22 to R-49, depending on climate.

Some cotton insulation manufacturers, such as UltraTouch Natural Cotton Fiber Insulation made by Bonded Logic, use recycled denim—as in blue jeans—to make insulation. This insulation is nontoxic and is resistant to pests, fire, mold and mildew. Reusing cotton as insulation also saves space that would otherwise be taken up in the landfills from discarded clothing and other cotton fabrics.

Vanderbilt has a score of green building initiatives including using cedar lumber for its building exterior instead of

PHOTO COURTESY OF VANDERBILT EQUITIES

Manchester Designer Outlets, an upscale designer outlet center, features green elements of construction and design, including experimentation with solar paneling, all conceived to provide a nontoxic shopping experience.

chemically pressure-treated wood, using paints and floor coatings without VOCs, installing building wiring that minimizes electromagnetic fields, and others.

PRUPIM USES GREEN POWER

PRUPIM (part of Prudential plc) is one of the largest real estate investment companies in the United Kingdom, with a global presence of 1,000 retail properties including such well-known units as Bluewater in Kent, United Kingdom; Manchester Arndale in Manchester, United Kingdom; Rue d'Antibes in Cannes, France; and the Mall at Cribbs Causeway in Bristol, United Kingdom.

The U.K. division of PRUPIM contracted with an energy procurement provider to purchase green power for 240 of its properties, thereby cutting back on 21,000 tons (19,000 metric tons) of emissions of pollutants per year.

The US$154-million contract provides green power to the properties at a hefty discount to current market rates. Combined Heat and Power plants produce the power, making it exempt from the U.K. Climate Change Levy, which adds to cost savings.

However, green power is only one of many sustainable practices that PRUPIM has in place. It has developed a framework for sustainability structured around the requirements of a typical environmental management system as required by BS EN ISO 14001:2004.

Each approach is specific to the property, although the company shares its best green practices among the properties to enable management to adapt efficiencies to multiple properties.

For example, PRUPIM was able to cut energy consumption at the Mall at Cribbs Causeway by 14 percent in one year simply by installing electrical sensors and timers to shut down unessential lighting in the parking garage at night. The cost to retrofit the lighting system now generates a rate of return of almost 40 percent per year for the first 10 years. Prudential, Capital Shopping Centres and JT Baylis own the property.

When water conservation became a priority at the same shopping center, changes were made to the external water feature, and passive infrared sensors were installed in the urinals, both of which helped reduce water consumption by 17 percent in one year.

The Mall at Cribbs Causeway also enables customers to save traditional forms of energy. It installed public electric car charging points in the underground Car Park K structure.

The shopping center's charging points offer drivers the opportunity to extend the range of their trip by allowing them to recharge their vehicles at the suburban shopping center, near Bristol.

Most new electric vehicles (EV) can travel between 40 and 80 miles (64 to 128 km) on one charge and do not burn fossil fuels for power. Instead, they use a powerful electric motor and banks of batteries for their power. An electric vehicle is 90

percent efficient compared to gasoline and diesel vehicles, which waste some of the energy through heat, noise and friction.

EVs charged with traditional electricity generated by coal-burning electric plants do indeed use fossil-fuel energy, but they do not produce GHGs while in operation. EVs that are charged from electricity produced from solar, wind or other renewable sources generate zero emissions.

PHOTO: MALL AT CRIBBS CAUSEWAY

BBC Two personality Brigit Strawbridge of the television series *It's Not Easy Being Green* helped launch the electric vehicle charging station at the Mall at Cribbs Causeway near Bristol, England. Strawbridge stars in the BBC Two program with her husband, Lieutenant-Colonel Dick Strawbridge, her son, James, and daughter, Charlotte, as they attempt to convert their 300-year-old building and garden into an ecologically friendly place to live.

Polling results consistently rank the environment as one of the top three priorities among consumers all over the world. Shopping centers and retailers have to heed to that call. Moreover, the shopping center industry is beginning to discover previously untapped potential for lowering operating costs, boosting sales and helping the environment at the same time. That is the win-win-win scenario the future has in store.

All of this adds up to a progressive greening of the retail sector. The retail industry was much less green in the 1990s than it is in the 2000s. There is little doubt that the transformation of the retail industry will continue well into the 2010s.

Chapter 12

The Cost/Benefit Equation

WHILE ATTEMPTING TO justify a return on capital invested in green tactics, retail real estate professionals often face a conundrum regarding the cost/benefit equation of green design-build.

Whereas it might seem honorable for private companies to spend private funds to improve the environment, retailers and commercial building owners also have to justify expenses and quantify efficiencies to ownership and shareholders when substantiating a green agenda.

INDUSTRY POLL

ICSC surveyed its members about sustainable design, development and operation practices in 2007. More than seven out of ten respondents were shopping center owners, managers or developers.

About 53 percent of the respondents said they employ tactics to reduce energy consumption while 76 percent indicated they were currently or were planning to switch lighting systems to more efficient types; for example, from incandescent to fluorescent.

Additionally, 41 percent of respondents said they have recycling programs in place and 36 percent use maintenance systems that emphasize sustainable operation.

Respondents also confirmed that the overriding factors when selecting building materials are performance and cost (88.9 percent), while sustainability on its own merits only comprises 3.4 percent of the total.

One caveat in interpreting the results of the survey is that many sustainable practices such as matters of energy efficiency, as tabulated in the survey, also reduce costs. This means that the survey respondents may have included sustainability factors in their responses relating to cost reduction.

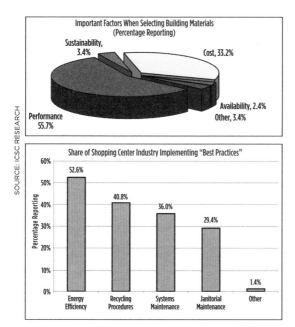

SOURCE: ICSC RESEARCH

The results of the survey highlight the importance of quantifying the cost/benefit equation of sustainability in order to be able to forecast how quickly the implementation of sustainable building practices will become common practice in the retail real estate industry.

A survey conducted by *Progressive Investor* magazine of 300 U.S. real estate investment trusts (REITs) comprising all real estate asset classes, revealed that 41 percent of them are actively pursuing energy efficiency and green building enhancements while an additional 27 percent are planning to institute green building programs.

In the building industry, cost-reduction techniques are implemented all the time, from the design phase to ongoing operations. Implementing these techniques in the operating phase requires major capital expenditures, such as in replacing HVAC equipment, adding new lighting systems, installing skylights, reroofing and introducing water recapture systems. Implementation is costly—but not always.

GREEN DESIGN–BUILD IS AN INTEGRATED PROCESS

What are the true costs to make these buildings green? How can these costs be amortized to achieve a reasonable financial benefit? Many design and construction project teams—as well as ownership—often ask themselves these questions. The cost/benefit equation is always in the minds of investors. They consider sustainable design as a separate, optional feature; something that if deemed financially feasible could be added to a project at an additional cost. Others disagree.

Many green design elements are not additive. They are simply good building practices to be incorporated into the design phase, and they will save costs and enhance the value of the building and the comfort of its occupants over the long haul. Complying with practices that do not pollute the environment almost comes secondary because what is good for the building is often the right thing to do to minimize environmental impact.

Many professionals consider green building tactics as added costs, but they deem energy-efficiency upgrades as an investment to recapture. Architect David Green notes that energy efficiency is just one element of good green building design.

"The same is true for the full range of environmental impact issues such as stormwater management, efficient water use, low-impact material selections and indoor environmental quality," said Green.

Green explained that the size and complexity of a shopping center's design and development team, coupled with the goal of designing a high-performance building, could only be approached with a strong, disciplined and integrated design process.

Green contends that an integrated design process differs from a conventional design process in that the conventional design process is very linear. At each step, issues are resolved to a point, and the work progresses to the next step.

Each next step takes the previous step as acceptable, and the process proceeds toward an end, which is typically established by building regulations or some other minimum health and safety standards. "That process is controlled by meeting, never exceeding, minimum standards," said Green.

He explained that an integrated design process begins in a nonlinear way. All stakeholders are brought into the process at the outset to help establish the goals for the project. Environmental goals are typically set against a baseline of standard practice.

The first steps are typically iterative and involve parametric studies to help find successive approximations to the solution by comparing the combined effect of multiple strategies. "The process leads to the final adoption of strategies, which in combination will meet or exceed the agreed goals of the project, including cost control," said Green.

Dr. Malcolm Lewis, PE, president of Constructive Technologies Group (CTG) Energetics, headquartered in Irvine, California, agrees in principle. CTG Energetics focuses on sustainability and energy efficiency in buildings and communities. "Sustainability in retail is typically about *people* first, *economics* second and *environmental responsibility* third," said Lewis. He explained that these factors are all important, but that a retail space that does not cater to people will not be financially successful, so the other goals never get a chance to matter. There is a way to do all three at the same time, Lewis believes.

According to Lewis, people desire appealing, exciting, comfortable spaces to be in and to be seen, to meet, to shop and to hang out. This first requires good design, but there is strong evidence that built environments that successfully integrate sustainability features will be more appealing to people and thus will be more economically successful.

Lewis noted in a position paper that these sustainability features focus on good indoor environmental quality (IEQ), which includes indoor air quality (IAQ), lighting and daylighting, thermal comfort, humidity control, acoustics and odor control.

The primary economic indicator of a successful retail environment is its sales volume per square foot, and this can be significantly affected by various IEQ factors, as described above, said Lewis. The other economic aspect is the control of costs for constructing and for operating the facility, including energy costs and operating and maintenance (O&M) costs.

The buying public is increasingly aware of and interested in the environmental impacts of the products and services they buy, wrote Lewis. This has strongly influenced the goods that are sold as well as the designs of the buildings in which they are sold.

Good sustainable design of their facilities offers retailers the opportunity to be responsive to this in ways that are also good business, Lewis noted in a research paper.

According to Lewis, the trend is toward designing retail environments that not only deliver environmental benefits but also document and promote the sustainability story.

"Whether or not retailers elect to tout the sustainability of their facilities, they are choosing to make them green because it is good business and good citizenship," Lewis predicts. Once perceived in this manner, the notion that green costs more, especially in an era of rapid cost escalation, tends to fade away.

COUSINS USES PURCHASING POWER

New construction represents the best opportunity to make a building or parts of it green without substantial incremental costs. Once buildings are designed, built, open and operating, building owners can often achieve some sustainability tactics simply through routine maintenance, such as changing the types of lamps it uses or using different, greener cleaning materials and buying in bulk.

Some green building initiatives—whether undertaken upon the conclusion of a piece of equipment's natural life or purchased for new construction—can be achieved for relatively the same costs as conventional (nongreen building) systems.

To achieve this, a building owner must show determination, be assertive and encourage cooperation with suppliers, particularly on big jobs where purchasing power influences an upgrade to green systems for relatively similar costs.

Wal-Mart does this when it decides it wants a particular lighting system that is highly efficient. The purchasing agent for Wal-Mart will go to lighting suppliers such as Sylvania and General Electric and request a custom-made system. Wal-Mart's suppliers are happy to oblige because they know a purchase for a large quantity of stores will justify any research and development costs involved.

Atlanta, Georgia–based Cousins Properties Incorporated, a company smaller than Wal-Mart but a relatively large real estate investment trust that became public in 1962, proved the feasibility of Wal-Mart's purchasing-clout approach.

In 2004, Cousins launched a program to install only sustainable reflective white roofs in existing centers (at the time a re-roofing was needed) and in new Avenue centers that Cousins is building. In the first three years, Cousins installed 1,417,650 square feet (131,700 sq m) of Sarnafil eco-friendly roofing systems.

According to John Rutte, PE, LEED AP, former Cousins vice president of development, Cousins made the decision to utilize Sika Sarnafil products on these Avenue projects because the light-colored reflective surfaces help the buildings stay cooler, thereby reducing energy use by its tenants' air-conditioning systems.

Because Cousins' Avenue projects are open-air lifestyle shopping centers, they require no cooling of their common areas in the summer or heating in the winter.

"Through careful review and evaluation of our roofing specifications and by cultivating collaborative relationships among our architect, general contractor and the

manufacturer, Cousins was able to utilize an environmentally friendly quality product with a life expectancy of more than twenty years," Rutte said. "Cousins paid about the same price as other roofing alternatives that do not soften our impact on the environment to the same extent."

For The Avenue Viera (Viera, Florida), Cousins installed a 306,000-square-foot (28,425 sq m) roofing system, and at The Avenue Webb Gin (Lawrenceville, Georgia), Cousins installed a 330,500-square-foot (30,700 sq m) roofing system over the retail stores. The design team selected the .048 mil S327 EnergySmart Roof thermoplastic PVC-polymer roofing membrane for The Avenue Webb Gin.

This mechanically fastened roofing membrane has polyester reinforcing to hold the screws and to prevent excessive elongation and sheet deformation, according to Tommy Earnest, a U.S. technical sales representative for the U.S.-based Sika Sarnafil company, a subsidiary of Canada-based Sarnafil Inc.

The membrane has a highly reflective surface designed for energy savings, and aids in reducing urban heat island (UHI) effect. EPA lists this roof under its Energy Star program for sustainable energy-efficient design. The roofs carry a 15-year warranty protection.

Aerial photo of The Avenue Viera, located in Viera, Florida (near Cape Canaveral), defines the holistic design of this lifestyle center and illustrates Cousins Properties' strategy to add reflective, cool, white roofs to properties that need re-roofing and to new properties. This sustainable practice helps Cousins' tenants lower their cooling costs.

PHOTO COURTESY OF COUSINS PROPERTIES INCORPORATED

More recent roofs installed at Cousins centers, such as The Avenue Murfreesboro (Tennessee), a 532,450-square-foot (49,470 sq m) roof, and The Avenue Forsyth (Forsyth County, Georgia), a 248,700-square-foot (23,100 sq m) roof—both installed in 2007—are Sika Sarnafil Sikaplan 45 (.045 mil) roofs.

These roofs share the same qualities as the S327 PVC membrane, but the Sikaplan 45 is a single-ply PVC roofing membrane. Sikaplan 45 meets the cool-roofing requirements of LEED, Green Globes, Energy Star and California Title 24.

The ideal way to implement green efficiencies—whether on expensive roofing systems, HVAC equipment or other major building expenditure—is to do it upfront in a new building or during a renovation, to ensure a proper payback during the building's natural lifespan.

SO, HOW MUCH MORE DOES GREEN COST?

A 2003 study entitled "California's Sustainable Building Task Force by Capital E, in Collaboration with the USGBC" concluded that the upfront costs for green design averaged only 2 percent and resulted in life cycle savings of 20 percent of total construction costs. The USGBC says that the average payback on designing and building green features is between 12 and 24 months. The USGBC boasts that the benefits of making buildings greener are:

- 30 to 50 percent energy savings
- 35 percent savings of carbon emissions
- 40 percent water savings
- 30 percent savings on solid waste
- 6.6 percent average improved return on investment (ROI)
- 8 to 9 percent decrease in total operating costs
- 3 percent higher rents
- 3 percent higher occupancy rates

These tempting statistics might encourage a real estate owner to blindly go green, but there is disagreement about just how much more it costs to make a property sustainable during the initial construction phase. "We've heard it's in the range of three to eight percent higher, said Timothy E. Gardels, CDP, vice president of design and construction for General Growth Properties, acknowledging that these costs have a payback during the life of a building and are not computed into the upfront costs.

According to J. Howard Nudell, CDP, AIA, OAA, president of Nudell Architects in Farmington Hills, Michigan, making a renovated property sustainable enough to achieve LEED certification affects two development costs—design and construction.

Dale E. Scott, CDP, senior vice president of Deerfield Beach, Florida-based SIKON Construction Corporation, agrees. "As the first step to effectively take a project through the planning process, the owner will need to assemble a project team consisting of design professionals and a LEED consultant," said Scott.

"Also, to assure the project budget and schedule can be met, a LEED-experienced general contractor becomes an essential part of the team right from the start of planning," he said, stressing the importance of controlling costs.

"If not closely monitored from the start, pricing on a green project will get out of control to a point the project will become economically not feasible," cautioned Scott.

According to Scott, a cost factor that people do not talk much about, but is occurring frequently on projects seeking LEED certification, is the general contractor's additional field supervision and project management time.

These are not "deal killer" costs, but the general contractor's general conditions costs must reflect additional personnel and project management time for a project that has to document LEED green building requirements, Scott contends.

Despite these added costs, Scott said that many developers and retailers that he works with have expressed a keen interest in adding green building features to their projects during the construction phase.

"Due to the popularity and emphasis on green buildings over the past couple of years—almost becoming an industry-wide buzz word in the past year—we are finding many owners are, at least, asking about building-green [features]," said Scott in December 2007.

Nudell said clients have expressed similar interest about sustainable design despite the extra costs. "We are still seeing more RFPs [requests for proposals] that call for design and construction measures to be incorporated into the project, which are likely to result in LEED certification," said Nudell, referring to his latest RFP for the redevelopment work on the mall interior of Forest City's Promenade in Temecula, located east of San Clemente, California.

In 2006, Nudell brought several LEED-accredited professionals (LEED AP) to his staff and encouraged members of his design team to seek LEED accreditation.

Getting up to speed on sustainable design appears to be a trend for architects all over the world—whether it relates to LEED, BREEAM or another green certification.

"We now have fifty-five LEED AP on staff," said J. Thomas Porter, CDP, AIA, of Thompson, Ventulett, Stainback & Associates (TVS) in Atlanta. According to Porter, many sustainable tactics are being added to design and construction projects all the time, whether or not the client decides to apply for LEED certification.

"Most of our projects go through a sustainability analysis," said Porter. "We often uncover several design elements that don't cost any more and make the project more sustainable."

There are some sustainability costs in the construction phase of a project that could be substantial and offer no financial payback, which influence overall costs, ac-

cording to some LEED-accredited professionals. One such cost involves recycling of construction waste if the material is not properly separated and reused.

"We reviewed the bids for demolition costs of one project and found that the recycling of construction material raised the costs by almost ten percent," said Gardels.

Some waste management suppliers are offering to recycle construction material at a higher fee, but they are not passing along the benefits when they resell the material to a third party as a profit center. In this case, it gives the builder bragging rights but no financial benefit.

According to Gardels, General Growth is continuing to explore the possibility of cost-neutral construction recycling with its general contractors, and he is not ready to conclude that the experience on one particular project is representative of what the company can generally achieve. "We have to educate our contractors," he said.

From a cost perspective, the financial efficiencies from recycling construction material come from reusing the material (such as recycling concrete) in the redevelopment. The savings of reusing material come from not having to purchase replacement material and transport it to the site or to haul away and dispose of the old material.

"Sustainable development can best be achieved without significant premium costs by setting goals in the earliest planning stages and engaging architecture and engineering consultants with notable sustainable design experience," said Kenneth G. Maynard, vice president of planning and design for General Growth Properties. "Integrated design drives both sustainable design solutions and cost efficiency."

General Growth did exactly that when it took over the former Lord & Taylor building at Park Meadows in the Denver, Colorado, metropolitan market and tore it down to make room for a Main Street-style outdoor retail development. Space at the site was tight for the mass recycling efforts that involved multiple contractors working at the same time, but that did not stop Gardels from fulfilling his company's green mission.

Gardels's team came up with a creative way to recycle construction waste from the common area, as well as from contractors working independently for the tenants. He hired a local waste management company to set up various dumpsters for both the tenant and landlord demolition contractors to share; to separate and recycle metal, concrete and other construction debris, rather than each contractor using a separate dumpster where all waste is deposited and then dumped in a landfill. This proves that implementing green strategies is not easy and often results in higher costs than traditional methods.

However, some costs can be minimized or offset by reducing other costs. For example, costs associated with construction waste management, to help divert part of the construction waste from disposal, can be substantially reduced if the material is grinded and reused as filler to level the site.

Some studies suggest that when designing and constructing a building from scratch, green building systems do not have to cost one cent more. One such study

by Davis Langdon released in 2004, entitled "Costing Green: A Comprehensive Cost Database and Budget Methodology," depicted green building costs by sustainable element and compared them to original budgets. This included projects built between 2001 and 2004.

In both this study and a follow-up study that Langdon conducted in 2006 and released in 2007, the LEED rating system was used as a parameter for determining costs associated with the sustainable design paradigm.

Langdon's 2006 study shows essentially the same results as its 2004 results. There is no significant difference in average costs for constructing green buildings as compared to nongreen buildings, according to both studies. Many project teams are building green buildings with little or no added cost and with budgets well within the cost range of nongreen buildings with similar programs, Langdon concluded.

However, many green building consultants note that the additional total design and construction costs are more in line between 1 and 3 percent for retrofitting a marginally efficient building into a green building (of minimum LEED level) when the project is undertaken as part of a major redevelopment and renovation as opposed to new construction. Incremental costs for making a project green depend on a multitude of factors.

THE COSTS FOR LARGE-SCALE PROJECTS

Forest City Commercial Group, a unit of Forest City Enterprises Inc., redeveloped the Northfield Stapleton master development plan in Denver with substantial green building innovations in both its office and retail components.

The USGBC recognized Forest City's achievements and awarded the Gold LEED certification for the core and shell design of the 3055 Roslyn Street office building and the LEED Silver for the core and shell of Main Street Shops at Northfield Stapleton, the retail portion of the development.

In addition to LEED certifications, representatives from Forest City took home the coveted ICSC MAXI Silver Award for integrating development and operations best practices with its marketing campaign, called Sustainability at Northfield Stapleton.

In the award entry, the developer outlined the costs to make the retail component sustainable. The estimated cost to do this was US$995,000, or 1 percent of the total net project cost, although these costs were not necessarily incremental in every case.

The developer averaged across the total square footage of Northfield's retail gross leasable areas and concluded that the total cost represented US$2.95 per square foot (US$31.75 per sq m). On a long-term net value basis, the property enhancements were estimated at US$3.25 per square foot (US$34.98 per sq m), an additional $0.30 per square foot (US$3.23 per sq m) using a return on investment (ROI) of 10 percent.

NORTHFIELD STAPLETON

Green Building Enhancements

Expense Summary

ITEM	EXPENSE
Consultants/building commissioning (service fees for design and implementation)	US$200,000
Insulation/waterproof (add foundation insulation and increase roof R-value over R-30)	US$200,000
Energy efficiency (high-efficiency furnaces, condensers, economizers, EMS)	US$150,000
Indoor environmental quality (enhanced ventilation, light and thermal control)	US$120,000
Landscape irrigation (install drip irrigation and "purple pipe" nonpotable system)	US$95,000
Glazing/skylights (specify Low-E coating for office windows/skylights)	US$55,000
Plumbing (reduce indoor potable water requirements > 25%)	US$55,000
Site lighting (reduce outer pole heights, metal halide w/full cutoff shields)	US$50,000
Bicycle facilities (full-protection bike racks and employee showers)	US$45,000
Paints/adhesives (specify materials with low VOCs)	US$25,000
Construction recycling (divert up to 75% site construction waste)	No cost premium
Recycled paving (recycled tarmac as asphalt subgrade – incentive credit is available)	No cost premium
Regional/recycled materials (specify local and high recycled content)	No cost premium
TOTAL EXPENSES*	**US$995,000***

* The capital requirement for sustainability is less than 1 percent of the net project cost.

Source: Forest City Commercial Group, Forest City Enterprises Inc., ICSC MAXI Awards

TRACKING GREEN COSTS

Doug Wiele, chief executive officer and founder of El Dorado, California-based Foothill Partners, was determined to quantify the incremental costs of developing his Uptown Monterey community center to LEED standards.

He had his accountants, his LEED-accredited advisor and his general contractor, Daniels and House of Monterey, California, tracked every cost pertaining to the redevelopment of a former grocery store site into Uptown Monterey. He asked them to segregate green costs from standard nongreen costs. He even had his project architect, Rauschenbach, Marvelli & Becker of Sacramento, California, track its time and any costs—soft and hard—to determine what was green and what was not.

The LEED-accredited advisors from Daniels and House and LP Consulting Engineers combed through every expense detail documented to achieve LEED points. And there were many. They diverted 2,100 tons of concrete and asphalt from landfills, and achieved 96 percent construction waste diversion to earn the project three LEED points. The deconstruction and salvaged material reused helped with three more LEED points.

Although the extra cost to deconstruct versus demolishing amounted to US$3,000, the market value of new wood displaced by salvaged wood saved the developer US$24,573. Steel framing helped the project achieve two more LEED points. The list goes on.

After he reviewed the final numbers, Wiele is convinced that the costs of going green on the redevelopment of his community center in downtown Monterey, California anchored by Trader Joe's are negligible. "I'm surprised by two things. One, that we've gotten this far and two, that it didn't cost us any more," said Wiele.

In fact, Foothill Partners achieved many LEED points at no extra cost. These included:

- Site selection (the project sits on a rebuilt urban site)
- Development density and community connectivity
- Alternative transportation with public transportation access
- Alternative transportation with parking capacity

PHOTO COURTESY OF FOOTHILL PARTNERS LLC.

The steel framing of Uptown Monterey community center in Monterey, California, helped the developer achieve LEED points in redeveloping the site as a green building. Although the extra cost to deconstruct versus demolishing amounted to US$3,000, the market value of new wood displaced by salvaged wood saved the developer US$24,573.

- Heat island effect minimized on the roof
- Water-efficient landscaping (reduced by 50 percent)
- Measurement and verification (tenant submetering)
- Storage and collection of recyclables
- Building reuse (maintained 50 percent of existing walls, floors and roof)
- Low-emitting materials, paints and coatings

According to Wiele, net capital costs for seeking LEED certification for the project were US$29,255:

UPTOWN MONTEREY

Net Capital Costs for Seeking LEED

Research funding: grants, rebates	US$ 1,840
Design charrette meetings	US$ 5,140
Designers and consultants	US$11,435
LEED administration	US$16,440
Pre-certification	US$ 5,840
LEED fees	US$ 4,300
Commissioning oversight	US$ 1,200
Subtotal of hidden costs:	US$46,195
Material and construction costs	(US$16,910)
TOTAL:	US $29,285*

*Excludes Pacific Gas and Electric Company (PG&E) rebates and life-cycle savings

Source: Foothill Partners

UPTOWN MONTEREY
BREAKDOWN OF ACTUAL MATERIAL AND CONSTRUCTION
COSTS TO SEEK LEED CERTIFICATION

Material	Type	Location	LEED Credits	Conventional Total	Green Total	Green Cost Premium	Green Actual
	Roof deck	Bldg. A/B	MR 4.1 MR 5.1	$0	$0	$0	$0
	Structural steel	Bldg. A/B	MR 4.1 MR 5.1	$0	$0	$0	$0
	Angle iron	Bldg. A/B	MR 4.1 MR 5.1	$0	$0	$0	$0
Metal	Anchors, brackets	Bldgs. A/B & C	MR 4.1 MR 5.1	$0	$0	$0	$0
	Rebar	Bldgs. A/B & C	MR 4.1 MR 5.1	$0	$0	$0	$0
	Bike rack	Bldgs. A/B & C	MR 4.1 MR 5.1	$0	$0	$0	$0
	Pipe	Fire sprinklers	MR 3	$0	$0	$0	$0
Roof	Tile	Bldg. C	MR 4.1 MR 5.1	$0	$0	$0	$0
	Built-up roof	Bldg. A/B	MR 4.1 MR 5.1	$0	$0	$0	$0
	CMU	Seat wall, trash enclosure	MR 4.1 MR 5.1	$0	$0	$0	$0
Concrete	Flyash	Bldg. A/B	MR 4.1 MR 5.1	$0	$0	$0	$0
	Slag	CMU wall, slab, sidewalks	MR 4.1 MR 5.1	$8,560	$8,960	$400	n/a
HVAC (premium costs)	5 ton units	All units	EAp2	$0	$15,000	$15,000	$1,500
	Batts - R13	Int. walls	MR 4.1 MR 5.1	$4,495	$5,606	$1,110	n/a
Insulation	Batts - R19	Ext. walls	MR 4.1 MR 5.1	$6,986	$9,960	$2,974	n/a
	Batts - R30	Ceiling	MR 4.1 MR 5.1	$24,494	$0	$0	n/a
Plaster	Exterior	Exterior walls	MR 5.1	$0	$0	$0	$0
Masonry	Stone veneer	Seat wall	MR 5.1	$0	$0	$0	-$2,100
	GL Beam	Roof structure	MR 4.1 MR 5.1 MR 6	$0	$0	$0	$0
Wood	SSI	Ceiling joists	MR 5.1 MR 6	$0	$0	$0	$0
	Framing	Bldg. C	MR 3	$13,193	$0	-$13,193	-$10,195
	Exterior doors	Exterior doors	MR 4.1 MR 5.1	$0	$0	$0	$0
Doors & Windows	Interior doors	Interior doors	MR 4.1 MR 5.1	$0	$0	$0	$0
	Windows	Windows	MR 4.1 MR 5.1	$0	$0	$0	$0
	Gyp board	Interior walls	MR 4.1 MR 5.1	$0	$0	$0	$0
	Paint	Lavatory walls	EQ 4.2	$77	$155	$78	$0
	Urinals	Lavatories	WE 2, WE 3.1	$2,700	$4,500	$1,800	$4,500
Finishes	Toilets	Lavatories	WE 2, WE 3.1	$2,200	$3.300	$1,100	$1,100
	Faucets	Lavatories	WE 2, WE 3.1	$1,650	$0	$0	$0
	Sinks	Lavatories	MR 4.1, MR 5.1	$0	$0	$0	$0
	Graywater reuse	Lavatories	WE 2, WE 3.1	$0	$0	$0	$0
Landscaping	Trees from local nursery	Exterior	WE 1.1, MR 5.1 MR 5.1	$0	$0	$0	$0
	Wheel stop	Parking lot	MR 4.1 MR 5.1	$0	$0	$0	$0
	Door mats	Exterior doors	EQ	$0	$0	$0	$0
Other	Entry floor frames	Exterior doors	EQ	$0	$0	$0	n/a
	Truck recharging	Loading ramp	ID	$0	$500	$500	n/a
	Construction waste	Project	MR 2	not in original estimate			-$1,041
	Salvaged stone	Courtyard	MR 1	not in original estimate			-$10,674
						$9,769 Estimated	-$16,910 Actual

As the project became a reality in 2008 and a source of pride for Wiele, he shared his experiences with other professionals interested in building to green standards at an ICSC meeting in Washington, DC in March 2008.

"In addition to this LEED certification [that we are seeking for Uptown Monterey], we are working on adding second-floor workforce housing on top of the retail, so the idea of LEED certification had some appeal to us [from the beginning]," said Wiele. His goal was realized in April 20, 2008, when Uptown Monterey became the first LEED-certified community shopping center in California.

The City of Monterey owns the underlying land where the project sits, and ground-leased it to GLC Foothill Monterey LLC, a joint venture between Foothill Partners Inc. and Granite Land Company of Sacramento, California.

WHAT'S THE PAYBACK?

Associated Food Stores (AFS) did a return on investment analysis upon completing the major interior, energy-efficient lighting system upgrade for its distribution center in Farr West, Utah. The project cost roughly US$725,000, but AFS anticipated about US$310,000 in energy savings during the first year of operation.

This project is expected to reduce energy consumption by an estimated 4,738,000 kilowatt-hours per year and has reduced the facilities' peak demand by 544.4 kilowatts, according to Reid Cram, project lead person for Lime Energy, who consulted with AFS and installed the equipment.

Cram believes that the negotiated and secured incentive from Rocky Mountain Power reduced initial capital investments for AFS and lowered the payback period for the investment to a mere one year.

The hefty savings do not take into consideration federal tax credits available from the U.S. Energy Policy Act of 2005, as Lime Energy completed the project in 2007, and it qualifies for tax credits.

Cram estimates that the annual environmental benefits of the project include eliminating emissions of 10.2 million pounds (4.6 metric tons) of carbon dioxide (attributed to climate change), 23,614 pounds (10.7 metric tons) of sulfur dioxide (the leading cause of acid rain) and 26,258 pounds (12 metric tons) of nitric oxides (a cause of smog and acid precipitation).

While the payback for AFS is respectable by almost any standard of measurement, it is not good enough for the toughest competitor in the packaged food and grocery business today: Wal-Mart. Wal-Mart's benchmark is a two-year payback. Period. The 24-month time frame determines whether Wal-Mart will move forward on a sustainable tactic or not, according to Wal-Mart's Charles Zimmerman.

A study by Turner Construction in its 2005 Green Building Market Barometer claimed that it costs less than 1 percent more in overall hard construction costs for adding green building enhancements during the construction phase to achieve LEED's minimum level of certification. A company aiming to invest in eco-friendly

programs needs to do the math and consider all angles. For example, Wal-Mart's feasibility study determined that it can make solar energy work for 22 of its stores in California and Hawaii, and it began implementing its plan.

Wal-Mart expects its photovoltaic panels will produce up to 30 percent of the energy requirements of those stores. Two factors make this feasible. One is the sunny climate in California and Hawaii, and the second is that these states are offering lucrative rebates because they have a goal of producing 20 percent of all energy from entirely renewable resources by 2020.

The pilot project that Wal-Mart will implement by 2008 will determine solar power viability for other Wal-Mart locations. The solar photovoltaic system is being accomplished through the SunEdison Power Purchase Agreement (PPA) model, whereby the solar supplier company allows its customers to purchase solar electricity, rather than solar equipment.

SunEdison finances, installs, operates and maintains the photovoltaic power plants for Wal-Mart. Under the win-win PPA model that Wal-Mart chose, SunEdison only charges Wal-Mart for electricity produced at rates equal to or below its existing retail prices.

Wal-Mart's solar systems are entirely driven by sunlight. They are silent, emissions free, highly reliable and complement existing utility power. Since the solar power plants have no fuel costs, the retail giant benefits by having long-term predictable energy pricing.

According to the Building Owners and Managers Association (BOMA), the cost of energy and water consumption comprises 28 percent of operating costs for office properties located in U.S. urban settings and 30 percent for suburban settings.

Costs of that magnitude can return quick payback in energy and water savings from initiatives that also make these buildings more sustainable.

But the benefits can also be intangible. Retail developers often compare the cost of green sustainable design to the perceived benefits, including the health and well-being of occupants, community friendliness and the economic benefits, not to mention the positive impact on the environment.

Improved indoor air quality (IAQ) is important to most building occupants, as is natural daylight filtered into an indoor environment, which can reduce the sick building syndrome. However, insufficient data exist to demonstrate this benefit in retail buildings as it does to the extent that offices and residences pose, where poor IAQ is found.

FAST-TRACKED ENTITLEMENTS

The benefits of sustainability are obvious for the municipalities in which the projects are located. These include less wind and water erosion and sedimentation of waterways during construction.

Sustainable buildings also place less demand on the community infrastructure for

potable water, sewage conveyance and power generation. For that reason, the Lowe's on Brodie Lane in South Austin, Texas, used its sustainability program as a key measure to expedite permitting after a long legal battle with the cities of Austin and Sunset Valley, and environmentalists.

According to the USGBC, when Lowe's presented the plans for the store that would use 40 to 70 percent less energy and 50 percent less water, the store was permitted in three months. It usually takes about 15 months to permit a store in Austin. The USGBC said Lowe's calculates a profit of US$85,000 a day from that store. Therefore, early permitting allowed the store to be built and open for business early, which saved US$3 million just by building the store quickly and to LEED Gold standards.

USGBC concluded that the store cost US$2.85 million to build, so in essence, Lowe's built a store at no cost, when considering the added profitability. The operating savings over building green retail buildings are real, but retailers and developers continue to seek case studies to demonstrate the quantifiable cost/benefit analysis desired.

WHAT DOES LEED REALLY COST?

Keith Smith, CDP, vice president of construction for Jacksonville, Florida-based Regency Centers, took part in the Regency green task force that studied the LEED system for incorporating green building practices into the vast development program of this developer of grocery-anchored centers. Smith believes the costs are manageable and reasonable.

Regency is taking on the project on a case-by-case basis. According to Smith, the developer will only include sustainable components that are appropriate for a given property. Smith said that Regency will evaluate everything available and will incorporate into the program only what makes sense.

He also claimed that Regency executives would ask themselves many questions in evaluating green practices before they approve them: Does this make financial sense? Does this make sense for the project? Do we have any avenues to recoup the expenditures, such as tax incentives, government subsidies or increased rental rates, because our CAM will be lower?

There are even advantages for Regency to reduce nonrecoverable operating costs. "We want to be prudent with our expenditure of money to make sure that at a minimum we're building projects that are more sustainable, have minimal impact to the environment and are favored by the communities surrounding each property," stated Smith. "We get a project and evaluate the low-hanging fruit. We will only do what is reasonable to achieve . . . what is right for the property, for our tenants and the community."

For example, if adding relatively inexpensive bicycle racks earns one LEED point, Regency might incorporate that "low-hanging fruit" into the program for appropriate centers. Regency management will also price each sustainable aspect toward

achieving LEED certification for the Greengenuity projects that the company has identified during the initial development phase.

Many LEED points can be achieved at practically no extra costs, such as creating bicycle storage, putting in water-efficient plants, adding a bus stop, using a LEED-accredited professional as part of the design and development team, and starting a share-a-ride program for store employees once the center is open and operating.

Other LEED points, although associated with extra costs, are available from simply having good business practices or complying with local ordinances and codes, such as recycling, proper stormwater management, pointing lamps downward to reduce light pollution, measurement and verification, and enhanced building commissioning to ensure the building is functioning as intended.

Yet, other LEED points are costly to implement, but once installed, they help the owner and tenants save on operating costs throughout the life of the building. Such green tactics make good business sense, as they can employ systems that reduce water use and optimize energy performance. This equipment can be lighting systems, HVAC equipment and cool reflective roofs.

"Our biggest challenge has been education within our company about sustainability," said Smith, referring to expanding awareness on how sustainable design and operation can lower costs and result in a superior building.

Smith explained that internal education with investment officers (asset managers), predevelopment and construction personnel, operations management and leasing agents is paramount. This is particularly important when communicating with tenants about their leased premises, some of which Regency turns over as a white box or a shell. Tenants need to understand what they are getting.

Leasing agents have a challenge to convey the value of green retail buildings to prospective tenants, according to Smith. "They have to say, 'We are giving you a more efficient building, with better insulated walls and roof, high-efficient HVAC and lighting, and for that there will be a higher cost in rent, which you'll be able to recoup through lower operating costs.'"

"We need to collect historical data to prove to tenants that this is all real," he added.

Regency plans that added costs involving new or renovated centers will run between 1 and 3 percent to achieve LEED certification—and it seems realistic.

"We already have solid estimates for the Shops of Santa Barbara [California] and the Shops on Main [Schererville, Indiana], and they both fall within our anticipated two percent of extra costs to make them green," Smith said.

"I am adding two percent to already budgeted soft and hard costs for several projects," Smith said about his budgets for coming construction projects. However, those initial added construction costs will have a payback during the operating phase. Energy efficiencies and water conservation yield savings for the building owner and the tenants. As shopping center operating costs are mostly recoverable through reimbursable common area maintenance (CAM) charges or through fixed CAM clauses quoted as part of total rent, the cost savings benefit the owner as well as the tenant.

If retailers typically pay 10 to 13 percent of retail sales in total occupancy costs, a sustainable design should yield higher market rents simply from the lower operating costs. Studies of this type are needed to help propel reasonable sustainable design as a standard business practice where everyone wins.

"One point is that retail lease structure is not always conducive to sharing energy investment cost/benefit. For example, the landlord cannot always realize the energy-savings payback benefits of a capital investment they might make in premium-priced equipment; rather, the benefit is realized by the retailers," said General Growth's Lisa Loweth. "Further, not all tenants take advantage of utility conservation measures at the store level that indirectly impact their costs."

In any event, the road to sustainability is largely unchartered, and progress is being made by both tenant and landlord, with benefits accruing to both parties.

"That said, there are many of the energy-efficient and sustainable design building components that are being used, and many shopping center developers are getting positive notoriety from their use of the 'green components' even though the project is not LEED certified—and that is not a bad thing," said Dale Scott.

"This includes incorporating some of the energy-efficient building components into projects that are not attempting to be green buildings," Scott asserted. "It just makes sense to do these things."

Chapter 13

Promoting a Green Image

IT **IS NO** longer sufficient for retailers and shopping center companies to have a green agenda in place or to simply implement a few green building tactics. They need to share their strategy with their stakeholders as well.

Customers, tenants, the community and other stakeholders want to know what private organizations are doing about going green. Shopping centers often tell their stories through news releases, advertising and by holding events that support the green movement. Retailers are doing likewise.

PHOTO COURTESY OF KRAVCO SIMON

The King of Prussia Mall in Pennsylvania lets customers know that it is helping reduce harmful emissions by using Global Electric Motorcars (GEM) battery-electric vehicles made by Chrysler to patrol the parking areas. A sticker on the vehicle prominently states "Ozone friendly."

Wal-Mart added this 386-hybrid truck, designed by the Eaton Corporation, to its fleet to save costs on fuel, to minimize its carbon footprint and to underscore its Sustainability 360 campaign. This vehicle will help Wal-Mart achieve its aggressive goal of improving its overall fleet efficiency by 25 percent.

Hybrid technology for this truck helps retain energy generated by the engine, storing it in the batteries. The truck sends the stored power through the motor and generator. When blended with engine torque, it improves performance, makes the engine more fuel efficient, and, in high speeds, sometimes operates with electric power only.

This process increases driving efficiency by 5 to 7 percent. The batteries power the heating, air-conditioning and electrical system when the engine is turned off. Eaton projects an improved miles-per-gallon performance that, when combined with less idle time, will result in about US$9,000 in fuel savings per year, based on an average cost of US$2.50 per gallon (US$9.46 per liter).

Green comes in many shades, and there is nothing wrong with informing stake-holders about the green tactics you are implementing. However, a word of caution: avoid greenwashing!

It is important for a store or shopping center to conduct a green audit to determine its environmental impact before embarking on a full-scale image-building public relations campaign. One objective of a green audit is to define the store or shopping center's carbon footprint to determine its tonnage of carbon dioxide emitted into the atmosphere. This is helpful in setting goals to reduce emissions and helps to measure success—a key to providing reliable data in disclosure reports or in communicating with the news media.

Wal-Mart first measured its global carbon footprint in 2005 and now reports through the U.K.-based Carbon Disclosure Project every year, benchmarking to calendar year 2005 as the base year. This assessment helped Wal-Mart set internal goals and to launch a multi-year public relations campaign called Sustainability 360, which began in 2007. This campaign gets out the message in many ways, from in-store signage to marked tractor trailer trucks that deliver merchandise to Wal-Mart stores.

JCPENNEY AND EPA RAISE PUBLIC AWARENESS

A bright idea hit the road in October 2007. JCPenney worked with EPA administrator Stephen L. Johnson's office to co-sponsor a month-long national tour to promote using energy-efficient lighting as an easy, effective and money-saving way for American households to help fight climate change.

Johnson kicked off a 10-city, 20-day Energy Star Change-a-Light bus tour at the Disneyland Resort theme park in Anaheim, California. The Change-a-Light campaign encouraged Americans to pledge changing out at least one inefficient lightbulb at home with an energy-efficient one. At Disneyland Resort, an EPA crew and volunteers boarded a state-of-the-art J4500 LX motor coach and rode it to New York, holding promotional events at various cities to get a message out about conservation. A 2007 EPA-model, clean-diesel engine, fitted with a particulate scrubber to remove gaseous exhaust and fueled by ultra-low-sulfur diesel, powered the bus. Motor Coach Industries, a large North American manufacturer of inter-city motor coaches, donated the bus.

"JCPenney encouraged the EPA's Energy Star Change-a-Light Bus Tour to stop at the new JCPenney store at Northfield Stapleton in Denver [for its grand opening] on October eighth," said Richard P. O'Leary, CDP, vice president and director of construction services for the JCPenney Company.

JCPenney and lamp manufacturer Sylvania gave two free Energy Star-qualified bulbs to everyone who took the Change-a-Light pledge. JCPenney also gave the first 500 visitors a reusable JCPenney shopping bag and refreshments during the grand opening of its store at the LEED Silver-certified Shops at Northfield Stapleton. The eco-minded event helped highlight that the store is JCPenney's pilot store

for a number of sustainable building components. EPA awarded JCPenney the Energy Star Partner of the Year in 2007 for excellence in energy management.

The Energy Star bus tour included stops at other shopping centers, such as Navy Pier in Chicago, Illinois; Faneuil Hall Marketplace in Boston, Massachusetts; and Manhattan's Union Square retail district. Sporting events such as a Broncos football game in Denver, Colorado, and a Falcons game in Atlanta, Georgia, also hosted tour events.

The EPA and the U.S. Department of Energy created the tour to raise awareness of the benefits of energy-efficient lighting choices. At each tour stop, an outdoor interactive education center was set up with interactive displays. The display conveyed the importance of our lighting choices and explained how to use and dispose of compact fluorescent lamps (CFLs) responsibly. It also made the connection between our personal energy use and Earth's climate. Just by using one Energy Star–qualified bulb, we can save about US$30 or more in energy costs over its lifetime.

According to the EPA, if every U.S. household changed one incandescent lightbulb to an Energy Star bulb, the United States would save US$600 mil-

PHOTOS COURTESY OF U.S. EPA

Top: EPA administrator Stephen L. Johnson (wearing white polo shirt) teaches children about the different shapes of compact fluorescent lightbulbs, including tubed, globe, spiral, covered A-shape, outdoor reflector, indoor reflector and candle, at a Disneyland event in Southern California. JCPenney cosponsored the educational display. Middle: An EPA event to promote the use of energy-efficient CFLs was set up at the popular Faneuil Hall Marketplace in Boston, Massachusetts, just outside the main entrance to Quincy Market. Locally sponsored tents included Osram Sylvania's, where people took the pledge and received one of 1,776 Energy Star–qualified CFLs, and Whole Foods Market, a retailer that is also considering collecting spent CFLs for recycling. Whole Foods Market gave away fresh bananas and apples to the public.

The bottom photo shows Navy Pier looking out onto Lake Michigan, where 500 people pledged to Change-a-Light through General Electric's "Hallowgreen" Web site. Participants were able to immediately go green by receiving a free Energy Star–approved bulb at this popular tourist-oriented mall near the famous Loop in Chicago, Illinois.

lion in energy costs each year, enough energy to light three million homes and prevent greenhouse gases equivalent to the emissions from more than 800,000 cars. Lighting accounts for about 20 percent of a home's electricity use. Energy Star-qualified lightbulbs and fixtures use about 75 percent less energy than standard incandescent lighting, and they last six to 10 times longer.

Energy Star, a joint program of the EPA and the U.S. Department of Energy, is designed to save money and protect the environment through energy-efficient products and practices. "By encouraging people to make smart energy decisions, President Bush and EPA are brightening America's future, one light at a time," said EPA administrator Stephen L. Johnson.

By the time the tour concluded, nearly one million Americans had pledged to change more than 2.6 million lights to help fight climate change. This represents a potential savings of nearly US$70 million in energy costs and prevents one billion pounds (453,600 metric tons) of greenhouse gas emissions.

Events such as this one and news media coverage of environmental issues are helping to shape public opinion about environmental concerns, and retail marketing executives are responding to this change.

Prominent red signs at Gap stores such as the one pictured at right at the Toronto (Canada) Eaton Centre ask, "Can the Next Generation Change the World?" This is an example of a corporate social responsibility campaign. This type of campaign, which for many retailers includes environmental responsibility, is on the rise all over the world as noted in Chapter 7.

MARKETING TO GREEN-BLOODED CONSUMERS

The majority (73 percent) of 100 chief marketing officers representing large U.S. retail companies, polled in a BDO Seidman Retail Compass Survey in autumn 2007, said they were increasing their marketing focus on green products.

More than one-quarter (26 percent) of the retailers said they were working closely with nonprofit organizations and promoting community service programs during the 2007 holiday shopping season. Half of those retailers were donating a percentage of sales, and as many as 31 percent were donating the entire proceeds from a specific product.

In 2007, San Bruno, California-based Gap Inc. topped its 2006 "red umbrella" charity promotion by offering red apparel products and donating a portion of the proceeds to help victims of AIDS in Africa. Gap earmarked a portion of the sales of merchandise it labeled as Product Red to donate to AIDS research and AIDS victims.

"The holiday season, when retailers are exposed to more consumers than any time of year, presents the prime opportunity to identify their brand with worthwhile causes, whether they be linked to charitable work or focused on environmental sustainability," said Catherine Fox-Simpson, a partner at BDO Seidman.

Underscoring that principle, Barneys New York launched a green advertising campaign in advance of the 2007 holiday season using such slogans as Give Good Green and Have a Green Holiday. Even the retailer's gift cards included slogans, such as Join the Green Revolution—We Have! and Green is Groovy.

ORGANIC COTTON APPAREL

The creative writers for the high-end retailer Barneys, now owned by an affiliate of Istithmar PJSC—an investment firm owned by principals associated with the Dubai, United Arab Emirates government—used a play on words to capture the attention of environmentally conscientious consumers with such phrases as "sensationally sustainable swag" and "orgasmic organic denim."

The luxury department store chain sells designer apparel, shoes and accessories for men, women and children—as well as home furnishings—in more than 35

PHOTO: R. E. MILIAN

stores. Its green catalog was printed paper recycled from 30 percent postconsumer waste, and soybean-based ink was used to print photos of the products. The eco-friendly merchandise that Barneys New York promoted included organic cotton T-shirts and free-range alpaca yarn hand-knit scarves.

However, Barneys is not alone in taking advantage of this consumer trend in *greening apparel*. The 2007 holiday season also brought 100 percent organic cotton jeans from the denim giant, Levi Strauss & Company, a pioneer in organic cotton denim since it first introduced a very limited line in 2005. Levi dyes its signature 501 organic jeans with natural indigo and sews recycled buttons and rivets onto organic Capital E jeans, which sell for a whopping US$245 at full retail.

Green consumers, though, have different budget needs. Wal-Mart's Sam's Club fulfills the lower-end budget needs by selling private-label organic jeans for only US$20 and T-shirts for under US$10.

Levi's next step was a full-scale launch of organic cotton jeans in all styles and colors, a revolution that dozens of manufactures of mainstream apparel will surely mimic.

IMAGE COURTESY OF GAP INC.

According to the Sustainable Cotton Project, farmers use one-third of a pound of pesticides to grow sufficient cotton to manufacture just one T-shirt. In fact, growers allocate almost one-quarter of all U.S. agricultural pesticides to produce conventionally grown cotton.

American Apparel, Nike and other apparel and footwear manufacturers are enticing retailers with clothes made from organic cotton, wool, bamboo and corn-based fibers, which will continue to make their way to shelves, racks and gondolas of retail stores across the world as consumers increase their demand for these sustainable products.

As high-volume retailers such as Victoria's Secret and Target begin to achieve success with organic apparel to the degree that food stores have already experienced

with special organic food lines, this eco-fashion trend is likely to move into the mainstream of U.S. consumers.

Today, fashion leaders such as Armani and Versace are embracing this trend as much as Diane von Furstenberg and Oscar de la Renta. This phenomenon is very different from the trend that began in the early 1990s when Esprit first rolled out organic cotton clothes and Patagonia launched its outdoor fleece sportswear line made from recycled plastic soda bottles.

The European consumer has generally been more focused on green products than American consumers have, but now both seem to be equally responding to environmentally friendly messages from manufacturers and retailers more than ever before.

CUSTOMERS' ATTITUDES ARE SHIFTING GREEN

The Natural Marketing Institute claims that U.S. consumers spent US$209 billion in 2005 on natural, organic and eco-friendly goods. The institute projects that figure will steadily climb to US$410 billion by 2010 and more than double again to US$845 billion by 2015.

PHOTO: R. E. MILIAN

The 2007 ImagePower Green Brands Survey revealed a significant shift in the collective consciousness of Americans, indicating that *green* is no longer an issue marginalized to fanatical environmentalists.

Nearly all Americans now display some green attitudes and behaviors, compared to a similar 2006 study conducted by the same consortium, which included WPP's Landor Associates, Penn, Schoen & Berland (PSB) Associates and Cohn & Wolfe (C&W), to track consumer behavior.

PSB's Internet Surveys Groups (ISG) conducted 3,029 interviews in April 2007, which represents a reliable sample of the American and British populations, for their respective perceptions of green. The study showed that 40 percent of the U.S. population believes that the leading environmental issue is global warming (climate change).

Teavana opened its first teahouse in Atlanta, Georgia, in 1997, and became an instant success by encouraging a healthy, alternative lifestyle. Stores like Teavana (featured above at the Galleria in Fort Lauderdale, Florida) are expanding rapidly in the United States to capture their share of the US$410 billion that the Natural Marketing Institute predicts U.S. consumers will spend by 2010 on natural, organic and eco-friendly goods. The Institute projects that figure will steadily climb to US$845 billion by 2015.

A similar survey conducted in 2006 by the same companies indicated that most U.S. consumers were unfamiliar with the concept of green. These consumers were not able to make the connection in 2006 as to how their actions affected the environment, while in 2007, as many as 20 percent blamed themselves for the state of the environment.

PHOTOS: R. E. MILIAN

According to the survey sponsors, the results of the 2007 survey seem to indicate that consumer-oriented companies (such as product manufacturers, shopping centers and retailers) must consider the next level of *greenness,* including all business practices involving consumer products from point of origin to the point of purchase. This includes raw materials, manufacturing process, product transport and the possibility for recycling the product.

Macy's sells this eco-friendly canvas shopping tote by Fossil for US$18.00 each, touting the reusable bag with an eco-themed print as being "good for the planet and good-looking too!" (Photo above)

Four out of ten Americans polled by GfK Roper in December 2007 said they would take reusable fabric bags to stores to prevent wasting disposable plastic bags. U.S. consumers used 91 billion plastic bags in 2007, and on a worldwide basis, consumers pick up an estimated 500 billion to one trillion plastic bags at stores each year, about about one million per minute. Billions of bags become litter, and some end up in ocean waters where they harm animals that mistake them for edible jellyfish.

It takes about 430,000 gallons (1.6 million liters) of fossil fuel to make 100 million plastic bags, according to Worldwatch Institute. In 2007, San Francisco, California, instituted a ban on nonbiodegradable plastic shopping bags used at large stores.

Costco and its main competitors, BJ's Wholesale Club and Sam's Club, do not give bags to customers. They simply reuse the cardboard boxes that the manufacturers used to ship the merchandise to the wholesale clubs. Costco Wholesale wants to take it a step further. It now sells reusable totes touting "Think Green" (top right). These bags are big—and inexpensive. A three-pack sells for US$3.

Costco hopes its Think Green bags catch on with its members so the company can ask suppliers to stop packing large merchandise in boxes and instead place the merchandise directly onto pallets. This would save on packing costs and reduce the strain on the environment.

In another study, conducted in December 2007 by GfK Roper and commissioned by Tiller LLC marketing consultancy, the results revealed that three-quarters of Americans planned to be more environmentally responsible in 2008 with half of those polled actually planning to make a New Year's resolution to live more of a green life.

Forty-two percent of the Americans polled said they would take reusable fabric bags to the supermarket to reduce the use of plastic bags, while two-thirds said they plan to cut back on using household chemicals.

Many commercial and household cleaning products contain hazardous ingredients, such as organic solvents and petroleum-based chemicals, which can release VOCs that remain in indoor air for a long time. Improper use, storage and disposal of these hazardous substances can affect the health of persons in the household and impact the environment.

The survey also found one-third of respondents felt guilty in recent years for not living a more environmentally friendly lifestyle. The GfK survey of 1,004 U.S. adults has a margin of error of plus or minus 3 percent.

KPMG LLP, the audit, tax and advisory firm affiliated with KPMG International, also conducted its own survey on American greening attitudes, and the results

coincided with the other two surveys cited.

Environmental issues increasingly figured into consumers' spending decisions, with a vast majority of the 2007 holiday shoppers expressing a willingness to pay more for eco-friendly gifts, according to the 2007 Annual National Shopping Be-

PHOTOS: R. E. MILIAN

⑤ Specialty leasing retail merchandising units (RMUs) at Westfield Garden State Plaza in Paramus, New Jersey, included (1) one promoting Organix Cosmetix and another (2) touting Nature's Comfort. Two miles away, the General Growth Properties Paramus Park mall featured (3) Organic Skin Care, an RMU that also promoted Organix Cosmetix (5). (4) At the Miracle Mile Shops at Planet Hollywood in Las Vegas, Nevada, an RMU promises "never again dry skin."

During the 2007 Christmas season, (1) Nordstrom department store at Westfield Garden State Plaza in Paramus, New Jersey, added special merchandise displays to feature organic cosmetics. (2) Macy's at Taubman Center's Fairlane Town Center in Deerborne, Michigan, promoted its Hotel Collection of towels made from 100 percent organically grown cotton. (3) Dillard's Inc. department store at the General Growth Fashion Show mall in Las Vegas, Nevada, promoted its Origin's Organics line. (4) A LUSH Fresh Handmade Cosmetics department sells British cosmetics, in which organic fruits and vegetables are blended into offbeat forms, such as solid shampoo bars, at the Macy's located at Simon Property Group's Menlo Park Mall in Edison, New Jersey. (5) Timberland sells canvas bags that encourage customers to help save the North Pole and posts signs on store windows at Westfield Garden State Plaza.

PHOTOS: R. E. MILIAN

havior Survey by KPMG.

"Some eighty-eight percent of the survey respondents were very concerned about the environment," said John Rittenhouse, a KPMG retail partner and national leader for operations risk management.

Rittenhouse added that 74 percent of the respondents indicated that they buy environmentally friendly products, 60 percent were willing to pay more for such items and 55 percent said they make a special effort to patronize retailers with a green reputation.

In December 2007, the Gordman Group randomly surveyed 815 U.S. shoppers by telephone for KPMG. The margin of error was plus or minus 3.5 percent. The message from the consumer appears to be consistent with every survey. Retailers that cater to environmentally concerned customers will continue to win their hearts and capture their business by promoting green products.

WIN THE CUSTOMER WITH P.O.P. DISPLAYS

PHOTOS: R. E. MILIAN

Two effective ways for shopping centers and retailers to target Earth-minded customers are through specialty leasing and displays of eco-friendly merchandise.

To capture the customer during the 2007 Christmas season, Westfield Garden State Plaza, New Jersey's largest shopping mall, in Paramus, licensed seven retail merchandise units (RMUs) to sell natural products catering to environmentally responsible and health-oriented consumers. In this manner, the shopping center filled any void that retailers did not satisfy.

Many traditional shopping center retailers also added special merchandise displays during the 2007 Christmas season to tout their green offerings.

Shopping center com-

In early 2008, Barnes & Noble Booksellers devoted an end cap, a retailer's most valuable space, to promote books touting the green movement.

panies that employ image-building campaigns to let the public know about their green agenda will likewise win over these customers and perhaps even win over retail tenants that have defined their own green agendas.

SUNRIDGE MALL RECYCLES

Retailers are promoting their green image and so are shopping centers. Mall companies are promoting a host of practices from recycling to purchasing electricity generated with renewable fuels.

Ivanhoe Cambridge began a comprehensive recycling program in 2007 at its Sunridge Mall and supported it with a marketing campaign. Sunridge Mall is the largest shopping center in North East Calgary, Alberta, Canada, comprising 160 stores and services including The Bay, Zellers, World Health Club and Canada's largest Sport Chek.

As with every well-conceived plan, Sunridge set a goal to increase the amount of waste to recycle from 16 to 35 percent after the first full year following the program's launch. To achieve that goal, Sunridge had to promote internally (to staff and tenants) and externally (to customers).

The organizers created a packet for the tenants, boldly labeled "Sunridge Recycles, Sunridge Mall's new environmental initiative," and distributed it to all merchants. The program, which began on May 14, 2007, gives Sunridge Mall the responsibility for collecting the tenants' trash as well as recyclables such as cardboard and paper.

Kelly Vieira, Sunridge's general manager, defined recycling as the collection, separation, processing and marketing of materials so they can be made into new products. Viera told her merchants, "It is a socially responsible way to help decrease dependence on raw materials by redistributing products that would normally end up in landfills."

Sunridge became the first shopping center to put together an organized recycling program that involves all tenants in the City of Calgary. Workers for the mall pick up recyclable and nonrecyclable refuse from the tenants once a day. They collect used oil, garbage and cardboard from food court restaurants more frequently.

At the end of the day, Sunridge's tenants can leave their recyclables outside their stores to be picked up by mall maintenance workers. During the day, there are several back-of-the-house locations where recyclables can be stored.

Recycling is only one of a series of sustainable practices that Ivanhoe Cambridge is rolling out at its centers across the world. "Like many things, sustainability is an evolution for Ivanhoe Cambridge that started with recycling at the center level,"

said Belinda Davidson, SCMD, director, regional marketing for Ivanhoe Cambridge's western region, responsible for shopping centers located across British Columbia, Alberta and Manitoba.

Green practices at the Canadian multinational operator of retail real estate have expanded to encompass many other environmentally friendly initiatives and will culminate with a LEED Gold building planned for the Vancouver market, according to Davidson.

Ivanhoe Cambridge's Sunridge Mall was the first shopping mall in Calgary to institute a full-scale organized recycling program. Prior to implementing the Sunridge Recycles program, Sunridge Mall recycled only 16 percent of all the waste the center produced. The property set a goal to increase that to 35 percent over the first twelve months of the program.

IVANHOE CAMBRIDGE USES GREEN POWER

Another green practice that Ivanhoe Cambridge successfully implemented is the use of renewable energy at many of its properties.

"In addition to supporting renewable power generation sources, Ivanhoe Cambridge has embraced recycling, detailed tracking of energy usage, conservation and other environmentally oriented practices," said Doug Harman, vice president, property services at Ivanhoe Cambridge.

The Canadian developer is doing its part to help fight climate change and create a healthier environment for future generations, with clean, renewable EcoLogo-certified electricity. In February 2007, Ivanhoe Cambridge signed an agreement with Bullfrog Power to purchase a minimum of 11,000 megawatt hours (MWhs) of green power annually to meet 30 percent of the electricity used to power the common areas of 13 of its shopping centers across Ontario. A megawatt (MW) is one million watts, and a kilowatt (kW) is one thousand watts.

This makes Ivanhoe Cambridge's use of green power in 2007 second only to Wal-Mart, Canada's largest purchaser of green power, which committed more than 20,000 MWhs.

"This agreement reflects both our commitment to environmental responsibility and to the future of the communities we serve through our shopping centers," said Kim D. McInnes, executive vice president and chief operating officer of Ivanhoe Cambridge.

In explaining Ivanhoe Cambridge's CSR philosophy, McInnes, who is also a member of ICSC's Board of Trustees, said, "We believe corporations have an important role to play in addressing the issue of climate change by reducing their emissions footprint and supporting renewable power."

Upper Canada Mall in Newmarket, Ontario—located approximately 31 miles (50 km) north of Toronto—is one of Ivanhoe Cambridge's shopping centers that promotes its commitment to environmental responsibility and to the future of their communities.

The power produced by Bullfrog's renewable energy generators on behalf of Ivanhoe Cambridge will reduce annual emissions of CO_2 by almost 8,000 tons (7,260 metric tons), nitric oxide (NO) emissions by 6.5 tons (5.9 metric tons) and sulfur dioxide (SO_2) emissions by 30 tons (27 metric tons).

While only CO_2 is a greenhouse gas, NO and SO_2 contribute to the formation of smog. NO should not be confused with nitrous oxide (N_2O), a general anesthetic, laughing gas and indeed a greenhouse gas, or with nitrogen dioxide (NO_2), the reddish-brown gas with a biting odor, which is another poisonous air pollutant.

"Ivanhoe Cambridge is demonstrating its leadership in environmental stewardship and taking real action to reduce greenhouse gas emissions and air pollution associated with conventional electricity generation," said Tom Heintzman, president of the utility company providing green power to Ivanhoe Cambridge facilities, in a news release that received wide exposure for the Montreal-based shopping center development company.

"This second green power purchase marks yet another step in Ivanhoe Cambridge's commitment to integrate sustainability into its culture and operations," Heintzman said. Bullfrog sources power entirely from generators that meet or exceed Canada's federal Environmental Choice program and the EcoLogo standard for renewable electricity.

Bullfrog's power comes from clean, emission-free sources such as wind power and low-impact waterpower hydro generators instead of coal, natural gas and oil, which are carbon-based fuels and release GHG.

Sky Generation has supplied Bullfrog Power with wind power from its existing Ferndale wind farm since 2005, and in 2006, two new turbines were erected to accommodate the growing demand for Bullfrog Power's green electricity service.

In addition to Upper Canada Mall, other Ivanhoe Cambridge properties participating in Bullfrog's Ontario renewable power grid are Bayshore Shopping Centre, Burlington Mall, Conestoga Mall, Devonshire Mall, Dixie Outlet Mall, Downtown Chatham Centre, Lynden Park Mall, Mapleview Centre, Oakville Place, Oshawa Centre, Quinte Mall and Tecumseh Mall.

In western Canada, Ivanhoe Cambridge joined the B.C. Hydro Power Smart Partner program, which is operated by B.C. Hydro. Ivanhoe Cambridge is purchasing renewable energy from B.C. Hydro for its British Columbia shopping centers.

PHOTO BY SPECIAL PERMISSION COPYRIGHT ©
ENMAX CORPORATION. ALL RIGHTS RESERVED.

Since 2004, Ivanhoe Cambridge has relied on wind power purchased from ENMAX Corporation to reduce energy expenses at six of its malls in Calgary, Alberta, and two office buildings.

Energy provided by windmills—erected at wind farms in southern Alberta, including McBride Lake, one of Canada's largest wind farms of which ENMAX is a 50 percent owner—now supply one-quarter of the properties' common area power, according to McInnes.

Ivanhoe Cambridge's six western Canadian shopping centers and two office buildings are consuming 24,000-megawatt-hours of renewable power annually, which is equivalent to removing more than 62.1 million car miles, according to ENMAX.

More than 2.5 million fully grown trees per year would have been required to absorb the CO_2 that these eight properties would have emitted had they used fossil fuel instead of this renewable form of energy.

The McBride Lake Wind Farm located near Fort Macleod in southern Alberta (below) generates electricity from renewable wind power to supply one-fourth of the common area needs of six Ivanhoe Cambridge shopping centers and two of its office buildings in Calgary, Alberta. Vision Quest Windelectric Inc. and ENMAX Green Power Inc. (Ivanhoe Cambridge's supplier of green power) jointly own the wind farm. The 76-megawatt electricity generating facility, which opened in 2003, produces about 235,000 MWh per year from 114 Vesta wind turbines. This is enough clean energy to reduce emissions of heat-trapping carbon dioxide gases by 235,000 tons (213,200 metric tons) per year.

All the while, Ivanhoe Cambridge—with a real estate portfolio consisting of more than 46 million square feet (4.3 million sq meters) of retail space and some 70 regional and superregional shopping centers—is using traditional public relations tactics to share the news about its environmental practices with tenants, customers and the community each property serves.

Headquartered in Montreal, Quebec, Canada, Ivanhoe Cambridge is the principal real estate subsidiary of the Caisse de dépôt et placement du Québec, one of the largest institutional fund managers in Canada. Four other prominent Canadian pension funds are also large shareholders of the company. René Tremblay, Ivanhoe Cambridge's president and chief executive officer, served as ICSC chairman from 2007 to 2008.

Another successful program for Ivanhoe Cambridge involved a highly visible campaign called Shopping As It Should Be, at Mayfair Shopping Centre in Victoria, British Columbia, Canada. The campaign won an ICSC MAXI Gold Award in 2007 partly because all of the messages were well integrated. Among these was a message of the center's green practices.

Mayfair Shopping Centre in Victoria, British Columbia, promoted Earth Day and the shopping center's sustainable practices, encouraging customers to "leave a smaller footprint." Mayfair also ran ads with its theme, "Light of Day," to inform the public that the shopping center uses daylighting to reduce energy consumption. The lights in the interior of the mall and in parking lots are regulated with automated photosensors. As the sun rises, the lights are dimmed until they eventually turn off. When the sun starts to set, the lights gradually turn on and become brighter as the sky darkens. Mayfair combined sales promotion with green practices to encourage customers to shop and recycle.

PHOTO COURTESY OF IVANHOE CAMBRIDGE

Mayfair Shopping Centre used Earth Day to promote its many sustainable practices, including the center's commitment to year-round energy conservation, and to increase environmental awareness with shoppers, retailers and community partners.

Mayfair Shopping Centre is demonstrating its green commitment through the Light of Day program. This initiative has drastically reduced energy consumption by using daylighting to illuminate the mall interiors.

Ivanhoe Cambridge installed this daylighting process at Mayfair during a lighting retrofit project in 2006 to make use of the natural light available from the significant skylight treatment throughout the property.

Sensors control the interior lights, automatically dimming them as the sun begins to rise high in the late-morning sky. "We feel it is important for businesses to do their part in helping to preserve our planet," said Ivanhoe Cambridge's Davidson.

FOREST CITY GREENHOUSE WEB SITE

As part of a wider environmental commitment, Cleveland, Ohio-based Forest City Enterprises launched a Web site devoted to sustainable living. Forest City calls the Web site "GreenHouse." It is colorful, interactive and fun, and Forest City uses it to communicate with tenants, partners and the residents of its housing projects. The site provides tips to be more sustainable, and it teaches what it preaches, focusing on 10 areas that the public can consider to help save the planet:

1. Recycle for reuse (encourages recycling from paper to plastics, even cell phones)

2. Power down (suggests many ways to reduce energy consumption)

3. Be water wise (advises ways to conserve water)

4. Don't dispose (provides tips to reduce material sent to landfills, such as using metal eating utensils instead of plastic and using reusable batteries instead of disposable ones)

5. It's in the bag (gives customers advice to consider when purchasing merchandise at stores; whether to ask for plastic, paper or cloth bags)

6. Get in tune (reminds the public that a tune-up for their vehicle can save gasoline and cut down on unnecessary emissions)

7. Drive less (recommends shorter trips, walking or using mass transportation instead of driving)

8. Go organic (plays up advantages of organic food and avoiding synthetic fertilizers and pesticides)

9. Buy local (explains how buying locally prevents items from being trucked from long distances, to minimize energy use and GHG emissions)

10. Clean green (suggests use of biodegradable, phosphate-free cleaning products that will not harm the environment)

Forest City also modified its tenant manual by adding a Sustainable Building Reference Guide. The guide informs tenants about green building features that the tenant should consider when building out its store's interior space, urging them to conserve energy and promote the health of building occupants.

Among Forest City's practices are the use of recycled paper and its use of soy- or vegetable-based inks on corporate materials such as business cards, letterheads and annual reports. Forest City also has an extensive training program to make sure its employees are aware of its strategy, reminding them to keep sustainability as a top-of-mind priority. Educating the retailers is part of that strategy.

Macy's, Bass Pro Shops Outdoor World, Harkins 18-screen theaters, and 60 specialty shops and restaurants anchor Forest City's Northfield Stapleton 1.2 million-square-foot (111,500 sq meters) project, 10 minutes from downtown Denver, Colorado, as previously referred to in Chapter 11. The LEED-certified Northfield Stapleton heavily promotes its green building design with ads, educates its tenants about environmental responsibility and offers incentives for tenants to become more sustainable.

SOURCE: FOREST CITY ENTERPRISES AND ICSC MAXI AWARDS

Northfield Stapleton's ads promote many aspects of their sustainability program. For example, the wind power ad explains how wind turbines provide a clean and renewable source of energy and eliminate 800,000 pounds (363 metric tons) of CO_2 emissions. The reflective roof ad shows how white and reflective roofs lower roof temperatures, keeping the inside of the building cool and reducing peak cooling loads by 10 to 15 percent.

The evaporative cooling system ad explains how cold water is sprayed into the airstream to cool as it evaporates and uses 75 percent less electricity than conventional air conditioning. The high-performance windows ad focuses on how windows at Northfield Stapleton provide improved insulation in both hot and cold weather, helping reduce energy consumption and adding natural lighting.

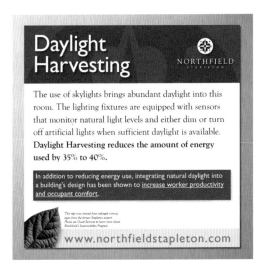

Northfield's daylight harvesting ad indicates how energy usage is reduced by 35 to 40 percent through use of skylights and sensor-monitored lighting fixtures, which not only regulate lighting based on available natural light but also regulate the on/off features based on room occupancy.

The high-efficiency plumbing fixtures ad explains how waterless urinals, low-flow sensor faucets and high-efficiency toilets work. These types of fixtures at Northfield Stapleton reduce water usage by more than 645,000 gallons (2.4 million liters) per year, enough to fill 180,000 bathtubs.

FCP GREEN

Representatives from First Canadian Place (FCP), an urban property on a sustainable site, owned by Toronto, Ontario-based Brookfield Properties Corporation, took home a MAXI Silver Award at the 2007 ICSC Fall Conference in New Orleans, Louisiana, for its clever multidisciplinary campaign to illustrate the center's green virtues.

Located in downtown Toronto, Ontario, FCP is an impressive 2.8-million-square-foot (260,000 sq m) mixed-use complex with 120 stores and a 72-level office high-rise. The PATH pedestrian underground tunnel connects the project to TTC subway stations, Go Transit, Via Rail and other office buildings in the central business district, making FCP an ideal project to minimize driving, although it has a parking garage.

The FCP Green marketing campaign included a series of special events to raise environmental awareness and involve the public in sustainable activities. A summary of FCP's events in April 2007 gives us an example of the creativity any shopping center can employ to hold events that appeal to the green-minded public:

- **Green Roofs: Garden in the Sky**
  Beth Anne Currie, green roof consultant and creator from Gardens in the Sky program, lectured about rooftop gardening as an ecological imperative for Greater Toronto.

- **Chatelaine: Green Goes Mainstream**
  Chatelaine magazine's Deborah Fulsang and Virginie Martocq discussed green style options, fashions and home furnishings.

- **FCP Shopper: Eco-Chic Fashions and Gifts**
  Cathy DeSerranno displayed fashions made with bamboo and organic cotton. The event also featured innovative examples of items produced with earth-friendly ingredients, dyes and packaging.

- **Webber Naturals: Rejuvenating the Natural Way**
  Joyce Tellier-Johnson, a naturopathic physician from Webber Naturals, taught various approaches to slowing down the aging process. The event was sponsored by Pharma Plus Drugmart.

- **Adria Vasil: Environmentally Friendly Products**
  From her book, *Ecoholic: Your Guide to the Most Environmentally Friendly Information, Products and Services in Canada*, Adria Vasil (columnist for *NOW* magazine) shared an inspirational sampling of the small steps to take to lessen a negative impact on the planet. The event was sponsored by Coles.

fcp
green

Earth Day® is April 22

Celebrate Earth Day® with FCP
April 16-30

fcpfirst.com or fcpevents.com
FOR DETAILS

SOURCE: BROOKFIELD PROPERTIES CORPORATION AND ICSC MAXI AWARDS

First
Canadian
Place

Shopping Centre

MIX BUSINESS WITH PLEASURE | **Brookfield** Properties
120 STORES, RESTAURANTS & SERVICES AT KING AND BAY fcpfirst.com

- **100-Mile Diet: Buying Canadian Local Food**
  Alisa Smith and J.B. MacKinnon, the authors of *The 100-Mile Diet: A Year of Local Eating*, explain their amusing and inspirational adventures making it through their one-year commitment to eat only food grown within a 100-mile (169 km) radius of their home. The event was sponsored by Coles.

- **The Tea Emporium: Green Tea**
  Shabnam Weber of The Tea Emporium cleared up some of the misconceptions about tea and offered information about it: What are the benefits of tea, and how will you best reap these benefits? Which teas are healthier? Which have caffeine, and which do not?

INORBIT MALL MITIGATES INDIA'S ENERGY CRISIS

Today India faces an energy crisis. There is a major shortage of oil-refining capacity, and the fast pace of development in India, coupled by the poor infrastructure to handle its needs, has resulted in power shortages of more than 25 percent of its needs.

Inorbit Mall's Save Power Have Power campaign helped support a growing concern about massive power consumption that is escalating in India. Launched in early 2007, the campaign also raised awareness about problems associated with climate change.

The enclosed shopping center used in-mall signs and outdoor ads to ask customers to lower air-conditioning use by turning up their thermostat and explained why it was turning up its own thermal controls "to save energy and to save the country." Inorbit Mall earned the MAXI Silver in 2007 for its efforts.

Shavak Srivastava, CMD, a principal of Square Foot Consultancy in Dubai, United Arab Emirates, and a consultant since 2003 to Inorbit Mall Ltd., a developer of several shopping centers in India branded as Inorbit, said the campaign was well received in Mumbai where the winning property is located.

He estimated the mall cut energy costs during the program by about 20

SAVE POWER. HAVE POWER

SOURCE: ICSC MAXI AWARDS, INORBIT MALL

percent, and the community rallied behind the cause partly because of Inorbit Mall's awareness ad campaign.

Everything Goes! Communication, a BTL communication agency, created and executed the energy conservation campaign.

"In a world of rapidly rising energy shortages, we hope the recognition helps us attain the position of an environmentally sensitive organization, which is something we feel strongly about," said Rajiv Bhatia, chief executive officer of Inorbit Malls (India) Pvt. Ltd., in an official statement in November 2007.

"The Save Power Have Power program was important for Inorbit because it was an initiative of the city [Mumbai] and the state [Maharashtra]," said Srivastava.

Mumbai, formerly called by its anglicized name, Bombay, is India's most populated city and is the capital of Maharashtra.

"As a responsible member of the community, we [Inorbit Mall] should take steps to support that," Srivastava said.

EDUCATING THE PUBLIC

The developer of Atlantic Station in Atlanta, Georgia, made green development and smart growth a prominent part of Atlantic Station's Web site and has included those messages in advertising pieces and the marketing of the retail stores and restaurants.

"We've found [the Web site] to be the most effective way of promoting all that is green about Atlantic Station since our site gets two to three million hits per month," said Liz Gillespie, SCMD, vice president of marketing for Jones Lang LaSalle, the managing agent for the retail portion of Atlantic Station. The website's address is: http://www.atlanticstation.com/concept_greenstar.php.

The site highlights the property's green initiatives and features extensive information about the environment and its association with the EPA. It also promotes special events at the property. Some Atlantic Station events, such as a book signing in October 2007 at a book promo for authors Newt Gingrich and former president and CEO of Zoo Atlanta, Terry L. Maple, highlight sustainability. Their book, *A Contract with the Earth,* reminds patrons of Atlantic Station's sympathy for the environment and helps to plug the Trust for Public Land & the Nature Conservancy, which signed on to cohost the event.

Any ad campaign that highlights the virtues of green design should address the audience in a mature, respectable manner. This audience is made up of customers who are sensitive to the environment and are seeking a real commitment. The communication needs to be straightforward and sincere. Only then will the customer truly appreciate your organization's green practices.

"Environmentalism and sustainable practices are not only things you do as an individual for a particular cause," the Atlantic Station Web site preaches, "they are also ideals you support as a member of a larger community."

Customers line up on May 26, 2007, at Pickering Town Centre in Pickering, Ontario, to exchange disposable plastic bags for "Be Seen, Be Green" reusable shopping bags. Inset: Aminh K. (9), a resident of the City of Pickering, display her "Earth Just Love It" poster, a winner of the shopping center campaign.

PHOTOS COURTESY OF 20 VIC

Chapter 14

ICSC Programs and Services

IN AN EFFORT to educate and share best practices in retail real estate, ICSC has embarked on a series of programs and services that address sustainability. This book is only one of them.

ICSC's green agenda includes courses that cover sustainable design and operation in several educational programs, including all of its weeklong schools around the world, the University of Shopping Centers and other programs.

Industry practitioners modified the test specifications to include best practices on sustainability in all of the ICSC professional certification programs, such as the Certified Shopping Center Manager (CSM), Certified Marketing Director (CMD), Certified Leasing Specialist (CLS) and Certified Development, Design and Construction Professional (CDP).

Periodicals, such as *Shopping Centers Today* and *Value Retail News*, have stepped up their coverage of retailers' and shopping centers' initiatives. These publications provide timely, in-depth explanations of this phenomenon to inform readers about newsworthy issues relating to green building practices. Textbooks and other book publishing activities within ICSC are adding this subject to the listing of topics in new releases.

Jon Ratner, 36, the son of Charles A. Ratner, president and chief executive officer of Forest City Enterprises, taught green building practices at the ICSC University of Shopping Centers, held in 2008 on the University of Pennsylvania's Wharton School campus in Philadelphia. Jon Ratner oversees Forest City's company-wide sustainability efforts. He inspires young and old to take a hard-line business approach while helping to improve the environment.

ICSC awards programs now recognize the contribution of green building design as part of the judging criteria. This includes the ICSC International Design and Development Awards, which presented an award in 2006 for the first time on sustainability, and the ICSC European Awards, with a ReSource Award category that combines the sustainability criteria with social responsibility and cultural preservation.

Through ICSC's global policy office—which interacts with local, state, province and federal governments mostly in the United States, Canada and the European Union—various committees of experts and interested ICSC members have been formed.

The ICSC Environmental Sustainability Subcommittee is a permanent subcommittee of the ICSC Global Public Policy Committee, consisting of volunteer members with expertise in a wide range of environmental and energy issues. The group investigates issues and advises the membership on appropriate initiatives. Members also serve as industry representatives providing feedback to municipalities, U.S. states, Canadian provinces and federal governments.

"There's a tsunami of environmental and sustainability issues coming our way," said Lawrence E. Kilduff, president of Mequon, Wisconsin-based The Kilduff Company and chairman of the ICSC Environmental Subcommittee. "The Environmental

Left: Mary Lou Fiala, ICSC chairman from 2008 to 2009, visited the Green Pavilion at ICSC's annual convention in Las Vegas, Nevada. The display showcased examples of green practices by retailers and shopping centers, and providing a central location for attendees to share ideas about sustainability practices that are sweeping the retail real estate industry. Below: In 2008, the ICSC Environmental Sustainability Subcommittee met in New York to discuss education, research and advocacy initiatives.

PHOTO ILLUSTRATION: R. E. MILIAN

PHOTO: R. E. MILIAN

Subcommittee wants to work proactively to educate the membership, municipalities, and other public and private partners, and continue to improve our industry's contribution to sustainability."

Another ICSC committee, the European Sustainability Working Group, is delving into several initiatives and is studying the impact of retail-specific green building standards applicable to various legislations in European countries. It plans to use a modified BREEAM system for measuring sustainable levels of retail-oriented properties.

ICSC's Global Public Policy office also represents ICSC members on environmental bills introduced in the U.S. Congress and monitors proposals that federal regulatory agencies and state legislatures raise from time to time in setting public policy.

ICSC also conducts research to quantify the green building movement of its members and keeps track of information published by many sources that affects retail real estate.

Sessions on sustainability are also being added to many ICSC meetings and conferences. In 2007, ICSC first brought sustainability to the forefront with a gigantic exhibition called the Green Pavilion at the ICSC Spring Convention (now renamed RECon) in Las Vegas, Nevada, and at the ICSC World Summit in Cape Town, South Africa. In 2008, the exhibitions were repeated in Las Vegas and taken to the ICSC European Conference in Amsterdam, the Netherlands, in April and to the ICSC Asia Expo in Cotai, Macau, in October.

ICSC also expanded the Trade Exposition In Las Vegas to include an entire Green Zone, dedicated to providers that offer environmental and energy-efficient products and services.

To help preserve the environment, ICSC requires its own suppliers and venue providers for its meetings and conferences to have a sustainability program in place. ICSC also introduced a logo to brand its various initiatives under the SEED acronym, which stands for "Sustainable Energy and Environmental Design."

PHOTO: AMANDA MOREAU/DDG

Chapter 15

Making the Site Sustainable

IN THE NEXT five chapters, we'll recap Chapters 1 through 14 by reviewing some of the key concepts of sustainability that relate to retail buildings as categorized by the LEED green building system.

All other green building systems measure these concepts as well, but they may fall in different categories. For example, LEED categorizes nighttime light pollution under *sustainable sites* whereas BREEAM categorizes it under *pollution*, a concept that LEED thoroughly recognizes but does not adopt as a category.

In this publication, we did not choose categories to support LEED per se over the other systems but rather selected one system for illustrative purposes. Most of the systems are perfectly adequate for measuring green building strategies, providing they are on a voluntary basis and give the retailer or developer the latitude to select what makes sense for the specific property.

SITE SELECTION

Sustainable site is a term that connotes many aspects that make the site where the building is located sustainable. This concept relates more to initial development or redevelopment as opposed to the operations phase of a retail facility.

We have heard the term *smart growth* used in various contexts for many years, but it does apply to some extent to both site selection that considers a denser population and to access to the infrastructure that supports urban living and commercial real estate.

In addition to choosing a sustainable site, the site itself can be constructed to be more sustainable. Sustainable sites tend to favor stormwater quality and quantity control, site cleanup, proximity of public transportation, minimizing light pollution and heat island effect, pollution prevention during construction and other adjustable features covered in this chapter.

By making smart decisions in the early planning stages of the site regarding where the retail facility will be located, developers can minimize operating costs and help the environment over the long term.

Depending on the climate, the building could be oriented to minimize or maximize solar heat gain and to capture the most sunlight for daylight harvesting purposes.

Another key concept in developing a sustainable site is to protect and, when needed, help restore natural habitat and maximize open green space.

DENSIFICATION AND CONNECTIVITY

Locating a project in an existing structure or using an urban infill strategy can preserve undeveloped land while minimizing sprawl. This strategy also responds to a new North American trend in mixed-use development that has existed in large cities all over the world, a trend we call live-work-shop-play lifestyle.

Densification is part of this trend and plays well in maximizing a real estate asset's funds from operations and property value. Building on to existing shopping centers often enhances returns because the existing center already has a built-in customer base and draws a critical mass. All of this also satisfies new urbanism and environmental trends and qualifies as a sustainable site.

When developers select sites in densely populated areas with access to public transportation, the site is sustainable because it encourages less carbon emissions when employees and customers use public transportation rather than using their own cars to get there.

ALTERNATIVE TRANSPORTATION

If the site is located in close proximity to alternative transportation that does not require the use of a single-occupied vehicle, the site may be deemed more sustainable than suburban out-of-town sites, where driving to and from the site becomes necessary. However, you have choices in that scenario as well.

Even a suburban site can be made more sustainable by providing feeder bus lines with access to local, regional and mass transit stations that serve a nearby metropolitan area. Retail developers can work with local and regional authorities as well as mass transportation entities to add public transportation to the site. This also helps retailers attract store employees.

Park-and-ride programs in buildings that have an abundance of parking with a portion assigned for commuting also encourage people to drive their cars less and to share rides either by using mass transit or by carpooling.

Another way a shopping center or office building discourages driving is by providing walkways, jogging tracks, bicycle paths, bicycle storage and changing rooms. These amenities encourage patrons and employees to move about in ways that require little consumption of energy or the release of GHGs.

BROWNFIELD REDEVELOPMENT

One of the best strategies involving sustainable sites is brownfield redevelopment: turning a contaminated, underutilized site into a safe, clean and environmentally friendly real estate full of vitality.

The downsides that have traditionally held back developers are the extra cleanup and insurance costs associated with building on a contaminated brownfield. However, government incentives are often available to help defray those costs.

On the positive side, many redeveloped brownfield sites tend to be centrally located with rock-bottom acquisition prices, and property values can skyrocket once the site is remediated and revitalized.

STORMWATER MANAGEMENT

Site improvements such as stormwater management are extremely important. Low-impact development (LID) should emphasize a stormwater management strategy that controls water at the source—both rainfall and stormwater runoff. This is called "source-control" technology.

Typically, this decentralized system distributes stormwater within a project site to directly replenish groundwater supplies. This eliminates sending stormwater on a path that gathers contaminants from paved surfaces and then flows into a municipal system of storm drainpipes and channeled paths, which force water downstream into a large stormwater management facility.

In developing or redeveloping a site, the most important thing you can do is to surround the building with permeable pavement, plantings or soil to allow stormwater to seep into the ground instead of flowing into municipal sewers. Many developers employ these simple and inexpensive techniques in place of the more expensive traditional culvert drainage strategies.

Use bioswales to reduce or slow the flow of stormwater from the parking lot pavement. Bioswales are landscaped grassy or vegetated channels designed to prevent erosion and filter stormwater, keeping harmful silt, automotive pollution, fertilizers and pesticides out of the storm sewers or watersheds.

Other stormwater techniques include designing rainwater cisterns, green roofs, wetlands and retention ponds intended to filter polluted stormwater runoff and divert it from the storm sewers. Proper stormwater management will mitigate the effect of groundwater shortages resulting from aquifers at risk, such as the Ogallala and the León Valley aquifers.

Aquifers are natural underground areas where large quantities of groundwater fill the spaces between rocks and sediment and provide a reservoir for valuable drinking water. The Ogallala aquifer is an underground body of water in the central United States that stretches from Wyoming to Texas and has been drying up over the past 60 years. The waterline has fallen more than 100 feet (30 m).

The southwest zone of León, Guanajuato, Mexico, where León City is located,

provides an example of potential environmental impacts that can affect groundwater when aquifer vulnerability is not taken into account in urban planning. Aquifers at risk in the León Valley threaten to contaminate the water supply of more than one million people.

URBAN HEAT ISLAND AND PERMEABLE PAVING

When developing or redeveloping a property, consider techniques to mitigate the urban heat island (UHI) effect. This phenomenon describes urban and suburban temperatures that are 2 to 10°F (1 to 6°C) hotter than nearby rural areas. The effect is primarily caused by dark surfaces such as roofs and parking pavements that absorb rather than reflect the sun s heat.

The types of materials used for the pavement and roof systems can also ease UHI effect. Reflective roofing material is now widely available and priced almost the same as a good-quality dark roofing material. Vegetated roofs—although somewhat costly—are becoming more common and are strongly encouraged in some municipalities.

Increasing the cover of trees and vegetation around a retail property is a simple, effective way to reduce the UHI effect. Trees provide a wide range of other benefits, including providing shade to cool the sidewalks and the building, enhancing the beauty of the property, absorbing GHGs and reducing stormwater runoff.

Cool paving materials also help to minimize the absorption of solar heat. The two principal types of cool paving materials are porous materials and light-colored pavers.

Permeable or porous pavements allow water to filter into the ground, keeping the pavement cool when moist. New technology has brought us permeable pavement constructed from concrete, asphalt and plastic lattice structures filled with soil, gravel or grass. Lighter-colored materials have higher solar reflectance. These materials absorb less solar radiation, thus remaining cooler.

Permeable paving or porous pavement can be applied to roads, parking lots and walkways to let water and air flow through the paving material. Typical hard-surface paving makes polluted water run off into storm drains and natural waterways. Porous pavement filters pollutants and allows rainwater to enter groundwater.

Specially designed flooring can be used to deviate water from the roof to drain into the building cisterns for recycling.

LIGHT POLLUTION

Light pollution is misdirected or misused artificial exterior light that generally projects upward instead of downward, where the lighting designer intended it to serve a specific purpose. Inappropriate application or installation of exterior lighting products generally cause light pollution. Why is this important, and should you even care? There are many reasons. The main one is that light pollution wastes

electricity, most of which is produced by carbon combustion and emits GHGs. However, there are more reasons.

Nighttime light pollution causes a glow over urban and suburban areas that spoils the views of the night skies that we humans have enjoyed since we first walked on Earth. Almost 90 percent of the world's population living in large urban cities located in developing and developed countries lives under skies dominated by light pollution, and half of those residents are unable to appreciate the beauty of a starry night from their homes.

PHOTOS: TARGET CORPORATION

Target achieved LEED certification for two of its stores in Chicago with innovative sustainable features such as sustainable sites previously used for industrial purposes, cleaned up by Target to meet LEED criteria, and the use of "green roofs" planted with vegetation to filter air pollutants, absorb stormwater and keep the stores cooler in the summer. One store is located on McKinley Park, at 1940 West 33rd Street, the other at 2112 Peterson Avenue.

Chapter 16

Energy and Atmosphere

TWO OF THE most important aspects of environmental sustainability deal with using renewable sources of energy and minimizing the burning of fossil fuels that damage the atmosphere, resulting in climate change.

Energy-related sustainability tactics are among the most efficient green building initiatives for retailers and shopping centers to implement because they not only help to reduce GHG emissions, but also result in substantial energy costs savings. These practices are truly a win-win.

Most of the energy that buildings use comes from electricity generated by gas- or coal-burning utility companies, which emit tremendous amounts of carbon dioxide gas. Reducing energy consumption is one way to reduce heat-trapping gas emissions. Unfortunately, most buildings depend on these electricity-generating plants, and the amount of GHGs emitted depends largely on the fuel these plants use to generate electricity.

However, many buildings are now able to source supplemental energy from renewable sources, which help reduce GHG emissions. Someday, the world will be primarily using renewable energy. We must prepare for this eventuality, which brings great advantages and some disadvantages.

A disadvantage to using renewable energy such as solar, wind and hydro is that it cannot be stored the same way as coal, gas and oil. From a national security standpoint, the United States has a vast Strategic Petroleum Reserve. The one-billion-barrel stockpile is the largest contingency reserve of government-owned emergency crude oil in the world.

The U.S. government can use any or all of it in the event of a war or other disruption to commercial oil supplies that threatens the economy. There is no such thing as a strategic solar reserve, at least not yet.

The United States can continue to maintain its stockpile of crude oil even if it largely switches to renewable forms of energy for regular consumption.

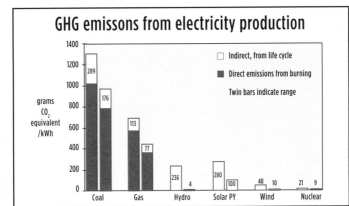

SOURCE: THE INTERNATIONAL ATOMIC ENERGY AGENCY (IAEA)

The Organization for Economic Co-operation and Development (OECD) and the International Energy Agency (IEA) have analyzed world energy use since 1971. Their published reports are designed to provide an understanding of energy use and emissions of CO_2 for more than 140 countries and regions by sector and by fuel type.

In a 2007 report entitled "Key Energy Statistics," the OECD estimates that GHG emissions worldwide from coal is 40.5 percent, from oil 39.5 percent, from natural gas 19.7 percent and from other sources 0.3 percent. According to the Australian Uranium Association's Uranium Information Centre Ltd., emissions of carbon dioxide from burning fossil fuels are about 25 billion tons (22.7 billion metric tons) a year worldwide, of which around 38 percent comes from coal, 21 percent from gas and 41 percent from oil.

The International Atomic Energy Agency (IAEA) states that emissions from electricity generation, a major contributor of greenhouse gases, account for one-third of total global GHG emissions.

The OECD and IEA expect that world energy demand will increase by more than 50 percent from 2005 to 2030. The projection takes into consideration the current world population of more than six billion and growing at the rate of 90 million a year. The OECD expects that by 2025 the world population will reach eight billion.

Thirty mostly developed countries, such as the United States, Australia, Japan and many European nations, make up the OECD. OECD countries account for slightly less than one-half of the world's primary energy supply and total consumption.

All indicators relating to producing energy by burning fossil fuels point to higher expenses, future scarcities and atmosphere pollution. Renewable energy is becoming a more viable alternative as time passes.

RENEWABLE ENERGY

Renewable energy sources will continue to play a bigger role in the design of buildings as well as what power plants use to generate electricity. Because these alternative sources of fuel offer such potential for the retail sector, now and in the future we should learn more about them and embrace their use.

Countries all over the world are exploring alternative sources of energy, and many retail buildings are drawing power from these renewable energy sources, from solar power to geothermal.

Governments of developed nations are trying to wean their countries off their dependence on fossil fuels while improving energy efficiency. With the price of crude oil hovering around US$100 a barrel and expected to rise in the near future, renewable resources of energy are becoming more practical to produce.

Two common sources of renewable are corn-based ethanol and biodiesel, made from farm crops such as palm oil and soybean oil. However, biofuels tend to require large amounts of land to cultivate, water to irrigate, chemical fertilizers to grow, and fuel-powered equipment to harvest.

This makes some crops unfeasible to make into biofuel. For example, biofuel made from wheat, rapeseed, soybean and sugar beets can cost more than US$100 per barrel to produce. Nevertheless, Europeans widely use rapeseed oil to make biodiesel because farmers can get more oil per land area devoted to cultivating than the land areas needed for cultivating soybean and wheat.

However, the more economical biofuels are made from corn, which costs roughly US$83 per barrel. Sugarcane costs US$45, and a relatively little known plant, jatropha, costs only US$43 a barrel to produce, at least when harvested in India.

Apart from the low cost, another benefit of producing biodiesel fuel from the oil of jatropha seeds is that this crop can be grown anywhere, including deserts and rock gardens. It needs little fertilizer and water.

Because jatropha is not edible, unlike corn and sugarcane, it does not take away from food crop resources. Jatropha appears promising, but more experiments are needed to determine its potential. Yet biodiesel is just one alternative able source of energy.

In addition to biofuels, renewable resources of energy are available in limited amounts from a number of technologies. Other common sources are solar, wind, hydropower and tidal (water), geothermal and biomass. These sources not only emit fewer pollutants into the atmosphere but also are renewable as they are easily replenishable for future generations.

Carbon fuel mainly consists of coal, oil and natural gas. Collectively they account for 90 percent of the total fuel used to create energy on Earth. Carbon fuels not only release climate-changing emissions but they also take millions of years to regenerate.

Today, the technology exists for using renewable sources of energy, but the supply line as well as the demand side is not geared up for a quick change from burning fossil fuels, which has been historically (and until fairly recently) a relatively inexpensive and abundant resource.

Preferred energy sources change throughout history. About 150 years ago, burning wood accounted for 90 percent of the world's energy needs, much like fossil fuels do today. Due to the convenience and low cost of fossil fuels, wood use fell behind and natural gas took its place.

As the tide turns on using fossil fuels, we will experience an increase in alterna-

tive energy sources. Many of the sources will need to be used in combination with others, as some are not always available. For example, on cloudy days, solar power cannot be easily harvested.

SOLAR POWER

Although the world of harnessing solar power is still "cloudy" today in terms of percentage of solar power produced, the future looks "sunny" for this type of renewable energy. In locales where the sun is plentiful, solar power has a role in green building operation, especially for space and water heating. This form of renewable energy is eco-friendly, as it generates no environmentally harmful by-products.

As noted in Chapter 9, many retailers are taking decisive action to install solar power systems at their stores and distribution centers. The most common way to harvest the sun's energy is by using photovoltaics, which convert solar energy directly to electricity. However, steam generators can also use solar thermal collectors for creating heat.

Photovoltaics consist of a photovoltaic (PV) cell, generally known as a solar cell, made from silicon alloys. The sun's rays emit photons that strike PV cells. Photons knock loose the electrons in silicones. As photons are absorbed, they generate electricity. Some photovoltaic systems use lenses to magnify the sun's rays as many as 500 times and require a fraction of the semiconductor used in older solar panels.

PV cells are similar to the batteries used to power appliances. They give off direct current (DC) and must be converted to alternating current (AC), using inverters to generate electricity to power buildings.

Today, photovoltaic equipment costs from US$2 to US$3 per watt to build. That is low compared to 1980 when it cost US$22 per watt. It may someday cost much less, thereby enabling technology and investment to increase solar power use all over the world. Today solar power accounts for only 1 percent of all energy used in the United States.

Germany now ranks first in solar power use despite its cloudy climate. Japan is not far behind. Germany's success began in 2000, when the government instituted policies for utility companies to give consumers a rebate for solar power they generate at their homes and send back excess power not used to the utility companies' public grid. Germany now has more than three gigawatts of solar power installed.

Piper Jaffray analysts follow companies that produce solar energy and anticipate that the industry will triple in size between 2007 and 2010 from about US$13 billion to US$40 billion in revenue.

WIND POWER

Wind is one of the oldest forms of renewable energy sources, harnessed thousands of years ago to power sail ships and grind grains. Wind is created through the natural

heating and cooling of Earth's land and water surfaces. However, it is not always available in abundance to rely on in every locale. When the weather is calm, there is little wind to generate power from wind turbines and other devices.

Wind power generators work in similar fashion to the windmills used centuries ago. The blades collect the wind's kinetic energy as the wind pushes them up and spins them. The moving blades turn a drive shaft that in turn rotates an electric generator, converting mechanical energy into electricity.

Wal-Mart and Chipotle have added wind-harnessing energy on a test basis (see Chapter 9), but the jury is still out on whether wind power makes sense for a single location rather than as part of a cluster of wind turbines that can generate large-scale power for a utility company. Whole Foods Market, a large user of green power, particularly wind power, purchases it wholesale from a utility company, rather than generating it at the stores.

Clusters of wind turbines, called wind farms, are used to produce wind power. One example sits outside Palm Springs, California, in Tehachapi, where the wind heavily blows during spring, summer and autumn because of hot air rising over the Mojave Desert and the cooler dense air rushing in from the Pacific Ocean taking its place.

Wind farms are typically located atop rounded hills, open plains, shorelines and between mountain ranges where wind funneling occurs. The top five users of wind power are Germany, Spain, the United States, India and Denmark. The latter generates 20 percent of its electricity consumption from renewable wind power.

WATER POWER

Hydroelectricity production can vary depending on the amount of accumulated precipitation. As dam gates are opened, a rush of water is released, creating tremendous force to produce power. However, most of the hydropower in the United States is concentrated in five states and half of the power generated comes from the U.S. West Coast states of Washington, California and Oregon. On the East Coast, New York ranks fourth with its mighty Niagara Falls, and Alabama ranks fifth.

In order to produce hydropower, several elements are needed, including a dam and a reservoir. Most U.S. dams serve the purpose of flood control or irrigation and do not produce hydropower.

Dating back to the 1800s, hydroelectricity is one of the oldest methods of producing electricity, and at the time, it replaced coal burning to generate power. Today, 7 percent of all power in the United States comes from hydropower and makes up three-quarters of the electricity generated from renewable resources.

The hydroelectric facility at Hoover Dam, powered by the running waters of the Colorado River, uses Lake Mead as a reservoir. It is an example of renewable hydroelectric power provided at relatively low cost to areas of Arizona, California and Nevada.

A Bulgarian developer, GTM Angel Balevski Holding, along with the well-known retail developer, Hamburg-based ECE Projectmanagement, Advance Properties Ltd. and Balkankar Sredets AF, plans to invest US$44 million in a chain of

hydro power stations to help power a mixed-use urban project the group is developing along the Iskar riverbed in Bulgaria.

The developer is targeting to complete the large-scale project, comprising an enclosed shopping mall, offices, apartments, hotels, a cinema and other entertainment facilities, by 2010. As projects such as Europe Park open in Bulgaria's capital city of Sofia, the shopping center industry will have valid examples of how hydropower can be employed in the shopping center industry.

Hydropower is one of the best renewable sources of fuel for electricity generation, as it is relatively inexpensive. Also, it leaves little or no waste products and does not pollute the water or the atmosphere.

TIDAL ENERGY

As long as the ocean tides continue to ebb and flow, converting electrical power from the tides is renewable energy.

The most laborious part of conversion is constructing a barrage, or large dam, across a river estuary to allow the water to flow through tunnels in the dam as the tide goes in and out, much like the way hydroelectricity is produced. The tide's motion can turn a turbine to help generate power.

The technology concept is simple. The dam has a sluice that is opened at high tide to allow the tide to flow into the basin. The sluice is then closed to keep the large quantity of water inside the dam. As the sea level drops, traditional hydropower technology is used to generate electricity from the elevated water in the basin.

Tidal energy does not pose sufficient environmental risk as nonrenewable energy does, but it can harm fish. When the sluices are open, fish safely swim through them, but when the sluices are closed, fish tend to seek out turbines in an attempt to swim through them, possibly being sucked through.

Tidal turbines need no fuel and produce no greenhouse gases or other waste. However, tidal power stations generate power only 10 hours a day, when the tide is flowing.

France's Rance estuary—built in 1966—is the largest tidal power station in the world.

GEOTHERMAL POWER

Geothermal energy comes from Earth's core, which has an extremely high temperature. An example of geothermal activity is the lava that erupts from a volcano.

The area immediately below the surface of Earth is generally cool like a cave that remains about 50°F (10°C) year-round. However, the temperature in the inner portions of Earth's layers, mostly made up of rocks and water, becomes hotter deep below the surface.

For centuries, humans have used geothermal energy from deep wells to heat

homes. This heated water or steam can also be pumped to the surface for reuse. Someday, in the not too distant future, many buildings will be heated utilizing thermal heat in the winter and cooled in the summer by using the more stable lower temperatures near the surface. (Refer to the Atrio Shopping Centre in Chapter 11.)

To heat or cool a building with geothermal energy, the geothermal gradient, which is the rate of temperature change with depth, must be precisely measured for the correct temperature to be brought into the building from different levels below the surface.

Geothermal energy is much like wind and solar energy. They are all more or less abundant, depending on the region. These geothermal resources, particularly those that conduct heat, are typically located near major plates known for earthquakes and volcanoes in the area known as the Ring of Fire surrounding the Pacific Ocean.

The Ring of Fire begins in Alaska on the western coast of North America and runs south to the southernmost part of South America. It also runs down the eastern part of northern Asia and all the way south to the southernmost part of eastern Australia, where the most geothermal activity takes place. This includes volcanoes, fumaroles, geysers and hot springs.

In the United States, there are only a few geothermal power plants, located in California, Hawaii, Nevada and Utah, and the power they generate collectively accounts for only 1 percent of the power generated in the United States.

However, geothermal heat pumps are gaining in popularity because they are energy efficient, environmentally safe, and cost-effective for heating and cooling, according to the U.S. EPA. The heat available deep inside Earth is sufficient all over the planet, and thus geothermal cooling and heating will likely become quite common in new buildings built in the 2010s and 2020s.

BIOMASS POWER

Biomass fuel is what Doc Emmet Brown used to power up his De Lorean DMC-12 sports car to fly up into the clouds in the science fiction comedy *Back to the Future II*. The scene made for good comedy when the film hit theaters in 1989, but today the future is here, and biomass is a reality.

Biomass is organic material, mostly made up of animals and plants, where the sun has stored its energy. As plants absorb energy from the sun, animals that eat them also retain the stored energy.

Biomass energy primarily comes from wood, crops, manure, waste and alcohol-based fuels. Wood can come either from harvested wood or wood waste, as in pulping liquor known as black liquor, which is the by-product from processing pulp to make paper and cardboard.

Municipal solid waste (MSW), manufacturing waste and landfill gas can be converted into biomass fuel. Ethanol from corn or sugarcane can also be converted to biomass fuel and can be used to generate electricity.

This waste is burned to produce steam for making electricity. The combustion releases some carbon dioxide but not to the extent of traditional fossil fuels. In addition, fossil fuels produce sulfur, which is attributed to acid rain, while burning biomass fuels does not.

NUCLEAR POWER

Nuclear-generated electricity is definitely an alternative to mitigating GHG emissions, but it is not truly a renewable source of energy. Uranium—the primary source of nuclear energy—is not renewable. Retail facilities cannot generate nuclear energy onsite. Instead, nuclear energy is an alternative for buildings only when utility companies add such power plants.

To produce nuclear energy, the United States and many other countries have to import uranium. Uranium is an extremely dense, metallic element found in rocks, in soil and in the ocean. Uranium is radioactive.

Nuclear power plants are currently in operation in about 35 countries, and many more plants are under construction. They do not emit carbon dioxide, sulphur dioxide or nitrogen oxides. However, the spent fuel waste ends up as a hot and highly radioactive solid mass that has to be handled with extreme care and sequestered for thousands of years.

According to the Australian Uranium Association's Uranium Information Centre Ltd., coal-fired power plants consume more than 3.2 billion tons (2.9 billion metric tons) of coal worldwide every year to produce 38 percent of the electricity. On the other hand, nuclear power plants use up only 61,000 tons (55,300 metric tons) of natural uranium to produce 16 percent of the world's electricity.

The United States produces and consumes 29.2 percent of the world's total nuclear energy. One concern voiced by many people regarding nuclear storage sites is the possibility that terrorists might attack one to wreak havoc over a large regional area. Such a scenario might cause a severe nuclear meltdown similar to the reactor accident at the Chernobyl nuclear power plant in April 1986.

Not all sustainability initiatives that reduce costs are limited to using renewable or nuclear energy. The mere effort of reducing consumption of fossil fuels is a sustainable tactic because doing so reduces greenhouse gas emissions.

OPTIMIZE ENERGY AT RETAIL FACILITIES

Energy-efficiency initiatives can range from simple conservation methods—such as lowering the thermostat by one degree in the winter—to purchasing and installing expensive energy management equipment and efficient HVAC equipment. According to the California EPA, lowering the thermostat by one degree in the winter saves 5 percent of energy costs.

Incandescent bulbs are out and compact fluorescent bulbs are in. One of the easiest ways to reduce energy is by relamping with energy-efficient bulbs. There are many types, each with their own level of efficiency and with a different lighting and coloring effect. This can make the selection of lighting a store or shopping center a well-thought-out process, as some lighting used for exterior purposes are not adequate for interior uses.

The incandescent lightbulb converts only about one-tenth of the electricity into light. Ninety percent of the electricity used by the incandescent bulb is wasted

One of the most popular compact fluorescent lamp (CFL) lightbulbs for use in the home and commercial settings is the corkscrew-shaped CFL, which lasts much longer than incandescent. A compact fluorescent has clear advantages over incandescent lightbulbs. CFLs use 75 percent less electricity, last six to 10 times longer, generate 70 percent less heat and produce 450 pounds (204 kg) fewer greenhouse gases (from power generated to supply an equivalent incandescent lightbulb). The CFL also saves consumers US$30 over the life of the bulb.

The U.S. EPA estimated that replacing an average incandescent bulb with a 25-watt CFL would save the equivalent of 100 pounds (45 kg) of carbon dioxide emitted into the atmosphere per year. This is equivalent to the emission of an average U.S. vehicle driving about 90 miles (149 kg).

However, CFLs contain mercury and have to be disposed of as hazardous waste to preserve the environment.

As of January 2007, only 6 percent of households were using the bulbs when

PHOTOS: R. E. MILIAN

When Wal-Mart sets its sight on having its customers reduce their carbon footprint, it can easily do so because of its sheer size. In 2007, the retail giant sold 100 million compact fluorescent lightbulbs.

Wal-Mart decided to push 100 million CFLs that year (up from the average 40 million units it had sold in 2005).

By October 2007, Wal-Mart had achieved that goal by lowering everyday prices, displaying the bulbs in valuable store end caps and printing educational brochures. Wal-Mart estimated that selling these energy-saving bulbs had the effect of taking 700,000 cars off the road or conserving the energy needed to power 450,000 single-family U.S. homes.

The retail price of CFLs had been ranging between double to as high as eight times the price of conventional bulbs depending on what retail store was selling them and whether the retailers discounted them below the manufacturer's list price.

However, when Wal-Mart started heavily discounting these CFLs, the price-setting impact crossed over all distribution points and made them less expensive for consumers and businesses. Also, selling 100 million compact fluorescent bulbs a year in the United States increased sales by 50 percent and saved Americans US$3 billion in annual electricity costs.

The CFL illustrates only one simple strategy anyone can use to lower energy consumption and protect the atmosphere.

DAYLIGHTING

One way to increase lighting without using bulbs or electricity is through daylighting. This involves the strategic use of skylights, which results in higher levels of lighting in the summer than the winter.

However, to obtain the optimum effects of daylight harvesting, a combination of photosensors, dimmers, dimmable daylight-mimicking metal halide lamps or fluorescent tubes (T5HO or T8s) used in combination with skylights are necessary.

The size and where the windows are placed as well as the use of clerestory and well-spaced skylights are also important for bringing natural daylight conducive to an attractive retail climate. This strategy helps to minimize the need for energy-consuming artificial lighting during the day. This combination of technologies tends to maximize energy savings.

There are many ways to cut power to lighting sources. One is the occupancy sensors used to turn lights on and off as people enter or leave the interior space. Another is to install high-efficiency electronic ballasts.

A type of ballast called "dimming ballasts" helps to reduce energy used in lighting. As natural light filters through the skylights, beginning at dawn and ending at dusk, they regulate the energy used every step of the way.

Wal-Mart and Costco Wholesale use this daylight harvesting technique. BJ's Wholesale Club uses skylights but only dims its lighting in two settings: full lighting during operating hours and 50 percent lighting during working hours for overnight cleaning and stocking. (See Chapter 9.)

Daylighting will reduce your building's electricity bill, help boost employee productivity and help increase sales, according to studies noted in Chapter 10.

EMS, FLOORING, INSULATION AND LOW-E WINDOWS

Individual switches or thermostats should not control retail buildings. Instead, energy management systems (EMS) use computerized monitoring and controls that automate the operation of equipment and lighting. This assures the equipment is used only when needed.

A good EMS can help reduce heating and cooling costs during operating hours by setting temperatures automatically, eliminating wasted run times and reducing power peak draw when energy costs are most expensive, even though peak charge times may last only a few minutes.

EMSs also help improve operating ranges for boilers and chillers and extend the life cycle of electrically powered equipment. To regulate the power a building demands under varying conditions, building monitoring systems use a power-monitoring harness, which tracks electricity used on a circuit-by-circuit basis.

Radiant flooring made with cross-linked polyethylene tubing uses water to heat and cool a building. Additionally, heat pumps produce chilled or hot water for the radiant slab and work with a dedicated outside air handler to heat or cool the building.

This can also act as an exhaust system to improve indoor air quality. When levels of carbon dioxide reach 800 parts per million (ppm), the dedicated outside air handler will turn on to do its job of refreshing the interior air. A Giant Eagle supermarket in Pittsburgh uses this system. (See Chapter 9.)

Extra care should be taken to keep the building properly insulated so that the HVAC system is not taxed. Proper insulation is critical when outside temperatures are extreme. R-values measure insulation properties; thus the higher the rating, the better the insulation property. R-values exceeding R-15 for roofs and R-31 for walls can trim energy costs.

Window design and insulation are also important. When reviewing the specifications for new windows, consider multiple layers of glazing and thickness of air space. With double-glazed windows, the air space between the panes of glass can affect energy use. A thin air space does not insulate as well as a thicker air space.

Low-emissivity (low-e) window technology is an essential component of green building design when window replacement or new construction is considered. Thin, transparent coatings of silver or tin oxide permit visible light to pass through but reflect infrared heat radiation back into the interior space. This reduces heat loss through the windows in the winter in cold climates, where passive solar heating is advantageous.

For milder climates, southern low-e windows that produce low heat gain coefficients are best in regions where summer cooling is more significant than winter

heating. Window shades and tinted glass have been used for decades to help keep a building cool in the summer. A new method called "electrochromic glazing" helps to reduce sunlight and heat transfer into the building interior. Electrochromic windows, or "smart windows," feature a new technology called "switchable glazing," which changes the light transmittance, transparency or shading of windows in response to environmental needs.

This method is an alternative to blinds. Sunlight, temperature or an electrical control can change these smart windows and smart skylights from transparent to heavily tinted with a mere flip of a switch that zaps an electrical current.

BUILDING SYSTEMS COMMISSIONING

When the construction documents for your development are completed and before your state-of-the-art systems are installed, the next most important step is commissioning. Hire an independent commissioning team early on—perhaps as early as when the design process is in progress—to check the design, installation, calibration and performance of your water and energy-consuming systems.

The key here is *independent*. Building commissioning is not a function the designer of the system should do. It is like getting a second medical opinion. Only then can you be assured that the project will meet the efficiency goals your designer and you set at the design stage.

It is best to install a system with the capabilities to monitor water and energy performance over the life of the building.

CFC REDUCTION

Reducing ozone depletion in the building sector has been a priority for more than two decades. In retail buildings, this applies to both HVAC and refrigeration systems. The goal in new buildings should be zero use of chlorofluorocarbon-based (CFC) refrigerants. For renovation projects, prepare a phaseout plan for CFC refrigerants.

This is particularly important for retail facilities that use a central plant with a chilled water system. They must be CFC-free or have a documented plan for phasing out CFC-based refrigerants.

OTHER CONSIDERATIONS

There are many tactics designers, construction managers and operators of retail buildings can employ to manage energy performance and protect the atmosphere. This is not limited to the building itself but also to the impact a building has on energy use. For example, a shopping center can use low-emitting and fuel-efficient

vehicles in security patrolling, maintenance trucks and other vehicular uses.

Retailers should consider how the merchandise reaches their stores and what can be done to lower the environmental impact from those deliveries.

Yet there are many more considerations. In order to affect energy consumption, designers and operators of retail buildings need to employ their creativity and skills. They need to be steadfast in their approach and cannot only think in terms of using less energy. "Energy reduction isn't just using less energy or producing less energy. It is also using eons-old techniques such as shades to lower air-conditioning costs or not using blacktop, which absorbs [the sun's] radiation more readily than other materials," said Benjamin A. Bross, LEED AP, design director of Mexican shopping center developer Constructora Planigrupo, S.A. "Energy reduction is looking at environmental contributors as well."

PHOTO: PAMELA LIPPE e4 inc.

PHOTO: R. E. MILIAN

Wal-Mart limits the amount of stormwater runoff at its Supercenter in Aurora, Colorado, with pervious pavement, on a testing area of the parking lot. This area has infiltration beds underneath the pavement to allow up to three inches of water to filter into the soil per hour. Inset: In the Scottsdale, Arizona, Supercenter. Wal-Mart uses countertops with photovoltaic panels to charge batteries to power the sink sensors, thereby saving water and energy.

Chapter 17

Water Efficiency

WATER, **ALTHOUGH PLENTIFUL** and replenishable in many areas, is a dwindling resource that must be managed and conserved—particularly in the United States and Canada, where suburban living dots the landscape with residential green lawns and commercial retail projects that devote acres of land to thirsty, lush landscaping. An enormous amount of potable water is poured on the ground each year to satisfy landscapes designed for beauty rather than practicality.

The U.S. EPA estimates that the average American family of four uses 400 gallons (1,500 liters) of potable water per day, with about one-third of that used to irrigate their lawns and gardens. By other estimates, the average family of four in the United States and Canada uses 6,400 tons (5,800 metric tons) of water per year. This compares with the average family in France, which reportedly uses half as much as North Americans.

Only 6 percent of the water the French use is for outside purposes such as watering lawns and washing cars, according to Centre d'Information sur l'Eau (CIEAU). Germans consume one-third, Swedes consume one-fourth and Danes consume one-eighth of the amount of water that North Americans consume on average.

As the world population expands, groundwater supplies are unable to sustain the demand placed by humans for fresh drinking water all over the planet. North Americans consume roughly seven billion gallons (26.5 billion liters) of water per day. Why do they consume so much by comparison to world standards? Suburban living and affinity for green turf has to be the answer.

Americans use a sizable portion of water for irrigation and waste it on sidewalks and as water runoff flowing into gutters. This is common when water restrictions are not preventing residents from irrigating lawns and landscaping.

In the building sector, half of the water is used for plumbing and fixtures with approximately one-quarter used for flushing toilets. The other half is used for irrigation of interior and exterior landscaping as well as for mechanical systems such

as HVAC, for example, the cooling tower that works in conjunction with chillers to cool a large building.

Droughts in many parts of the world including the United States are forcing governments to institute water restrictions, and summer 2007 had one of the most severe restrictions in memory. The 2007 drought across North America resulted in restrictions in the U.S. Southeast in Alabama, Florida, Georgia, North Carolina and South Carolina; in the Midwest in Ohio, Michigan and Minnesota and in the West in Arizona, Colorado and Nevada.

Some restrictions limited outside irrigation to even or odd days or to once-a-week watering while others imposed stiff fines for letting water run off into the street. Las Vegas even banned front lawns in new residential developments.

WATER-EFFICIENT LANDSCAPING

Retail stores and shopping center companies can consider a number of tactics to conserve water. One method is a drip irrigation system, which slowly sends water directed to the roots where it will do the most good and results in minimal runoff.

Some property managers use a rainwater capture system to avoid irrigating landscaping with utility-supplied potable water or fresh water pumped from wells.

A more sophisticated system is HydroPoint Weather Trak controller, which calculates sprinkler needs by analyzing grass type, soil composition and weather. This data is beamed to the unit by satellite and regulates the operation of the sprinklers for optimum use.

One of the best and least costly solutions for property managers and developers is to install drought-tolerant plant material indigenous to the area that is able to withstand periods of drought. This is the foundation of *xeriscaping*, which entails creating a lush and colorful landscape by planting slow-growing, drought-tolerant plants intended to conserve water and reduce frequency of landscaping maintenance work.

Xeriscaping also involves other gardening principles, such as planning and designing for water conservation, selecting low-water plants and groupings of plants with similar water needs, irrigating efficiently, using soil amendments to retain moisture near the roots, using mulch to reduce evaporation and to keep the soil cool, and mowing, weeding, pruning and fertilizing properly.

WATER USE REDUCTION

Inside stores and shopping centers, the public restrooms are among the biggest users of water. Toilets are continuously being upgraded to minimize pressure and water use. In 1950, a toilet's single flush consisted of seven gallons (26.5 liters) into the bowl. Since 1995, toilets have been mandated by law in many jurisdictions to use no more than 1.6 gallons (six liters) per flush.

New technology is being employed in restrooms including waterless urinals, low-flow automated faucets, aluminum and non-polyvinylchloride (PVC) plastic piping that does not emit harmful gases and low-flow dual-flush toilets. (See Chapter 11.) These toilets are intended to use the entire 1.6 gallons to flush solid waste and to use half that amount for flushing urine.

In restroom sinks from Wal-Mart to Home Depot, special sensor-sensitive faucets are being installed to prevent water dripping down the drain unnoticed and excessive water use. (See Chapter 9.)

PHOTO COURTESY OF ALTOON+PORTER ARCHITECTS

PHOTO COURTESY OF TURNBERRY ASSOCIATES

Top: Twenty-two buildings feature more than 70 different facades, detailing a collage of Old World and contemporary architectural styles, in Town Square Las Vegas, a 1.5 million-square-foot (14,000 sq meters) shopping, dining and entertainment lifestyle center that opened in November 2007.

The center features six acres of desert landscaping complete with desert plants, trees and rock mulch. The developer installed a mixture of low-water use plants and drought-tolerant xeriscaping and outfitted them with an underground drip irrigation system, the most effective system for sending water to the roots of the plants with minimal waste. About 6,000 square feet (560 sq meters) of artificial grass spans the park, and a pond helps to create a psychological effect that contrasts with the desert surroundings. The project, located south of Mandalay Bay, is a joint venture development of Aventura, Florida-based Turnberry Associates and Las Vegas-Nevada based Centra Properties.

Left: The Gardens on El Paseo in Palm Desert, California, an upscale lifestyle center, incorporates a natural xeriscaped design. The center was developed by Davis Street Land Company and designed by Altoon+Porter Architects. The architects' design reduced water needs in the landscaping by 50 percent and in the building by 20 percent.

INNOVATIVE WASTEWATER TECHNOLOGIES

One important consideration in water conservation is the sources of withdrawal. Tap water purchased from the municipality or utility company is the most expensive water and when used for irrigation or flushing toilets is not efficient, although many organizations rely totally on tap water for all its water uses.

Groundwater pumped from a well is another source, but there is a limit to groundwater because a drop in precipitation can drastically lower the level available if use is not curtailed.

All potable groundwater must be protected. Nonpotable groundwater may be made potable if treatment technologies can purify it from effluent and saltwater intrusion.

Consider other sources. The sources of surface water, which include rivers, lakes, wetlands, and oceans, can be tapped into, but these are often expensive to process and have limited uses.

The reuse of water also results in real savings because reused water costs about one-fourth of potable water in many areas.

Directly collecting rainwater and storing it is becoming more prevalent in green building techniques because increasing the volume or the percentage of water recycled and reused is a sustainable approach to water conservation.

Graywater is the water that runs down the sink, the dishwasher and the washing machine in a home. This water may be reused for nondrinking purposes, especially landscape irrigation. There are graywater conservation systems that recycle restroom water from the sink by filtering and cleaning it to be reused in flushing toilets and urinals.

Mixed-use buildings that combine residential, offices and hotels with retail can benefit greatly from this technology, as water from showers and laundry is processed into graywater to use in toilets and cleaning processes.

Chapter 18

Materials and Resources

THE **LIST OF** approved materials and resources that underscore a sustainable building is just as long as the list of those that are discouraged. The objective is to recognize the difference and carefully weigh the pros and cons of each.

The focus in this chapter is to examine the use of materials sourced locally or regionally, especially those made from renewable resources. The preference is for materials that are salvaged or recycled.

CONSTRUCTION WASTE MANAGEMENT

Recycling waste and construction debris is another component of the green building category called "materials and resources." Construction waste recycling is the separation and reusing or recycling of recoverable waste materials generated during construction and remodeling.

Packaging, new material scraps and old materials and debris all constitute potentially recoverable materials. Likewise, appliances, masonry materials, steel, wood, doors and windows are recyclable.

In the past, most construction waste would go into landfills, increasing the burden on landfill loading and operation. This is no longer the case. The first step in a construction waste-reduction strategy should consist of good planning, which entails the planned reuse of construction debris, such as grinding and pulverizing concrete and using it as fill. (Refer to The Shops at Don Mills in Chapter 11.)

An effective construction waste-reduction program requires on-site separation to separate, store, grind and reuse the material. If it cannot be reused on the site, it should be sold and trucked away.

Initially, this will take some extra effort and training of construction workers. Once the general contractor and subcontractors understand your goals, on-site separation and reuse can be accomplished with little or no additional cost after subtracting the savings from reusing or income from reselling recycled material.

BUILDING REUSE

Green building architecture seeks to reuse a building rather than raze it, if possible. Typically, a building reuse means leaving the main portion of the building structure and shell in place while performing a *gut rehab*. (See Chapter 11 on the Yorkdale Shopping Centre expansion.)

Repairing or rebuilding the interior of a building rather than tearing it down preserves natural resources. This includes raw materials, energy and water resources required to build new. It also prevents pollution that would have occurred with the extraction, manufacturing and transportation of new materials as well as avoiding solid waste of building material that would have been dumped in landfills.

RECYCLED CONTENT

Anything that can be recycled should be, according to green built standards. This includes newspaper, white paper, cardboard, chipboard, glass, tin, aluminum, metal, plastic and even oil.

Materials you purchase should require low maintenance, be long lasting and have a minimal negative impact on the environment. When selecting materials and considering resources involving sustainability, there are some basic principles to consider. Materials must meet certain performance requirements that endure and ensure safety within the built environment, such as resistance to moisture and biocontamination and at the same time have no negative impact on the natural ecosystems.

REUSED OR RAPIDLY RENEWABLE MATERIALS

Reused, salvaged or rapidly renewable material is important. Materials that minimize waste are also essential. An example of rapidly renewable materials is certified wood in accordance with Forest Stewardship Council guidelines. Salvaged wood such as reuse of form lumber for framing and sheathing is also acceptable. Nonwood products made of recycled materials are possible substitutions for original wood.

STORAGE AND COLLECTION OF RECYCLABLES

Recycling is a process of collecting, sorting and processing solid waste and other discarded materials for use as raw materials intended to make new products. When planning resources, the storage and collection of recyclables as well as the waste to be directed to the landfill are all critical considerations.

The retail facility should have an easily accessible dedicated area for recycling paper, cardboard, glass, metals, plastics and even batteries. There should be an area set aside for storing hazardous waste until qualified contractors can dispose of it properly.

SOURCING LOCAL AND REGIONAL MATERIALS

When selecting materials and resources for a building or its ongoing operation, check to see where they were manufactured and how far the material will be transported to the site.

This will not only save on costs but will also cut down on extra fuel and GHGs emitted into the atmosphere from the transportation of these materials and resources from the point of origin. It is best to try to obtain materials that have been extracted, harvested, recovered or manufactured within several hundred miles of the building site.

AVOID HARMFUL CHEMICALS

In exterior settings, sustainable practices are just as important as ensuring indoor environmental quality in the building interior because the wrong products—often used for interior cleaning and other uses—can leach and cause damage to the environment.

In shopping centers, synthetic and chemical fertilizers should be minimized or not used at all when attempting sustainable landscaping practices. Going green means using organic-based fertilizers. The same goes for using organic herbicides to kill unwanted grass and weeds as well as organic pesticides to exterminate insects.

Organic-based products have enzymes that work in harmony with the environment to ensure proper root growth of plant material. Turf grass can green up in seven to ten days with organic fertilizers, and unlike many synthetic products that produce instant results and fade soon after, the organic products will continue nurturing the lawn for up to twelve weeks.

Another sustainable technique that requires no substance to be introduced to the lawn at all is core aeration. Often the top four inches (10 cm) of soil beneath the turf becomes compressed, preventing air, water and nutrients from reaching the grass roots.

Aerating lawns with a powered aerator produces a number of holes, at least four inches apart, greatly enhancing the ability of lawns to absorb the nutrients and restore beauty and vitality.

Citibank prototype for London, United Kingdom bank locations emphasizes recycled materials including ceiling tiles, furniture, accessories, upholstery, millwork and window shades.

PHOTO COURTESY OF CITIBANK

Chapter 19

Indoor Environmental Quality

POOR INDOOR ENVIRONMENTAL quality has been associated with the *sick building syndrome* (SBS) for several decades. As far back as 1984, a report released by the World Health Organization (WHO) suggested that as many as 30 percent of the buildings worldwide may be responsible for some form of SBS.

Physicians have diagnosed patients with a specific building related illness (SBRI). This type of diagnosis needs a combination of findings to confirm. It includes the clinical testing of a patient to match symptoms, with laboratory confirmation of contaminants in the building itself.

SBRI includes humidifier fever, asthma, Legionnaires' disease, fiberglass dermatitis and toxicity from overexposure to carbon monoxide (CO) gases or formaldehyde (HCHO). For example, to confirm if a sick building occupant is suffering from over exposure to CO, a physician would order lab tests of COHb of the patient's blood. At the same time, building management is expected to have tests conducted by qualified experts to determine if there is a significant presence of dangerous levels of CO.

INDOOR CHEMICAL AND POLLUTANT CONTROL

Today, the subject is better understood, and building operators know that many factors can contribute to poor indoor environmental quality. Among the most common are toxic molds, extreme contamination by dust mites or other microbes, chemical or biological contamination, and other forms of indoor environmental conditions.

Toxic mold, mildew and fungus as well as bacteria, viruses and insects or their metabolites can cause respiratory illness and fungal disease when they become airborne inside a building. The condition can be more detrimental for those who spend a great deal of time in a contaminated building, typically employees.

OCCUPANT COMFORT AND DAYLIGHT VIEWS

Other contributors to making building occupants uncomfortable, although they are perceived to a lesser extent, can include such elements as inappropriate lighting, unpleasant sound acoustics, unbalanced heating, cooling and ventilation systems and other sources.

Daylighting promotes human health and well-being, but to do this effectively, buildings need to be designed and configured properly. In North America, this can include elongating the retail building along an east-west axis. Light from a high source is preferred to direct sunlight, which can create uncomfortable brightness in isolated spaces. Diffused skylights help but clerestory windows, if used, are typically clear.

Poor environmental quality affects building occupants in different ways. Some people appear to be immune to poor conditions and exhibit no signs of symptoms. Others will complain of a host of symptoms ranging from eye, nose and throat irritation to stress, headache, asthma, itchy skin, fatigue and even irregular bowel movements.

INFECTIOUS AIRBORNE CONTAMINANTS

The inviting atmosphere inside enclosed shopping malls and stores draws thousands of people daily, but as with a sampling of any size, some of these people are likely to be sick and in a contagious state. Bacteria and viruses fly through the air we breathe on dust particles and respiratory droplets that act as an aerosol spray when people cough, sneeze, laugh, burp, talk—and even as they exhale.

These infectious contaminants glide through the air inside crowded stores and malls for other unsuspecting patrons and employees to breathe in as everyone shares the common indoor air they believe is fresh and healthy. That is when airborne transmission of respiratory diseases and viral infections occur.

Bacteria cause some of these infections while viruses cause others. For example, strep throat is caused by a common type of bacteria called streptococcus that spreads by touch or as an airborne contaminant. Viruses cause smallpox, chicken pox, tuberculosis, the flu (influenza) and the common cold. All are airborne contaminants. They are flying around, exchanging themselves from human to human.

Infectious airborne contaminants can affect the health, comfort and well-being of building occupants and visitors, and the productivity of workers, according to Aileen M. Marty, MD, FACP, a physician, scientist and professor of emerging infections on special assignment with Battelle. Battelle is an Arlington, Virginia–based international science and technology enterprise that explores emerging areas of science and works with government and industry worldwide.

"Air duct systems often become contaminated with dust, bacteria, pollen and other debris," said Marty. "If moisture is present, the potential for microbiological growth such as mold, bacteria and amoeba is increased, and spores or vegetative cells from such growth enter the building's occupied spaces."

According to Marty, these contaminants may cause allergic reactions or clinical diseases such as Legionnaire's disease or other illnesses.

Indoor air quality at enclosed shopping centers is often compromised by the very nature of these buildings because multiple tenants often rely on common HVAC systems that can quickly spread contaminants throughout the property.

Proper indoor air circulation and filtration help improve the indoor air quality. While filtration can help remove spores and many types of bacteria, some airborne viral pathogens are so small they can pass through filters.

"The single best thing that building operators can do to minimize health risks and promote indoor environmental quality is to ensure that air duct systems are properly installed, maintained, cleaned and operated; and that furniture and equipment do not block the HVAC system's air circulation, temperature control, and pollutant removal activities to function properly," Marty said.

THERMAL COMFORT

Thermal comfort is a general interior condition that building operators strive to maintain. They do this to satisfy the average person who is wearing clothing that is neither too heavy nor too light and who can still feel comfortable inside a building while performing routine functions.

Thermal comfort should be focused on the customer who is on a routine shopping visit, although in a work setting. Thermal comfort of workers can lead to improved productivity.

Various factors contribute to thermal comfort or lack of it. This includes air movement, air temperature, relative humidity and other interior climate controls that result in comfort for most people, although this can vary from person to person.

RELATIVE HUMIDITY AND MOLD PREVENTION

Relative humidity (RH) in an indoor setting is important not only to provide building occupants with a comfort level that allows them to enjoy and thereby prolong their shopping activity but also to mitigate indoor contaminants. RH for human comfort ranges between 30 percent and 60 percent. RH above 70 percent may cause condensation on cold surfaces, which may form mold or bring on corrosion and other moisture-related deterioration on the building surfaces.

The North Dakota State University (NDSU) Extension Service warns of health symptoms and the effects of mold. They include watery or itchy eyes, sore throat, stuffy nose, coughing, skin irritations and some may trigger asthma attacks.

Molds typically like to grow on organic materials such as drywall, wallpaper, wood, carpet and soap scum. Mold must be removed because nonliving mold can also cause health threats.

A low RH creates different problems such as potential damage to expensive musical instruments, deterioration of some types of merchandise and packaging, static

electricity, cracking and peeling of painted surfaces, and shrinking and warping of doors, furniture, floors and building materials made of wood.

Indoor air quality tends to get worse with the presence of moisture in indoor settings. This condition tends to worsen over time. Walls, floors and ceilings of a shopping center in which relative humidity is high tend to harbor and culture bacteria, molds, mildew, fungus, virus and insects. However, it is not moisture alone that causes these conditions. Two other substances help create a destructive mold condition, mold spores and organic matter.

"Every type of fungus has its optimum [relative humidity] moisture level of preference to thrive and grow," said Gerhard Haas, Ph.D., Fairleigh Dickinson University professor with the Biology Section of the School of Natural Sciences in Teaneck, New Jersey. "Indoor air should not be too dry or too humid. If too dry [below 30 percent], your skin can feel dry and flaky, and become susceptible to skin rashes, your nasal passages and sinuses dry out, the throat becomes itchy and irritated and can lead to colds and flu.

"When it is too humid [consistently above 55 percent], dust mites and other insects thrive, mold can grow uncontrollably, mildew can stain wall coverings and fabric window treatments and overall affect IEQ. About forty to fifty percent RH is ideal."

The American Society of Heating, Refrigerating and Air-Conditioning Engineers (ASHRAE) Standard 62.1-2004 recommends that relative humidity in building interiors be kept under 65 percent to mitigate conditions that can lead to microbial growth. On the other hand, a poor level of relative humidity can cause respiratory infections and allergies.

INCREASED VENTILATION

To make the interior space comfortable and livable, adequate ventilation is critical. Effective ventilation involves both airflow into the interior space as well as out of the interior space. Exhaust ventilation, in particular, helps to remove contaminants from the building's interior.

Some buildings provide as little as five cubic feet per minute (cfm) per occupant of outdoor air for ventilating the interior, which some experts consider inadequate to satisfy the health and comfort of building occupants.

MINIMUM IAQ PERFORMANCE AND TOBACCO SMOKE

Criminal laws and occupational safety and health regulations are banning tobacco smoke all over the world. The first countrywide ban was Ireland in 2004. Italy followed the next year. Since then, many nations are passing legislation to prevent building occupants from suffering from the harmful effects of second-hand environmental tobacco smoke, which include an increased risk of heart disease, cancer, emphysema and other chronic and acute diseases.

Meanwhile, retail building operators that are not protected by law to enforce this

indoor environmental hazard must institute programs of their own to protect non-smoking building occupants. One way is to institute a smoking ban or to restrict it. Another is through better indoor air circulation.

Notwithstanding tobacco smoke, ASHRAE recommends a minimum of 15 cfm of outdoor air per building occupant for ventilating the interior of many types of buildings and a minimum of 20 cfm for office buildings. The ASHRAE Standard 62-1989 specifies that outdoor air between 15 and 60 cfm should be supplied per person to each room in a building. The range depends on the activities that normally occur in that room.

Energy-efficient HVAC systems as per the ASHRAE Advanced Energy Design Guide are quite popular with green building advocates because of their reliability.

Much of the blame for poor indoor environmental quality has been squarely aimed at poor air circulation or the inadequacy of a building's ventilation system to draw from exterior fresh air to replace the stale and contaminated air circulating inside the space.

However, it is more than that. The materials used in the building's interior and other chemicals brought into it often result in outgassing that lowers the environmental quality for the building's occupants.

The barriers in a built environment that keep out unwanted elements—rain, snow, wind and extreme temperatures—also serve to prevent unhealthy conditions from escaping from the interior space.

LOW-EMITTING MATERIALS

Hazardous, toxic, inorganic, organic and biological pollutants can contaminate the built environment and breach the safety of building occupants.

Volatile organic compounds (VOCs) are emitted as gases from many building materials and supplies, whether solids or liquids. VOCs include a variety of chemicals, some of which may have short- and long-term adverse health effects.

A wide array of products numbering in the thousands emits VOCs. These range from paints to cleaning supplies. All of these products can release organic compounds while you are using them, and to some degree, when they are stored. Concentrations of VOCs are up to ten times higher indoors than outdoors, which is a reason why VOCs are important for retail building professionals to guard against.

Ensuring indoor environmental quality is not as complicated as it seems once the parts of an interior space are analyzed for possible contaminants. To do so, let us explore what constitutes the building's shell and the components of the building's interior structures.

BUILDING FRAME AND ROOF

Let us begin with the shell. Buildings have a frame usually of steel or reinforced concrete with columns that are sprayed with fireproofing insulation. Those built

prior to 1973 in the United States, and later in other countries, contain asbestos. If asbestos becomes loosened (crumbled or pulverized) as in friable asbestos-containing material (ACM), the microscopic fibers remain in the air for long periods of time and can become permanently lodged in the lungs of building occupants.

Retailers and developers prefer a flat roof design for shopping centers and adjacent or freestanding retail stores. Equipment such as antennas, exhaust vents, air handling units (AHU) and HVAC rooftop units nicely sit on the roofing membrane hidden from the view of the customers.

The integrity of these roofs can often be compromised. It becomes an entry point for water intrusion from rain, melting snow or faulty plumbing, and the water can damage interior walls, flooring, ceiling and other components such as store displays and furnishings.

Worse, interior space can become contaminated with moisture-loving mold to cause a host of health-related problems. In addition, openings in roofs cause reentry of flue and other exhaust gases to deteriorate the environmental quality of the space.

CEILINGS AND WALLS

A building that uses sustainable materials promotes the health of its occupants. Covered ceilings improve the appearance of a store or shopping center and help to hide air ducts, wiring, plumbing, etc. However, some of the material used in and near ceilings can affect environmental quality when paint, chemicals and other substances contaminate the ceilings.

For example, acoustical plaster sprayed on ceilings may contain crysotile asbestos (banned in 1978). Other types of ceilings include hung tiles made of various materials.

Testing of ceiling tiles has revealed elevated levels of polychlorinated biphenyls (PCBs). The U.S. Congress banned the domestic production of PCBs in 1977.

The interior and exterior walls of building structures are susceptible to contaminants. Some have vapor barriers, others do not. Mold infestation can adhere to walls and pose a health risk as thermal movement of water condenses on the building envelope.

Most interior walls and many ceilings are made up of gypsum board, which is otherwise known as drywall, wallboard and plasterboard. Gypsum board can be fire resistive and can come in single-layer or multilayer to minimize sound transmission. This material is now manufactured with environmental concerns in mind, such as preservation of natural resources, waste management and recycling, issues of reclamation, etc.

In the United States and Canada, almost all of the material used to manufacture gypsum board is currently from recycled paper and other now safe synthetic origins, such as reused waste material, desulphurization of flue gases from fossil fuel burning and others, eliminating the transfer of this waste to landfills.

Though drywall may be safe, the paint finishes or wall coverings can be made with toxic ingredients. These can include lead in paints and toxic glue used in applying wallpaper that leaves residual toxic fumes absorbed in indoor air for months. Fumes also result from pesticides and solvents in paint and joint compound.

It becomes important to use low-biocide paint or the least toxic adhesives when covering walls with wallpaper. Some wallpaper textures attract dust mites, fungal toxins, animal allergens and excretory residue of insects such as cockroaches.

Even plastic wallpaper, especially if exposed to heated air or nearby radiator heat, can cause harmful outgas. When using wall tile, consider the tile itself and the tile-setting cement or adhesive. Low-odor, nontoxic, water-based adhesives are available for hard-composition wall and floor tile containing no acrylic additives.

Some molds in indoor environments produce chemicals known as *mycotoxins* that can make people with weak immune systems sick. A common health concern from exposure to mold is asthma and allergy in susceptible people. This is the reason why it is important to help prevent mold from accumulating on the grout of wall tile by choosing mold-resistant grout types and cleaning it periodically.

Reused and recycled material, a major consideration in building design, applies to wall and floor covering. Some wall tiles are now made from recycled glass and concrete. Others are made of recycled marble, granite and glass chips. Yet others are made with renewable leather, natural rubber and tree bark. All these types of reused materials are considered green, which gives an architect many varieties of wall and floor covering to choose from when specifying green-building design.

GREEN CLEANING PRODUCTS

Various cleaning fluids and air fresheners have negative environmental effects. A few commercially available air fresheners merely mask smells instead of neutralizing or removing odors.

Some also coat the building occupants' nasal passages and diminish their sense of smell. Housekeeping and maintenance contractors should be trained and informed about the importance of using safe and green alternative products made from non-toxic ingredients.

Words such as *sustainability* and *green products* have entered the lexicon of shopping center maintenance managers.

"Our clients are insisting on green cleaning products that are safe and environmentally sensitive," said Emerson E. Russell, president and chief executive officer of Emerson Russell Maintenance Corporation (ERMC) Total Facility Services in Chattanooga, Tennessee, which handles many shopping center accounts.

Client feedback led Russell to create Green Clean, a program he started at four shopping centers in St. Louis, Missouri, then began rolling out across all 162 properties that ERMC maintains, over a three-year schedule.

"We're moving to Green Clean, first and foremost because we felt it was the right

thing to do," said Russell. "It's one of those 'win-win' scenarios that benefit the shoppers, air travelers, or office workers in our properties, the local communities we serve, our own employees and especially the environment." ERMC has more than 4,000 employees throughout the United States.

ERMC contracted with Spartan Chemical Company Inc., a manufacturer of chemical specialty maintenance products and industrial degreasers, to supply all green products.

Spartan's green products support the use of renewable natural resources. These products include Spartan's BioRenewables glass cleaners, which contain agricultural raw materials, and Tribase all-purpose floor cleaner. Both products are by-products of soybeans and corn, as opposed to petroleum-based. Spartan Green Solutions is a product line featured by Spartan.

Spartan offered ERMC a product named Consume, a non-pathogenic bacteria product known as bioaugmentation because it digests organic matter, which is also used in the cleaning process. ERMC and Spartan also implemented various methods to reduce the use of paper and plastic. ERMC is now using a biodegradable paper alternative.

Biodegradable alternative product specifications and suppliers are available through EPA's Environmentally Preferable Purchasing (EPP) program in conjunction with the U.S. General Services Administration (GSA).

GSA publishes the "Cleaning Equipment, Accessories, Janitorial Supplies, Cleaning Chemicals and Sorbents" catalog to help government purchasers compare the environmental attributes of cleaning products. For more information, visit: http://www.gsa.gov/gsa/cm_attachments/GSA_BASIC/sch79ib_R2H73-l_0Z5RDZ-i34K-pR.pdf.

For cleaners and degreasers to be approved by GSA, they must be readily biodegradable (60 percent to 70 percent biodegradable within 28 days), have low toxicity and contain no phenolic compounds or petroleum solvents.

These green products should comply with the Organization for Economic Cooperation and Development's definition of ready biodegradability, and should not constitute a hazardous waste, as defined in 40 CFR Part 261, when offered for disposal.

Some third-party certified environmentally preferable products already come endorsed as sustainable. Some well-respected third-party sources are Green Guard, Green Seal, FloorScore, the Carpet & Rug Institute's Green Label Plus program, American Association of Textile Chemists and Colorists (AATCC), American Society for Testing Materials (ASTM), etc. The EPA Comprehensive Procurement Guidelines and GreenSpec also reference some products as being green.

The important requirement when selecting cleaning products is not to settle for second best when it comes to safety. Various cleaning chemicals on the market are not only harmful to IAQ but they can also wreak havoc with the environment when disposed of improperly. It is preferable to use products that contain biodegradable emulsifiers derived from naturally grown plants that are environmentally safe, phosphate-free, noncaustic and noncombustible.

FLOORS AND SUBFLOORS

Vinyl asbestos tiles (VAT) have not been used in the United States since 1980 but are still widely present in past installations all over the world. Carpets are attractive and comfortable but are a source of dangerous levels of IAQ contaminants ranging from the adhesive used to tack them to the hard floor to every indoor organic and biological contaminant that settles on them. These contaminants can become airborne from the slightest movements of building occupants.

Consider flooring materials that are natural, nontoxic, and environmentally friendly, and those that come from renewable resources. If using carpets, some manufacturers make them with recycled materials, many carefully selected for low VOC emissions.

Look for cradle-to-cradle recycled carpet, which means the material of old worn-out carpet is recycled into new carpet rather than disposing of it. The caprolactam pellets, which are a form of recyclable nylon, can be recycled without sacrificing aesthetic and performance quality. The objective is to avoid the estimated 4.6 billion pounds (2.1 million metric tons) of carpet sent each year to landfills.

If wood flooring is used, AFC-certified wood dedicated to environmental and socially responsible trade practices is popular with proponents of green building design.

Popular new wood floors are made of bamboo. There are also store floors made of cork, which comes from the bark of cork oak trees in the Mediterranean, and are renewable in 10 to 12 years.

Cork floors have certain advantages. They absorb sound and are soft to walk on—almost like a hard carpet. Cork floors are also naturally hypoallergenic. To ensure the best possible indoor air quality when choosing material for flooring, look for material that does not release carcinogenic or other toxic fumes over time.

Adhesives engineered with polyether technology are better than urethanes and silicones, both of which can emit an odor affecting air quality in confined spaces. Aldehydes, N-methylpyrrolidon, dibutyglycol and other organic acids are emitted from some adhesives and should be minimized in a green built environment. An aldehyde is an organic compound containing a terminal carbonyl group.

The foundation below the floor surface should consist of plain concrete without curing agents such as accelerants and retardants.

One by-product of the incineration process is *fly ash*, which contains a high concentration of heavy metals and may have to be disposed of in hazardous waste landfills. Fly ash is reused in producing Portland cement and grout, structural fill, parking lot subbase, aggregate, roofing tiles, paints, metal castings, and filler in plastic and wood products. Although found to be safe in many cases, exercise caution when using fly ash or toxic additives in building design. Moreover, avoid using tar-based or petroleum-based waterproofing sealers.

Subfloors should be made of untreated reinforced concrete. Untreated concrete floors should be sealed with cement-based nontoxic material, and have a smooth finish.

As with walls, when ceramic floor is used, use cement mortar with cement-based grout that has no acrylic additives. Cement *thin set* has no fungicides and is recommended for some installations.

GASES

Interior air should be tested for radon (Rn) gas, which remains low and stagnates due to its weight (eight times heavier that air). The decaying of radium, thorium and uranium produces Rn.

Excessive radon exposure can kill human cells and cause cancerous tumors. Therefore, all floor cracks from where radon gas rises from below Earth's surface should be sealed.

Combustion of gas from smoke of wood burning, coal, tobacco and even emissions from motorized engines produces carbon monoxide (CO). Fortunately, tobacco smoking and coal burning is rarely permitted but was quite common in the past.

Do not allow motor vehicle engines to run idle in enclosed parking structures. Other gas-powered tools and equipment should be started and switched off outside the building envelope. This includes hedge trimmers, lawn mowers, blowers, snow throwers, weed eaters, pressure washers and others.

DOORS, WINDOWS AND FURNISHINGS

Sustainable door and window frames can be anodized aluminum, porcelain, steel or enameled metal, glass or solid renewable wood with nontoxic sealer. Presswood should not be used. Do not use pentachlorophenol wood preservative.

Windows should have metal-bound felt or hard vinyl stripping and be able to be opened. Thermally broken and double-glazed windows are preferred.

If plywood must be used, use the exterior type in building interior furnishings and installations because it contains less formaldehyde (HCHO). Alcohol-based shellac is acceptable when applying a moisture barrier wood finish. Also, beware that certain pressed wood-based products emit HCHO, which occurs in the atmosphere with the oxidation of methane gas and other VOCs. HCHO is a colorless gas that can irritate the skin, nose and throat. It causes headaches, nausea and breathing problems, and prolonged exposure can cause depression.

Some stationary fixtures, furnishings and equipment emit a variety of VOCs and semivolatile organic compounds (SVOCs).

It is wise to install low-emitting materials, and some manufacturers have the Greenguard Certification Program conduct an independent, third-party testing to qualify their products and materials as being low emitting.

IAQ MANAGEMENT PLAN DURING CONSTRUCTION

Construction debris, construction dust, chemical fumes and off-gassing materials can pose a health risk to building occupants breathing the lingering air when construction is taking place in a commercial building open for business.

This is why it is important to have a plan in place for preventive job-site practices to eliminate these risks and reduce residual problems after the building is open for business and operating as a retail facility.

A construction general contractor must develop a thorough plan. Everyone must agree to this plan before the work commences. Areas to consider include material substitution and storage, regular monitoring of activity, air quality and safe cleanup.

The LEED green building rating system requires that the project meet at a minimum the requirements of the Sheet Metal and Air-Conditioning National Contractors Association (SMACNA) IAQ Guidelines for Occupied Buildings Under Construction standards of 1995.

This plan should include job-site preparation, demolition plan, construction, indoor air quality control, site and noise protection, monitoring procedures and cleanup after the job has been completed.

This plan must also take into account that employees and patrons must be protected during construction around a retail establishment that is open for business. The plan must also address personal property, which includes store fixtures and merchandise available for sale.

PHOTO: STARBUCKS

Starbucks' new 20,000-square-foot, open joint rain screen design by VaproShield is located in the Lakewood (Washington) Towne Center, originally built in 1958 as the Villa Plaza Shopping Center. The cladding system is a Parklex pre-finished wood panel product made by Finland. The system redirects water and wind in order to control runoff and prevent infiltration into the building structure while allowing the sun's rays to be filtered. It minimizes heat in the summer but does not cast a shadow in the winter.

What's in Store?

SUSTAINABILITY IS LIKELY to remain a world priority for many years. And there are good reasons for this. The world population growth and industrialization of populous countries such as China and India are likely to drive the need for continued conservation of natural resources and to help mitigate harmful GHG emissions.

The current path of climate change we have experienced in the past two decades is like a large ship moving in one direction then trying to abruptly turn around at sea. It would take a long time because the turnaround curve is wide and cumbersome.

Many nations in the developed world, such as Australia, Canada, France, Japan, Germany, the Netherlands, the United Kingdom and the United States, are committed to reducing their emissions of greenhouse gases drastically in the next five years.

"It is simple, really. Human health and the health of ecosystems are inseparable."

Dr. Gro Harlem Brundtland, former Chair of the World Commission on Environment and Development and former Prime Minister of Norway

Along with other determined developing nations, they will overcome hurdles—to help lessen their use of fossil fuels—that today might seem insurmountable. This may include using renewable sources of energy or refining methods to sequester their carbon dioxide byproducts effectively.

However, developing countries are still on track to become more significant contributors to climate change because of their growing appetite for carbon-based fuels and rampant industrialization evidenced in the first decade of the 2000s.

Current population trends indicate that Earth will experience a substantial population gain, and as a result, developing countries will continue to produce more material, more food and consume more energy and water to satisfy this grow-

ing population base. In the process of doing so, and unless a major switch to using renewable energy occurs, developing countries will release more GHGs into the atmosphere.

This added strain will likely counteract any progress by developed nations to decrease their own emissions. The net effect could still record emissions at dangerous and historically high levels through 2015, according to climate change observers.

The U.N. Framework Convention on Climate Change (UNFCCC) is meeting in Bali, Indonesia, to hash out a new comprehensive agreement that many observers hope will involve reduction of polluting emissions by all nations and would truly mitigate global warming.

Even if the Bali talks produce a meaningful successor to the Kyoto Protocol, which reduces GHGs for the combined nations of the world in the 2010s at or below 1990 levels, the damage already done to the atmosphere is not immediately reversible.

It will take decades—perhaps even centuries—before the effects of any reduction of heat-trapping gases become evident in world temperatures and reduce the level of catastrophic weather-related events, glacial retreating, loss of coral reefs and other consequences of climate change that we experienced in the 2000s.

No one—not even climatologists representing the IPCC—can guarantee how long it will take to turn back the clock to undo the greenhouse effect that has accumulated over Earth during the past 150 years, especially the accelerated level of climate change that occurred in the past two decades.

New and more restrictive legislation is likely to be passed by governments all over the world. Regulations to protect the environment will continue to make their way into building codes for the next decade much the same way as it occurred during the 1990s when accommodating the disabled greatly influenced changes in local codes.

Science will bring new methods of generating renewable energy and find new ways to recycle and reuse waste. Technology will make things possible that now appear economically prohibitive in the same manner that solar energy was once considered too expensive to harness. Energy from crude oil was too inexpensive in the past to motivate modern industry to consider alternative sources of energy, but that has now changed.

Just as our communication methods have changed since the 1990s (using cell phones instead of landline phones and sending e-mail instead of mailing letters), so too will our energy consumption and our use of alternative renewable energy sources change in the 2010s.

There will be a cost to pay for reducing our carbon footprint, but the world economies will likely absorb it without affecting growth. The IPCC estimates that stabilizing climate-changing emissions to an acceptable level would cost anywhere between 1 and 3 percent of the world's gross domestic product (GDP).

At first, people thought the green building movement was a fad. Now, most industry practitioners realize that this is no fad. The green building movement

will continue to flourish as professionals become better educated about the benefits building owners and tenants can reap from high-efficiency buildings and the potential for improving the comfort and health of building occupants. In fact, the movement is likely to gain even greater momentum in the 2010s, so prepare for it.

Through its research, McGraw-Hill Construction estimates the green building market will reach US$10 to $20 billion by 2012. These high investments should come with a lucrative payback for instituting efficiencies in subsequent years. That is what the retail real estate industry should strive to achieve.

Retailers—led by Wal-Mart, Target, Starbucks, Best Buy, JCPenney, Whole Foods Market and others—that have demonstrated the benefits of being green will revolutionize retailing in the 2010s to satisfy a new breed of educated and demanding consumers.

More important, the change in attitude by present generations of shopping center professionals and executives of retail chains toward more eco-friendly practices coupled with the receptiveness of young people today will become the catalyst for change.

Humans are adaptive and inventive. If humans can construct buildings that are as tall as mountains and as comfortable as paradise, so too can they drive change that does not compromise the environment.

Gro Harlem Brundtland's dream for developing buildings and communities "that meet the needs of the present without compromising the ability of future generations to meet their own needs" can indeed become reality.

And a convenient truth.

PHOTO: R. E. MILIAN

Glossary

UNDERSTANDING THE TERMS and concepts of a green agenda is the first step toward recognizing that many sustainable green tactics are economically achievable and result in immediate, enduring benefits for those undertaking them. Below is a quick reference guide to sustainability issues covered in this publication.

American Association of Textile Chemists and Colorists (AATCC) A trade association that sets standards for environmentally friendly carpets, furnishings and fabrics.

American Society for Testing Materials (ASTM) A source of environmental ratings for adhesives, air filters, ceiling tile coatings, humidifier pads, paints, and polymeric surfaces such as vinyl, epoxy, rubber flooring and laminates.

American Society of Heating, Refrigerating and Air-Conditioning Engineers (ASHRAE) An organization that sets building standards relating to heating, ventilation and air-conditioning while promoting building sustainability.

biodiversity Biological diversity refers to the number, variety and variability among living organisms from all sources (terrestrial and aquatic/marine) and takes into consideration genetic diversity, species diversity and ecological system diversity.

biofuels Fuels derived from renewable raw materials, such as corn, sugarcane, tree bark, black liquor and residuals from logging.

bioswales Landscape elements situated near paved areas and filled with vegetation, compost and/or riprap designed to prevent fertilizers, insecticide, automobile fluids and other forms of pollution from surface runoff water that may be released to the watershed or storm sewer.

Building Research Establishment Environmental Assessment Method (BREEAM) Widely used in European countries but primarily in the United Kingdom as one of the leading measurements of green building and environmental compliance of existing laws.

brownfield Real property, the expansion, redevelopment or reuse of which may be complicated by the presence of a hazardous substance, pollutant or contaminant,

which needs to be professionally remediated. Cleaning up and reinvesting in these types of properties have a significant upside to compensate for the risks and extra costs for insurance and site cleanup.

building commissioning (Cx) *See commissioning (Cx).*

cap-and-trade system A system that mandates to cap the amount of carbon dioxide that a company is allowed to emit and provides for allowances beyond the cap that can be traded (sold or bought) on the open market. *See also emissions trading.*

carbon allowances The amount of carbon dioxide a company is allowed to emit. Excess allowances can be sold in a cap-and-trade system.

carbon cycle A series of processes involving photosynthesis, decomposition and respiration by which carbon cycles from various depositories, such as the atmosphere, ocean, soil and living organisms.

carbon dioxide (CO_2) A gas formed during combustion of organic matter and various natural processes. It is the most significant contributor to climate change. Trees consume carbon dioxide through photosynthesis and emit oxygen.

carbon disclosure Voluntary reports that companies provide to disclose greenhouse gas emissions data as well as business risks and opportunities relating to climate change.

Carbon Disclosure Project (CDP) An independent not-for-profit, U.K.-based organization used by S&P 500, FT 500 and FTSE 250 companies as well as smaller companies around the world to disclose current and projected carbon dioxide and other greenhouse gas emissions and other elements of environmental footprint. CDP publishes information about the reporting companies pertaining to the implications for shareholder value and commercial operations presented by climate change. The information is available to investors, shareholders, corporations and the public.

carbon footprint The amount of carbon dioxide and other greenhouse gases, in tons, that a store, shopping center or company emits into the atmosphere.

carbon monoxide (CO) A colorless, odorless and tasteless highly toxic gas produced from the partial combustion of carbon-containing compounds, notably in internal-combustion engines. Exposures can lead to significant toxicity of the central nervous system and heart.

carbon neutral A building, shopping center or store that emits zero level of carbon dioxide and other greenhouse gases. This can be achieved by using only renewable energy sources such as solar, wind or hydro, or by a combination of energy sources that balances the amount of carbon released with the amount sequestered. This could involve planting trees elsewhere that absorb an equal amount of carbon dioxide produced or by carbon offsets purchased from a third party.

certified wood A forest certification often given to wood products by a disinterested party after inspecting forest management and use to evaluate ecological, economic and compliance with social standards for sustainable forestry.

climate change *See global warming.*

commissioning (Cx) A necessary systematic process involving a series of tests of building systems to ensure that a building performs in accordance with the design, intent, contract documents and the owner's operational needs. Usually referred to as building commissioning, it is a mandatory requirement for LEED certification of commercial buildings, but it is rarely included as part of the typical design and construction process.

corporate social responsibility (CSR) Companies with stated principles focused on human rights, workers' rights, ethical business practices, and community support.

CSR *See corporate social responsibility.*

cultural preservation A movement by shopping centers intended to instill pride, protect, restore and honor the cultural diversity or ancestry of a locale and community. This may include but is not limited to language, music, dances, buildings, sacred or important cultural sites, arts and crafts, and other forms, which bear historical relevance.

ecosystem The complex system comprising all plant, animal, fungal and microorganism life and their association to the nonliving environment dependent upon each other and interacting as one ecological unit.

effluents An outflow of water from a natural body of water or from a man-made water basin. Man-made effluents are generally considered polluted water, such as the outflow from a sewage treatment facility or wastewater discharge.

embodied energy The total energy that can be attributed to bringing a building or other item to its existing state. It includes the energy consumed in raw materials, processing them and manufacturing composite items as well as transporting materials to the site, the energy consumed in the construction and operation of the building all the way up to its disassembly and deconstruction.

emissions trading The selling and buying of permits issued to a business or a country that allows them to emit a certain amount of greenhouse gas. *See cap-and-trade system.*

EMS *See environmental management system and energy management system.*

energy management system (EMS) An automated and computer-aided system used by building operators to monitor, control and optimize the performance of heating, ventilation and air conditioning (HVAC) systems, lighting and other appliances, and equipment that use electricity.

environmental footprint The extent to which a store, shopping center or company negatively affects the environment. This can be from the amount of greenhouse gas it emits into the atmosphere to the extent of rainwater runoff from the property that later pollutes lakes, streams and waterways.

environmental management system (EMS) A system used by a company to guide specific competencies, behaviors, procedures and policy for implementing a responsible environmental policy.

Environmental Protection Agency (EPA) An agency of the U.S. (or state) government charged with protecting human health and safeguarding such areas of the natural environment as air, land and water by conducting assessments, providing education, enforcing environmental laws and setting administrative policy.

flue gas The air or smoke rising from a chimney after combustion in a burner below. It will usually consist of mostly nitrogen (typically more than two-thirds) derived from the combustion of air, carbon dioxide and water vapor as well as excess oxygen. It can include pollutants such as particulate matter, carbon oxides, nitrogen oxides and sulfur oxides, and other chemical pollutants.

forest certification A certification for wood products (certified wood) given by a disinterested party after inspecting forest management and used to evaluate ecological, economic and compliance with social standards for sustainable forestry. Forest Stewardship Council is one such organization allowing the FSC trademark to identify FSC-certified wood.

Forest Stewardship Council (FSC) An international organization that promotes responsible stewardship of the world's forests and certifies wood products in more than 70 countries to meet FSC standards, which are labeled as FSC-certified wood and carry the FSC trademark.

fossil fuels Energy fuel from plant and animal residues formed under high temperature and pressure below the ground over of millions of years through a chemical and physical transformation. These fuels can be liquid such as oil, gaseous such as natural gas and solid such as coal.

geothermal Relating to heat generated in or near the core of the earth or cooling slightly below the earth's surface.

Global Reporting Initiative (GRI) A system of guidelines widely used in Europe to report on a company's sustainability efforts and carbon footprint.

global warming The warming of the earth's atmosphere from the release of greenhouse gases, potentially capable of catastrophic effects ranging from shifting weather patterns and storms to melting of the polar ice caps, which will raise sea levels. Also referred to as climate change.

green audit An inspection and analysis of a store, shopping center or company to define its impact on the environment. It is intended to reduce energy usage and greenhouse gas emissions and promote the health of building occupants.

green building A building standard intended to achieve building efficiency with renewable energy, water conservation techniques, waste management and materials selection that attempt to minimize the negative impact that buildings can have on

human health and the environment through specially focused development, design, construction and operating techniques.

Green Globes A Web-based, simple-to-use self-assessment auditing tool created by the Green Building Initiative (GBI), popular in Canada, the United Kingdom and the United States.

green image A perception by the public that a retailer, shopping center or company has taken a position and has implemented practices to help preserve the environment.

greenwashing The ill-advised practice of a company representing itself as a fully sustainable business when it is not so through disseminating disinformation to present an environmentally responsible public image.

greenhouse gases (GHGs) A term for a collection of global-warming gases such as carbon dioxide (CO_2), methane (CH_4), nitrous oxide (N_2O), hydrofluorocarbons (HFCs), perfluorocarbons (PFCs) and sulphur hexafluoride (SF_6).

GRI *See Global Reporting Initiative.*

groundwater Water beneath the earth's surface appearing in spaces between soil particles and rock, sometimes found in aquifers. It can be liquid but can also include soil moisture, permafrost (frozen soil), immobile water in bedrock and deep geothermal or oil formation water.

ice cap A dome-shaped mass of glacier ice that spreads out in all directions; usually larger than an ice field but smaller than 19,000 square miles (49,210 sq km) wide.

ice sheet A dome-shaped mass of glacier ice that covers surrounding terrain, such as the Greenland and Antarctic ice sheets, and is larger than 19,000 square miles (49,210 sq km).

International Organization for Standardization (ISO) The Geneva, Switzerland–based organization founded in 1947, representing standards from 146 countries.

ISO 14001 A global standard guiding the efficiency of corporate environmental management systems (EMS) set by the International Organization for Standardization. The ISO 14001 standard was officially published on November 15, 2004.

krill Abundant crustaceans resembling small shrimp in ocean waters all over the world but very prevalent in Antarctic waters. Nonpredatory fish feed on krill and other types of plankton, making krill an important part of the food chain.

land use The human use of a parcel of land for a certain purpose such as to build residential houses, commercial buildings, agriculture, forestry or recreational parks. Permitted land use refers to zoning restrictions regarding what the land may be used for.

landfill A site where household, commercial and industrial waste is transported by truck for disposal. Waste is generally spread in thin layers and then covered with soil. Also referred to as land waste disposal or dump.

Leadership in Energy and Environmental Design (LEED) A green building rating system widely accepted as a benchmark in North America for the design, construction and operation of high-performance green buildings. Buildings can apply to the U.S. Green Building Council or an affiliate organization for various levels of sustainability ratings by proving performance in five key areas of human health and environmental contribution: sustainable site development, water savings, energy efficiency, resources and materials selection, and indoor environmental quality.

life cycle assessment (LCA) The process of assessing the human health and environmental impacts of a product, equipment, process or service from the time it is first used or installed until it is disposed of or removed.

low-carbon economy A world economy driven to mitigate the effects of climate change that is anticipated in the future when emissions of carbon dioxide from burning carbon-based fuels such as coal, natural gas and oil are expected to be frozen worldwide and significantly reduced. Advocates expect that sometime during the period that follows a low-carbon economy, all carbon-based fuels will be phased out, which will result in a zero-carbon economy or post-carbon economy.

methane (CH_4) A colorless, flammable, nontoxic form of greenhouse gas. It is formed naturally from the decomposition of organic matter and is a major component of natural gas extracted from geological deposits for fuel and industrial uses. Wetlands, livestock and energy are sources of methane emissions into the atmosphere.

National Environmental Policy Act (NEPA) U.S. law that is the foundation of environmental policy.

nitric oxide (NO) The most common form of nitrogen, emitted by motor vehicles into the atmosphere where upon being exposed to sunlight, it combines with oxygen to produce NO_2 (a pollutant) and other nitrogen oxides. *See nitrogen oxides.*

nitrogen (N) A common gas in the atmosphere and an element found in water and soil. Excessive concentrations in water can lead to increased biological activity, through eutrophication. Nitrogen is added in treating wastewater to aid in the breakdown of soluble organics. *See nitrogen oxides.*

nitrogen oxides (NO_X) A generic term for a group of gases made up of nitrogen and oxygen in varying amounts, such as nitric oxide (NO), nitrogen dioxide (NO_2), nitrous oxide (N_2O) and dinitrogen trioxide (N_2O_3), produced during combustion at high temperatures. These oxygen compounds of nitrogen are colorless and odorless except that N_2O—a greenhouse gas—mixes with particles in the air to form reddish-brown smog over urban areas that results in acid rain and climate change. The primary sources of NO_X are motor vehicles, utility companies that produce electricity and other sources that burn fossil fuels. *See nitrogen.*

notional building A version of an actual building subject to the same occupancy and plant operation patterns as the actual building. The notional building is modi-

fied to conform to a clearly defined set of standards to help establish a benchmark to measure the performance of the actual building.

PCBs *See polychlorinated biphenyls.*

pH A measure of the concentration of protons (H+) in a solution resulting in acidity, alkalinity or any range thereof. The "p" stands for Potenz, a German term for "power" or "concentration." The "H" stands for the hydrogen ion (H+). Generally, pH value is an approximate number measured between 0 and 14 that indicates whether a solution is acidic (pH less than 7), alkaline (pH higher than 7) or neutral (pH = 7).

polar ice cap A high-latitude region of land or water covered in ice, also known as a polar ice sheet.

polychlorinated biphenyls (PCBs) A family of 209 synthetic congeners, similarly structured organic chemicals. They range from oily liquids to waxy solids. Some are toxic and others are not. They are used as coolants and lubricants in transformers and other electrical equipment, such as hydraulic fluids and as plasticizers, carbonless copy paper ink, dyes and pigments. PCBs are harmful when released into the environment as waste by-products of chemical manufacturing and incineration.

primary energy Fuel obtained directly from primary energy sources such as coal, natural gas, oil, uranium, hydro and solar energy.

Programme for the Endorsement of Forest Certification (PEFC) An international forest certification system used to document that wood retrieved from a forest has been certified as sustainable.

postcarbon economy *See zero-carbon economy.*

R-value The insulation properties of certain building insulation materials. The higher the R-value, the greater insulation.

renewable energy Energy derived from natural resources such as sunlight, wind, tides and geothermal and naturally replenished in a relatively short period. Renewable energy such as solar power, windpower and hydroelectricity typically does not emit large amounts of greenhouse gases.

sealant A substance used to fill or close small gaps and cracks in another material, such as drywall or windows. It is generally a viscous material that becomes solid, preventing penetration of air, gas, noise, dust, fire, smoke or liquid from one location to another.

secondary energy Energy produced by converting primary or another secondary form of energy, such as electricity, steam, hydrogen and refined petroleum products.

spent fuel A hot and highly radioactive waste product emanating from nuclear fuel that has reached the end of its useful life in a reactor, after about three years, and has to be removed and stored.

sustainability The conviction that today's generation of industries, governments and the people of Earth should consume and preserve natural resources in a manner so as to allow future generations to sustain the same quality of life as we do today. The term is sometimes used synonymously with social responsibility and encompasses economic, social and institutional qualities of life to be sustained over time by corporate initiatives.

sustainable development A development that meets the needs of the present generation without compromising the ability of future generations to meet their own needs.

Sustainable Forestry Initiative (SFI) A North American forest certification program endorsed by PEFC.

triple bottom line Companies or investment returns that factor social and environmental responsibility as well as financial results into the business model.

volatile organic compounds (VOCs) Any organic compound that interacts in atmospheric photochemical reactions such as methane, a greenhouse gas. When released into the environment, VOCs can damage soil and groundwater and contribute to indoor pollution as well as pollute the atmosphere. Some VOCs have odors such as gasoline, alcohol and solvents in paints.

zero-carbon economy A world economy (also known as post-carbon economy) in which all carbon-based fuels such as coal, natural gas and oil are completely phased out and prohibited, and replaced with renewable sources of energy. Advocates driven by the intent to stop the effects of global warming anticipate this economy to occur sometime in the 21st century. A zero-based economy follows a low-carbon economy.

About the Author

 **Rudolph E. Milian, SCMD, SCSM,** is senior staff vice president for Professional Development Services of the International Council of Shopping Centers (ICSC). He is responsible for ICSC's programs and services involving industry best practices through education, professional certification, books, publications and periodicals. Mr. Milian's shopping center career spans more than two decades, having previously held positions in on-site, regional and corporate shopping center marketing, property management and asset management. Earlier he was an executive with a retail chain.

PNC BANK, WASHINGTON TOWNSHIP, NEW JERSEY
PHOTO: R. E. MILIAN

Index

Fruits & Passion store, located at
Ibn Battuta Mall in Dubai, United Arab
Emirates, is a Canadian retailer founded
in 1992. It offers a unique environmentally
sound retail concept that demonstrates
a commitment to quality by appealing
to the five senses.

PHOTO ILLUSTRATION: R. E. MILIAN

The
RetailGreen Agenda

**Sustainable Practices for
Retailers and Shopping Centers**

"The book helps you understand the scope and provides access to a long list of initiatives and tactics."

—**Arcadio Gil Pujol, CSM, CMD, CDP**, Managing Director
LaSBA, S.A., Madrid, Spain

"An excellent primer on sustainable efforts by developers and tenants alike. The author has captured the current state of affairs, and while firmly endorsing responsibility, does not reach doom and gloom."

—Joseph Pettipas, **LEED AP, IDC, ARIDO, IIDA,**
Vice President and Practice Leader Retail and Hospitality
Hellmuth, Obata & Kassabaum, Inc. (HOK Canada), Toronto, Ontario, Canada

"A must read for any architect and shopping center manager to understand how their visitors and communities relate to buildings."

—**Mario Castro Frías, CSM, CMD, CDP,** Vice President, New Project Development
Allard Industries Ltd., Santo Domingo, Dominican Republic

Advance Acclaim for The RetailGreen Agenda

"A good introduction to the various ways in which sustainability is being addressed by the real estate sector."

—**Benjamin A. Bross, LEED AP,** Design Director
Constructora Planigrupo, S.A., Mexico City, Mexico

"This book provides a thorough review of the environmental issues and the practical and effective measures retailers and shopping centers are employing to lessen their impact on the environment and contribute to healthy communities."

—**David V. Green, AIA, LEED AP,** Principal
Altoon + Porter Architects, LLP, Los Angeles, California, USA

"Good introduction to the topic of sustainable development in general and its potential for application to retail development in particular."

—**John Rutte, PE, LEED AP,** Vice President, Development
Cousins Properties Incorporated, Atlanta, Georgia, USA

"An optimistic approach to encourage leaders of the industry to 'do the right thing.'"

—**Michelle Corti,** Master's Class 2008, D. Bren School of
Environmental Science & Management
University of California, Santa Barbara, California, USA

"An absolute must for anyone contemplating or starting a sustainability program in the retail industry. It will solidify your concerns and reasons for starting the program and give examples and best practices from those paving the way."

—**Jeffrey M. Bedell, LEED AP, CEM, CPP,** Vice President, Operations
The Macerich Company, Santa Monica, California, USA

"Good reference for the shopping center sector that allows benchmarking and knowledge about what is being done by the shopping center industry."

—**Elsa Rodrigues Monteiro,** Head of Institutional Relations,
Environment & Communications
Sonae Sierra, Lisbon, Portugal

"Great source of information; explains a very complex issue in an easily understood and educational manner."

—**Richard P. O'Leary, CDP,** Vice President, Director of Construction Services
JCPenney Company, Inc., Dallas, Texas, USA

"An excellent overview of the situation."

—**Lisa Loweth,** Vice President, Sustainability
General Growth Properties, Chicago, Illinois, USA

D0806975

THE
RETAIL GREEN
AGENDA

Sustainable Practices for Retailers and Shopping Centers

Rudolph E. Milian

International Council of Shopping Centers